ACID® Pro 6 Power!:

THE OFFICIAL GUIDE

D. Eric Franks

THOMSON

COURSE TECHNOLOGY ™

Professional ∎ Technical ∎ Reference

ISBN-10: 1-59200-977-8
ISBN-13: 978-1-59200-977-0

Library of Congress Catalog Card Number: 2005931913

Printed in the United States of America

07 08 09 10 11 PH 10 9 8 7 6 5 4 3 2 1

THOMSON

™

COURSE TECHNOLOGY

Professional ■ Technical ■ Reference

Thomson Course Technology PTR, a division of Thomson Learning Inc.
25 Thomson Place
Boston, MA 02210
http://www.courseptr.com

Publisher and General Manager, Thomson Course Technology PTR:
Stacy L. Hiquet

Associate Director of Marketing:
Sarah O'Donnell

Manager of Editorial Services:
Heather Talbot

Marketing Manager:
Mark Hughes

Senior Editor:
Mark Garvey

Marketing Coordinator:
Meg Dunkerly

Project Editor/Copy Editor:
Cathleen D. Snyder

PTR Editorial Services Coordinator:
Elizabeth Furbish

Interior Layout Tech:
Digital Publishing Solutions

Cover Designers:
Mike Tanamachi and Nancy Goulet

Indexer:
Sharon Shock

Proofreader:
Kim V. Benbow

} Acknowledgments

Special thanks go out to Cathleen Snyder for her editorial dedication and hard work following this project through from start to finish. This book would also not be possible without the support of the Thomson Course Technology staff, specifically Mark Garvey. Finally, the author would also like to thank Sony Media Software for their technical review and support.

} About the Author

D. Eric Franks is a writer and editor living in Ocala, Florida. As the Director of Technical Education at Digital Juice, he works with other broadcast professionals on instructional media, including print, audio, and video productions, online training, and live presentations. Previous industry jobs have included technical writing for Sonic Foundry and Ulead Systems, as well as a stint as *Videomaker* magazine's technical editor for a number of years.

TABLE OF Contents

} Introduction

Sophisticated yet simple, Sony Media Software's ACID® software puts the ability to create professional-quality music using almost any modern computer in the hands of the masses. The ACID software is, first and foremost, fun; you can produce something that sounds pretty good the very first time you fire it up. (In fact, if you haven't already done so, by all means put this book down and go try it out.) This initial ease and simplicity masks the fact that the ACID program is a powerful and professional-level tool ideally suited to song composition and film scoring, among other uses. This book intends to comprehensively cover these higher-level features and show you how to use the software in real-world situations. Whether you are a new-wave multimedia designer creating engrossing content for the 'Net or an old-school producer in a traditional studio, these pages aim to show you how to take full advantage of ACID. And get this: You can even make money with the ACID application.

What Is ACID?

The ACID 6.0 software from Sony Media Software is the most popular and advanced loop-based music creation and remixing tool ever created. It is also the first successful tool of is kind, pre-dating Apple's "revolutionary" GarageBand by nearly seven years. It doesn't require any particular musical talent (beyond a good ear) and it needs no special equipment (beyond a basic computer). The ACID software is a fully capable stand-alone tool, yet it meshes perfectly with studio hardware and other software multimedia applications. As an artistic tool, it is stunningly easy to create catchy tunes within an hour of installation. And it all starts with the loop.

Loops are short sections of music or a performance that are saved into standard media files on your computer. They are the building blocks of ACID songs. The first loops were created by physically connecting short sections of audio tape end to end with sticky tape, thereby creating physical loops of magnetic tape. When run over the playback head in a tape player, this creates an infinite loop of audio, which was an interesting artistic trick for some performers. Modern computer-based composers use loops in more sophisticated and pragmatic ways. Typically, loops are recorded in such a way that when the loop ends, it can immediately begin seamlessly playing the start of the file again, potentially forever—hence the name "loop." Recorded by professional musicians, loops allow you to take a drum set, a bass line, and a lead and put them into a new and original composition. Because there are many thousands of loop libraries available, the creative possibilities are almost endless. And since the individual loops are created by some of the world's top musical talents, the quality can be top shelf, regardless of whether you can play a note of music yourself. ACID isn't just a crutch for folks with little or no musical ability; the program also helps performers create their own loops and thus expand their range of tools and expression.

The ACID application is primarily a musician's tool, with song creation, recording, and multi-track mixing being the primary focus, but many other professionals and serious hobbyists will also find it extremely useful. The software is ideally suited for multimedia professionals who need to create original music for Shockwave and Flash presentations. Video and film professionals will find no tool better suited to scoring: I've heard ACID loops in everything from television commercials to the Bollywood film *Asoka*. DJs and mixmasters can use the software to remix songs in amazing new ways, even in demanding and exciting live performance venues. And of course studios and musicians will find the multi-track mixing and recording features second to none. The powerful effects sitting behind the ACID application's apparent simplicity enable you to create truly professional material.

One of the most amazing aspects of the software is its apparent simplicity. Don't let that fool you: There's a lot going on under the hood. Beat matching, tempo adjustment, key matching, and mixing are only a few of the things that you might never notice as you use ACID. Once you've explored the program for a while, get ready for the next level with complex effects, digital video, MIDI, cutting-edge compression algorithms, CD burning, 5.1 surround-sound audio, and Internet publishing. That's what this book is about.

About This Book

This book takes you beyond the basics and into guru-level procedures that utilize the ACID 6.0 software to its fullest potential. The program is more than a toy, although it can certainly be more fun than a video game. This book is targeted at the intelligent user who is ready to use the ACID software on the job in the commercial sector or as a tool for artistic self expression. The clear and solid examples in the first few chapters will quickly allow the non-technically inclined reader to express their creativity more fully. On the other hand, technically savvy non-musicians will find the chapters on introductory music theory invaluable in moving beyond casually playing with ACID and into serious music composition. And for those of you who are both techno-wizards with software and maestros in the recording studio, this book is going to show you the most efficient techniques to maximize the application's power.

We will start with the fun stuff. As previously mentioned, you can definitely pump out some pretty amazing tunes within minutes of popping the ACID CD into your computer. And you really should play for a bit immediately after you install the program (and before you read another word). The first goal of this book is to familiarize you with the nuts and bolts of the ACID software. Thanks to the well thought-out user interface (UI) and program workflow, the application can be mastered fairly quickly.

The second goal of this book is to go beyond the basics and into true music creation. Most people never create a song that is more than a bunch of music clips (loops) that sound good together, layered track onto track. It shouldn't end there, however. Just as a good story or novel has an arresting introduction, a dynamic exposition, perhaps a shocking conclusion and a satisfying denouement, so a good song also has structure. To use another analogy, just because you can type doesn't mean you can write a great novel. The middle section of this book focuses on music and music theory, with a heavy emphasis on how to effortlessly express your musical ideas using the ACID program.

The final goal of this book is to get into some of the more technical aspects of the software. From burning industry-standard CDs to producing highly compressed MP3 files for the Internet, publishing and sharing your music is the ultimate goal. In the process, this book will cover everything you need to know about maximizing the quality of your music after the creative process is over. In addition, it will show you how to polish your masterpieces using effects processing. There are also a hundred other fascinating topics that you can dive into, from amazing MIDI technology to recording your own vocals and solo jams. This book is all you need to get you on your way.

What's New in Version 6.0?

All versions of the ACID software do the same basic thing: Create and remix loop-based music. Some of the changes with the 6.0 version are under the hood, with new rendering and processing algorithms that will be largely invisible (and inaudible) to us mortals, but which are nonetheless significant. Other changes will be more dramatic and will actually change the way you work on a daily basis. And there are some completely new features with this version that ACID veterans will want to play with right away. Because Sony Media Software marketing covers all of the new features in the ACID 6.0 software extensively in their promotional materials and on their Web site (follow the Comparison link on the main ACID 6.0 page), I am only going to highlight a few additions that I found particularly impressive.

❋ The new "high-performance multi-threaded audio engine" might be the most intangible new feature in version 6.0, but it might also be the most significant. Professionals working in high-end studios will notice the difference when working with 24-bit/96-kHz or even 192-kHz audio (which can bring even muscular computers to their knees). The new audio engine also lets you record multiple tracks and MIDI simultaneously.

❋ You can now mix different media files on the same track, which is a new feature that will at first baffle old-school ACID users. It might be slightly disorienting at first, but the old one track/one loop philosophy of all of the previous versions of the ACID software was really a limitation. The new workflow really takes the loop–track–mixer logic of the product to its most flexible level. And, of course, you can still continue to limit yourself to one loop per track if you really want to.

✻ You'll also notice a new Clip Pool, which will go a long way toward unbaffling ACID veterans who find the new track model confusing. The Clip Pool sorts all of the different media files that you can use on a track.

✻ Composers will appreciate the ability to work intuitively with musical sections of music, such as verses, refrains, and bridges. Need to start verse 2? Now you can copy and paste from verse 1 and get on with the variations very quickly using a new type of region called a Section.

✻ The ACID software has always been a loop-based composer first and a MIDI tool second. Although this may be historically true, with the 6.0 release, the new MIDI editing features in the program really take the software into new territory. If you have been using the ACID application for mixing but using another tool for MIDI composition, the new features are well worth learning and might ultimately streamline your audio production workflow greatly.

✻ Did I mention the new audio engine? It shows up in so many of the new features that it is hard to overemphasize its importance. One other area you will notice it right away is in the real-time effects processing on audio signals coming into the application. Professionals will find that they can finally substitute software for much of the hardware they have gotten used to over the years, getting one step closer to the all-in-one DAW in a box.

Which ACID Is Which?

Sony Media Software has released a number of different versions of the ACID program, from a free version to the more expensive professional version. As you might expect, you get what you pay for, although I can recommend without hesitation that you try one of the free demo versions if you have any reservations.

ACID XMC is an inexpensive product that is designed to introduce beginners and hobbyists to the ACID family by Sony Media Software. You might find it on the store shelves at Best Buy, or you can download it directly from Sony Media Software. After you get the application, you can also grab some demo songs from ACIDplanet.com. You will certainly get a taste of the application and be able to create some very cool stuff, but you will fairly quickly run into some of the limitations of this program. Sony Media Software may offer some good deals on upgrading to a higher version from the XMC version.

ACID Music Studio is the base level of the application that this book covers. If you are even mildly serious about producing quality music, there is no question that you need to own at least this version of the ACID program. Full-featured and powerful, ACID Music is reasonably priced to fit the budget of the interested amateur musician and composer, yet can still produce professional-level output. ACID Music also comes with a CD of basic loops.

ACID Pro is the high-end version of the software that is appropriate for studios, professionals, and prosumers. As with other versions, stepping up to this version when you are ready is a simple matter. Uncompromising quality and the technical tools you need to get the job done make this an awesome addition to any multimedia professional's audio rack. The ACID Pro application also comes with a CD of basic loops.

The following table highlights some of the major differences in the different versions of the ACID software.

	ACID XMC	ACID Music Studio	ACID Pro
Tracks	10	Unlimited	Unlimited
Disc-at-Once CD Burning	No	Yes	Yes
Bit Depth	16/48-kHz	16/48-kHz	24/192-kHz
Multiple Sound Cards Support	No	No	Yes
5.1 Surround Mixing	No	No	Yes
Effects (Included)	None	Express	XFX 1, 2 and 3
Video	No	Yes	Yes
DirectX Plug-In Automation	No	No	Yes
Volume and Panning Automation	No	Yes	Yes

	ACID XMC	ACID Music Studio	ACID Pro
Effects (FX) Automation	No	No	Yes
Adjustable Stretching	No	No	Yes
Save Tracks to Individual Files	No	No	Yes
ASIO Driver Support	No	No	Yes
MIDI Recording/Piano Roll	No	Yes	Yes
Media Manager	No	No	Yes
Flash Import	No	Yes	Yes
Grooving	No	No	Yes
Folder Tracks	No	No	Yes
VST Effects and VSTi	Synths	No	Yes
Nestable Tracks	No	No	Yes
Groove Quantization	No	No	Yes

* Source: http://www.sonymediasoftware.com

❄ **ABOUT ACID**

Unsure of which version of the ACID software you own? From the Help menu in the program, select About Sony ACID. The dialog box that opens details not only the type of product you have purchased, but the version and build number as well. When you are ready to upgrade, you might be able to purchase a new license online and instantly convert your current version to a more advanced version.

Reading This Book

This book is designed to serve as both a tutorial and a reference. You should plan to have this book open at the same time ACID is running because there are many examples and procedures that only make sense in the context of using the program. Learning by doing is always the best study method.

❄ If you have never used the ACID software before, you want to work through the examples (after playing with the program for a couple of hours) in the first two chapters fairly carefully to master the basics.

❄ If you already have a good feel for the program, you might want to browse through the first two chapters and see whether it all seems familiar. It shouldn't be a waste of time: There are a few surprises, shortcuts, and expert tips scattered throughout the basic material.

❄ Veteran ACID users with limited formal musical training might want to concentrate on the music theory chapters and the new features, and otherwise use the book as a comprehensive reference.

There are a few conventions that might make using this book easier. The first is the Note feature. Notes usually contain additional information that is particularly important to understand. Anything critical to understand but likely to be lost in the hundreds of thousands of words that comprise this book might be set off as a Note.

NOTE

Do not taunt Happy Fun Ball.

Tips, on the other hand, are not so critical. Tips usually contain information and ideas to make your life easier or enhance the ACID software's performance. Sometimes an entire procedure can be executed with a single keyboard shortcut, and such a shortcut will frequently be highlighted in a Tip.

TIP

Sony Media Software's ACID application is most enjoyable when the volume is turned up to 11.

Getting Additional Help

Readers of this book should not forget (nor underestimate) the quality of the documentation that came with the program from Sony Media Software. This text should be seen as a supplement to these primary references and not as a substitute. Read the manual, pause the mouse cursor over unfamiliar items in the UI to get ToolTips, watch the status bar at the bottom of the program, and don't forget to use F1 for specific context-sensitive Help on almost anything. Finally, check out Sony Media Software's Web site and user forums. The discussions that occur on ACIDplanet.com can often be nearly as interesting as the music that shows up there.

http://www.sonymediasoftware.com

http://www.acidplanet.com

1 } A Song Is Born

The goal of this chapter is to introduce the basic features of Sony Media Software's ACID® program and explain how they function in practical use. The procedures described here are the fundamentals. We'll talk about laying down tracks, trimming, and mixing, among other things. Along the way, we'll define the terms and illustrate them with a host of examples. This is a fun chapter that is not very deep. You should be able to breeze right through it and come out with some very fun sonic doodles that sound pretty darn good at the end. Most importantly, the techniques you learn here are the ones you will use on a daily basis, in every project.

The best way to use this chapter is to turn on your computer, run the ACID software, put this book in your lap, and try the procedures as you read. Some procedures are so easy that they won't seem worth the trouble, but you might as well go ahead and try them anyhow. Many of the concepts we'll be describing throughout this book simply cannot be understood without hearing them for yourself. We'll start at the beginning, lay down some tracks, and do a little mixing. The final section explains how to save a song so that you can publish it and share it with others.

From start to finish, this chapter shows you how to begin a project and output a final song. We're going to start with four quick definitions—projects, loops, tracks, and events—and then immediately move into practical examples.

❄ **START PLAYING!**

One of the primary goals of this book is to be motivational, to get you excited about the ACID software and ultimately about music. With that in mind, I want to stop you right here: Have you played with the application yet? Don't worry, we'll get to work soon enough. But if you haven't played around with the program yet, close this book, run the program, use the Explorer window to find your loops, and drag-and-drop a few into your timeline. We'll see you back here in a few hours.

Building Blocks

The ACID software uses specific terms to convey specific ideas. It's important to understand what "the program," "the manual," and "the Help" mean when referring to program-specific terms because the meaning of each term might be quite different from how it's used in the real world (although those real-world meanings often offer a clue). Here are a few fundamental ideas that need to be discussed.

Projects

The first step in composing a song with the ACID software is to create a *project*. When you first run the program, a new project is loaded automatically. Every time you use the program, you're working on a project. The projects you'll save on your computer contain all of the information about your composition, such as the key, tempo, and audio files used. Project files control every aspect of your song, including which sounds are used, how they're mixed together, and what effects modify the sound.

ACID project files have the .acd extension and are only recognized by the ACID software. That is, they cannot be opened or played back in any other applications. Although a project saves information about your composition and the sounds that make it up, a project file is *not* a song and cannot be played back as such on a media player, over the Internet, or on a CD player.

The great thing about working with projects, instead of editing actual audio files on your computer, is that you're not actually changing any clips on your computer. This editing process is non-destructive, and it lets you edit and experiment with sounds without fear of changing the original clips. You primarily edit ACID project files and not loops or clips, although you can do that as well. When you're done with your project, which is made up of loops, clips, and effects, you can save it to another format that can be burned to a CD or published on the Internet. This is called *rendering*, and it's the process of creating an actual song. Actually, because the ACID software is also a video-scoring tool, the final render might even create a new movie file.

> **SAVE YOUR WORK**
>
> When you start a new project, the first thing you should do is save it. Select Save from the File menu and type a name for your project. Saving is also the last thing I do before I shut down the software at 3 a.m. It's a habit. I save all the time, reflexively, especially when something aurally wonderful has just happened (you'll know when). Periodically, I'll also save versions of a project as I work, especially when it's taking a new sonic direction. I just tag an 001, 002, 003 to the end of the filename, methodically. That way, I always have something to go back to if a particular path gets hopelessly muddled.
>
> My motto is: *Save early, save often.*

If you haven't done so yet, let's start a project. If you have the ACID software running right now, you're in a project already. To start a new project, go to the File menu, select New (or press Ctrl+N on your keyboard), and click the OK button. This opens the New Project dialog. (You'll learn some more details about some of the other parts of the New Project dialog in just a few pages.) The first thing you want to do is save: File menu > Save. The first time you do this, you'll have to enter a filename and then click OK. Excellent: You now have a perfectly silent musical composition.

Clips and Loops

A file is the most basic unit a typical computer user works with. Files can be text documents (.txt), pictures (.bmp), or songs (.mp3). Media files (see Figure 1.1) are just files that contain audio, video, digital music, or pictures. In the context of modern multimedia production work, media files are often referred to as *clips*. Within the ACID software and in this book, media files and clips are the same thing. Clips that can be used in the application are video, audio, or MIDI in nature. Audio files are central to the ACID software, of course. Some typical audio file formats that can be used in the application are .wav and .mp3.

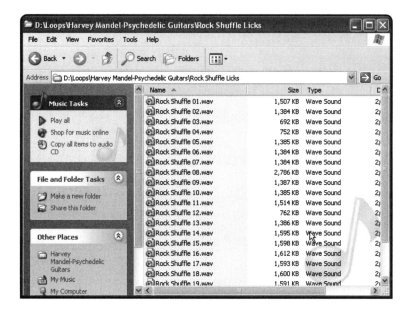

Figure 1.1
A file folder in Windows Explorer that contains Windows audio files in the .wav file format.

Loops are specially recorded audio files, usually fairly short in duration, that you can play back using just about any Windows media player, such as Winamp or even the Windows Media Player. A loop is structured so that when it's played back, the end of the loop immediately and seamlessly leads back into the beginning of the loop. Most loops can be played over and over again infinitely, sounding as if they're much longer continuous recordings.

Loops are normal audio files and are commercially available from multimedia companies for use in loop-based music tools. ACID loops from Sony Media Software actually contain a little more information than a typical .wav file, such as key and tempo information. This makes them particularly easy to use in the ACID software. You can use Sony Media Software loop libraries with many other multimedia applications, such as video editing applications or Flash animation tools, and loops from other companies can also be used in the ACID software. In fact, the ACID software is a killer app that's so dominant that many other companies produce *ACIDized* loop libraries containing the extra musical information needed to integrate with the ACID software. Many other companies also have software that can read ACIDized media properly, such as Apple's GarageBand.

Let's add a loop to your project. The Explorer window should be visible at the bottom of the program, and it should look very familiar if you've ever used a Windows computer. Click on the hard drive that contains your loops, find the folder where you've stored them, and then drag and drop a clip into the timeline (see Figure 1.2). You've just created a track.

Figure 1.2

The Explorer window and the main timeline. Drag files from Explorer to the timeline to create a track.

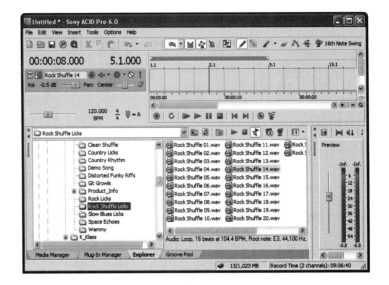

Tracks

In a traditional bricks-and-mortar studio, engineers record the audio of a song as separate *tracks*. Physically, tracks are narrow bands on an audiotape that run parallel to each other for the length of the tape. Recording the various parts of a song to separate tracks on the same piece of tape means perfect synchronization can be achieved, and the tape can be played back while a new part is recorded to one of the blank tracks.

Another feature of multitrack recording is that the audio engineers can adjust and mix the individual tracks and record that mix to another tape. Musically, a track corresponds to a single part or performance in a song. For example, guitar, drums, and vocals can all be recorded to separate tracks. Tracks don't necessarily contain a single instrument voice. For example, a track could contain an entire orchestral wind section or a combined drum and bass section.

> ❋ **PARADIGM SHIFT**
>
> Perhaps the single biggest change between the ACID 5 and ACID 6 products is the new ability to insert any loop into any track. In other words, tracks are no longer defined by a single clip. This is a fundamental change in both workflow and signal processing that will change the way you work on a daily basis. Of course, until you get used to this change, you can voluntarily restrict yourself to the one track/one clip paradigm, but the flexibility of the new structure is very powerful.

Tracks in the ACID application (see Figure 1.3) are exactly analogous to tracks in a studio or on an audiotape, although they are infinitely more flexible. An ACID track can contain one clip, which might be an individual instrument corresponding to a track laid down in a recording studio. An ACID track might also contain different clips, instruments, and parts, however. Tracks are a very powerful organizational tool when used wisely, even though you can basically insert clips anywhere you want into any track you want. The number of tracks is unlimited and can include MIDI songs or even video, although there are some minor limitations to mixing different types of media in a track.

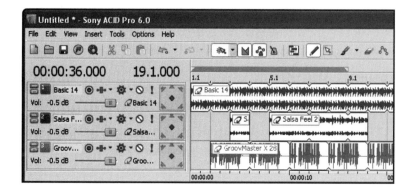

Figure 1.3
Three tracks, with a drum beat on Track 1 ("Basic 14"), a piano part on Track 2 ("Salsa Feel 2"), and a bass line on Track 3 ("GroovMaster X 28").

Every track has a number of important controls in the Track Header section on the left side (see Figure 1.4). You can use the controls on the left side of the tracks to adjust, mix, and otherwise modify an audio track with special effects. Many of these controls correspond to faders and knobs typically found on the mixer board in a conventional studio. (See Chapter 6, "Mastering the Mix," for more on mixers in the ACID software.)

Figure 1.4

The controls available in the Track Header.

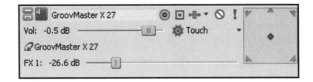

* **Minimize/Maximize/Restore buttons.** Changes the height of the track between three preset values. Many aspects of a track's appearance can be customized. Track size can be controlled by using the Minimize, Maximize, and Restore buttons in the Track Header. The lower edge of the track in the Track Header can also be dragged to change the size. Finally, the vertical scroll bar on the right side can be used to zoom in and out of the timeline, changing the height of all the tracks. Tracks can be all different sizes. The width of the Track Header can be changed by dragging the narrow bar that separates it from the timeline.

* **Track Number/Color/Pitch.** The track number is the order of the track from the top down and is located in the top-left corner. The track number is simply a numerical indication of the track order from top to bottom. The track order, and thus the track number, does not affect the mix or sound of a project. Track color can be changed by right-clicking the colored square in the Track Header, selecting Color from the pop-up context menu, and then choosing a color from the submenu. The color of the waveform of the events inserted into the timeline is determined this way as well. This color is used for your reference only. One possible idea is to make all bass tracks the same color, all percussion tracks another, keyboard tracks another, and so on. Pitch shifting information is also displayed in this area of the track. See Chapter 9, "Loops," for a discussion of loop and track types.

* **Track Name.** Defaults to the name of the clip, but can be changed. By default, the name of a track is derived from the name of the source file. You can change this name by double-clicking it and entering a new one. While it is not necessary to change the track name, it is definitely a good idea to change it if you are going to use multiple clips in a single track.

* **Arm for Record button.** Click this button to arm a track for recording. Clicking this button does not actually start the recording process, which is started with the Record button on the Transport bar below the timeline.

* **Bus/Device Selection button.** This sets the routing for the track to one of the busses or devices. The ACID audio signal can be sent through any number of real devices (such as multiple soundcards), virtual devices (busses in the ACID application), or effects (FX), just as an audio signal can be sent through a device in a real studio (such as a guitar through a phaser pedal). Although this can seem a bit confusing at first, all of this routing gives you a lot of flexibility and power to control the mix. The Bus/Device Selection button isn't visible on the track unless

you have more than one soundcard on your computer or have inserted an additional bus or FX into the project. See Chapter 6, "Mastering the Mix," for more information on grouping tracks together into a bus.

❋ **Track FX button.** Click this button to add effects to a track. See Chapter 7, "Grooves and FX," for more information on adding and modifying a project with effects.

❋ **Automation Settings button.** This button sets up the touch mode of the track when recording effects automation. This controls the strength of an effect or other parameters of the effect over time, and the automation feature records your adjustments of the various sliders in real time as you play back the project.

❋ **Mute and Solo buttons.** These buttons silence a track or make it the only track playing. Click the Solo button on one track to hear only that track. Click another Solo button on another track to hear both of those tracks. Click multiple Solo buttons to play several "solo" tracks at a time. Likewise, click the Mute button on a track to silence it. Multiple tracks can also be muted at the same time.

❋ **Volume and Pan sliders.** In all projects, the Volume slider controls the output volume of the track in the mix. For stereo projects, a Pan slider is available. For 5.1 surround sound projects, a Surround Panner replaces the Pan slider.

❋ **Multipurpose fader.** This slider will appear (see Figure 1.5) when you have inserted a new effects bus to route signals through in a project. You can click the Multipurpose Fader Mode button to assign the track to a bus (Bus A) or Assignable FX (FX 1). Assignable FX are discussed in greater detail in Chapter 7, "Grooves and FX."

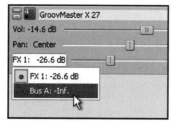

Figure 1.5
The Multipurpose fader is used to control volume, panning, and FX level.

Events

Events are containers in a track on the timeline and are the most basic unit of editing in the ACID program. They contain clips (media files) and can be moved, mixed, and modified. Events control the mixing and occurrence of sounds in your project. Think of them as windows into a clip, and don't confuse them with the clips themselves. When you dragged a clip to the timeline, you created a track automatically, but it's still empty. Here's how to add your media to the mix and create an event:

Figure 1.6

The Draw tool.

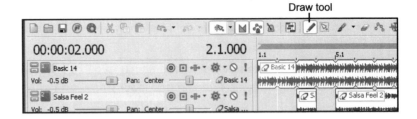

1. Make sure the Draw tool, the pencil on the toolbar, is selected (see Figure 1.6).

2. Click the track and drag from left to right.

As you draw an event, you see the waveform appear, and there are periodic notches in the borders. We'll discuss this in more detail later, but for now, press the spacebar to hear what it sounds like. In Figure 1.7, the clip Shuffle 2.wav in the Explorer window is used to create Track 1. The event in the track represents the sound of the clip as a waveform. It also controls how the clip is used in the project, setting which part of the entire file is played, how many times it repeats, and when it occurs, among other things. Clips appear in the Explorer window. When you insert a clip into a blank part of the timeline, you add it as a new track. You can also drag clips to existing tracks. Occurrences of a clip in a project are known as *events*.

Figure 1.7

A clip in the Explorer window is used to create the track on the timeline, which in turn contains an event that controls how the clip is mixed into the project.

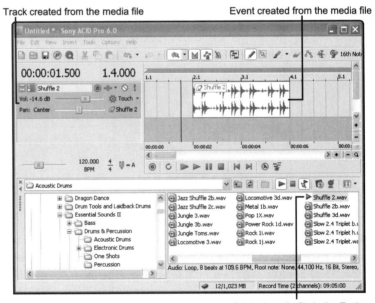

Nothing that you do to an event, neither distortion nor deletion, will ever change the actual clips stored on your computer. Instead, events control every aspect of how the ACID application plays back and mixes a sound file into a project and then the final song. Trimming an event does *not* trim the clip saved on your computer. This kind of non-destructive editing gives you an open license to create aural mayhem on your machine, safe in the knowledge that your source clips aren't being modified.

❋ **REVERSING EVENTS**
You can reverse events on the timeline: Right-click the event and select Reverse from the menu or just press U on your keyboard.

An event can be shorter than the clip it contains, in which case only a portion of the loop is mixed into the project. An event can also be longer than the loop it contains, in which case multiple repetitions of the loop are mixed into the project. Figure 1.8 shows a number of different events created from the same clip. Track 1 (top track) contains an event that's exactly the same length as the loop file, so it repeats only once. Track 2 uses the same source loop, but its events use only short sections of the total file. Track 3 also uses that source loop, but its event is three times longer than the original file, and therefore it repeats three times.

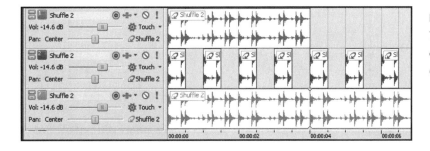

Figure 1.8
Three tracks with a number of different events that all use the same clip.

All You Need to Know

And that, in a few pages, is all you need to know:

1. Start a new project.

2. Create some tracks by dragging clips onto the timeline.

3. Draw events on the timeline to create music.

If this was all new to you, now is the time to take a break and begin your addiction to the ACID program. Otherwise, let's explore some of the details we've glossed over so far.

Projects

When you edit in the ACID application, you're editing a project with the ultimate goal of rendering a song. Creating, opening, and saving of projects are discussed in detail in this section.

Creating a Project

After you've launched the ACID software, select New from the File menu or press Ctrl+N. The New Project dialog (see Figure 1.9) has a number of options that define your project.

Figure 1.9

The New Project dialog. All of the information on the Summary tab is optional.

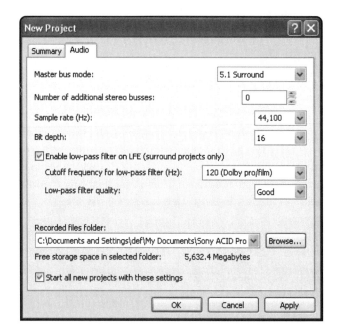

All of the information on the Summary tab is optional. The Audio tab contains properties that affect the quality of the project's output:

* **Master bus mode** (see Chapter 6, "Mastering the Mix,") determines whether your project is a simple stereo project or in fancy 5.1 surround sound. At this point, we'd highly recommend that you start out with a stereo project because that will be complicated enough to mix. Besides, you'll certainly want to downmix a 5.1 project to stereo for compatibility anyway.

* **Number of additional stereo busses** (see Chapter 6, "Mastering the Mix,") determines how many busses are available to group tracks together or for Assignable FX. This number depends on your hardware setup (such as the number and type of soundcards), and on how many groups of tracks you'd like to create. Don't worry if the concept of busses and whether you need them is mysterious at this point; additional busses are easy to create and can be

added at any time. More information on busses and why you might want to use them is available in Chapter 6. More information on Assignable FX and how they work is available in Chapter 7, "Grooves and FX."

❋ **Sample rate** is one of the two fundamental parameters that control the final objective quality of the audio file that you render from your project. The sample rate is measured as the number of samples per second (Hz). 44,100 Hz (44.1 KHz) is the same quality as a music CD and most ACID loops, and that's the default setting in the ACID software. You'll want to select 48,000 Hz for DVD audio projects. Higher numbers mean higher quality and larger final file sizes, while lower numbers make smaller files that may be more suitable for distribution on the Internet. Although it's convenient to set up a project sample rate in this dialog, it's not necessary. The final song's sample rate can be set independently when you render it after the project is finished.

❋ **Bit depth** is the other fundamental parameter that determines the quality of a song, and it's measured as the number of bits per sample. Having more bits per sample allows you to save more information about the sample, yielding a higher-quality file. 8-bit depth represents each sound pressure measurement (on a microphone or out of a speaker), with only 256 possible values (2^8). 16-bit depth samples have a much greater resolution, with 65,536 possible values (2^{16}). Bit depth is important to both file size and quality, and it's discussed in greater detail in Chapter 12, "Publishing." For now, a bit depth of 16 is fine because that's CD quality and is the bit depth of most loops. If your source media uses a bit depth of 16, selecting a bit depth of 24 offers no advantages or improvements in quality.

❋ **Low-pass filter options** are only available for 5.1 surround projects and are dealt with in more detail in Chapter 6.

❋ **Recorded files folder** sets the default location for audio files you record using the ACID software.

❋ **Start all new projects with these settings** will create new projects with your customized changes. If this is not selected, the ACID factory defaults will be used.

❋ **CALCULATING FILE SIZE**

From the bit depth and sample rate, you can calculate the final file size. For one second of uncompressed CD-quality audio:

(44,100 Hz × 16 bits) × 2 stereo channels = 1,411,200 bits

Or, because there are 8 bits in a byte:

(1,411,200 bits / 8) = ˜176,400 bytes

If you want your project to always use the same settings, and they're different from the ACID software's default settings (stereo, 44 kHz, 16-bit), select the Start All New Projects with These Settings option at the bottom of the dialog.

Saving Your Project

Immediately after you create a new project, you can save it as a project file on your hard drive. Until you save a project, no information or changes you make will be permanent. To save a project:

1. Select Save from the File menu, or press Ctrl+S.

2. The first time you do this, the Save As dialog opens. Browse for the desired location on your hard disk drive (HDD) and enter a name for the new project. The name will have the format MYPROJECT.ACD, replacing MYPROJECT with whatever name you choose. The .acd extension is required for ACID project files.

3. Click the Save button when you're finished.

After you save the project, you can make future saves by pressing Ctrl+S. You should get into the habit of pressing Ctrl+S whenever you've made a change that you like. Better to save as frequently as possible than to lose your work due to a power failure or some other glitch. To create a copy of a project, select Save As from the File menu and enter a new name. This is a great way to create different versions of the same song.

 WHEN TO USE RENDER AS

The Save and Save As commands are used only to save proprietary ACID project files (.acd). When you're ready to create a media file that can be played back outside of the ACID application, burned to a CD, or published on the Internet, use the Render As command.

Change Project Properties

Although you can set up the project properties when you create a new project, you can also change these settings at any time. Furthermore, you can always change the settings on the Audio tab when you make a final render:

1. Select Properties from the File menu, or press Alt+Enter. You can also click the Project Audio Properties button on the Mixer window (see Figure 1.10).

2. On the Summary tab, enter the optional song composition, engineering, and copyright information. Some audio file formats you create for publication will save this information along with the song. Otherwise, this information is used for your personal reference.

3. On the Audio tab, enter the number of additional stereo busses. This is important if you have multiple audio outputs, such as multiple soundcards.

4. Also on the Audio tab, set up the quality of the song. The default settings for the sample rate (Hz) and bit depth are 44,100 Hz (44.1 kHz) and 16-bit, which is CD quality. These settings can all be changed when you create the final version of the song for publication.

5. Set a default location for your recorded files. While it is not strictly necessary, paying a little bit of attention to this now will save you the headache of tracking down your recordings later.

6. For future convenience, select the Start All New Projects with These Settings item to always load new projects with these changes.

7. Click the OK button when you're finished.

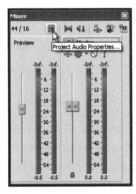

Figure 1.10
The Project Audio Proper-ties button on the Mixer window.

Exploring Loops and Previewing

After you start a new project, you see the ACID workspace and a completely empty timeline with no tracks on it. Because events are what you mix into a final song, and they're created from loops on your computer, locating loops is the first step in creating a song.

You locate loops using the ACID application's Explorer window. This window looks and operates just like Windows Explorer and is just as easy to use. The left side of the window contains the Tree view, which allows you to browse through drives and folders, while the right side contains the List view, which displays folders and clips. By default, the Explorer window is located in the Window Docking Area at the bottom of the ACID software's user interface (UI). If it's not, select Explorer from the View menu or press Alt+1.

Although you can drag clips directly into the ACID workspace from Windows Explorer, the ACID Explorer window displays more loop-related information and allows you to preview loops automatically. You can (and should) preview loops while playing back a project, so you can audition them to see whether they fit the creative vision for your song. There are a small number of buttons along the top of the Explorer window, pictured in Figure 1.11:

Figure 1.11
The Explorer window toolbar. The Auto Preview button is an on/off toggle. Clicking the View button cycles through the different view options, while clicking the arrow next to the button displays a menu of options.

* To display information about a selected loop, click the arrow next to the Display button in the Explorer window and select the Summary View item from the menu.

* To preview the selected loop file automatically, click the Auto Preview button in the Explorer window. If you enjoy extra mouse clicks, you can preview loop files manually using the Play and Stop buttons.

* When you have a folder of loops that you particularly like or that you use frequently, click the folder to select it (in either the left or right panel) and click the Add to Favorites button. This creates a shortcut to that folder in the special My Favorites folder, found in the root of the Tree view.

The basic routine when you're adding media to a project is to play back the project (or loop play a smaller portion of it) and preview clips in the Explorer window one at a time (possibly using the arrow keys on your keyboard to move, pause, and preview the files in a folder) until you find suitable loops. Of course, this isn't an entirely random process. As you become more familiar with your loop library, you'll be able to zero in on what you need much more quickly.

LOOPS ON YOUR HARD DRIVE

Most loop libraries come on CD-ROM discs. The ACID Explorer window allows you to browse for and preview clips in any location on your computer, including on floppy disks (remember those?) and external memory devices. Typically, though, CD-ROM drives aren't as fast as your computer's hard disk drives (HDD). Because you'll be previewing loops frequently, it's highly recommended that you copy your loop libraries to your HDD. Although clips such as loops can take up a lot of space, you'll save a lot of time by having them on your HDD. Not to mention that you won't need to swap discs in and out of your CD-ROM drive.

Event Basics

Events and the loops they create are the bricks you use to build songs in the ACID program, so creating events is the most important skill to master. Fortunately, it isn't very difficult at all. Drawing or painting is the metaphor that is used in the ACID software for visually describing how music is created on the timeline. This is why the two primary tools used to create events are the Draw and Paint tools. The rest of this section covers all of the basic event operations, such as copying, pasting, and moving events around a project.

Creating a Track

All audio events, video events, and MIDI events are contained in tracks on the timeline. Therefore, you need to create a new track before you can create an event. To create a track, browse for and preview clips in the ACID Explorer window, and then double-click one to create a track.

When you add a new track to your project, the software adds it as the last track. You can also add clips to the timeline, creating a new track wherever you drop each file (provided you don't drop it into an existing track). Once the software creates a track and it's visible on the ACID timeline, it's ready for you to insert events into it.

Creating an Event with the Draw Tool

Finally, we get to the meat and potatoes of ACID music composition: the creation of events. The easiest tool to use is the Draw tool, which is selected by default when you first run the ACID software.

To draw an event, click the Draw tool button on the toolbar or press Ctrl+D. This is the default tool, so it may be selected already. Then click on the timeline and drag the mouse cursor horizontally from left to right to draw an event, as pictured in Figure 1.12. (Right to left will also work, if you prefer.)

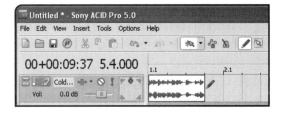

Figure 1.12
Using the Draw tool to draw an event on the timeline.

Events can be any length at all. Most events in a project are based on loops that can be repeated. Loop-type events that are created will loop automatically when the event extends beyond the length of the original clip. A small notch at the top and bottom of the looped event marks each repetition (see Figure 1.13).

Figure 1.13

This event contains three repetitions of a clip. The notches at the top and bottom of the event indicates each loop.

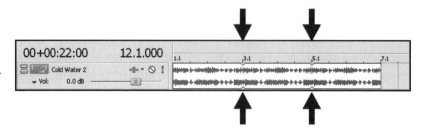

❋ **SNAP TO IT**

One thing you'll notice almost immediately about drawing events is that you can't exactly draw them anywhere you want. Instead, the event tends to want to begin on one of the vertical grid lines, and tends to want to end on another one. This behavior is called *snapping*, and it's designed to make sure events line up with the project's beat. You can toggle snapping on or off by pressing F8.

Using the Paint Tool

The Paint tool is not unlike the Draw tool, in that you still drag the mouse on the timeline to create events. Click the Paint tool button on the toolbar, or press the D key repeatedly until it's selected. Then click on the timeline and drag the mouse cursor horizontally to paint an event. The Paint tool has four uses:

❋ **Painting across tracks.** Although the Draw tool only works horizontally within a single track, the Paint tool works across *all* tracks. This can be a timesaver in some situations, but mostly it's just incredibly fun to doodle around with the Paint tool, creating a song instantly. Try this out in a live performance, painting events just in time before the playback timeline cursor arrives.

❋ **Creating multiple events with a single stroke.** Typically this is useful with a short One-Shot clip, such as a single kick drumbeat. When you drag the mouse on the timeline while using the Draw tool, a single instance of the loop is drawn no matter how far the mouse is dragged. When you use the Paint tool, you create a single event for every grid line that you drag across. By zooming in and out on the project (roll your mouse wheel), you can set the grid spacing to be once every measure, once every two beats, once every beat, or some other spacing. Then, to use the kick drumbeat example, you could use the Paint tool to quickly insert a kick on Beat 1 of every measure, on Beats 1 and 3, on every beat, or periodically at any grid spacing you zoom to.

❋ **Erasing.** Right-click an event using the Paint tool to erase sections of the event. The amount of the event that's erased is equal to the space between two grid lines, and is therefore dependent on grid spacing and zoom level. Snapping must be turned on for this to work.

❋ **Joining events.** Events that are split, or that are in separate pieces, can be rejoined by painting across the split or gap between them.

The Paint tool is very efficient, and you should definitely play around and learn how to use it. Although it's not as intuitive to some as the Draw tool, it's more powerful in many situations.

Multiple Clips in a Single Track

So far, we've kept things pretty simple while only talking about inserting a single clip into a track, but it is possible to put multiple files into a track. One reason for doing this might be that you want to keep all of your recorded bass parts organized in a single track. Once you have multiple clips in a single track, however, you have a dilemma: When you use the Draw tool to create an event in the track, which clip is going to be drawn? Let's start by adding three events to a track. You can do this by dragging multiple files to the same track from the Explorer window. Or you can right-click the track and select Properties. This opens the Track Properties dialog box (see Figure 1.14), which can be another target for dropped clips.

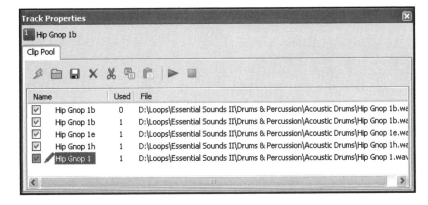

Figure 1.14

The Track Properties dialog with multiple clips. Notice the pencil icon next to one of the files on the list.

> ❋ **Note**
> You'll notice that one of the clips listed in the Track Properties dialog has a pencil icon next to it. You guessed it: This is the particular clip that will be drawn into the event in the track you are working with. This can be a little confusing at first, since the track name is, by default, the same as the first clip you used to create the track. In other words, you could be working in a track named "Rock Shuffle 01," but drawing events into that track named "Rock Shuffle 02" or anything else (see Figure 1.15).

Figure 1.15

A track's name can be entirely different from the name of the clip listed on the Paint Clip Selector.

Track Header

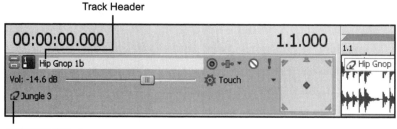

Paint Clip Selector

> ❋ **Note**
>
> An easier way to select the clip that is going to be drawn into the track is to select it from the Paint Clip Selector (see Figure 1.16). So, in this example, maybe you'd want to name your track "Rock Shuffle," but to see which clip was going to be drawn, you'd look at the name listed in the Paint Clip Selector. It might be a little confusing at first, especially to ACID old-timers, but if you are conscientious about track organization and naming, this organizational flexibility can really be a big help.

Figure 1.16

The Paint Clip Selector on the Track Header determines which clip is going to be painted into the track.

> ❋ **Note**
>
> Besides project organization, the multiple clips in a single track model also gives you a powerful new way to control how effects are mixed into the signal flow of your project. In other words, instead of thinking about a track in terms of an instrument or part, you could instead think of the Reverb track as where you'll want to put everything with a particular reverb effect. In almost all situations, it is better to use an Effects bus for this purpose, over in the Mixer window, but it is a possibility.

Snapping

Snapping is a default behavior in the ACID software. It's a huge timesaver because it synchronizes loops to the beat automatically. Snapping applies not only to moving events, but also to event creation and trimming (see Figure 1.17). There will be many times when you won't want an event to snap to the visible grid lines, and there are two main solutions to this: Turn off snapping or zoom in on the project. There are three ways to turn off snapping:

Enable Snapping button

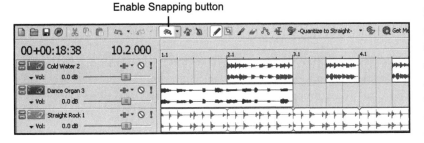

Figure 1.17

Events line up with the vertical grid lines on the timeline. Also notice that the beats in the drum part tend to line up with the grid lines as well. This is all automatic as long as snapping is turned on.

❋ Click the Enable Snapping button on the toolbar to toggle it on or off. Snapping is on when the button is pressed.

❋ Press the F8 key. This is a shortcut for the Enable Snapping button and toggles this function on or off.

❋ To disable snapping temporarily, click on an event and then press the Shift key without releasing the mouse button. Now you can drag the event with snapping disabled temporarily.

Moving and Trimming Events

You can move events around on a track easily by dragging them. Events must remain within their original track (that is, you can only drag events horizontally). Once again, the leading edge of the event snaps back and forth to the grid lines as it's dragged. You can drag events over other events on the timeline, covering them up.

Trimming events is about as easy as moving them. Move the mouse cursor over an event edge. When the cursor changes from a tool icon (such as the pencil icon for the Draw tool) to the trim cursor (see Figure 1.18), drag the edge of the event toward the center of the event to shorten it, or away from the event to lengthen it. Again, the edge you're trimming snaps to the grid lines. Events that you're trimming are always selected, which is indicated by an event background color other than white.

Figure 1.18

As you move your mouse cursor over the edge of an event, it will eventually turn into a trim cursor, indicating that you can now drag the edge of events to trim them.

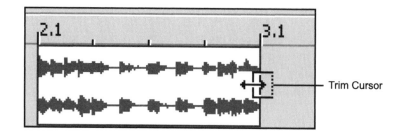

Trim Cursor

Waveforms

A waveform is a visual representation of a sound file. In ACID events, waveforms are visible in the Chopper window and the Track Properties window, among other places. Ultimately, you edit in the ACID application by ear, but you can make very precise cuts, splits, and trims simply by looking at the peaks and valleys of a clip or event.

❋ The size of a peak indicates the amplitude (loudness) of the sound.

❋ Stereo clips have two parallel waveforms that represent the two stereo channels. The top waveform is the left channel, and the bottom waveform is the right channel.

You can use waveforms to identify where the beat falls in rhythmic music. The two events in Figure 1.19 display the waveforms of two different clips. The top track has a spoken-word clip. The bottom track contains a drum part and displays clear periodic peaks in the waveform that line up with the beats marked along the top of the timeline. By zooming in and out on the timeline or in another window, you can see more detail in the waveform and make more accurate edits.

Figure 1.19

The top event is monophonic, and the bottom one is in stereo.

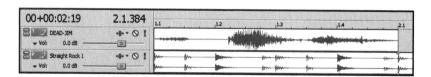

❋ **WHAT ARE SFK FILES?**

The ACID software calculates and draws the waveforms of clips at the time of insertion. For short clips (like most loop files), this is extremely fast and you might not even notice the delay. The waveforms for longer clips, typically entire songs or the soundtrack to a video file, take much longer to draw. In these situations, the application stores the waveform drawing on your hard drive as an .sfk file for future reference. For example, if you inserted suppers_ready.mp3 (roughly 23 minutes long) into a project, the ACID software would calculate the waveform, which might take a few dozen seconds, and save it to suppers_ready.sfk. You can delete these small .sfk files at any time because the ACID program will recreate them as necessary.

Slip Trimming

When you're trimming an event, the event edge moves to cover or reveal a clip. For example, when you trim a drum part with a kick beat on one, the kick remains on beat one, even though the event gets longer or shorter. In slip trimming, the relative distance of the clip from the edge being trimmed remains the same. In other words, the media within the event moves along with the trim and changes relative to the project, the timeline, and the beat.

Take a look at Figure 1.20 for a visual explanation. The top event is the original event. The second track shows what happens if you drag the edge of the event (trim it) longer. The last track shows the results of a slip trim to the same position. The event is the same length as the one in Track 2, but the media within the event is in a different position. Notice that the loop notch is also in a different position, and that the mouse cursor is a slip trim cursor.

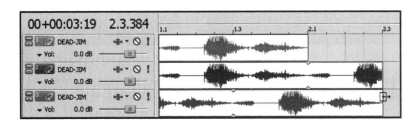

Figure 1.20
The third track shows the results of a slip trim. You can see the slip trim cursor on the last event, which is a reversed regular trim cursor.

You can engage slip trimming by pressing the Alt key while dragging the edge of an event. Watch for the mouse cursor to change from the regular Draw or Paint tool cursor to the special slip trim cursor when the Alt key is pressed.

Shifting the Media within an Event

The media within an event can also be shifted and moved relative to the project while the event itself remains stationary. In Figure 1.21, the first track has a single event in it. The track below it has an identical event, but the media within it has been shifted. Notice that the waveform of the event in the third track is in a different position than in the first track, even though the event remains in the same position on the timeline. The mouse cursor also changes to a shift cursor. This is simply a variation of slip trimming.

You can shift the media within an event by pressing the Alt key while dragging inside an event. The mouse cursor changes to the shift cursor when the Alt key is pressed.

Chopper Window

The Chopper window is a special tool that you can use to perform a precise trim of a clip and insert the trimmed portion into the timeline. The advantage of using the Chopper window is that you can trim an event in more detail without zooming in on the project timeline. There are also a number of other tools in the Chopper window that make trimming easier.

Figure 1.21

The waveform of the third event is shifted to the left, but the event itself remains in the same position when you slip trim.

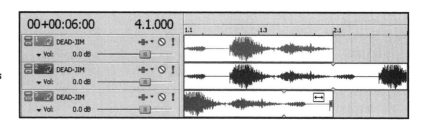

To view the Chopper window, select Chopper from the View menu or press Alt+2. The Chopper window displays the entire clip of the selected track. Click on a different track to load a different clip into the Chopper. To trim and insert events into the timeline using the Chopper:

1. Drag the mouse on the waveform in the Chopper window. This creates a selection region that's highlighted.

2. Position the timeline cursor on the main timeline where you would like the new event to be inserted.

3. In the Chopper window, click the Insert button.

You can see in Figure 1.22 that the selection area in the Chopper window is also highlighted on the main timeline, representing the location of the event to be inserted.

Figure 1.22

The selected area in the Chopper window is inserted into the timeline at the cursor's position.

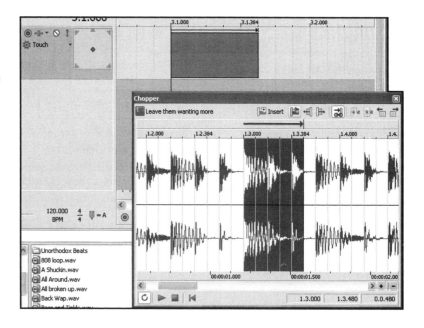

There are many more features, including (but not limited to) markers, regions, and spacing out events at regular intervals. See Chapter 4, "Polishing Up," for more information on trimming events using the Chopper, creating interesting variations on a clip by splitting it up creatively.

Zooming

Zooming is a fundamental skill that's easy to master. Zooming helps you work on the timing of your project in more detail. At extreme levels of zooming, you can make microsecond-level and even sample-level changes in event placement and trimming. Zooming also subdivides the project into finer grid lines (see Figure 1.23), giving you more control over event placement and trimming, yet it continues to offer snapping to the existing song structure.

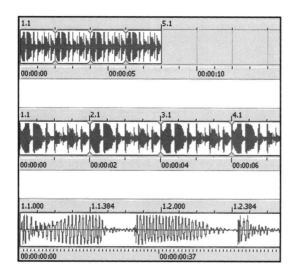

Figure 1.23
The grid lines in the top example are at every measure. The second example is zoomed in a bit, and the grid lines fall on each beat. The final example is zoomed in much further and shows even more detail in the pictured event.

There are a number of different zooming methods. Zooming in on the timeline horizontally means that less time is visible, but you can see more detail in the waveforms. Zooming out horizontally shows more of a project and gives you an overview of the song. Vertical zooming changes the track height. More information on zooming is found in Chapter 2, "Getting Around."

Copying, Cutting, and Pasting Events

The standard Windows functions of copying, cutting, and pasting all work in the ACID software as you'd expect them to. As with Windows, copying or cutting an event places the data on the Windows Clipboard temporarily. The Copy, Cut, and Paste items are all available on the Edit menu. The standard Windows shortcuts apply (Ctrl+C for copy, Ctrl+X for cut, Ctrl+V for paste). Copying leaves the original event on the track, while cutting removes it. You can also right-click an event and select Copy or Paste from the context menu (see Figure 1.24). Once you have some data saved to the temporary Windows Clipboard, you can paste it into a new location.

Figure 1.24

Right-click an event to display a context menu that contains the Copy, Cut, and Paste commands (among others).

When you're pasting an event, click on the timeline to move the cursor to the location where you want the pasted event to begin. The cursor snaps to the nearest grid line, meaning that the pasted event is snapped into synchronization with the project automatically. Snapping can be turned off (F8), or for more precise placement, you can move the cursor using the left and right arrow keys on your keyboard.

Another way of pasting in the ACID application is by using the Paste Repeat command (see Figure 1.25). This allows you to paste an event multiple times quickly, either end to end or with a defined interval between repetitions. To Paste Repeat an event from the Clipboard:

Figure 1.25

This event was Paste Repeated five times.

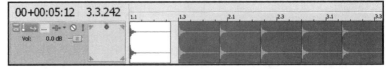

1. Click on the timeline to move the cursor to the location where you want the pasted event to begin.

2. Select Paste Repeat from the Edit menu or press Ctrl+B.

3. In the Paste Repeat dialog, enter the number of times you want the event to be repeated in the Number of Times to Paste box.

4. Select a paste spacing option and enter a spacing interval in the Paste Every box, if applicable.

One final pasting technique is the Paste Insert command. This command is very powerful, but it can be a bit intimidating because it shifts events in every track in your project. In short, Paste Insert pastes the Clipboard data into a project at the cursor position, moving every event in every project out of the way and down the timeline to the right. Events that are bisected by the timeline cursor are split. To Paste Insert an event from the Clipboard:

1. Click on the timeline to move the cursor to the location where you want the pasted event to begin.

2. Select Paste Insert from the Edit menu or press Ctrl+Shift+V.

In a regular Paste operation, the event is pasted directly over anything that's underneath it. In a Paste Insert operation, everything is moved out of the way and nothing is overwritten (see Figures 1.26a and 1.26b). Paste Insert is related to ripple editing (discussed in more detail in the next section), but it's unaffected by whether ripple editing is turned on or off.

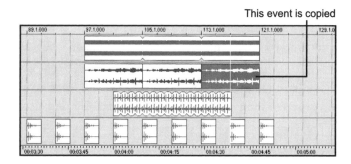

Figure 1.26a

This is the how the timeline looks before the Paste Insert operation is executed. The event that has been copied is highlighted.

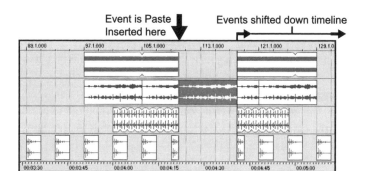

Figure 1.26b

With Paste Insert, the insertion point is marked and all of the other events in the project are moved down the timeline.

MOVING EVENTS OUT OF THE WAY
Ripple editing and the Insert Time command also move events down the timeline and out of the way.

Ripple Editing

Ripple editing, a term taken from the world of film, refers to moving clips out of the way when new clips are inserted earlier in a movie. Sometimes called a *film-style insert*, this means that no footage is lost or covered up by the inserted clip. This process lengthens the total length of the project. The result is not unlike executing the Paste Insert command. The important difference is that ripple editing operates on only a single selected track and Paste Insert works on the entire project, as illustrated in Figure 1.27. Both operations work from events that have been copied to the Windows Clipboard (Ctrl+C or Ctrl+X).

Selecting Multiple Events

There are three basic ways to select more than one event at a time. The first two are standard Windows operations:

* Press and hold the Shift key to select a range of events. In this operation, you click on one event, press the Shift key, and then click on another event. Both events are selected, as well as any events that fall between them. This includes events on the same track and events on different tracks. Imagine drawing a rectangle with the two clicked locations defining two of the corners. Every event that's covered by this imaginary rectangle is selected when the Shift key is pressed.

* Press and hold the Ctrl key while clicking on multiple events. Every event is selected individually and added to the selected group as long as the Ctrl key is pressed. Clicking a selected event again will deselect it.

* The Selection tool on the ACID toolbar can also select multiple events. Click the Selection tool button on the toolbar, or press the D key to cycle through the various editing tools. To select multiple events, click and draw a rectangle on the timeline, as pictured in Figure 1.28.

* Create a section in the music and move the entire section by dragging its bar. Sections are dealt with in more detail in Chapter 3.

Events are selected as the boundaries of the rectangle touch them, across multiple tracks and anywhere in the project. When you're using the Draw tool, you merely need to click and drag to move an event. When you're using the Selection tool, you need to click once to select it, and then click again and drag to move it. This also works when you're selecting multiple events: Click and draw the selection area, release the mouse button, click one of the selected events, and drag to move all of them.

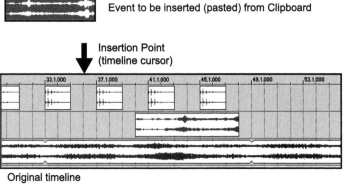

Event to be inserted (pasted) from Clipboard

Insertion Point
(timeline cursor)

Original timeline

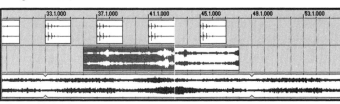

Paste (Ctrl+V)

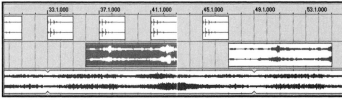

Paste with Ripple Edits

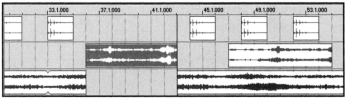

Paste Insert (Ctrl+Shift+V)

Figure 1.27
A comparison of normal Paste, Ripple Editing Paste, and Paste Insert operations.

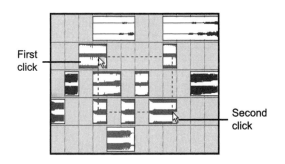

First click

Second click

Figure 1.28
Holding the Shift key and then clicking two events selects all of the events in between. The rectangle outlined by the dashed line shows which events are selected.

> ❋ **COMBINE FOR EFFECTIVE SELECTING**
> Use a combination of these operations to most effectively select the events you want. For example, you could use the Selection tool to select a broad range of events, switch to the regular Draw or Paint tool, press and hold the Ctrl key while going back through the events, and click on the ones you don't want to select.

Duplicating Events

Duplication of events is a close relative of copying and pasting. In combination with selecting multiple events, this is one of the most useful ACID skills you can acquire. Not only is it useful for a repetitive copy-and-paste task involving a single event, but you can duplicate entire sections of a project. Repetition in a song is an important structural element that cannot be ignored.

To duplicate an event, select the event by clicking on it. Press and hold the Ctrl key and drag the event to a new location. The original event remains in place, while a new event is created and moved to a new location. This is essentially a copy-paste operation, all in one quick action. The events in the top part of Figure 1.29 were all selected using one of the multiple selection methods discussed previously. Then the Ctrl key was pressed as the events were dragged to the right down the timeline. This instantly duplicated all of the events and repeated them, leaving the original events as they were.

Figure 1.29

All of the events in the top example were selected. Then the Ctrl key was pressed while dragging one of the events. This instantly duplicated all of the events.

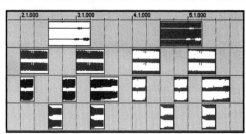

Playback and Mixing

Playing back a project or part of a project will quickly become second nature as you work with the ACID program. Mixing, on the other hand, is a surprisingly complex skill that cannot be overlooked in any project. It's pretty important to work with volume and panning to control the mix early in a project, but mixing is also probably the last and most important variable to finalize before a song is published or committed to a CD.

Project Playback

You preview a project and play it back by using the Transport controls just below the timeline (see Figure 1.30). What you hear when you play back a project is the sum total of all of the events, as mixed together by the ACID software. The position of the playback is indicated both by the timeline cursor and by the position numbers at the top of the Track Header.

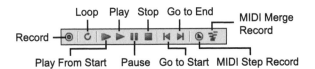

Figure 1.30

Project Transport controls are just below the timeline.

Because this is such a common operation, there are a number of important shortcuts that make this process easier:

❊ Press the spacebar to start and stop playback at the timeline cursor position.

❊ Press Enter to pause playback. The difference between stopping and pausing is that stopping returns the playback to the original timeline cursor position, while pausing freezes playback at the current position (and resumes it from there).

❊ Press Shift+spacebar to start and stop playback from the beginning of your project.

❊ Use looping playback to isolate smaller sections of the project.

Looping Playback

Looping playback means playing back the same short section of a project over and over. This becomes especially important once a project gets longer than 10 seconds or so. Although that short section is playing back over and over, you can simultaneously make small changes to the project and hear the results without delay.

Engage looping playback by clicking the Loop Playback button on the Transport bar. This is a toggle button: Looping is on when this button is clicked. Or press the L key to toggle looping playback on and off. (Q also works as a shortcut.) The portion of the project that's looped is indicated by the Loop Region bar at the top of the timeline. To create a loop region (see Figure 1.31), drag the mouse on the Marker bar. Click the Play button on the Transport bar when the timeline cursor is inside of the loop region, or just hit the spacebar.

Figure 1.31

The Loop Region bar is gray when looping is turned off and dark blue when turned on.

> **PLAYING BACK LOOP REGIONS**
>
> The loop region plays back only from within the loop region or earlier. Playback that begins before the loop region eventually enters the loop region, and looping will occur when playback reaches the end of the region. Playback that begins after the loop region never enters the region, and therefore never loops.

Monitoring the Mix

It's also important to monitor the mixing of all of the events and tracks by watching the Mixer window (see Figure 1.32) as the project is played back or events are previewed. By monitoring the project visually in the Mixer window, you can prevent clipping errors where the volume is too loud. This can cause distortion and ruin a song. The Mixer window is visible by default when the ACID program is run. If it's not visible, select Mixer from the View menu or press Alt+3.

Figure 1.32

This is an exploded view of the Mixer.

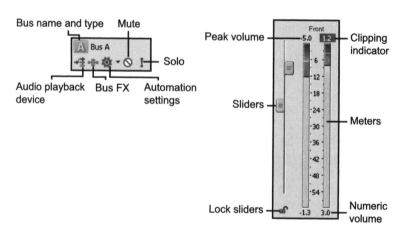

The Mixer window is subdivided into a number of master control panels, each of which has a fader and a small number of other controls. You'll use these control panels to adjust the mix and the routing of the audio signal through the ACID program. The controls correspond to similar controls found on mixers in the real world (see Chapter 6, "Mastering the Mix"). By default, the Mixer window displays a Preview bus and a Master bus.

❄ The Preview control panel only sets the volume for clips as they're previewed from the ACID Explorer window. Although this doesn't affect the mix of the project, the initial volume of a track is determined by the Preview volume. As with the other faders in the Mixer window, a numeric value for the volume is displayed below the fader. The Preview control displays both stereo channels, but you cannot divide the fader to control the volume of each channel independently.

❄ The Master control panel controls the final volume of the overall project. You can also add FX to the Master control panel to affect the whole project.

❄ Busses are different routes that the audio signal can take through the ACID software's virtual mixer. The Preview bus and the Master bus are available by default. If you have multiple soundcards, you can create additional busses to route signals through. For example, you could have the entire project routed out one soundcard through the Master bus, and have one of the solo tracks route out through another soundcard, perhaps to a pair of headphones used to monitor that track. FX and audio plug-ins can also be routed through their own busses. To route a bus to specific hardware, click the Playback Device button on the Bus toolbar. Busses can also be routed through other busses. More information on configuring busses is available in Chapter 6, "Mastering the Mix."

❄ Individual tracks can also be assigned to a bus. This is especially useful when you want to group tracks together to apply the same FX scheme to them as a unit.

❄ Busses are named automatically, but you can rename a bus name by double-clicking it and entering a new name. Typically, hardware busses are named using the letters of the alphabet. Assignable FX busses are named according to the effect or effects used.

Clipping

Clipping means the volume is too high. This happens when the total volume of all of the events in a mix combines to make the volume greater than 0 dB. The problem with this isn't that the volume is too loud and will irritate your neighbor, but that it has exceeded the possible range for the digital data. Information that occurs above this volume level is lost, which generally results in a poor-quality mix. Clipping should be avoided at all costs. Indeed, it's considered to be a mixing error.

A REASONABLE VOLUME

The maximum usable volume is a contentious issue. Suffice it to say that any volume less than 0.0 dB is technically acceptable, but pushing the mix all the way to 0 dB doesn't leave any room for future additions to a project. Keeping it below −10.0 dB always gives you a safety margin, but there's no real reason to use that number rather than any other reasonable value.

Clipping is displayed as a red decibel warning just above the Mixer's Master meters (see Figure 1.32). Normally, the decibel rating displayed in this area is not highlighted in red and serves as a peak volume indicator. The decibel values are reset every time playback is stopped and restarted. To reset these values during playback, click on the peak volume indicator.

Master Volume

The simplest way to solve clipping problems is to lower the Master Volume fader. This fader is divided into two halves, left and right, which control the volume to the left and right stereo channels:

* ❉ Click and drag the middle of the slider to move the sliders together.
* ❉ Double-click either slider control to align them together (if apart).
* ❉ Use the lock at the bottom of the slider to lock the two halves together relative to one another.
* ❉ The up and down arrow keys on the keyboard can be used to control the volume as well. Press Shift+up or down arrow to control the left slider, and Ctrl+up or down arrow to control the right slider.

The Master Volume isn't usually the best way to solve clipping problems, although it's certainly the easiest way. Clipping can often be an indication of a song that needs to be remixed in a more complex way. Because the Master Volume levels reflect the entire frequency spread of a project, clipping and poor mixes can happen because a project has too much bass or treble. In other words, clipping can happen even if the project doesn't sound too loud. Volume, panning, and equalization should all be considered as potential solutions to clipping problems. Regardless of whether your project *sounds* too loud, clipping should always be fixed.

Track Volume

The way tracks in a project are mixed together is determined by the combined volume of all of the tracks. Each track has a Multipurpose fader that controls the volume by default (see Figure 1.33). Drag the slider left and right to control the volume (gain) of the track. The precise volume is indicated numerically to the left of the fader. Since this is a Multipurpose fader, you can use it to control not only the volume, but also the panning and FX volume of the track.

Figure 1.33

The faders on these tracks
all control the volume.

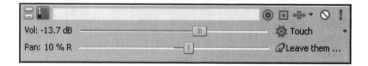

TRACK VOLUME
The initial volume of a track is determined by the volume of the Preview fader in the Mixer window at the time the track is created.

Panning

Panning is the balance between the two stereo channels. For example, panning 100% left means that the audio comes out of the left speaker only. This is an important and often overlooked aspect of ACID mixes. Blasting every loop out of each stereo channel at 50% can result in boring mixes and can cause clipping problems, whereas moving a saxophone solo track 70% to the right can make a mix sound more realistic, as if the performers are actually standing onstage in front of the listener. Careful track panning can also add space to a song, making it seem bigger in the room (although you don't want it to sound like you have a piano that's 50 feet wide). All in all, panning can be a subtle but important way to improve a song.

Fading Events

You can fade into or out of individual events by using the Fade Envelopes on either side of any event. Sometimes referred to as ASR (*Attack Sustain Release*) Envelopes, they're the easiest way to fade continuous events smoothly. To use ASR, move the mouse cursor over either upper corner of an event. When the cursor changes to the Fade Envelope icon (see Figure 1.34), drag the envelope toward the center of the event. The curved line represents the fade, and the duration of the fade is indicated by the grayed-out end of the event. Right-click the Fade Envelope, select Fade Type from the context menu, and then select a shape from the submenu. You can also access these shapes by right-clicking the upper corner of the Fade Envelope.

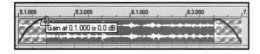

Figure 1.34

This event has Fade Envelopes on both ends. You can see the fade cursor and the numeric gain on the left side.

Envelopes

Envelopes are used in the ACID application to animate volume and panning in real time. You can use them to fade a track in and out gradually, or to move a sound across stereo channels. You can fade effects (FX) in and out using envelopes. Finally, you can use envelopes to fix localized clipping problems without adjusting the entire track's volume and panning. Envelopes are track-level objects and control the volume and panning of an entire track, but ultimately the track output is controlled by the placement of events within the track. Therefore, envelopes are closely associated with the occurrence of events in a track.

Envelopes appear as colored lines in tracks on the timeline (see Figure 1.35). A flat line indicates an unchanging volume or panning. Lines at an angle indicate a rising or falling volume, or a pan from left to right (left=top, right=bottom). By default, all ACID projects can use volume and pan envelopes. FX automation envelopes can be used if FX (audio plug-ins) are added to the Mixer as Assignable FX busses or if they are added to the Track Header. See Chapter 7, "Grooves and FX," for more information.

Figure 1.35

Four possible envelopes on a track. Hold the mouse cursor over a node to see a ToolTip that identifies the envelope.

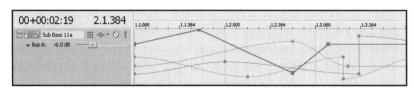

❄ WHAT COLOR IS YOUR ENVELOPE?

Envelopes are color-coded in the ACID program. Blue=volume, red=pan, and all other colors=FX.

In Figure 1.35, no events are visible in the track to make the illustration more clear. In an actual project, an event would also be inserted somewhere in this track to take advantage of this rather artificially complex tangle of envelopes. Without an event, there's no output from a track, and therefore no reason to automate the volume, panning, or FX with envelopes.

To use envelopes, right-click on a track and select Insert/Remove Envelope from the context menu. Then select the type of envelope to insert or remove (such as volume). Or, you can press Shift+V (volume) or Shift+P (pan).

To remove envelopes from a track, right-click the track and select Insert/Remove Envelope from the context menu, or toggle it with Shift+V and Shift+P. Then, from the submenu, select the envelope that you want to remove. Active envelopes have check marks next to them.

Envelopes can remain active (that is, affect a track's output) and still be invisible. To show/hide envelopes, select Show Envelopes from the View menu. From the submenu, select the particular envelopes you want to show/hide. You can instantly show or hide the Volume and Pan Envelopes by pressing the V or P key. These shortcut keys insert new envelopes if a track doesn't already have an active envelope of the corresponding type. They never remove an envelope, however.

The small square boxes on an envelope are called *nodes* and are used as animation key points. An envelope is the line between two nodes, either straight or with a curve, indicating a smooth animation of the volume or panning (see Figure 1.36).

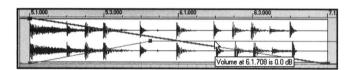

Figure 1.36
The event in this example pans from left to right (Pan Envelope goes from top to bottom) as the volume gradually fades in (Volume Envelope starts on the bottom and rises to the center). Each of the envelopes has two visible nodes with a straight envelope line between them.

You can easily modify envelopes and nodes with just a few clicks:

❋ Double-click an envelope to add a node.

❋ Drag nodes up or down to change the volume or panning. You can also drag the line between two nodes to move both simultaneously.

❋ Drag nodes left or right to reposition them.

Creating MP3 Files

The final step in any ACID project is the creation of a song. Up to this point, the project has been saved as an ACID project file (.acd), so the only way to hear it is to play it back from within the ACID software. To make the song available universally, you need to save it to a standard multiclip format. The process of creating a multiclip from a project file is called *rendering*. The format you choose affects the size of the clip, the quality, and how accessible it is to other people:

* If you want to create an audio CD that others can play on their home stereos or car CD players, the standard Windows .wav format is a good choice. The quality is very high, but these files are far too large to e-mail to friends or post on the Internet.

* If you want to publish your song on the Internet, the MP3 audio formats are a good choice. Small file sizes (at the price of some quality) make this format ideal for e-mail and iPods as well.

Currently, one of the most popular formats is the MPEG-1, Layer 3 format, or MP3. This certainly isn't the only format you can use, nor is it necessarily the best. It's very widespread, however, and it's an excellent format if you want to share your song with others. To render an MP3, follow these steps:

1. Select Render As from the File menu to bring up the Render As dialog (see Figure 1.37).

2. Choose a format from the Save As Type list. In this case, choose MP3 Audio.

3. Enter a name for the song in this format: mysong.mp3. The project's name is the default name.

4. Choose a compression template from the Template list. This is a complex balancing act between quality and file size, with the size increasing as the quality does. For now, 128 Kbps, CD-quality audio is a good choice, yielding a fairly small file with acceptable quality.

5. Browse for a location to save the file and click the Save button.

Render times can vary, depending on the length and complexity of the project, but typically it takes only a few seconds. (Video renders can be significantly longer.)

Rendering formats, maximizing quality versus compression, and tweaking all of the various settings for rendering are covered in much more detail in Chapter 12, "Publishing."

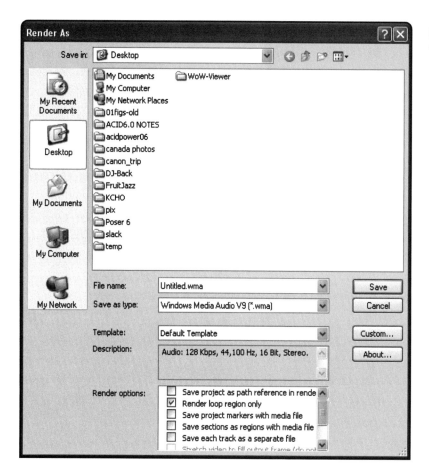

Figure 1.37
The Render As dialog.

2 } Getting Around

Familiarity with Sony Media Software's ACID® interface is critical to getting the most out of this software. The ACID workspace is logical and efficient, and it's designed with a specific workflow in mind. Understanding this workflow and the underlying design will maximize your experience with the ACID software.

Fortunately, learning how to use the workspace, or user interface (UI), is a simple process. This chapter serves as a full introduction to all of the various parts of the ACID UI. In later chapters, we'll explain how to use individual controls and windows more fully as they become relevant.

A Visual Tour

The UI is broken up into three major sections, as illustrated in Figure 2.1. Significant portions are taken directly from Microsoft Windows design principles. This isn't theft on the part of the Sony Media Software engineers, but rather a good use of tools that you're already familiar with. Getting to know the overall layout will make using the ACID program (and reading this book) easier.

The three major sections are as follows:

❊ **Menu and toolbar.** These are standard Windows features that you're probably comfortable using. The menus contain very nearly all of the commands that control the ACID application. The toolbar contains a smaller subset of more frequently used commands and can be customized to display your choice of buttons.

❊ **Timeline.** Timelines are almost universal in multimedia and animation applications. Time increases as you progress toward the right side of the timeline, allowing you to align events in a project visually. One important aspect of the ACID software's timeline area is the Track Header at the far left. Although it's not a part of the timeline proper, the Track Header contains many special controls.

❋ **Window Docking Area.** Below the timeline is the Window Docking Area. This is a broad catchall area that can contain all of the smaller sub-windows that do the real work in the ACID software. These sub-windows don't need to remain in this lower region. You can drag them anywhere on the screen you want.

Figure 2.1

An overview of the ACID user interface (UI).

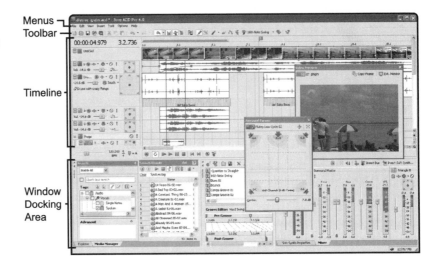

These three areas are discussed in more detail later in this section.

Windows Standards

Many of the menu and toolbar items in the ACID application are standard features of any good Windows application. The main menus at the top of the UI are the most complete list of available commands in the software.

The ACID application makes extensive use of shortcuts to speed up editing. Many of these shortcuts follow standard Windows conventions. For example, you can execute the Copy command by pressing Ctrl+C. Likewise, you can execute a Save command by pressing Ctrl+S.

Beyond the standard Windows commands, each ACID menu shortcut is identified to the right of that command. For example, you can display all of the various windows in the application instantly by using the commands on the View menu, or by using the associated keyboard shortcuts. Figure 2.2 shows the View menu.

To view the Explorer window, press Alt+1. Notice the V next to the View > Show Envelopes > Volume menu item, indicating that all you need to do is press V to toggle the Volume Envelope on and off. Although you can navigate most ACID menus using keyboard shortcuts, only a limited subset of commands have hotkey shortcuts that can be executed without navigating menus.

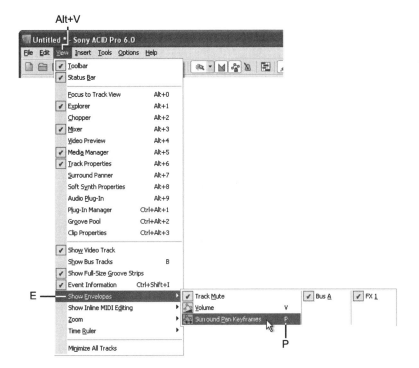

Figure 2.2
Press Alt+V (View menu command), E (Show Envelopes item), and then P to toggle the Pan Envelopes. Volume Envelopes can be toggled by pressing V at any time.

As you'll start to notice as you work with the ACID software, the user interface is both simple to use initially and incredibly deep and complex. Showing and hiding envelopes is just one example:

❄ Pressing capital V (Shift+V) will show and hide Volume Envelopes in the selected track.

❄ Pressing lowercase v will show and hide all Volume Envelopes across all tracks.

This behavior extends to Pan Envelopes as well: Just substitute P and p into the previous operations.

Timeline

The timeline forms the bulk of the ACID UI. This is where your project is laid out, left to right, in chronological order. The various sounds or loops that you use to create a song are mixed together in tracks from top to bottom. There's no hierarchy to the tracks, as far as dominance in your mix is concerned. All loops that overlap vertically are mixed together to form the audio that's played back from the ACID application. The timeline is made up of many separate parts (see Figure 2.3).

The basic layout of the timeline is functional and easy to get used to:

❄ ACID tracks correspond to audio tracks in the real world. In a traditional recording studio, a recording engineer can record multiple parts in a studio session to different tracks on a tape, such as a drum track, a saxophone track, a bass guitar track, and a piano track.

Figure 2.3

The various parts of the timeline.

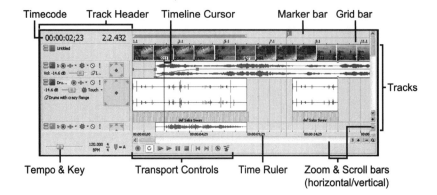

Because each track is independent of the others, the engineer can then modify and mix those tracks individually. ACID tracks operate in a similar way, but they're actually much more versatile. An ACID track might have an audio recording, a MIDI composition, or a video component.

❊ The timecode at the upper left of the UI specifies the current position of the edit cursor (Time at Cursor) in a selected format, including specific measure and beat information.

❊ You can adjust the tempo and key of the project in the area just below the Track Header, which is the vertical column to the left of the main timeline in Figure 2.3.

❊ The Marker bar, Grid bar, and time ruler all help you align events and organize a song. You can change the particular units that are displayed according to your personal preferences.

❊ The zoom and scroll bars are important and easy to use, allowing you to see more detail in a project or navigate quickly to a new location.

> ❊ **CURSORS, FOILED AGAIN!**
> There are two basic cursors in the ACID application. One is the standard Windows mouse cursor, which most frequently appears as an arrow. In the software, the straight vertical line that runs from the top to the bottom of the timeline is the edit cursor.

Navigating the Timeline

Moving forward and back on the timeline moves you forward and back through time in your project. The edit cursor marks the current position and is the focus of any actions that you take. For example, when you press the spacebar, the project begins playing back from the edit cursor's position. If you paste an event into a project (Ctrl+V), it will be pasted at the edit cursor's position. Clicking anywhere in the timeline area moves the edit cursor to that position.

Horizontal Scrolling (through Time)

You can navigate the timeline by using the horizontal scroll bar at the bottom. This allows you to view different parts of the project, and it's independent of the edit cursor (that is, the edit cursor doesn't always need to be on the screen).

❄ Use the arrow buttons on either end of the scroll bar to move left or right through a project.

❄ Drag the scroll bar to move left or right.

❄ Press and hold the Shift key and use your mouse wheel to move left or right.

❄ **MOUSE WHEELS**

The wheel in the center of a Windows mouse is referred to as the mouse wheel, wheel button, or scroll wheel. Many Windows applications now take advantage of the mouse wheel for scrolling and zooming. I don't want to sound like a mouse salesman, but once you've used a mouse with a wheel, you'll wonder how you ever lived without it. This is doubly true in the ACID application.

Vertical Scrolling (through Stacked Tracks)

Eventually, a project will have enough tracks stacked up that it's difficult to view all of them at once. You'll need to move up and down through the various tracks in a project:

❄ Use the arrow buttons at the top and bottom of the vertical scroll bar.

❄ Drag the vertical scroll bar up and down.

❄ Press and hold the Ctrl key and use your mouse wheel to move up and down.

Zooming

Zooming in and out on the timeline is one of the most fundamental skills in the ACID application. Fortunately, zooming is very easy, especially if you have a mouse with a wheel button.

Project Zooming

Zooming controls the accuracy of your editing in the ACID software. Zooming in on a project allows you to see greater detail in an event's waveform or perform edits within very small fractions of a second, right down to the audio sample level. Zooming out allows you to get a better overall feel for a project, allows for much faster navigation, and lets you copy large sections of the project and paste them to other locations. You'll constantly be zooming out to move around a project and then immediately zooming back in to make a precision edit:

❄ Use the + or – button on the horizontal scroll bar.

❄ Drag the edge of the horizontal scroll bar.

❄ Use the mouse wheel button.

Figure 2.4 shows two different zoom levels of the same project.

Figure 2.4

Zooming out allows you to see more of your project (top), while zooming in allows you to see more detail. Notice the time scale at the bottom of the two screen grabs: The top grab displays 15 minutes of a project, while the bottom grab spans two minutes.

Zoomed out

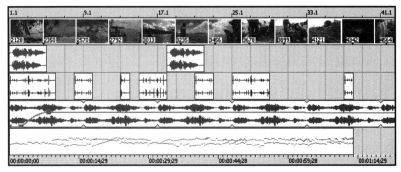

Zoomed in

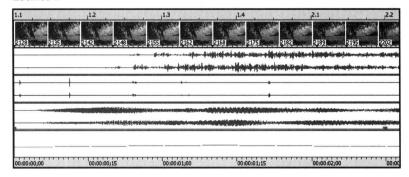

Track Zooming

Less important than project or timeline zooming is track-level zooming. This simply controls the height of the tracks in the ACID software (see Figure 2.5), allowing you to see more tracks at one time (zoomed out) or more detail in a track (zoomed in):

※ Use the + or − button on the vertical scroll bar.

※ Click the area between the + and − buttons and drag up or down.

Transport Controls

The Transport controls (see Figure 2.6) operate like standard media file playback or VCR controls. You'll use these buttons to move the edit cursor around on the timeline, and to control playback and recording in a project. A few Transport controls are also available in the Explorer and Chopper windows.

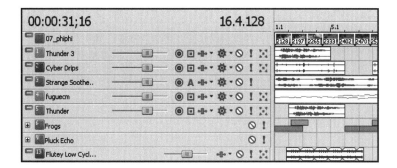

Figure 2.5

Zooming out using the vertical zoom/scroll bar makes the tracks shorter in height and allows more tracks to be viewed at a time.

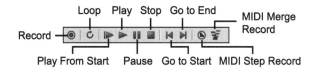

Figure 2.6

The Transport controls handle playback and navigation around your project.

Tracks

Tracks are analogous to audio tracks in a multitrack recording environment. The digital tracks in the ACID application are extremely flexible organizational tools where you will lay out the clips that make up your project. Each track can be associated with a particular media file, whether audio, video, or MIDI. Tracks can also contain a number of different clips, if you want; for example, you could put all of your different bass clips into a single track. Track-level controls include effects, volume, panning, and other important aspects of how the application mixes a media file into a project. Tracks can be expanded, minimized and grouped, organized and nested into related Folder Tracks.

When you add media files into a project, a new track is created for the file, which is now treated as a clip in the ACID software. For example, depending on the type of audio media you add, one of three clip types is created to accommodate it: Loop, One-Shot, or Beatmapped. When you add multiple different media files to a track, multiple clips are created and made available to be painted into the track.

Each track has two major parts: the Track Header on the left and the timeline portion of the track on the right (see Figure 2.7). The Track Header serves as the control panel for the track, with Volume faders and FX controls, and is analogous to the track controls on a mixer board in a recording studio. The main timeline portion of the track is where the song is drawn and most editing takes place.

Figure 2.7

Tracks are stacked on the timeline and divided into two parts: the Track Header and the main body of the track on the timeline.

Track Header   Timeline

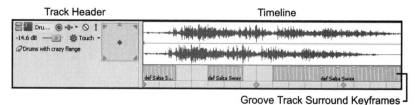

Groove Track Surround Keyframes

Folder Tracks

You can group tracks together into nested Folder Tracks, which is an important organizational trick that will keep your timeline workspace manageable. How you use Folder Tracks is up to you, but a good example might be to put all of your bass elements into one Folder Track set, your keyboards into another, and your percussion into another set. Or you could break it up by melody and harmony. Folder Tracks can contain other Folder Tracks, so you can create quite a bit of structure with this important tool. There isn't a right or wrong way to do it and the Folder Track structure does not change the mix of a project, although you can mute and solo groups of tracks in a Folder Track.

To create a Folder Track, right-click in the Track Header and select Insert Folder Track (Ctrl+ Alt+F). Name the new Folder Track and then drag any tracks you want into the new hierarchy. You can group your tracks however you'd like—for example, grouping all percussion parts or vocals together. The Minimize and Maximize buttons then collapse and expand the tracks to conserve space and make your projects more manageable (see Figure 2.8).

Figure 2.8

Tracks can be organized and grouped together into Folder Tracks. In this image, you can see Folder Tracks ("Pianos" and "Synths") within another Folder Track ("Keyboards"). All can be minimized to a single very narrow track.

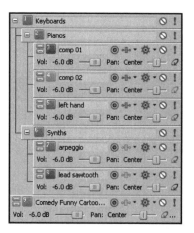

Events

Events are the most fundamental objects on the ACID timeline. You can think of events as containers for media files or as windows into a media file. A single event can contain multiple repetitions of a media file or only a small portion of a much larger file. Events are drawn or painted onto the timeline and represent the project's output visually. Depending on the zoom level, events also display the sound in a media file with a waveform drawing (see Figure 2.9). This waveform shows the amplitude (that is, loudness) of the sound waves over time, making visual edits possible. You'll very rapidly begin to recognize what you hear in the waveforms you see, making it possible to cut precisely between two drumbeats, for example.

> ❄ **FILE > CLIP > EVENTS**
> We are going to call any audio, MIDI, or video file on your computer a "media file" or just "file." Once a media file is in a track in an ACID project, we'll refer to it as a "clip." An "event" is what you create when you select and paint a clip (or part of a clip) onto the timeline.

Figure 2.9
Events contain media files and control exactly how they occur in a project. This event has four repetitions of a loop, and fades in and fades out.

Envelopes

Envelopes aren't exactly independent objects in the ACID program. Instead, they overlay events in a track, controlling the volume, panning, and effects in real time. Envelopes allow you to fade in and out of a loop or pan across stereo channels. For example, a purple Volume Envelope that starts in the middle of a track and moves down toward the bottom indicates a volume that gradually decreases over time and fades out (see Figure 2.10). Technically, envelopes are track-level objects; they operate on events and typically correspond to specific events in a track. For this reason, envelopes can be locked to events (that is, move as the events move) by making sure the Lock Envelopes to Events button is clicked (or by selecting Lock Envelopes to Events from the Options menu).

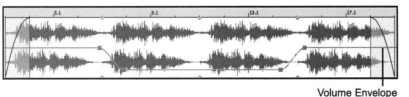

Figure 2.10
A Volume Envelope on a track over an event.

Volume Envelope

Marker Bar, Beat Ruler Bar, and Time Ruler Bar

Surrounding the timeline are a number of rulers and bars that help you measure and subdivide your project (see Figure 2.11).

Figure 2.11

These bars help measure and subdivide a project.

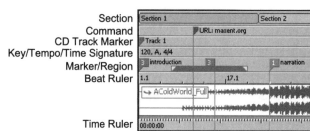

* The **Section bar** contains all markers and regions that you can use to organize and quickly navigate around a project. Sections are added by pressing Shift+S after first defining a loop region.

* The **CD Track Marker** lets you drop CD track markers when your ACID timeline and project encompasses an entire CD. This allows you to create an entire seamlessly mixed CD, for example, and add track divisions that your listeners can navigate to on their CD players. CD track markers are added by pressing the N key.

* The **Tempo/Key/Time Signature bar** holds all of the project-level tempo, key, and time signature change markers. Press T to insert a tempo change marker, K for key, or Shift+T for both. All of those shortcuts open the same dialog anyhow.

* The **Marker bar** contains all markers and regions that you can use to organize and quickly navigate around a project. Markers serve as snapping points for the cursor and events in a project. Press M to drop a marker and R to create a region from a selection.

* The **Beat Ruler** is divided up into measures, beats, and time, in the following format: measure.beat.time or 00.00.000. You can change the beat spacing, but the detail that's visible in a grid depends on the zoom level in a project. Beat lines serve as snapping points for the edit cursor and events in a project.

* The **Time Ruler** appears along the bottom of the timeline and is independent of the grid. It serves only as a reference to time and can display time in a number of different formats (for example, SMPTE timecode of HH:MM:SS:FF).

* The **Time Marker bar** lets you add markers to your project at absolute points in time that do not change with the tempo. You can add hit markers to the Time Marker bar by pressing H on your keyboard.

Toolbar

The toolbar (see Figure 2.12) contains a small subset of the total number of commands available in the ACID software. These buttons are the commands that you use the most frequently, giving you faster access to them. The ACID toolbar defaults to 20 or so common buttons, but you can now customize the toolbar however you like. From the Options menu, select Customize Toolbar to get started.

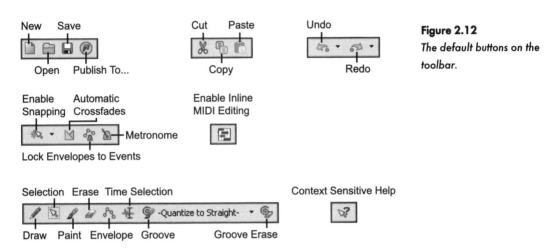

Figure 2.12
The default buttons on the toolbar.

To show or hide the toolbar, select Toolbar from the View menu. The check mark next to the Toolbar item on the View menu indicates whether the toolbar is visible.

You can display the name of a button (and the command it executes) by holding the mouse cursor over it. The ToolTip that pops up also appears over many objects in the application and often displays the associated shortcut keys.

The default toolbar is Sony Media Software's best guess as to what the user might want to do most frequently. The ACID software also allows you a significant amount of customization to fit your personal work habits, such as by specifying the particular command buttons that appear on the toolbar. To customize the toolbar:

1. From the Options menu, select Customize Toolbar.

2. In the Customize Toolbar dialog (see Figure 2.13):

   ❊ Select a button from the Available Toolbar Buttons list and click Add to add a new button.

   ❊ Select a button from the Current Toolbar Buttons list and click Remove to remove a button.

3. Click the Close button when you're finished.

Figure 2.13

Customizing the toolbar.

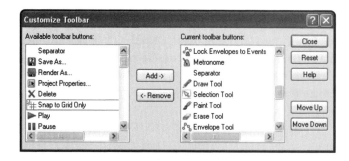

You can change the order of the buttons on the toolbar. Select individual buttons on the Current Toolbar Buttons list in the Customize Toolbar dialog, and then click the Move Up or Move Down buttons.

Window Docking Area

The Window Docking Area at the bottom of the ACID UI is a catchall area designed to conveniently organize many of the smaller windows in the software. You can find the full list of the 12 windows that are associated with the Window Docking Area on the View menu. A check mark next to a window's name indicates visibility; clicking a window's name changes whether it's visible.

> **SHOW AND HIDE**
>
> To make the various windows visible, press and hold the Alt key and then press the number keys 1–8 along the top of your keyboard. Three additional windows use Ctrl+Alt+1, Ctrl+Alt+2, and Ctrl+Alt+3 as shortcuts.

Docking Windows

The "docking" part of the Window Docking Area means that you can lock the various windows into place and organize them into tabbed windows at the bottom of the UI. This implies that there must be an undocked state for all of these windows, and indeed there is. You can drag any window to and from the Window Docking Area, and then resize and position it anywhere on the screen (see Figure 2.14). This allows you to customize the look and feel of the ACID software to suit your working style.

* To drag a window off of the Docking Area, click on the handle on the left side of the window and drag it out of the Docking Area (typically toward the top of the application).

* To return a window to the Docking Area, click the title bar and drag it back to the Docking Area until it snaps into place.

Floating Mixer window

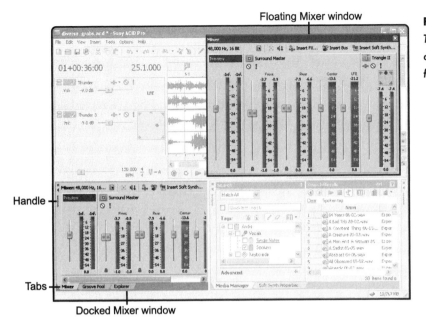

Figure 2.14
The Mixer window in its docked and undocked (or floating) states.

Handle

Tabs

Docked Mixer window

Organizing the Window Docking Area

The purpose of having a Docking Area is organizational. The Docking Area organizes the various windows in two distinct ways. First, you can divide the Docking Area itself into a number of different regions. Second, each region in the Docking Area can contain any or all of the various windows, stacked in a tabbed arrangement. Typically, the Docking Area is divided into two (or sometimes three) regions, with each region containing one or two windows.

The Window Docking Area in Figure 2.15 is divided into three regions, allowing convenient access to all of the possible windows. Notice that the Video Preview and the Mixer windows are in their own regions. In this case, this keeps these windows visible at all times for previewing and monitoring project playback. You can rearrange windows in the Docking Area by dragging them by the handle on the left side.

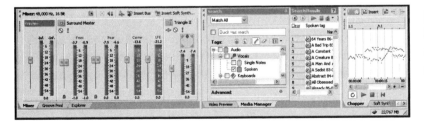

Figure 2.15
Here, the Window Docking Area is divided into three regions.

* To stack windows in the same region, drop a window's handle directly on another window's handle.

* To place a window in its own region in the Docking Area, drop the window's handle anywhere in the Docking Area away from any other window's handles.

Although it's possible to have each window in a separate region or all of them in a single region, it's probably best to stack some less frequently used windows in the same region.

LAY IT OUT
Layout considerations include frequency of use and available screen real estate. Although the exact layout is entirely up to you, in a good layout you rarely ever need to resize or move any of the windows.

Resizing Windows

You can resize the various windows by dragging their edges in and out. Windows can be resized in either a docked state or a free-floating state. The entire docking region can be made taller or shorter by dragging the bar that separates the Transport controls from the Window Docking Area. In all cases, watch for the mouse cursor to change to a resize cursor when it's over the correct location for resizing. You can also toggle the Window Docking Area on and off by pressing F11 on your keyboard.

SAME AS IT EVER WAS
The ACID software saves the window layout that you've customized. When you restart, it remembers all of the changes you've made.

Defining the Windows

Each of the windows in the ACID application is a miniature application in and of itself. In the next few pages, we will simply define the purpose of each of these windows. More detailed explanations will be saved for later chapters as each window becomes relevant to your project.

Focus to Track View (Alt+0)

Although it is not technically a window in any formal sense of the word, the main timeline and track area in the ACID software forms the canvas that you'll paint your song into. You can shift the focus of the program back to the main Track view by pressing Alt+0 (the Alt key and zero). This is an important shortcut for those of you who are mousephobic, because it returns you back to the main timeline when working in all of the other windows in the program (see Figure 2.16).

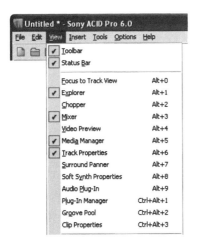

Figure 2.16
The View menu contains all of the commands for revealing and hiding the various windows in the workspace.

SHORTCUT SHOW

The shortcut key presses listed for each of these windows shows them and does not hide windows that are already visible. You can hide (in other words, close) windows from the View menu or by clicking the close button in the upper-right corner of each window.

Explorer (Alt+1)

The ACID Explorer window functions exactly like Windows Explorer, and it allows you to locate and manage media files on your computer. It also allows you to preview a selected media file by clicking the Auto Preview button (see Figure 2.17), and it gives you additional information about the selected file in the Summary view at the bottom of the window. You can add media files to new tracks in a project by double-clicking them or by dragging them to the timeline from ACID Explorer. You can also add media files to existing tracks by dragging them onto tracks already on the timeline.

Chopper (Alt+2)

The Chopper window (see Figure 2.18) is a miniature audio-editing tool that allows you to trim audio files. It's completely non-destructive, meaning that any changes you make in the Chopper don't change the original source media file. The Chopper allows you to select shorter sections of a media file quickly and accurately, and then insert those sections into a track as events.

Mixer (Alt+3)

The Mixer window allows you to monitor your project and route audio signals to various channels and effects. The ACID software's virtual mixer contains many of the same features and controls

Figure 2.17

The Auto Preview button in the ACID Explorer window.

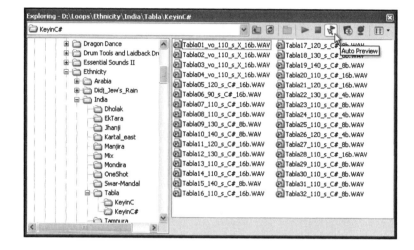

Figure 2.18

The Chopper window displaying an audio file.

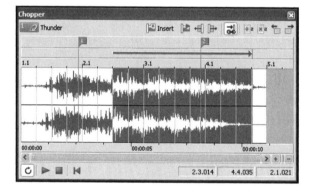

as a mixing board in a recording studio. Preview volumes, output volume, and FX routing are a few of the operations that you can control in the Mixer window (see Figure 2.19).

Video Preview (Alt+4)

The Video Preview window (see Figure 2.20) allows you to preview the video component of a project. With the appropriate hardware (such as a FireWire card and DV camcorder), the output from this window can be sent to a television monitor (see Chapter 11, "Video"). There are no editing controls in this window.

Media Manager (Alt+5)

One of the most important and useful windows in the ACID program is the Media Manager (see Figure 2.21). Although you can use the Explorer window to browse around your loop libraries just as you do in Windows Explorer, the Media Manager is the pinnacle of efficiency. It isn't entirely intuitive to use at first, but taking the time to set up a database and learning how to use

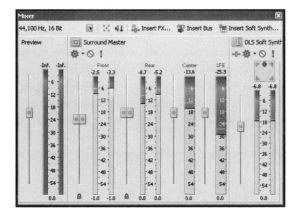

Figure 2.19
The Mixer window. Typically, it's less complex than the pictured 5.1 Surround project, but it can be a powerful tool for controlling complex hardware bus arrangements and effects routing.

Figure 2.20
The Video Preview window.

the Media Manager is well worth the effort. Better still, continued use makes your database easier to use over time.

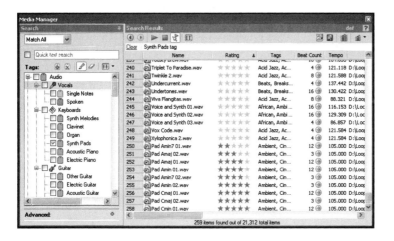

Figure 2.21
The Media Manager is essentially a database and searching tool.

Track Properties (Alt+6)

The Track Properties window displays all of the relevant information about a track and the clip or clips it contains (see Figure 2.22). Different types of clips have different types of properties. For example, MIDI clips have very different properties from audio clips. Video tracks don't have any properties to display in this window. One of the most important parts of the Track Properties window is the Clip Pool, which is a tool that determines which clip will be painted into the track timeline when multiple clips are in a single track.

Figure 2.22

The Track Properties window displaying information about a track and the various clips it might contain.

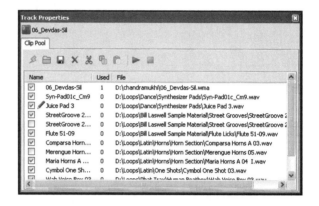

Surround Panner (Alt+7)

The Surround Panner (see Figure 2.23) lets you set the position of a sound as it's distributed to the five speakers in a 5.1 array. The virtual position of the sound is indicated by an orange diamond with lighter keyframe dots lining its animated path over time. You can also set the center channel and LFE volume in this window.

Figure 2.23

The Surround Panner with an animated position diamond and associated keyframes.

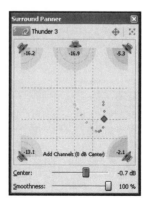

Soft Synth Properties (Alt+8)

The Soft Synth Properties window opens the controls for the soft synth plug-in you've selected for a particular MIDI track. Soft synths often have dials and knobs that mimic real-world synthesizers, but they can look like just about anything (see Figure 2.24).

Figure 2.24

The Delay Lama soft synth interface in the ACID Soft Synth Properties window.

Audio Plug-In (Alt+5)

You'll use audio plug-ins and FX to modify the sound of a project. You can use them to fix, clean up, sweeten, or otherwise improve the audio, or you can use them to change a sound more artistically. Each audio plug-in or effect has its own individual array of controls (see Figure 2.25) and is displayed in the Audio Plug-In window. This window is identical for both track- and project-level FX controls. You can find it by pressing the FX button on the UI.

Plug-In Manager (Ctrl+Alt+1)

The Plug-In Manager is a very simple window (see Figure 2.26) for organizing your plug-ins. Because you can have a lot of plug-ins, this window makes it convenient to see them all.

Figure 2.25

*One set of possible
controls that can appear in
the Audio Plug-In window.*

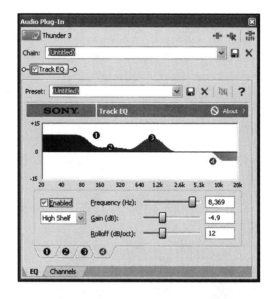

Figure 2.26

*The simple folder tree
structure of the Plug-In
Manager.*

Groove Pool (Ctrl+Alt+2)

The Groove Pool window (see Figure 2.27) is a powerful tool you can use to syncopate your tracks. Use the Groove Pool to organize and edit your grooves, and to add them to your project at the track level.

Clip Properties (Ctrl+Alt+3)

The Clip Properties window (see Figure 2.28) shows all of the information associated with an individual clip (media file). While some of this information is inherent in the file itself, such as whether it is an audio file or a MIDI file, many of the properties can be changed to affect how

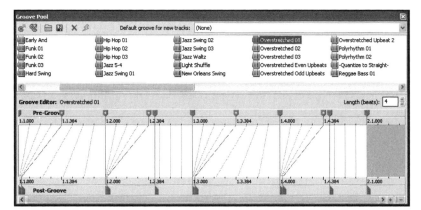

Figure 2.27
The Groove Pool with the browser window on the top and the Groove Editor on the bottom.

the clip is used in your project. For example, you could define the clip as a loop so that it repeats automatically on the timeline or set it up as a one-shot so that it doesn't. You can also define the tempo and key of the clip as it is used in the ACID application here.

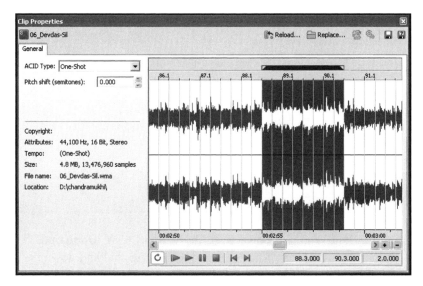

Figure 2.28
The Clip Properties window lets you view and change all of the characteristics of a clip as it is interpreted by the software.

Top Ten Shortcuts

Although it's impossible for you to memorize the entire list of available shortcuts in the ACID software, always remember that the application uses keyboard shortcuts extensively. If you find yourself using the mouse to click buttons, or navigating the same set of menus and submenus again and again, there's probably some type of shortcut. The mouse wheel navigational shortcuts are especially useful, although judging by the exhaustive use of keyboard shortcuts in the software, you might get the impression that the folks at Sony Media Software have an irrational fear of mice. See Sony Media Software's Help file or PDF manual for a complete list of shortcuts. Table 2.1 shows the shortcuts I find myself using literally every single time I use the ACID program.

Table 2.1   Handy Shortcuts

Keypress	Result
Mouse wheel	Zoom horizontally in and out on a project (also up and down arrow keys)
Shift+mouse wheel	Scroll through a project horizontally
Ctrl+drag an event (or events)	Duplicate selected events and move them to a new location on the same track
Spacebar	Play; start/stop playback
F8	Turn snapping on and off (or even better, temporarily disable snapping with the Shift key)
D	Change Edit tool (frequently used by pressing D to switch to the Selection Edit tool and then Ctrl+D to switch back to the Draw tool)
K	Insert key, tempo, or time signature change
M	Insert marker
S	Split an event (or events) at edit cursor position
V	Insert Volume Envelope (or view/hide Volume Envelopes)

This list could be topped by the standard Windows commands Ctrl+Z and Ctrl+Y (Undo and Redo), as well as Ctrl+C (Copy), Ctrl+X (Cut), and Ctrl+V (Paste). Of course, holding down the Ctrl key (or Shift key) allows you to select multiple events. And don't forget the Windows motto, "Save early, save often." Use Ctrl+S to do this.

Chapter 2 Quiz

1. Your ACID project is laid out chronologically in the:

    A. ACID Explorer

    B. Toolbar

    C. Timeline

    D. Your ACID project will never be laid out chronologically.

2. You can scroll horizontally on the timeline by:

    A. Using the arrow buttons on either end of the scroll bar

    B. Dragging the scroll bar left or right

    C. Holding the Shift key while moving your mouse wheel

    D. All of the above

3. The Window Docking Area can help you organize smaller windows in the ACID software. (T/F)

4. The Chopper window is used to:

    A. Trim audio files

    B. Solo audio files

    C. Increase the volume of audio files

    D. Deselect audio files

5. The Video Preview window allows you to play a video game inside of the ACID application. (T/F)

6. The shortcut to start and stop playback is:

    A. D

    B. F8

    C. Enter

    D. None of the above

7. Audio plug-ins modify the sound of a project. (T/F)

8. The detail that's visible in a grid depends on:

   A. The zoom level

   B. How many events you have on the timeline

   C. How many tracks are in your project

   D. The number of effects you use per track

9. The toolbar contains every command available in the ACID software. (T/F)

10. The Transport controls move the edit cursor around the timeline. (T/F)

3 } Composition

A well-composed song is more than a collection of sounds and loops thrown together on a whim. And it's more than just a beat, a bass, and a beautiful melody. Good songs, like good stories, have structure. We can divide a story into a beginning, a middle, and an end. It's made up of words, sentences, and paragraphs. We can view a song's structure in the same way, in terms of its component parts: beats, measures, and phrases. Sony Media Software's ACID® software has the tools to help you create that structure.

Although you should feel free to violate any and all rules in the name of art, even the most abstract avant-garde composers benefit from a basic knowledge of music theory and composition. Of course, this is a technical book so we'll only skim the surface of this artistic topic, thus you should broaden your musical composition skills with a book dedicated to that subject.

This chapter details some of the more interesting features of the ACID application and shows you how to create a song in a number of different genres. As you work through the examples, you should save the finished projects to use as templates for your own creations.

Song Structure

Just as a good story has a beginning, a middle, and a satisfying conclusion, many genres of music are based on some type of structure. At the largest level, you can break down a song into verses and refrains. You can then subdivide the verses and refrains into smaller musical phrases and ideas. At the lowest level, you find individual measures, which are in turn composed of notes and beats. Each level of organization is important in telling the complete story.

You can easily see the largest level of structure in the verse-refrain pattern of a standard pop song. Throw in an introduction and maybe a short solo break, and you have a complete song. The next few pages will demonstrate how to use markers to annotate a song and give it an underlying structure. Through clever use of duplication, you can build a pop song out of only two or three musical phrases.

The most common large-scale structure heard in popular music today is the verse-refrain-repeat structure. This structure is also very common in any sing-along type of song, such as church music or Christmas carols. The verses usually tell some sort of story, either individually or as a group, and each verse is different from the others. The refrain, or chorus, usually contains the main point of the song, often contains the words in the title, and is repeated more or less word for word every time. Although most composers avoid boring the listener intentionally, the predictability of this simple structure makes popular music more accessible. The listener can pick up the refrain very quickly and hum or sing along. Repetition can also make a song more memorable and catchy.

From simple children's songs to church music, the verse-refrain-repeat structure allows us to sing along, because everyone can pick up the repeated refrain quickly. We can assign letters to the various parts of a song to identify them. Let's label the verses with an A and the refrain with a B. A typical song might look as follows:

Verse	Refrain	Verse	Refrain	Verse	Refrain
A	B	A	B	A	B

The popular music you hear on the radio is rarely composed of only a few verses and a refrain. Most songs add a third element to spice up the mix, which we'll label C. The band Genesis had a hit song and album in the '80s that followed this pattern:

A B A C A B

This translates to verse-refrain-verse-break-verse-refrain. The break, or C, signals a major shift in the music. (This allowed the band to perform extended solos during live performances.) The return to the verse (A) and then the final refrain (B) gives the song a very satisfying resolution and ending. Of course, Genesis didn't invent this Biblically ancient and simple pattern with their song and album "ABACAB," but its widespread use in everything from acid jazz to zydeco cannot be overstated.

Songs often have more than just three parts. Extending the structure of a song is as simple as adding more letters. The point of using this type of notation is to demarcate the structure and highlight repetition. In improvisational music, especially jazz, a bandleader can unobtrusively mouth the letter "F" to the band to tell them the F section of the song is next. This helps to maintain the structure of the song, while still giving each performance a freedom of form. (He could have said "D" or whichever part he wanted them to play next.) Repetition, when used correctly, does *not* automatically mean a boring song. It's the first step in transforming the ACID software from a toy into a tool for creating songs.

In the very early stages of a project, the software allows you to divide the timeline into rough sections using timeline markers, regions, and an explicit Section tool.

The structure you create serves as a sketch or outline for the song, giving you visual clues about how it's coming together. This process isn't strictly necessary, but it can help you create satisfying, well-constructed compositions. If you've only been fooling around with the ACID program up until this point, you'll be pleasantly surprised by how much sophistication you can add to your projects with just a little structure.

Creating Structure

You can create a visual structure for a song by using visual cues such as sections, regions, and markers. These timeline cues allow you to outline the song and plan for future sections. They serve as quick navigation tools to move around the timeline and let you select, copy, and move entire blocks of your project to new locations. Sections, regions, and markers are all important for planning and structure in the early stages of songwriting, as well as for identifying specific occurrences of sounds and events.

Section Labels

The Section bar sits above the timeline and lets you demarcate areas of your project that correspond to musical sections such as verses, refrains, or the ABC sections we discussed earlier. Another popular and useful naming convention could be to name sections by guitar chords, if that is appropriate to your project. A typical section might last four measures (four bars) or eight measures, or any other length, depending on the style of music you are composing. For example, a traditional 12-bar blues composition might logically have sections that have a 12-bar duration. Or you might want to use shorter four-bar sections, three to each 12-bar pattern. Because ACID sections are completely inaudible, your own personal workflow will decide how you use sections to create structure. In our 12-bar blues example, it would certainly be easier to copy and paste 12-bars to move on to the next part of the song, but maybe you'd find it easier to create more variation with the four-bar sections.

Creating Sections and Labels

To add a new section (and a corresponding label), press Shift+S on your keyboard (see Figure 3.1). This will make the Section bar visible at the top of the timeline and create a new section at the edit cursor, with a length that matches the loop region, whether or not the loop region is actually at the edit cursor position. The new section is not just a simple visual cue that marks off part of the song, but it actually includes the events and envelopes on the timeline. That is, you have created a real section in your ACID project that contains everything in every track below it. The colored bar on the Section bar that shows you where the section extends is the section label.

You can also drag the edges of the section label to shorten or lengthen it. As with most elements in the ACID software, you can right-click the section on the Section bar to perform all of the relevant operations on it, such as renaming it or changing its color.

Figure 3.1

Press Shift+S to create a section above the timeline.

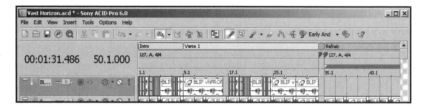

Working with Sections

As previously mentioned, sections are real structural parts of your project. When you grab the section label at the top of the timeline on the Section bar and drag it to a new location, everything on every track in that section will move with the section. This makes it almost effortless to duplicate arbitrarily large sections of your project in an instant. Because repetition is such an important part of song composition, this is indeed a very powerful tool and technique. There are a couple of options on the context menu for the section label that I want to highlight. Right-click the label to see this menu.

- ❄ **Delete** completely removes the label and the section itself, including everything on the timeline.

- ❄ **Remove Label** simply deletes the label marker on the Section bar, but leaves everything on the timeline intact.

- ❄ **Clear Events** deletes all of the events on the timeline within the section, but leaves the label intact and unchanged on the Section bar.

The convenience of working with sections cannot be overemphasized. When you are first working with sections, however, especially in an already mature project, you can almost instantly completely destroy huge sections of your project spanning dozens of tracks and possibly hundreds of events and edits. No worries: Press Ctrl+Z to undo any damage done.

> ❄ **SHIFT+S IS FOR SECTION**
> The simplest way to add a section is to first define the duration of the section using the loop region and then press Shift+S on your keyboard.

Markers

You can use markers to note anything useful in a song. One common use for them is to mark cues or transitions in a song. Because you can delete markers easily, you can use them as temporary placeholders in a composition. To jump to the location of a marker instantly, just press the associated number key on your keyboard. This type of navigation is limited because you can only set 10 markers that you can jump to, 0 through 9. (The total number of markers is unlimited, but only the first 10 will be numbered and can be accessed by pressing the number keys at the top of the keyboard.) The ACID software assigns numbers to the markers in the order of their creation. This allows a renamed marker to assume double duty, serving as both a numerical navigational element and a structural marker as renamed by the composer.

Creating Markers

To add a marker, right-click the Marker bar above the timeline and select Markers/Regions from the context menu. Then, select Insert Marker from the submenu (see Figure 3.2). Even easier, you can add a marker instantly by pressing the M key.

Figure 3.2

Right-click the Marker bar to insert a marker.

Markers are automatically numbered 1–9 and then 0 as you add them to a project. You can continue to add more markers, but they're not numbered after the tenth (0) marker is added.

 M IS FOR MARKER

The simplest method of adding markers is to position the edit cursor at the place where you want to insert a marker and then press the M key.

To instantly navigate to a marker, press one of the number keys 1–0 at the top of your keyboard (not on the number pad). You can quickly name (and rename) a marker to more clearly identify its purpose. Right-click a marker and select Rename from the context menu, or just double-click the marker. Then you can type or edit the name of the marker. Click away from the marker or press the Enter key to finish. Names are for your reference only. Figure 3.3 shows a number of markers used to identify the verse-refrain structure of a song.

✳ **MORE MARKERS**

Markers are, of course, general-purpose flags that can be used to identify anything. You can add markers on the fly during playback by pressing the M key. You can then go back later during editing, name these markers, and use them to snap and line up events.

Figure 3.3

Named markers define the structure of a song.

Moving and Deleting Markers

You can move markers by dragging them to any location. By default, markers are numbered according to the order in which they're added. Because you can drag a marker to any location, it's possible (and even likely) that markers with lower numbers may appear later on the timeline and seem out of order. Markers will snap to grid lines when snapping is turned on. To disable snapping temporarily, press and hold the Shift key while you drag.

There are three ways you can delete markers in the ACID software:

❋ Right-click a marker and select Delete from the context menu.

❋ To delete multiple markers, create a selection area by dragging the Time Selection tool on the Marker bar, right-clicking a marker, and selecting Delete All In Selection Area from the context menu.

❋ To remove all markers in a project, right-click a marker and select Delete All from the context menu.

LOOP REGIONS

You can create a loop region (time selection) instantly by double-clicking the Marker bar between any two markers. This applies to all markers, including key, tempo, region, and time markers.

Regions

Regions are related to markers in that they're used to create structure and instantly recreate loop regions (time selections). Region markers are green and come in pairs. (Regular markers are orange.) Regions are numbered along with markers automatically. Pressing the number key that corresponds to a region selects that region automatically. You'll use the two green markers that identify a region to recreate a loop region in a project (see Figure 3.4), which is used to control looping playback or to identify shorter sections of a project to be rendered (saved as a song).

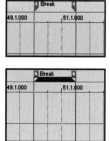

Figure 3.4
Right-click the Marker bar to insert a region. Regions are identified by two green markers. The loop region (time selection) in the lower image is dark blue and is used to loop project playback repeatedly.

To add a region, drag on the Marker bar to create a time selection (loop region) of the desired size. Then right-click the time selection and select Insert Region from the context menu.

 R IS FOR REGIONS
The easiest way to create a region is to create a loop region first by dragging on the Marker bar, and then pressing R.

Regions share many properties with markers, such as renaming, automatic numbering, and deleting. Working with regions is not unlike working with markers, except that they come in pairs:

❋ To create a region, set the loop region where you want it and press R on your keyboard.

❋ To name a region, right-click the left region marker of a pair and select Rename.

❋ To delete a region, right-click either region marker of a pair and select Delete.

❋ To move the entire region (both region markers with the same spacing between them) to a new location, hold the Alt key while dragging either region marker.

❋ To set the loop region between the two markers, double-click on the Marker bar anywhere between the markers. You must have looping turned on for playback to loop. This allows you to preview a shorter section of your project repeatedly, while simultaneously making adjustments to the project.

Time Markers (Hits)

Time markers are very different kinds of markers that you'll use to create or define structure in a song. The reason time markers are so different is that they can be completely unrelated to the parts of the song itself. They're markers that are dropped in reference to real-world measurements of time in terms of minutes and seconds and maybe even frames, whereas a song is divided into measures and beats. The beats in turn are determined by the tempo (number of beats per minute), which can vary wildly. One very important use of time markers is for film and video scoring, where you'll want to drop markers on frames that will not change location, no matter what happens to the tempo of the song.

Time markers are purple and appear on a dedicated Time Marker bar below the timeline. Because time markers are true to the measurement of time in the real world, they're ideal for syncing audio events in a project with video events. Time markers snap to units of time, not to the grid marks at the top or the timeline (see Figure 3.5).

Figure 3.5

The Time Marker bar with associated time markers at the bottom of the timeline.

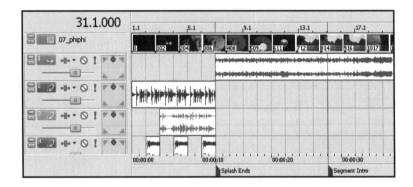

To add a time marker, position the edit cursor at the location where you want to drop a marker. Then, select Time Marker from the Insert menu. You can also press H as a keyboard shortcut.

> ❋ **H IS FOR HIT**
> Press H on your keyboard to drop hit (time) markers below the timeline. You might think that T would have been a better choice, but that is what we use for Tempo Change markers. If you dislike any of the comprehensive default shortcuts, go to the Options menu and select Customize Keyboard.

As with other kinds of markers, you can rename and delete time markers by right-clicking them to access the context menu. You can drag time markers to a new location and use them for navigational purposes as well (again, from the right-click context menu).

Musical Phrasing

How long should a verse or refrain be? As with all discussion of structure in this and the next chapter, there are some widely followed guidelines in much of today's popular music. Of course, you should feel free to violate these guidelines at will for your own projects, but a basic understanding of these principles is important to the creative process.

Beats

When you count along with a song, you're usually counting the beats. These beats aren't necessarily related to the drums or rhythm section of a song, they can be strong or weak, and they don't even need to be heard out loud.

Musical notation and time signature define beats in a very precise way. The speed or tempo of a song can be expressed in terms of the number of beats per minute (BPM). The BPM of most popular songs can range from a slow 80 BPM in a sad ballad to more than 200 BPM in frenetic dance music. You can play just about any style of music at just about any tempo (see Figure 3.6), so it's an overgeneralization to say that dance music is 120 BPM. (It frequently is, though.) On the timeline, you often see beats as sharp peaks in the waveform of events in percussion parts. As a matter of fact, the ACID software can often find beats in songs automatically, such as when it beat matches an imported track. (See Chapter 9, "Loops.")

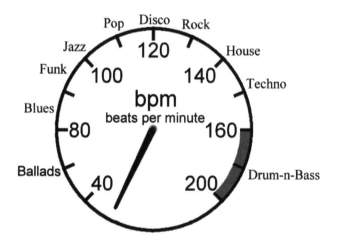

Figure 3.6

The tempos of some popular musical styles. This is only a rough guide, and each style covers a large range of possible tempos.

Measures

Musically, we can group beats together into measures. In western popular music traditions, groups of four are common. When something called a quarter note (1/4) equals one beat, we call this ubiquitous time signature *common time*. This is the default time signature in the ACID software, and it's represented by 4/4 in the lower part of the Track Header. (See the following section.) Most loops from Sony Media Software, and indeed from most loop content companies, are recorded in 4/4 (or less frequently in 6/8).

We can also refer to measures as *bars*. Because this is how we structure music, it makes sense that the ACID timeline is also divided into bars and beats. If you look at some sheet music, it looks like the top part of Figure 3.7. The bottom of the figure shows how the same music looks in the ACID application. Very similar, no?

Figure 3.7

Typically, measures are separated by lines in a score. The ruler at the top of the ACID timeline divides time into measures, beats, and ticks (with 768 ticks in a beat).

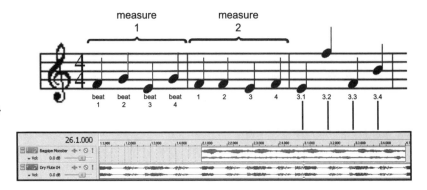

Time Signature

The bottom number in a time signature is called the *beat value*, and it represents the type of note that gets one beat in a measure: 1 = whole note (1/1), 2 = half note (1/2), 4 = quarter note (1/4), and 8 = eighth note (1/8). The top number in the time signature denotes the number of beats in the measure. So 4/4, or common time, means that there are four beats in a measure and the quarter note gets the beat. 6/8 means that there are six beats in a measure and eighth notes get a single beat. For most people, it's a bit complicated to think about this mathematically, but each time signature has a distinctive sound.

It's important to remember that the time signature is unrelated to the tempo of the music in any way. It's a relatively unimportant concept in the ACID software, as long as you're generally working with popular western music and loops. Once you start exploring other genres, time signatures can get rather wild. Indeed, some of the most interesting music in the world involves musicians playing in two different time signatures simultaneously, with the various parts dividing and coming back together again in complex ways. We aren't going to teach that here or even pretend we know how to do that sort of thing ourselves. Suffice it to say that the relationship between the time signature of a project and the time signatures of its various loops is important and can be very interesting. For more information, see the section on setting the number of beats in a loop in Chapter 9, "Loops."

Project Time Signatures

There are two ways to set the time signature of your project (see Figure 3.8):

* ❋   Click the Project Time Signature button and select a signature from the list (such as 2/4 or 4/4).

* ❋   Click the Project Time Signature button, select Other, and type in a time signature in the Custom Time Signature dialog.

The beat value is limited to the definitions of the kinds of notes that can be played: whole (1), half (2), quarter (4), eighth (8), sixteenth (16), and thirty-second (32).

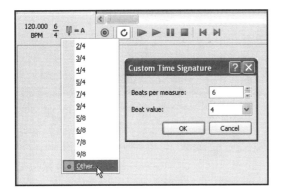

❋ **TIME SIGNATURES**

Both ACID projects and ACIDized loops have time signatures. By looking at the properties of a dominant loop in your project, you can figure out the original time signature and adjust your project accordingly. Or you can experiment with the complexities of multiple time signatures and really mix things up.

The grid on the timeline is divided to visually aid composition based on a time signature and, by default, the Ruler Marks will change depending on the time signature. You can change the grid spacing to accommodate different kinds of projects—for example, a video project—in which case the spacing will not change when you change the time signature (see Figure 3.9). To change the grid spacing, select Grid Spacing from the Options menu or right-click any blank area on the timeline and select Grid Spacing. Then, from the submenu, select the note value that you want the grid lines to fall on. Because you can snap event edges to grid lines, this can also make placing events on the beat much easier. Changing the grid spacing doesn't alter the project audibly in any way, and the inherent time signature that a loop was created in doesn't change. Changing the grid will help with composition and organization, and it sets the snapping behavior of events on the timeline.

❋ **RULERS AND GRIDS**

Notice that the grid marks might not necessarily line up with the ruler at the top of the ACID timeline. (For example, try setting Grid Spacing to Triplets.) The ruler divides the project into measures, with four beats subdivided into thousands of a second: 1.3.937.

Figure 3.9

Some time signatures and how the grid spacing might represent them. A single measure is displayed. Grid marks are visible only if the zoom level is high enough to reveal them.

Changing Time Signature Mid-Song

You can also change the time signature at any point in a project. Mid-song time signature changes are represented by blue markers at the top of the timeline (along with tempo and key changes). To change the time signature mid-song:

1. Move the edit cursor to the position where you want the time signature change to occur.

2. Go to the Insert menu and select Tempo/Key/Time Signature Change (or press Shift+K on your keyboard).

3. Enter the time signature you want to change to in the Tempo/Key/Time Signature Change dialog (see Figure 3.10).

Phrases

Just as measures are made up of beats, measures make up less formal groupings called *phrases*. A phrase can be as large as a verse or even an entire section (such as the A section of ABACAB), or as small as just a few measures. There's no strict rule about the length of a phrase, but again, the number 4 frequently turns up in phrases composed of 4, 8, 12, or more measures. Additionally, shorter phrases can be combined to create longer phrases. And phrases form the larger sections A, B, and C, which are combined into complete songs.

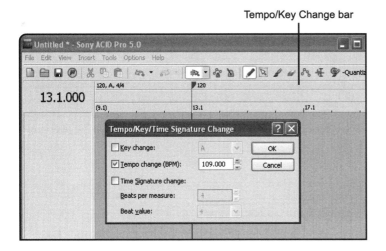

Tempo/Key Change bar

Figure 3.10
Changing the time signature mid-song.

In summary, songs are broadly divided into sections, which may be split into less formal phrases, which are in turn composed of measures, which are made up of beats. Whew!

One example is the 12-bar blues phrase, which is very (very!) common in popular music. This is the grouping of 12 measures into a single complete phrase. You'll almost certainly recognize this structure if you've ever listened to blues, jazz, or rock music. You can probably predict where the phrase is going and where it will end. Again, this predictability is part of the appeal of this simple structure. You couldn't set up the listener to expect the next bar in the phrase and then creatively surprise the ear if this phrasing wasn't so prevalent. See the next chapter for more information on creating a 12-bar blues phrase in the ACID program.

Tempo

Tempo is the speed of a song and is completely unrelated to the time signature. It's expressed in beats per minute (BPM) and can be changed easily to fit the mood of a song. In real music and in the ACID software, the tempo can also be changed mid-song. The software defaults to 120 BPM, which is fairly typical for popular music. Generally speaking, tempo in written music is usually indicated by the number of beats in a minute (see Figure 3.11), so estimating the tempo of a song from its score is a straightforward conversion.

Project-Level Tempo Changes

You can set and change the initial tempo of the project at any time, but it's best to plan out your song from the start. Tempo is important to the type of song you're creating and can set the overall mood of the piece. The default tempo for any new project in the ACID application is 120 BPM.

Figure 3.11

Tempo can be indicated in beats per minute (BPM) in written music and in the ACID software.

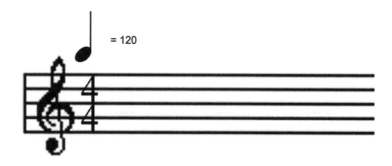

To change the tempo of a project:

1. Double-click the Tempo indicator at the bottom of the Track Header.
2. A box appears around the tempo and the cursor flashes. Enter the new tempo (see Figure 3.12).

Figure 3.12

Manually entering a new project tempo by double-clicking the Tempo indicator.

You can also change the tempo by dragging the Tempo slider next to the numerical indication of the tempo. As with many other sliders in the ACID software, holding down the Ctrl key will make the slider move with more precision.

TEMPO AT THE CURSOR

The Tempo indicator displays the tempo at the edit cursor's position, and it doesn't necessarily indicate the tempo of the project (unless the cursor is positioned at the very beginning).

Changing the Tempo on the Timeline

You can also change the tempo at any point in a project. Mid-song tempo changes are represented by blue markers at the top of the timeline (along with key changes).

To change the tempo mid-song:

1. Move the edit cursor to the position where you want the tempo change to occur.

2. Go to the Insert menu and select Tempo/Key/Time Signature Change (or press T on your keyboard).

3. Enter the tempo you want to change to in the Tempo/Key/Time Signature Change dialog (see Figure 3.13).

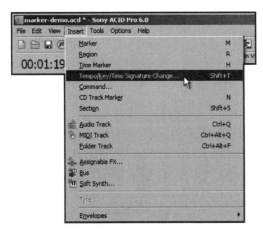

Figure 3.13
Changing the tempo mid-song.

❄ **SLOW DOWN**
Clustering a larger number of tempo markers together allows you to incrementally yet gradually increase or decrease the speed of a song.

The Tempo/Key Change bar may not be visible until the first time you change the tempo or key from the Insert menu. Once the Tempo/Key Change bar is visible, you can make changes directly on the bar.

To change the tempo mid-song from the Tempo/Key Change bar:

1. Right-click the Tempo/Key Change bar at the point where you want the key to change.

2. From the context menu, select Insert Tempo Change.

3. Enter the tempo you want to change to in the Tempo/Key Change dialog.

You can also change the tempo of the project at a specific marker using the Tempo slider at the bottom of the Track Header. Click on an existing Tempo/Key Change marker to select it (or move the edit cursor to the marker's position), and then drag the Tempo slider. If no tempo changes have been made anywhere in the project, the slider alters the project's (initial) tempo.

> ❄ **T IS FOR TEMPO**
>
> The simplest and fastest way to change the tempo is to move the cursor to the position where you want the tempo to change and then press the T key.

Changing the tempo doesn't alter the pitch or key of a song or loops, within reason. Yes, the ACID software is an almost magical application and its engineers are truly Wizards of the Code, but there are limits to this technology. Some distortion may occur if the project tempo is radically different from the original tempo of the loop. You can most easily hear this with vocal parts. The original tempo (and other information) of a loop from Sony Media Software is displayed in the information bar along the bottom of the Explorer window when the file is selected (see Figure 3.14) in beats per minute (BPM).

Figure 3.14

The original tempo of the selected loop is displayed at the bottom of the Explorer window.

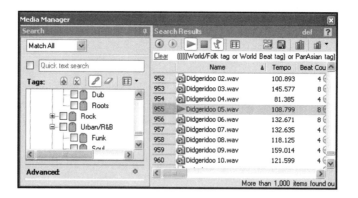

Matching Project Key to a Loop

If there's one dominant loop in your project that must be 100% undistorted in any way (such as a solo vocal track), you can match the tempo of the project to that loop. This is best planned out well in advance and done as early in a project as possible.

To match a project's tempo to a loop's tempo:

1. Right-click the Track Header for the loop whose tempo you want to use.

2. From the context menu, select Use Original Tempo.

The tempo of the loop is also displayed as a part of the menu item (see Figure 3.15).

Figure 3.15
Matching the project tempo to a loop's tempo.

Adjust the Tempo to Fill a Length of Time

There's one other extremely clever method of setting the tempo of a project. Let's say you've composed the perfect background music for a 30-second commercial spot. The only problem is that the music runs for 35 seconds at 120 BPM. Speeding up the tempo will make it run faster, but how much do you need to increase it? Guessing and experimenting will get you the right answer eventually without too much work, but the ACID software has a feature that lets you adjust the tempo automatically using just one marker.

To match a project's tempo to a set length of time:

1. Add a marker to the end of the music.

2. Position the edit cursor at the desired length of time.

3. Right-click the marker and select Adjust Tempo to Match Cursor to Marker.

If you position the cursor before the marker (see Figure 3.16), the tempo is increased and the total duration of the music is shortened. If you position the cursor after the marker, the tempo is slowed and the total duration of the music is lengthened.

Figure 3.16

In this example, a 35-second project is shortened to the same duration as a 30-second piece of video.

Another way to adjust the tempo is with the Fit to Time command on the Edit menu. Using the previous example, our current project is 35 seconds, but it needs to be 30 seconds. From the Edit menu, select Fit to Time, type 30 in the New Length text box, and click OK.

This procedure is most effective when the change in duration of the project is relatively small percentage-wise, yielding a correspondingly small change in the tempo. Although the total project duration is always changed by this procedure, it can be used anywhere in a project. This means that you can use it to synchronize musical changes with video action. Place a marker at a completed musical transition, put the cursor at the location of the action in the video that corresponds to that transition, and then select Adjust Tempo to Match Cursor to Marker to synchronize.

Many times, when working on a score for a video, a composer will work from the video to the music, "spot" the film, and drop "hit markers" (a.k.a. absolute time markers) at points where she would like something musical to happen (a change in mood or tempo perhaps). Then she'll match the musical segues (particular measure and beat intersections) to those markers. Dropping markers with the M keyboard shortcut is the ideal way to proceed.

Key

Most people never move beyond playing with the ACID software as a simple toy. Which is perfectly fine, of course! But if you're ready to make serious music, this section is vital. Again, as in the previous section, the musical ideas discussed here are simple and should be seen as an introduction to music theory in light of ACID technology. None of these concepts should be viewed as rules that you need to follow. You certainly don't need to be a musician to work with the application, but some knowledge of musical notation is necessary if you want to use it to its fullest potential.

The key of a song is sometimes described as the *root note* that it's based on. The key of a note determines its pitch, or how high or low it is. The key of a song sets which notes of a scale are going to be used, depending on the harmonics of the piece (see Figure 3.17). For example, a P.D.Q. Bach piece in C Major would use a certain subset of all of the possible notes in a scale. The harmonics largely determine whether the song sounds pleasing to the ear. This is strongly influenced by culture. For example, a harmonic European scale is completely different from a harmonic Indonesian one.

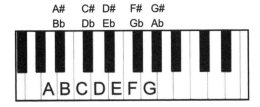

Figure 3.17
The key of a phrase or song can be any note from A to G#, as seen on this piano keyboard.

When you start a project, the entire song is in a single key (A by default). This is the root note of the song. The root note defines the key of the song, but interestingly, that note might never be used in the entire song. The key determines which notes on the scale will sound good together (to a Western ear, at least) and how chords are formed.

Typically, loops are recorded in a specific key or root note. Generally speaking, loops that sound good together are in the same key, and loops that are of different keys clash and sound dissonant. (Of course, dissonance can be very desirable artistically.) The ACID software does a lot of background work that's transparent to the user, converting loops in different keys to match in a project. You can change the key at the project (song) level, at the track level, at the loop level, at the event level, or even mid-song or mid-loop. If it isn't already clear to you, this is a stunningly powerful capability that greatly expands your musical options.

> ❄ **IN KEY OR OUT**
> It's important to note that the key of a song and the key of a loop don't necessarily need to match in order to sound good together. While the ACID program tries to change the key of a loop to match a project automatically, this can be overridden and controlled manually. See Chapter 9 for more information.

The tonal distance between two adjacent keys can be a whole step, as it is between A and B, or it can be a half-step, such as between E and F (see the next section). The key can also be modified by sharps and flats. Flats (b) are a half-step lower, and sharps (#) are a half-step higher. (It may be easiest to think of the black keys on the keyboard as the sharp and flat notes, although this isn't strictly true.) So, a song could be in the key of B, or a half-step lower in the key of Bb. The key of Bb can also be described as the key of A#. You can see that there's no black key between B and C on a piano. While it's not incorrect to talk about B# or Cb, it's often easier to refer to B# as C, because they're more or less equivalent notations.

Chords and Intervals

Chords are made up of two or more notes played simultaneously, and they're responsible for much of the emotional feel of a song. For example, major chords tend to sound happy and minor chords sound sad (to a Western ear, anyhow). The key doesn't define chord intervals, but it's important in determining the structure of a chord. In the ACID software, the creation of chords is rather limited by what actually sounds good based on the loops you select. However, it's a good idea to know a little about chords and structure because some loops, especially pads, are based on chords. These loops are usually named after the chord or structure. For example, Pad Dmaj 02.wav is composed of a D Major chord. Strummed and even plucked guitar parts are often described in terms of chords, and these also sometimes correspond to the name of the loop. Arpeggios are variations of chords, with the notes spread out over time instead of being played simultaneously.

There are a total of 12 keys on a piano keyboard, from A to G#, and this represents 12 half-steps or intervals. We can describe the distance between two notes in terms of steps. The distance between E and F is one half-step or one semitone, while the distance between D and E is one full step, one tone, or two semitones. We can then describe a chord in terms of intervals, or the distances between the various notes that make up the chord. For example, a chord called a C Major triad could be described as a C root note, a second note four semitones higher, and another note seven semitones above the root. Expressed numerically, a major triad might be described as a 0-4-7 chord. Unfortunately, life isn't so simple.

Intervals

Typically, intervals aren't expressed in terms of the number of semitones distant from the root note. Instead, musicians use terms such as *major 3rd* and *perfect 5th* to describe specific intervals (see Figure 3.18). While the system isn't entirely intuitive, it's logical and well constructed. A perfect 5th is one of the most useful intervals in popular music. In fact, when it's pounded out on a heavy-metal guitar, it's the basis of the power chord.

A perfect 5th is really an interval of seven half-steps or semitones. The Indigo Girls often harmonize in thirds, meaning one voice is just a bit below or above the other. It sounds nice and harmonic, while a 2nd (two semitones) or a 4th (five semitones) tends to sound slightly harsh.

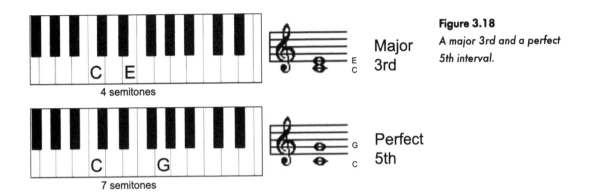

Figure 3.18
A major 3rd and a perfect 5th interval.

Table 3.1 describes the names of all of the possible intervals. Notice that an interval of six semitones has two names, depending on how you write it on the staff. There are many cases where it's possible to represent a given interval in two ways. For example, an interval of eight semitones could be from C to Ab or from C to G#. These two representations are harmonically equivalent.

Table 3.1   Intervals

Semitones		Interval Example in C
1	Minor 2nd	C and Db
2	Major 2nd	C and D
3	Minor 3rd	C and Eb
4	Major 3rd	C and E
5	Perfect 4th	C and F
6	Augmented 4th	C and F#
	Diminished 5th	C and Gb
7	Perfect 5th	C and G
8	Minor 6th	C and Ab
9	Major 6th	C and A
10	Minor 7th	C and Bb
11	Major 7th	C and B
12	Octave	C and C

Major Triad
A major triad is a simple chord created from a perfect 5th interval and a major 3rd interval. It has a happy sound and can be abbreviated as C Major, Cmaj, or even just C (see Figure 3.19).

Figure 3.19
Two different major triads.

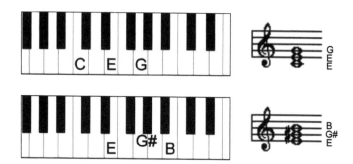

Minor Triad

A minor triad is a major chord with the second note lowered a half-step (flat). This means that the second note is three semitones lower than the root, also known as a minor 3rd. This chord sounds sad and depressing. A C minor 3rd is abbreviated C minor, Cmin, or Cm (see Figure 3.20).

Figure 3.20
A C minor triad.

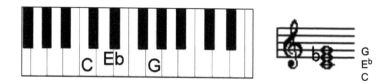

Key Progression

The key of a piece of music is the root note it's written in. If you want to write an interesting song, the key should change occasionally. Unfortunately, it's all too easy to just keep plugging away in the ACID software and never change the key.

The sequence of key changes in a song is the *key progression*. For example, a typical blues progression might be C for four measures, switch to F for two measures, back to C for two, G for one, F for one, and finally back to C for two measures. This 12-bar blues pattern, illustrated in Figure 3.21, is very common. Moving up the key of a song can often step up its emotional intensity, while lowering the key can have the opposite effect.

KEYS AND CHORDS

In this book, key progressions are distinct from chord progressions. Key progressions involve only changes from C to Eb to F# and so on, while chord progressions involve changes from major to minor (among other harmonics).

Figure 3.21
A typical 12-bar blues key progression.

Limits

The ACID software does an excellent job of changing the original tempo and key of a media file without distortion, but there are limits to how much a file can be stretched and changed. If you don't compensate for speeding up the tempo of a loop, the pitch will shift up, making vocals sound like they're coming from chipmunks. Likewise, lowering the pitch will make a media file play slower. The ACID application takes care of this. It can maintain the pitch while the duration is being stretched, or maintain the duration while the pitch is being shifted.

There are limits, however. When a loop is manipulated beyond a certain point, it begins to sound strange and distorted. Vocal loops are especially prone to these distortions, because we're so used to hearing voices every day.

Remember that this limit also applies to media files when they're inserted into a project in a different key. For example, when the project key is C and you want to use an ACIDized media file with a root note of A, the loop is transposed to match the project automatically. This results in a pitch shift of +3. The ACID software also has a pitch-shift limit of +/− 24 semitones, but distortion usually occurs well before you reach this limit. There are four places where you can change the key in ACID: project, track, event, and loop.

Project-Level Key Changes

You can change the fundamental key of the project at any time, but it's best to plan out your song from the start as much as possible. The default key for any new project in the ACID application is A, but this is easy to change (see Figure 3.22).

To change the key of a project:

1. Click the Key button at the bottom of the Track Header.

2. From the context menu, select the key you want to use.

Mid-Song Key Changes

The key can also be changed on the fly at any time in the project. Mid-song key changes are represented by blue markers at the top of the timeline (along with tempo changes; see Figure 3.23). You can drag key change markers with your mouse to reposition them.

Figure 3.22

Changing the project's key from A to D.

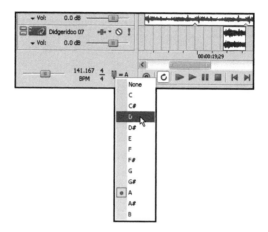

Figure 3.23

Changing the key mid-song.

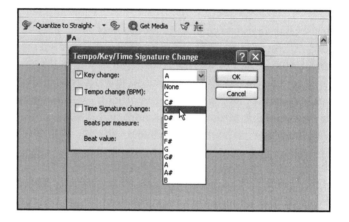

To change the key mid-song:

1. Move the edit cursor to the position where you want the key change to occur.

2. From the Insert menu, select Tempo/Key/Time Signature Change.

3. Enter the key you want to change to in the Tempo/Key/Time Signature Change dialog.

The Tempo/Key Change bar might not be visible until the first time you change the tempo or key from the Insert menu. Once the Tempo/Key Change bar is visible, you can make changes directly on the bar.

To change the key mid-song from the Tempo/Key Change bar:

1. Right-click the Tempo/Key Change bar at the point where you want the key to change.

2. From the context menu, select Insert Key Change.

3. Enter the key you want to change to in the Tempo/Key/Time Signature Change dialog.

You can also change the key after the key change marker is inserted by clicking the Key Change button at the bottom of the Track Header. The key changes at the current position of the edit cursor. You can also use the Key Change button on the Track Header. Click on an existing key change marker to select it (or move the edit cursor to the marker's position). Then, click the Key Change button and select the desired key from the context menu.

We hope you can see the great variety of key changes you can make in your song. As with many concepts in this book, it's a lot easier to understand what the heck we're talking about when you hear it. So if you aren't playing with the ACID software already, now would be a great time. Add a simple tonal loop (that is, not a drum loop) to the timeline, paint a brief section, and then change the key to hear the results.

❋ **K IS FOR KEY**

The simplest and fastest way to insert a key change is to move the edit cursor to the desired position and press the K key, followed by the key that you want to change to. For example, press K and then G to instantly change the key to G.

Loop-Level Key Changes

Commercial loops from Sony Media Software (or any loops that have been ACIDized; see Chapter 9) contain key or pitch information, and they're adjusted to match a project's key automatically when they're inserted into it. You can change the key or root note of a loop as it occurs in a project by modifying the loop's properties after it's been inserted into the project. This change affects only the loop and is non-destructive. That is, it doesn't change the audio file on your computer. Again, the root note of a loop allows the ACID software to adjust the pitch automatically to match a project, but this can be overridden. To change the root note of a loop:

1. Insert a loop with key information into a project. Most commercial loops from Sony Media Software will have this information.

2. Right-click the track that contains the loop and select Properties from the context menu to open theTrack Properties dialog.

3. Right-click the clip you want to change and select Clip Properties to open the Clip Properties dialog.

4. Click the Stretch tab.

5. From the root note list, select the new key for the loop.

Although all of the methods for changing the pitch are fundamentally the same, changing the root note of a loop as it occurs in a project is probably the last method you should use. The default root note information in an ACIDized loop was saved there by the artist who recorded the loop. This provides important information, both to you and to the ACID software itself, about the inherent and natural key of the audio file. In most cases, it's probably better to change the key of the track that contains the loop instead of changing the loop's root note in the Properties dialog, even though the results are identical. See Chapter 9, "Loops," for more information about the root note of a loop.

Blues

Anyone who listens to any form of popular music in the United States will instantly recognize a 12-bar blues phrase, whether or not they know to call it that. This particular song construction sounds so familiar because of its venerable roots, which extend well back to the blues and earlier. The blues is one of the most fundamental and characteristically American forms of music. The great thing about studying the blues is that its basic form isn't hard to understand, and yet it can serve as a springboard to jazz, rock, and many other kinds of music.

This isn't to suggest that the blues is in any way simple or unsophisticated. In fact, it's one of the most expressive and emotionally rich genres, and it's a great foundation for your own instrumental and vocal solo improvisations. A basic blues chord progression might look like Figure 3.24 in a root (project) key of F.

Figure 3.24

A full 12-bar pop progression, F7/F7/F7/F7 - Bb7/ Bb7/F7/F7 - C7/Bb7/F7/ C7/, in the ACID program. Notice that when you're changing the key to Bb, you actually need to select A# in the ACID program. which is tonally equivalent for our purposes.

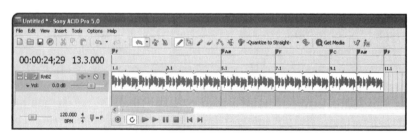

The pattern illustrated in Figure 3.24 is frequently referred to as a *blues chord progression*, but in reality it's only a key progression. The chord structure, for example, could remain a constant dominant 7th. The ACID software doesn't automatically allow you to select the type of chord used, but if you throw in some loops from a blues loop CD, especially a good bass line, you should get excellent results. The pattern works well with many jazz and pop bass lines as well (see the next section, where we'll walk through an example), so go ahead and experiment. Again, the prevalence of this phrase, and even its inclusion in this book, might suggest that it's not the most creative pattern in the world. So feel free to funk it up.

Pop Progression

One of the most basic key progressions in popular music, and one you'd surely recognize if you heard it, looks something like Figure 3.25. Or at least it looks like this when you're starting from a root (project) key of C.

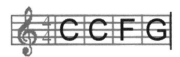

Figure 3.25
A very basic pop music key progression.

The keys of C, F, and G are the three "Pillars of Pop," and this key progression has been used extensively since the birth of rock and roll. As such, you probably don't want to overuse it too much, but it makes for an excellent learning example in the ACID application. It's also great for setting up the listener's expectations and then smashing them to pieces with your own unique stylings.

Link Wray

It is impossible to say who invented the blues or rock and roll or any other style of music, but there are often brilliant and innovative individuals at the transition points that become closely identified with taking a style to the next level. So it is with Link Wray, who can be considered the father of the power chord (a C chord with an interval of a 5th, noted "C5") and the rock and roll sound. His song "Rumble" from 1958 is often cited as the first use of the power chord, but his distorted electric guitar sound was probably just as influential on the emerging art form. Link Wray died in November, 2005, at age 76.

Creating a Pop Progression

Just for an experiment, try the following procedure in a brand new project, before you have even selected any clips to use in a song. After you are done creating this basic pop progression, go find a solid rock drum and a straight ahead bass line and fill up the timeline. Instant song: just add loops. To create a pop progression in the software:

1. Start a new project.

2. To change the key of the entire project to C, click the Tuning Fork Key button at the bottom of the Track list and select C from the pop-up menu.

3. Right-click the time ruler at Beat 1 of Measure 3, represented by 3.1 on the timeline, and select Key from the context menu.

4. Select F to change the key to F.

5. Move the playback cursor to Measure 4, Beat 1 (4.1), and change the key to G.

6. Change the key at the 5.1 point back to C.

Set the loop bar to encompass the first four measures, and draw an event from a simple bass line in a track in the project. The simpler the bass line is, the easier it is to hear the key changes. If you add a basic beat and a piano, the song sounds nearly complete, if a bit boring. Even at this very simple level, you can already hear the familiar pop pattern. The project ends up looking like the one illustrated in Figure 3.26.

Figure 3.26

A simple pop progression as it appears in the ACID software.

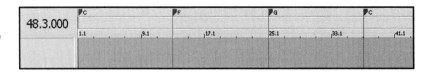

Remember the dominance of the number 4 from the "Musical Phrasing" section? Four beats in a bar, with four bars in a phrase. One of the most common phrases in pop music is 12 bars long. It's a simple matter to extend the simple C/F/G/C phrase you just created into a full-blown pop song (see Figure 3.27). Try out this example and save it as a template for your own future use. Then, when you come home from work and you're feeling tired, fire up the ACID software and open the template for some instant pop doodles.

Figure 3.27

A full 12-bar pop progression, C/C/C/C - F/F/C/C - G/F/C/C, in the ACID software. A simple bass line loop (8thnotesimple1.wav) has been added to the project so you can clearly hear the results of these key changes.

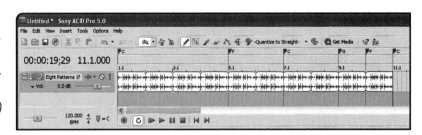

Track-Level Key Changes (Pitch Shift)

Track-level key changes alter the basic key of every event that occurs in a track (see Figure 3.28). A key change can also be referred to as a *pitch change* or *pitch shift*. Events in the track still respond to event-level pitch-shifting and to project-level key changes. To pitch-shift a track:

1. Right-click the empty part of a Track Header.

2. From the context menu, select Pitch Shift Track.

3. From the submenu, select Up Semitone or Down Semitone.

Track Pitch Shift

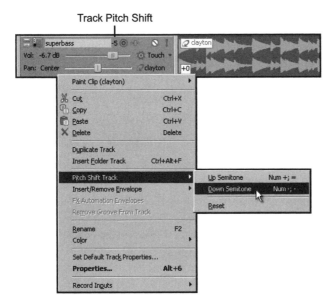

Figure 3.28
Pitch-shifting a track (changing its key).

Event-Level Key Changes (Pitch Shift)

Changing the key of individual events (see Figure 3.29) in an ACID project adds a new creative level to song composition. In the ACID application, changing the key of an event is called *pitch-shifting*. The effect on an individual loop is identical to using a project-level or track-level key change. To pitch-shift an event:

Figure 3.29

Pitch-shifting an event (changing its key). This event has been shifted up one semitone.

Pitch Shift on event

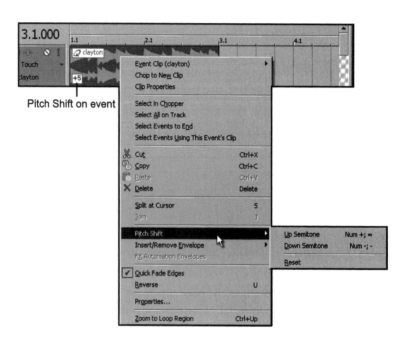

1. Right-click an event on the timeline.

2. From the context menu, select Pitch Shift.

3. From the submenu, select Up Semitone or Down Semitone.

> ❄ **MORE QUICK PITCH SHIFTS**
>
> To quickly pitch-shift an event, click on it and then press the + or − key on your number pad repeatedly.

Radical Event-Level Key Changes

Through meticulous splitting up of a loop into one- or two-note events, you can create entirely new melodies through the use of event-level key changes (see Figure 3.30). While the distortion caused by such drastic changes might limit this process somewhat, it can help you avoid the bane of all loop-based music composition: *too much repetition*. We humans are pattern-recognition machines, so altering loops and events to break up the pattern is an important part of keeping your songs interesting.

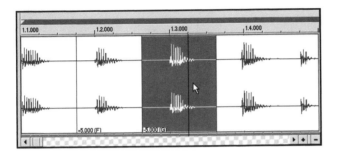

Figure 3.30
A single event that covers one repetition of a loop split into four events. Some of the events have been pitch-shifted to create the C/F/G/C pattern.

To create intra-event key changes:

1. Draw an event into a project. It might be easier if you limit the event to the length of the loop (that is, one loop).

2. Zoom in on the event until individual beats or notes can be seen in the waveform.

3. Press F8 to turn off snapping.

4. Click on the event between two notes. The edit cursor moves to this position.

5. Press the S key to split the event into two events. The events can be split further for more flexibility.

6. Select the newly created events, and change the key by repeatedly pressing the + or − key on the number pad.

It's not necessary or even useful to split the event between every single note. Once the event has been split and modified, you can duplicate the split events as a group to easily repeat the pattern by selecting all of them and then copying and pasting them. You can also hold down the Ctrl key as you drag the loops to copy them, which is sometimes convenient when a small number of clips need to be duplicated a short distance away.

❋ **THEMES AND VARIATIONS**
Although you can create unique melodies from scratch with this method, perhaps the best use of it is to modify a loop so that it's not so repetitive. Alter small sections of the event in simple ways, creating a more natural and interesting sound as the loop is repeated throughout a project.

Chord Progressions

Changing the key and creating key progressions is a simple and powerful technique in the ACID software. Some of the most interesting progressions also develop and release tension by changing the structure of the musical chord itself, while at the same time changing the key. Key progressions are distinct from chord progressions, however, and creating complex chord progressions in the application isn't a realistic possibility. This isn't a limitation of the software, since a chord might be an inherent part of a loop.

Whether a chord, arpeggio, or melody is major or minor is determined by the loops you choose in the ACID software. It's impossible to change a loop from major to minor in the same way that you might change the key from F to A. It might be difficult to find loops that will fit into a particular progression. This doesn't mean that you cannot take creative advantage of the powerful nature of chord progressions in the ACID application.

There are three ways you can create chord progressions in the ACID software: Hunt down loops with the proper chord structure, create your own chords from simple loops, or create your own chords with real-world instruments and record them into the application. None of these methods is particularly easy, but the results are well worth the effort.

Chord Progressions from Preexisting Loops

To create chords from preexisting loops, you just need to purchase a CD with the proper loops. Unfortunately, this severely limits your creativity. It's almost impossible for any single loop CD to provide even the most basic and popular chords in any quantity. There are some good chorded pads on some techno and electronica CDs that might contain some useful chords (see Figure 3.31), but by and large, the selection is far too limited to be useful.

Figure 3.31

The Explorer window displaying some loops that might work in a chord progression. As with other chorded-type loops, the names of the chords are part of the loop's name.

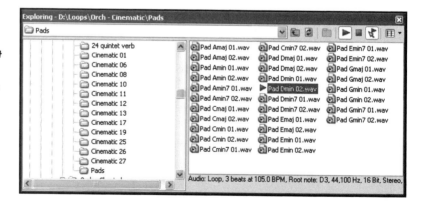

One possibility is to use a major version and a minor version of an audio file to create a chord progression. Again, you need to be fortunate enough to find an appealing loop with the appropriate harmonic variations to get this to work, but even a simple major and minor version can produce a satisfying chord progression. For example, take a look at the chord progression shown in Figure 3.32.

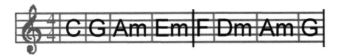

Figure 3.32
A simple but effective chord progression.

Setting up the key changes is a simple matter. The trick is to insert both the major and minor versions of the audio file into the project in two tracks. Then, the major version is used for the C, F, and G sections, while the A, D, and E sections use the minor version, producing Am, Dm, and Em chords (see Figure 3.33).

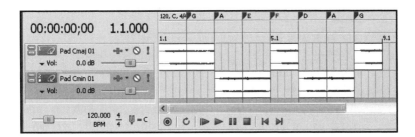

Figure 3.33
A simple chord progression using a major and a minor variation of an audio file.

Chords and harmony are very complex topics that extend well beyond major and minor descriptions, and well beyond the scope of this brief chapter. Although changing a loop from major to minor is impossible from within the software, you can use some simple monotonal loops to create chords, and you can then modify these chords into progressions.

Creating Chords with Simple Loops

It's possible to take certain harmonically simple loops and stack them into different tracks to create chords, as pictured in Figure 3.34. This is a very interesting and creative method that allows you to create all sorts of major and minor chords. It's especially well suited to electronic and dance music, where rich, strange sounds are highly valued. This technique is limited in more conventional acoustic projects because the chords end up sounding artificial.

To create chords from events:

1. Insert a harmonically simple loop into a new project.

2. Right-click the Track Header and select Duplicate from the context menu. Repeat so that you have three tracks (or however many notes you need in the chord) that all use the same loop.

3. Draw in an event in each track.

4. Select each event and use the + and − keys on the number pad to change its pitch.

Figure 3.34
Tracks of the same loop stacked to make a C major triad and a C minor triad.

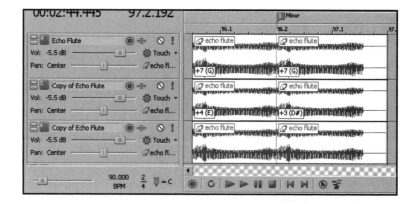

You have quite a lot of flexibility in creating a chord. It might be convenient to arrange the tracks in the order that the notes appear in the chord, with the first track holding the highest-pitched note and the last track holding the lowest-pitched note, but this isn't necessary. Chords also don't need to be stacked in order to occur simultaneously. Instead, you can create arpeggios with this same technique, but it's not really necessary to use multiple tracks if the notes don't actually overlap in time. See the earlier section, "Chords and Intervals," for more information.

> **DOWNMIXING CHORDS**
>
> Once you've created a satisfying chord, it might be useful to mix down the multiple tracks that make up the chord to a single track, or even to render the tracks as a new loop file. This allows you to use this chord in other projects, and it saves RAM and processor cycles.

Chapter 3 Quiz

1. You can use markers to:

   A. Color your tracks

   B. Create a visual structure for your song

   C. Play back ACID loops

   D. Add effects to your project

2. You can move markers by dragging them to any location. (T/F)

3. You can delete markers by:

    A. Right-clicking a marker and selecting Delete

    B. Selecting one or more markers with the Selection Edit tool, right-clicking a selected marker, and selecting Delete All in Selection Area

    C. Right-clicking a marker and selecting Delete All

    D. All of the above

4. Pressing the number key that corresponds to a region deletes that region. (T/F)

5. Regions do not share any properties with markers. (T/F)

6. To set the time signature for your project:

    A. Click the Project Time Signature button and select a time signature from the list

    B. Click the Project Time Signature button, select Other, and type in a time signature

    C. Both A and B

    D. Neither A nor B

7. The tempo represents the speed of the song. (T/F)

8. You can change the tempo of a project by:

    A. Double-clicking the Tempo indicator

    B. Dragging the Tempo slider

    C. Selecting Tempo/Key/Time Signature Change from the Insert menu

    D. All of the above

9. ACID projects have no default key. (T/F)

10. Changing the key of individual events is called *pitch-shifting* in the ACID software. (T/F)

4 } Polishing Up

Previous chapters have covered the basics of song composition. When we remember a song, we usually are thinking about a kind of summary of the song: its melody, bass line, or the words to the refrain. There's a lot more to a finished song, however, like an introduction, break sections, solos, and, of course, a conclusion. The compositional ideas presented in this chapter are the difference between a good song created in the ACID® application and a finished one. This is a short chapter and the concepts covered here are simple, but no song is truly complete without using the techniques we'll discuss. Later in the chapter, we'll take a look at the Chopper tool and how it can help you create variation in your song. The chapter concludes with some advice on long-term project management that will allow you to revisit finished songs at a later date.

Introductions

Like the introduction to a story, the intro to a song should say something about what is ahead. It might have a catchy hook to entice the listener to keep listening. On the other hand, a slow fade-in, creating mystery and building tension, can be very effective for some genres. As discussed in the previous chapter, most songs have some type of structure, whether it is a verse-refrain structure or a 12-bar blues pattern. Most songs do not launch directly into these patterns right away, however. Instead, a song frequently opens up with a brief introductory phrase. Like the overture to an opera, the introductory phrase often briefly quotes or references other parts of the song, most frequently the melody.

Making Space for an Intro

Because we'll often create the introduction out of parts from the main song, it is pretty difficult to know what the introduction is going to sound like in the early stages of composition. Waiting until after a song has matured a bit to create the introduction poses a different problem, however: How can you add material to the beginning of an ACID project? Of course, you could use the

Selection tool to select every event in the project and move them as a unit down the timeline, but there are better ways to move complex projects around.

One of the easiest ways is to insert some time (that is, some empty measures) at the beginning of a project, moving the rest of the project right down the timeline. Essentially, this is a Ripple Edit and is similar to a Paste Insert.

To insert time:

1. Move the timeline cursor to the beginning of the project. The easiest way to do this is to click the Go to Start button on the Transport bar, or better still, press Ctrl+Home on your keyboard.

2. From the Insert menu, select Time.

3. In the Insert Time dialog, enter the amount of time to insert.

In most cases, you will only want to insert whole measures of time (such as 4.0.000—see Figure 4.1) and not partial measures (such as beats or ticks). ACID time is, by default, formatted as measures.beats.ticks (with beats in 1–4). 12.3.500 would insert 12 measures, three beats, and 500 ticks (500/768). Because the real-world amount of time inserted is based on the tempo of the song (in number of beats per minute), a second of time could be any number of beats. Your introduction can be any length, but in most popular music it will be four, eight, or 12 measures (or some multiple of four). There is no need to follow this convention, but it might be helpful for planning purposes. Furthermore, because you can render parts of your project, such as everything from 10 measures to the end, it is easy to compensate for silence at the beginning. Often this is desirable as a pre-roll for live performances and recording.

Figure 4.1

The Insert Time dialog and the gap it creates in the timeline.

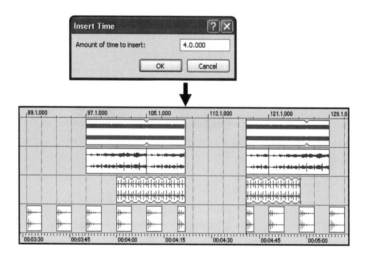

Types of Introductions

There are, of course, many possible types of introductions, including fanfares, overtures, a brief quotation of the melody (often without vocals), and even a simple fade-in. Because we'll often compose the introduction from elements of the song that already exist, the multiple-selection-and-copy techniques discussed in Chapter 2, "Getting Around," are ideal for quickly creating an introduction. If you do use a copy-paste operation, consider using a Paste Insert (or a Ripple Edit) to create the space you need at the beginning of the project, instead of manually inserting time and then performing a more conventional Paste command.

❊ Quoting the refrain or main melody is a very good introduction. As a kind of summary, introducing the theme or *idée fixe* can really add emphasis to a song and even create anticipation.

❊ Adding instruments one at a time is actually a variation of a fade-in. It is pretty common to use the percussion and the bass line in the introduction to establish a song, but solo vocal lines are also effective.

❊ Use FX to mute or muffle the song during the introduction, creating an interesting electronic intro. A very slow flange can create an introduction that sounds as if you are hearing the song over a shortwave radio, before the main body of the song explodes. The easiest way to do this might be to group the tracks you want to use into a single bus, and then apply the flange to the bus.

These are just a few ideas to get you started with the introduction. In creative reality, the possibilities are unlimited.

Fading In and Out

A fade-in can be executed using a combination of Volume Envelopes and slowly adding instruments (tracks) one at a time. Although you could simply add Volume Envelopes over the beginning of a song, before you create a dedicated introductory section, you will lose the first verse or refrain. It's still probably a good idea to insert time and create a dedicated introduction.

Track Fades

We discussed Track Envelopes (both Volume and Pan) in Chapter 2. Remember that the volume of a track is unaffected by a Volume Envelope that is in the vertical center of the track. To create a fade-in:

1. Click a track to select it.
2. Press the V key on your keyboard.

3. Double-click the Volume Envelope at the end of the introductory section to add a node (keyframe).

4. Drag the first node on the envelope to the bottom of the track.

Dragging a node down decreases the volume, while dragging it up increases it. Hold the mouse cursor over a node to see a ToolTip displaying the numeric value that modifies the track volume. As shown in Figure 4.2, the envelopes can cross multiple events and do not need to begin fading at the beginning of the project. Events that do not begin exactly at the start of the project need to have three envelopes nodes to create a proper fade-in, or they won't start in silence at the beginning of the event.

Figure 4.2

Multiple Volume Envelopes and staggered instrument introductions can create a simple beginning to a song.

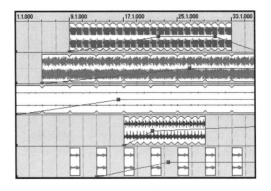

❋ V IS FOR VOLUME

Pressing the V key on your keyboard (or P for panning) actually does two things. First, it inserts a Volume Envelope in a track (if one doesn't already exist). Second, if a Volume Envelope already exists on the selected track, it shows or hides all Volume Envelopes. For example, if you press V once in a track with no Volume Envelopes, a Volume Envelope will be inserted *and* all other Volume Envelopes in the project will be made visible. Pressing the V key again will hide all Volume Envelopes.

By default, the line between two nodes on an envelope is straight (linear). You can more precisely control the type of fade by changing the shape of this line. Right-click the envelope line anywhere on or between the two nodes. Then, from the context menu, select Linear Fade, Fast Fade, Slow Fade, Smooth Fade, or Sharp Fade (see Figure 4.3). Selecting Hold from the context menu creates a flat line by adding another node and is equivalent to no fade or change in volume.

A check mark next to a menu item indicates the type of fade selected. The shape of horizontal lines (that is, unchanging volume/pan) cannot be set, although you could change the shape of a horizontal line and then later drag the node to create a fade.

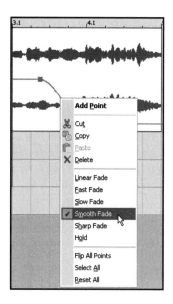

Figure 4.3
The five types of fades.

Event Fades (ASR)

Volume and Pan Envelopes (as well as FX Envelopes) are track-level envelopes. That is, they run across an entire track, affecting every event in that track. You can also quickly fade individual events in or out using Event Fade Envelopes, otherwise known as Attack-Sustain-Release (ASR) Envelopes. To create an event fade, move the mouse cursor over the upper left or right corner of an event. The cursor changes to the special event fade cursor (see Figure 4.4). Drag the Fade Envelope in toward the center of the event.

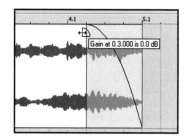

Figure 4.4
The mouse cursor changes to a special cursor when positioned correctly. The end of the fade is displayed in a ToolTip (where the change in gain is 0.0 dB). The faded portion of the event is visually faded as well.

By default, the black envelope line that the ACID software draws on the event is curved. Like track-level envelopes, we can change the shape of the envelope. Both types of fades (track- and event-level) sound the same in the final mix. To change the shape of the Event Fade Envelope, right-click the envelope and select a fade type from the context menu. Then, from the submenu, click on the shape of the fade you want (see Figure 4.5). From top to bottom, these correspond to track envelope Fast, Linear, Slow, Smooth, and Sharp fades. If you right-click when the event fade cursor is visible (see Figure 4.4), the event fade type menu appears immediately as the context menu, eliminating the need to first select a fade type from another menu.

Figure 4.5
Event Fade (ASR) Envelope type shapes and their corresponding names.

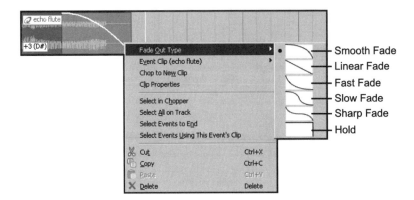

Quick Fade Edges

Quick fade edges are related to the other types of fades in name only. While we use Event Fade and Track Volume Envelopes to control the mix of events in a project, the ACID software uses quick fade edges to prevent clicks and pops that might be associated with the harsh edge of an event, which may sharply cut into a loop. The quick fade edge is so short in duration that it is not normally visible on an event unless the zoom level is very high (see Figure 4.6) and cannot be heard. The clicks and pops it prevents are very audible, however, so it is a good idea to leave this feature toggled on by default. To toggle quick fade edges on/off, right-click an event and click Quick Fade Edges from the context menu.

Figure 4.6
Quick fade edge on the end of an event. Notice that the beat ruler that measures the timeline only displays a very short duration of time and thus a very short fade edge.

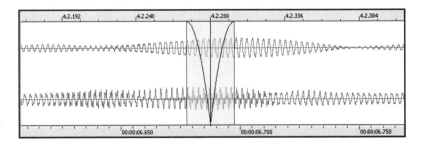

Like other toggled menu items in the ACID program (such as snapping), a check mark indicates that quick fade edges are active. You can set the precise duration of the quick fade edge (and whether it is used by default on all events in a project) in the Preferences dialog (see Figure 4.7).

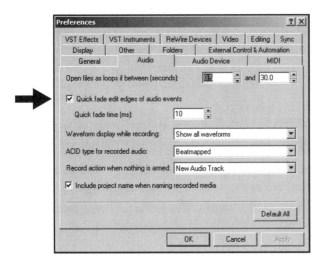

Figure 4.7
The Audio tab in the Preferences dialog contains the quick fade options.

To set the quick fade duration:

1. From Options, select Preferences.

2. In the Preferences dialog, click the Audio tab.

3. Make sure that Quick Fade Edit Edges of Audio Events is selected.

4. In the Quick Fade Time (ms) box, enter the duration of the quick fade in milliseconds (thousandths of a second).

Conclusions

One of the most common conclusions to a song is a fade-out. Fading out is just as easy as fading in and is accomplished by using envelopes on the track or event level. Although conclusions are generally easier to compose than introductions, it is best to have a dedicated ending to your song. In other words, don't just fade out the final refrain as it repeats endlessly into the night. Instead, try repeating the refrain just one more time (or a short portion of it) and then fade it out, perhaps rapidly. There are other types of finales, however, and a simple fade-out may be an indication that the composer just couldn't think of anything else to do. A fade-out, then, might be simply a sign of laziness or an artist running up against a deadline.

In the broadest terms, the end of a song should sound like the end. It should be satisfying and have a nice resolution. Because music is such a big part of our lives, the listener can often predict when a song is about to end based on familiar devices used in popular music. Of course, we don't want to create standard, boring tunes, but following a few of the conventional styles can make a song sound complete.

End on Beat 1

It is a little counterintuitive, but one very effective way to end a song is by ending it on Beat 1. As with many of the discussions in this book, it is rather difficult to describe this in words, but if you fire up the ACID software and try it out, you'll be surprised at how simple and clear this ending is. In order to effectively find Beat 1, you need to zoom in far enough on the project to find the individual beats and split the events. It might also help if you turn snapping off (F8), because this will snap to grid lines and you may want to cut somewhere else. To end on Beat 1:

1. Turn off snapping by pressing F8 on your keyboard.

2. Move the timeline cursor to the end of the project. Click the Go to End button or press Ctrl+End on your keyboard. This moves the timeline cursor to the edge of the last event.

3. Zoom in until only one measure (or less) is visible. Use the mouse scroll wheel or the zoom arrows at the bottom of the timeline.

4. Drag the edge of the event that you want to use as the ending hit, moving it until the first beat is visible in the waveform. You can use the grid marks as reference, but ultimately you are going to need to estimate where the note on Beat 1 falls by looking at the waveform of the event (see Figure 4.8).

Figure 4.8

Finding Beat 1 and cutting after the audible beat in an event is fairly simple if you zoom in far enough on the timeline.

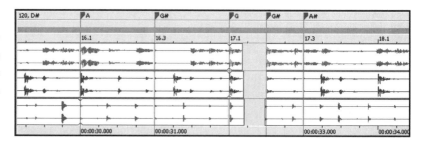

Extending the event farther and then splitting it between notes is sometimes easier than simply extending an event. Click the event to move the timeline cursor to the split position, and press S on your keyboard. Use an Event Fade Envelope (ASR) to more seamlessly trim the edges of the event, especially if there isn't a clean break between Beats 1 and 2. This particular technique is highly dependent upon finding loops that are suitable, but there are a surprising number of loops in many different genres that will work. You can also repeat this technique on multiple simultaneous events across multiple tracks for a more coordinated ending. Finally, you can use events

on other tracks to hide the inevitable extra notes that you simply cannot trim from other loops that
do not have crisp breaks between Beats 1 and 2.

Big Finale

There are certain key progressions (discussed in Chapter 3) that very clearly signal the end of a
song, especially in western popular music. One of the most classic is a progression that gradually
falls by half-steps for a measure and then finally quickly rises back to the root note in two beats
to a resolution. Rockers have used this phrase from day one (and earlier, of course) in songs such
as Bill Haley's "Rock Around the Clock." Try setting up a project finale that looks like the one
pictured in Figure 4.9, matching the key change markers, to listen to this instantly recognizable
pattern.

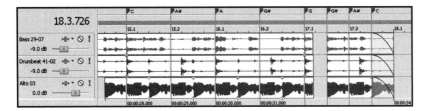

Figure 4.9
*Big finale in a project key
of C. Notice how the grid
bar organizes the key
changes in the number of
measures as well.*

This particular technique is also highly dependent upon finding suitable loops. In Figure 4.9, a
simple bass line with repeating notes works particularly well. In some cases, you may be able to
isolate a single note in a loop to use with this progression. Chord progressions are also extremely
effective in creating a sense of resolution in a song. The ACID software is not particularly well
suited to creating unique chord progressions from monotonic loops, but you should take advantage of this when you can (see Chapter 3, "Composition").

Mixing and Merging Songs

Albums (and to a lesser extent CDs) are sometimes unified works, much as a symphony is a unified
collection of individual movements. At times, this large-scale structure is a part of the initial goal
of the artist. At other times, the big picture is not visible until the component parts are finished.
Whenever the inspiration to group songs together into a larger theme strikes you, the song order,
introductions, and conclusions are important to creating the complete structure.

The ACID application is certainly not limited to electronic music creation, and a huge variety of
acoustic loops and samples are available to prove this point. But techno, ambient, new age, and
other electronica are some of the genres that are particularly well-suited to the mixing and merging
of songs. Either two at a time or as CD-length continuous mixes, mixing is much more than beatmatching. Mixing is most important in the introductions and conclusions of mixed songs, although
a unifying theme or instrumentation is often an important element.

Beatmapping is not the only consideration when mixing, but it is an important one. The software defaults to 120 BPM for all projects, and unfortunately, many artists use this tempo over and over again for dance music. This has the side effect of making beatmapping very easy. Hopefully, your music uses a variety of tempos and tempo changes, but this means that you will need to match tempo and beats (that is, beatmap) in the conclusions and introductions of mixed songs. The process of beatmapping varies depending on whether you are mixing finished (rendered) songs or ACID projects.

Mixing Rendered Songs

Mixing finished songs has applications well outside of original song creation in the ACID software. Mixing songs using material ripped from commercial CDs is an industry unto itself, and it can be a great way to make spectacular mix CDs for your own use. The application definitely allows you to do things that you would not be able to do with two turntables, although a live mix using 12-inch platters is much more of a performance art.

The first step in mixing two audio files in the ACID software is to beatmap each of them using the Beatmapper Wizard. Once you have done this, you can insert both songs into an ACID project. The tempo of both songs will automatically be adjusted to match the tempo of the project, and mixing is then simply a matter of mixing the two tracks together. You should set the tempo of the project to one song or the other (right-click the Track Header and select Use Original Tempo), or you could set a distinct tempo somewhere between the original tempos of the two. Most effectively, you can use multiple closely spaced Tempo Change markers (press T on your keyboard) to gradually alter the tempo of the overlapping mix section.

The mixed portion of the two songs does not need to be limited to the few measures of the introduction or the conclusion. Splitting the events that contain the songs into smaller parts can allow you to do many creative tricks with a mix. The Chopper window is especially useful in targeting smaller sections of a long song with regions that you can quickly insert into the mix. See the "Chopper Trimming" section later in this chapter for more information.

Mixing Projects

Working at the project level gives you even more creative control in mixing. It is possible to open two copies of the ACID software, select all of the events in one project, and paste them into another, creating one project from two. However, this can be a cumbersome way to mix two songs. Instead, it is better to pick a few key tracks or instruments from one project to mix together into the second. Fading pads in and out, or introducing the drums from one song into the other, is very effective. This mixing does not need to take place only at the boundaries between two songs, but it's especially easy to mix throughout a project. This is so easy and effective that you can create an entire CD without discernable song breaks. Although the application will automatically match the tempo of properly beatmapped songs to the tempo of the project, there may be situations in which you want to change the tempo of your compilation CD over time. When the songs have very different tempos, for example, you can create gradual tempo changes from one song into another by using multiple closely spaced Tempo Change markers.

Breaks and Bridges

Breaks and bridges are short sections of a song that connect the main parts of the song together. A break may be as simple as a pause in the music, although it is definitely a pregnant pause that builds quite a bit of tension. Bridges can be longer, and are frequently instrumental sections in pop songs between one of the refrains and a verse. Bridges can be used in a live performance to highlight solo instruments, and might be formally labeled as a separate section. For example, the C section in Genesis' song "ABACAB" might be described as a bridge (see Chapter 3, "Composition") and was used for solo improvisations in live concerts. In this discussion, *breaks* are defined as very short sections, lasting two or fewer measures, that build tension and then explosively release it. *Bridges* are defined as longer sections that might contain solos, but always contain some kind of major change.

Break It Down

One of the most arresting types of breaks involves complete silence followed by a rapid and explosive build back into the main song. In electronic music, the build may be a frenetic snare drum that rises in volume back to the main song. Surprisingly, this is so effective that it sounds like the snare and the song increase in tempo as the break proceeds, even though they usually don't. This is very difficult to describe in words, although it is instantly recognizable in music.

Like the Beat 1 conclusion discussed previously, a break that begins on Beat 1 can be very effective (see Figure 4.10). The pause on Beats 2, 3, and 4 is very tense, and the return to the song on Beat 1 of the next measure creates powerful anticipation in the listener. One variation on this can include silencing all instruments except the drums. Breaks can be much longer, but you may lose the listener beyond two measures or so. On the other hand, a break may also be as short as a half-beat, starting on the AND of Beat 4 (such as one-and, two-and, three-and, four-BREAK, one-and...). In any case, the return of the song after a break can result in a huge release of tension.

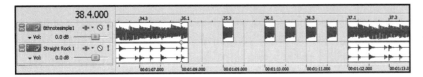

Figure 4.10

A break beginning after Beat 1 in Measure 35 (35.1.000). The break continues for two measures, with the baseline (Track 1) broken up for variety, and the song returns on 37.1.000.

You will find a number of different loop styles that are particularly useful as break loops:

* **Hits.** These are musical blasts or crashes that emphasize the beat very strongly. Sometimes called *verbs*, hits are often labeled as such in loop names (such as Horn Hit Loop.wav). Look for One-Shot drum loops and crashes as well. You can also create your own hits by carefully splitting a loop file to isolate a single note or chord.

* **Rolls.** These are typically done on the snare drum. A roll is a very rapid sequence of beats that can build into the return of the main song. Using the Track Envelope to increase the volume through the roll event can significantly increase the tension. The effect can be so enthusiastic as to create the illusion of a tempo increase, although this is rarely the case. Like hits, rolls are often labeled as such (Snare Roll.wav). With some effort, you can create rolls from existing drum parts. See the upcoming section on using the Chopper for an example.

* **Fills.** A roll is actually a repetitive version of the fill. Fills are usually a radical change in the drum pattern and may be labeled as such (such as 4-4 Fill 39-02.wav).

An important part of a break is the return to Beat 1 in the next measure. Most loop files loop infinitely and fit together from end to beginning. This is ideal for coming out of a break, because you can use Beat 4 of one of the loops that was silenced during the break as the lead back into that loop. See Figure 4.11 for an example.

Figure 4.11
A full-featured break beginning on Beat 1 (23.1.000), lasting two measures and returning with a roll (Track 4 – Straight Snr Roll), an intro back into the piano part (Track 3 – E Grand 02), and a crash (Track 5 – BD Crash 2) on Beat 1 (35.1.000).

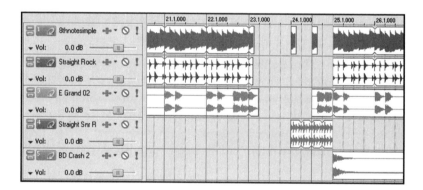

Bridges and Solos

In this book, bridges are longer sections of music that differ from the main part of the song. In popular music, a bridge might be an instrumental bridge and can serve as a time for solo sections between vocal refrains and verses. While a bridge may be quite radically different from the rest of a song, it still needs to fit together with the overall scheme. You can often use a break to introduce a longer bridge section. Bridges are more diverse than short breaks, and it is difficult to describe any specific techniques for creating an effective bridge. However, you should look for loops that are in "solo" or "one-shot" folders on your discs.

Spicing Up Solos

The best and most interesting solos are original performances you have recorded into your ACID project. As mentioned, there are some solo loops of longer-than-average length in some collections of commercial loops. It may also be possible to split up a shorter loop into a number of parts, rearrange them, and use key changes to create an entirely new sound.

Solo instrumental sections or vocal rap sections in a non-rap song are very common examples. There is no particular secret to creating an effective solo section. Just treat it as you would any other part of a song's structure (see Chapter 2).

Loops that are well suited to solos are often found in solo folders on loop discs, or even on discs composed only of solos. Solo loops are longer and may be in One-Shot folders also. While many solos on loop discs are just fine as-is, you can also significantly modify a solo for variety, as pictured in Figure 4.12.

❋ Split a solo event between notes and rearrange the split pieces. Press the S key on your keyboard to split the original event at the timeline cursor's position.

❋ Change the pitch of the individual events split from the main event. Click on an event and press the + or − keys on the number pad to change the pitch.

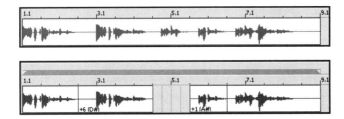

Figure 4.12
The top image shows the original solo loop. The bottom image shows the same loop file split into a number of pieces. Many of the pieces have also been pitch shifted up or down to create an entirely new solo.

Chopper Trimming

The Chopper is a window that specializes in letting you trim your events. In many cases, trimming directly on the timeline may be the easiest way to edit your events. The advantage to using the Chopper is that you can leave your project at a lower zoom level for easier navigation and then use the Chopper at a higher zoom level, allowing you to make precise splits and trims on the waveform without constantly zooming in and out.

The Chopper has a number of other features that make certain edits much easier. It's a powerful time-saving tool, but unfortunately it's largely ignored by most ACID users. Understanding what it is used for and how it is used is definitely one of the marks of an ACID Guru. Let's start by looking at the Chopper window layout (see Figure 4.13).

❈ The timeline displays the waveform of the entire media file and grid marks for snapping.

❈ Turning snapping on and off in the main program also affects snapping in the Chopper.

❈ Zoom in and out on the Chopper timeline with the mouse scroll wheel or the + or − buttons to the right of the horizontal scroll bar, or by dragging the edge of the horizontal scroll bar itself.

❈ You can change the units on the grid bar in the Chopper by right-clicking the waveform, selecting Grid Spacing, and then selecting your desired grid spacing. You can change the time ruler along the bottom to display your choice of units as well.

Figure 4.13

The Chopper window has a short timeline that covers the duration of the media file.

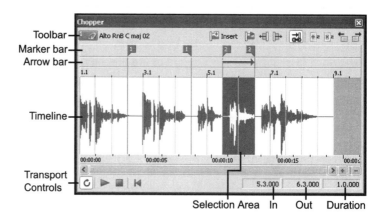

A basic event insertion using the Chopper works something like this:

1. Create a selection area by dragging on the Chopper timeline (see Figure 4.13).

2. Position the main UI timeline cursor where you want the insertion to occur. You can see the selection area and arrow from the Chopper window at the main timeline cursor position.

3. Click the Insert Selection button on the Chopper toolbar. An event appears on the timeline corresponding to the selection area in the Chopper.

As mentioned, there are a number of reasons why you might want to insert events this way. For example, you might want only four seconds of a five-minute media file. With larger disk drives being widely available and people saving entire CDs to their hard drives, it is not uncommon to use a whole song as the source media file for a track. It is likely that in your own creations, however, you will want to use only small portions of these songs as looping events. The power of the Chopper is that you can open an entire song and then create multiple regions for the various smaller parts of the media file, without drawing the whole darned event into the main timeline window.

❋ To create a region, drag on the Chopper timeline to create a selection area and press the R key on your keyboard.

❋ To recall a region, press the associated number key along the top of your keyboard (not on the number pad).

❋ Regions are saved when your project is saved, and are associated with the clip and not the media file. (Other tracks using the same event will not have the same region information.)

❋ Regions and markers added in the Chopper also show up in the Clip Properties dialog (and vice versa). You can save regions (and markers) to the media file so that you can access them in other projects by clicking the Save File button in the Clip Properties window.

The Chopper toolbar contains a number of tools to enable selection modification and timeline cursor movement (see Figure 4.14).

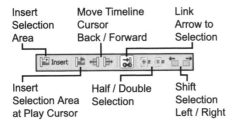

Insert
Selection
Area

Move Timeline
Cursor
Back / Forward

Link
Arrow to
Selection

Insert
Selection Area
at Play Cursor

Half / Double
Selection

Shift
Selection
Left / Right

Figure 4.14
The Chopper toolbar.

The Chopper's Arrow bar and arrow represent the total length of time that is inserted into the timeline, regardless of the selection area. By default, the arrow and the selection area are always the same length. Click the Link Arrow to Selection button on the toolbar to toggle whether the arrow and the selection area are independent or not. The reason for doing this is shown in Figure 4.15.

❋ If the arrow is equal to the length of the selection area, the ACID software inserts the events back to back in a looping fashion.

❋ By making the arrow longer than the selection area, you can insert events in a periodic fashion, with a time interval between them, by repeatedly clicking the Insert Selection button.

❋ There isn't really much reason to make the arrow shorter than the selection area. When you insert events this way, the entire selection region is still inserted, but the timeline cursor is only advanced to the arrow's position. The next insertion will therefore cover up the event

Figure 4.15

The effects of the arrow on inserting events from the Chopper. In each case, four events were inserted and a fifth is ready to go, as displayed on the main UI timeline.

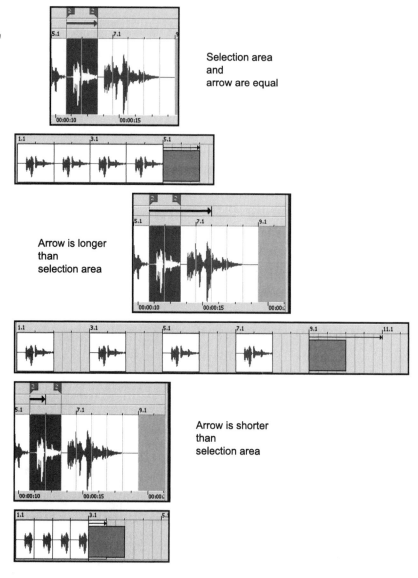

Selection area and arrow are equal

Arrow is longer than selection area

Arrow is shorter than selection area

portion that extended beyond the arrow. This is identical to simply inserting a shorter selection area with the arrow linked to the area, with the exception that the last event inserted would have been longer. This is also a fast way of creating stutter effects without changing a selection size, but you might want to use an audio effect for that anyhow.

One simple example of how you can use the Chopper effectively is by changing a drum line to create an interesting break:

1. Find and select a beat in the Chopper. In the example (see Figure 4.16), the initial kick is selected.

2. Click the Link Arrow to Selection button so that this feature is turned off.

3. Drag the mouse on the Arrow bar to extend the arrow to 1.3 in the Chopper. This is two full beats.

4. Place the timeline cursor on Beat 1 of the measure where you want the break to begin.

5. Click the Insert Selection button and repeat. This example uses six repetitions.

6. Click the Link Arrow to Selection button so that this feature is turned on. The arrow is now the same size as the selection. In the example, it equals one beat.

7. Insert the selection to create back-to-back loops. In the example, a kick roll is created that serves as an introduction back into the resumption of the main percussion pattern at 9.1.

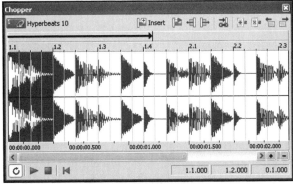

Figure 4.16
The Chopper can be used to break up a beat and create rolls.

The initial kick is isolated in the chopper.

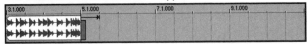

The arrow in the chopper determines the spacing.

The selection from the trimmer is inserted six times.

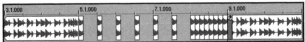

At 7.3 the arrow equals the kick. No space is inserted and a kick roll is created.

Figure 4.16 shows the results of this procedure. Drum breaks and rolls are common in many styles of music. The regular periodic nature of Chopper event insertions makes creating these sorts of patterns easier.

You can also work backward from events on the timeline and into the Chopper. Right-click an event on the timeline and choose Select in Chopper from the context menu. The portion of the media file that makes up the event on the timeline determines the default selection area in the Chopper.

Project Management

Besides the actual process of finishing up the musical parts of the song, ACID project management becomes more of a concern as a project matures. For example, once you have a song that you really like, you can use the Save As command to create a new version of the song that you can continue to modify, safe in the knowledge that the original is preserved. Because project files are relatively small, there is no reason not to archive projects or the evolution of a project over time. You'll certainly wish you had when your label wants you to start work on your second album.

Backing Up Projects

The ACID software can back up projects automatically as you work. This gives you some security in case the original file gets deleted or corrupted, as files sometimes do. You can open these .acd-bak files with the File > Open command. Backup files can be created automatically every time you save the project if you select the Create Project File Backups on Save (.acd-bak) item in the Preferences dialog on the General tab (Options > Preferences).

Recovering Projects

Normal project files (.acd) reference the media files on your computer and point to their locations. If these files are moved or their names are changed, the software will not be able to reference them. For example, if you use the file D:\loops\funk\bass04.wav in the original project and then move it to your E:\ drive, the ACID projects that reference this file can't find it in its original location.

When you open a project that references files that have been moved, the application will prompt you with a warning message noting that the files cannot be found (see Figure 4.17). The easiest way to recover these broken links is to select the Search for Missing File item and click the OK button. In the Search for Missing Files dialog, it might be faster to narrow the ACID search by specifying the new HDD containing the files in the Look In list. After the ACID program has found the file, click the OK button to end the search, even if the entire drive has not been searched. If the relative locations of the other files in the project remain the same (that is, you have moved *all* of your loops to a new drive or location), the software will find the remainder of the media files automatically. If not, the application will prompt you again for each file that has been moved to a new location or been renamed.

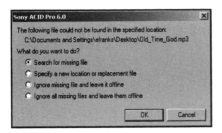

Figure 4.17
The dialog that enables you to search for missing files.

Saving Projects with Embedded Media

You can also save projects with the media embedded within a single compressed file, allowing you to more easily transfer a project to another computer. The project file containing the media can be quite large (easily over 10 MB), but because it is zipped and compressed, the total file size is smaller than if you simply copied all of the files uncompressed to a new location.

> ❊ **COPYRIGHT**
> It is NOT legal to distribute a song with embedded media in it for other people to use if it uses loops from a loop library. This violates Sony Media Software's copyright, for example, which explicitly forbids redistributing their loops.

To save a project with the media included, select Save As from the File menu. From the Save as Type list, select ACID Project with Embedded Media (.acd-zip). Enter a name, browse for a location to save the file, and click the Save button. The new zipped project file has a special extension, but it is simply a zip file nonetheless. You can prove this by changing the extension name to *.zip and then opening the archive in Windows Explorer (in Windows XP). You can then see and access all of the original project files, just as you would any files in a compressed archive.

Chapter 4 Quiz

1. You want the introduction of your song to:

    A. Catch the listener's attention

    B. Refer to the melody or other phrases in the song

    C. Both A and B

    D. Be the longest part of the song

2. You can create fade-ins by:

    A. Adjusting the Volume Envelope

    B. Adjusting the Pan Envelope

    C. Turning down your speakers

    D. All of the above

3. Drawing an event fade affects an entire track. (T/F)

4. Creating fade-outs is more difficult than creating fade-ins. (T/F)

5. Quick fade edges are used to:

    A. Adjust the panning of an event

    B. Prevent clicks and pops at event edges

    C. Create grooves with fast tempos

    D. None of the above

6. The ACID software defaults to a tempo of 120 beats per minute, but you are free to adjust this. (T/F)

7. The Beatmapper Wizard helps you mix two songs together. (T/F)

8. Breaks and bridges in songs are used to:

    A. Ensure your song reaches the minimum length required to be considered a song

    B. Tie the parts of your song together

    C. Save CPU power if your PC is slowing down

    D. All of the above

9. The Chopper is useful for trimming your events. (T/F)

10. You should never back up your project until you are completely finished. (T/F)

5 } Recording Vocals and Instruments

Perhaps the most challenging yet rewarding part of composing a song in Sony Media Software's ACID® software is creating your own unique sounds and loops. One of the best aspects of loop-based music creation is that all of the prerecorded commercial instruments and parts you put together are high-quality professional recordings. It's like having a room full of top-flight studio musicians at your beck and call to back up your performances. Fortunately, the application has all of the tools you need not only to record a lead guitar or vocal track, but also to edit and enhance those performances. The good news is that the ACID program is a fantastic software tool for recording that is simple enough not to get in the way of your groove. The bad news is that many computers are not ideal high-fidelity recording devices, so we're going to talk just a little bit about hardware in this chapter. Finally, we'll also take a look at some fundamental ways you can improve the quality of your sound, especially in a simple home studio environment.

Hardware

For the home studio enthusiast as well as the professional musician, quality is all about gear, and gear costs money. Most home studio enthusiasts have at least a decent soundcard and stereo system that allows them to produce some pretty amazing output with the ACID software, but recording input is another matter; the plastic microphone that came packaged with your soundcard is really only a step above using your telephone as an input device. Although it is well beyond the scope of this book to give specific recommendations on how to set up a professional studio, we can offer a little advice to the novice. The following section on hardware recommends some improvements that the interested amateur or enthusiast might find helpful in creating a decent home recording studio without building a booth and covering the walls with acoustic tile.

Noise

The single biggest problem with recording outside of a dedicated studio is noise. Besides the basic considerations of keeping the dog quiet and the windows shut to keep out traffic noises, a surprising number of background noises in a home can ruin a recording. Chief among these is the refrigerator, which you may not notice turning on and off until you are listening to the playback with your headphones on. There are even more insidious noise generators that you can't hear with your ears, including the hum of electricity in the wires of your house, not to mention the mess of noise-generating electronics known as the personal computer.

Environmental Noise

Unfortunately, when using the ACID software, your computer can be a primary source of background noise. There really isn't much you can do about the whir of fans and the click of the hard disks without isolating your computer box from the monitor, mouse, and microphones. You may be able to isolate your computer in a cabinet beneath your desk, making sure that your computer continues to have adequate air circulation for cooling purposes. If you are really a techno-geek, you could install a whisper-quiet water-cooling system on your PC for around $100.

 HOT BOX

Use extreme caution when putting your PC in a cabinet. Maintaining air circulation to keep your PC cool is critical. If you do put your PC in an isolating cabinet, overheating is easy to diagnose: Your computer will suddenly start to crash more often and for no apparent reason. Although an occasional crash from overheating is rarely fatal to a PC, it is not particularly good for it either.

The ACID software comes with some filters that you can use to improve and minimize constant background noises (such as some of the EQ plug-ins and the Noise Gate plug-in), but you use these only after the damage has already been done. Use these tools only when absolutely necessary. Highly directional microphones can also be useful if you simply cannot isolate your computer.

It's best to place the computer box in another room and run the wires to your semi-isolated environment. This is not as hard as you might think with wireless keyboard and mouse technology. Wireless desktop sets come in two varieties: IR optical and radio. IR (infrared) keyboards only work on a line of sight from the keyboard (transmitter) to the receiver attached to your computer, although you can buy some devices called *IR blasters* to relay the signal. Radio remote keyboards typically work through a single wall to a computer that is a short distance away (usually less than 15 feet). There are different frequencies and technologies (including Bluetooth) that you should explore. Unfortunately, there is no way to know whether any particular device will work in your situation until you get it home, hook it up, power up all of your gear, and give it a try, so you should make sure you can return your purchase if it doesn't work. The last piece of this remote studio puzzle is your display, which is not a problem because 25-foot VGA-display extender cables are widely available to get from your computer to your monitor.

Getting the microphone in close to the subject of your recording is an excellent way to diminish the prominence of environmental noise. The closer the better, but watch out for explosive consonants (such as "p") and sibilants (such as "s") in vocal performances by using a pop filter (baffle), which you can easily create with a coat hanger and a nylon stocking. By getting the microphone in close, you can lower the gain on the recording device, which will certainly reduce background noise levels.

Electronic Noise

Although vocal and analog instrument recordings need the best possible acoustic environment, electronic instruments that feed directly into your hardware will not suffer from a noisy studio or basement. Because you can plug keyboards, theremins, electric guitars, and MIDI devices directly into the back of your soundcard, you don't have to worry about the dog barking during recording. This does not mean that you are home free, however; computers are amazingly electronically noisy. Between the power supply, the hard disks, and all of the various components, a lot of electronic interference flows around inside of your computer. This noise can be picked up and cause a low-level hum directly on the soundcard (especially cheaper ones) or even through the cables that come from your instruments and especially from microphones. Again, Sony Media Software makes some plug-ins that you can use to eliminate this constant hum after the fact, but this is a last-ditch rescue technique. Another desperate solution is to set the level of the incoming signal as high as possible, raising the noise floor in recording to a level where the signal drowns out all of the various hums, making them essentially inaudible. (See the following section on recording in the ACID program.)

Higher-quality (and of course more expensive) soundcards targeted at musicians and recording engineers are much more electronically quiet than the more widely available general-purpose cards. In addition to being internally quieter, these cards are frequently better shielded from external electronic noise sources, including other components within the PC. Finally, professional soundcards often have a breakout box (BoB) of some type that brings your connections out from behind the computer. Ideally, you could run this BoB from your control booth into your recording studio, which at least isolates where electronic noise can get into your cabling.

USB Sound Devices

Beyond the soundcard with a breakout box, some soundcards actually exist outside of the computer itself. This can be a good way to isolate the computer from noise and is really great if you want to record audio to a laptop. One personal caution, however: While recording to a laptop is a great when you are in the field and can't haul your main computer with you, most people find actually editing audio or video on a laptop to be a miserable experience. Yes, it can be done, and some people even have a laptop as their primary machine, but touchpad mousing and small-screen squinting is really not all that fun—even if the marketing brochures make it look cool. The only other limitation to USB soundcards is that the digital cable run is still limited to about five meters. You can double this range with a powered USB hub, but you aren't going to get much more than that.

There are a number of other sound devices that hook up to your computer through a digital USB connection, which can be an excellent way to maintain a clean digital signal between your recording device and your computer. One example is the JamLab Personal Guitar System from M-Audio. This is a small box that lets you plug an electric guitar straight into your computer and has some neat effects that come with it. This product and others like it are a full magnitude better than jacking into your soundcard's mini-plug for getting guitar into your computer. In many situations, for example when using dynamic microphones, a device like this can also act as a very effective and quiet preamp, boosting the signal enough so that it is useful.

Cable Runs

All consumer soundcards use 1/8-inch mini-plugs for mic and line inputs. Without getting too far into the technical details, suffice it to say that this is an unbalanced connection, which means that your cable runs are limited in length and that the potential for electronic interference is very real. We'll talk about microphones in just a minute, but as soon as you start shopping for a mic, you'll immediately notice that any decent mic has a three-pronged connection known as an *XLR* or *Canon connection*. This is usually (but not always) a balanced connection that, when used with a balance XLR cable, eliminates line noise and lets you run cables 25, 50, or even 100 feet or more. Because your microphone is almost certainly going to have an XLR connection, you should definitely buy an XLR cable so that you can take advantage of its balance cable potential. Even if your soundcard has only a 1/8-inch mini-plug input, it is still worthwhile to use balanced cables for the majority of your cable run and then use an XLR-to-mini-plug adapter in the last few inches to your computer. Finally, because very nearly all microphones are monophonic, you may need to perform a little troubleshooting in the ACID software to determine the best way to use the channels when recording. One very serious problem to watch out for is that some XLR-to-mini-plug adapters cause phasing problems when combining a monophonic balanced input across stereo left and right channels. The solution is simply to record a mono input in the ACID software, almost always the left channel only. For example, when you press the Record button in the Record dialog, from the Record device drop-down list, select Microsoft Sound Mapper (Mono, Left Channel—see Figure 5.1).

Figure 5.1

To avoid phasing problems from microphones and adapters, select mono recording on the Track Header.

Detecting Problems

The first step in detecting unwanted background noise is to watch the meters in the ACID software's Record dialog. When you are ready to record, if there is a constant flicker of green at the bottom of the meter, even below 57 dB, it means there is some kind of background noise, either environmental or electronic. One solution to this is to reduce the gain in your audio hardware's mixer on the device that you are recording from until you have eliminated the flicker. Don't turn the gain down so far that you don't record the quietest parts of what you want to record. Not having the meters peak very high may not be a problem, because you can always turn up the volume once the track is in the ACID software. If you do record some background noise, turning up the volume on a track will also increase the volume of the background noise. You may have to juggle lower recording levels against recording some small amount of background noise. Obviously, you'll want to experiment and get the kinks worked out before you get your highly paid and tempestuous musicians into the studio.

At times it is simply impossible to control background noise completely. In these cases, you can use a number of powerful audio effects (FX) plug-ins to eliminate noise in post-production in the application. Noise Gate is a straightforward effect that will set the lowest level of noise that can be heard in a track and only works during the quietest sections. Compression, in conjunction with Noise Gate, can increase the volume without increasing background noise (see Chapter 7, "Grooves and FX"). You can also use the various equalization (EQ) plug-ins to good effect to diminish background noise that occurs at a particular frequency, effectively eliminating a 60-Hz hum behind 1,000-Hz vocals, for example. Finally, Sony Media Software also sells a separate Noise Reduction plug-in that is tailored to this kind of work.

❋ **LAST RESORTS ONLY**
Although these effects are of the highest quality and are used by professionals in almost every project, these solutions are all last resorts. It would be better not to have the noise in the first place. There is no substitute for a high-quality recording, and the phrase "We'll fix it in post" is a joke more than anything else.

External Solutions

Although this is a book about the ACID software, one solution you should consider is to record to a dedicated device such as a tape deck (preferably a digital audio tape [DAT] deck), an MD player, or even into your camcorder. Although this means that you won't be using the ACID application as your recording studio and you'll lose some convenience, going this route can help you completely avoid the many noisy complications that are inherent in recording into a computer. Using even a mediocre microphone and a Walkman-type tape recorder can often produce better recordings than a soundcard on a noisy computer. Problems can arise with tape playback speed and synchronization if you use an analog device, however. Recordable MP3 players and MD players avoid syncing problems by recording digitally, but because these data formats are compressed, your recording will be of poorer quality (although it may still be better than a background hum). Small DAT machines solve both problems by recording CD-quality audio (or better) in a precise digital format. These machines become more affordable and widely available every year. As with MP3 and MD recording, you can also often transfer these machine's recordings directly into your computer through a pure digital connection (if your hardware supports such a connection), such as digital optical, coaxial, S/PDIF, or FireWire. Finally, you could also use a mini DV camcorder to create high-quality digital recordings that can be transferred to your computer digitally. Although you probably cannot justify purchasing a camcorder primarily for your audio studio, you can add audio recording to your self-justification list of why you need to buy a camcorder. It cannot be stressed strongly enough that you *must* use an external microphone if you use this method, as camcorder motors and electronics are often internally even noisier than your computer and are easily picked up by onboard microphones, which defeats the whole purpose of using a dedicated recording device in the first place. Even moving the camera one meter away will almost certainly completely isolate it from an externally connected microphone. Look for a mic jack (and a corresponding headphone jack) if you decide to use a camcorder.

Another benefit to not using the ACID software to record is that there are a few acoustically nice places to record around just about any house. Walk-in closets with racks of clothing are acoustically dead and usually are very nice for recording. Another great location is inside of your car. Of course, your neighbors are going to think you are nuts, but, honestly, they probably already suspect as much anyhow.

Using one of these solutions eliminates one of the great features of the application, however, which is that you can record directly into the timeline of the ACID software in perfect sync while playing back a project. The rest of this chapter focuses on recording into the application using your computer's soundcard.

Microphones

The quality of your microphone determines the quality of your recording. Professional-level microphones are available starting at around $100 U.S. and are really worth this relatively minor investment. Unlike your computer, which was probably already out of date by the time you got it home from the store, a good microphone will last a lifetime, and many musicians have a favorite mic they have been using for many years. Many types of microphones are available, depending on the intended use. It is not really within the scope of this book to detail microphone choice, but we'll present a few general ideas to get you on the right track. Obviously the plastic microphones that come with many soundcards and computers are not well suited to recording quality music. If this is your first serious microphone purchase, we highly recommend that you talk to the salespeople at your local music store. You can probably save money by ordering on the Internet, but spending an extra $10 to talk to an expert is worth it. Tell them what you want to record (for example, voice or acoustic guitar) and what the destination device is so they can also tell you about the cables and adapters that you'll need. The service at local shops is usually quite good, and they might even allow you to buy a mic, try it out for a week, and bring it back if it isn't exactly what you need. Another advantage to buying locally is that the people at these shops might even be interested in what you are trying to do and will have a wealth of advice beyond just microphones.

❄ PREAMP

Most microphones, especially dynamic mics, need their signal boosted a bit. Some sort of microphone preamp is often a required piece of hardware in your signal path, especially when going into a computer soundcard. Simple but effective microphone preamps typically cost around $100.

We can divide microphones into two broad categories: condenser and dynamic. In short, condenser microphones work by transforming the pressure of sound waves in the air into an electrical signal with a metal plate that changes in capacitance as it moves closer to and farther away from another plate. Dynamic mics use a coil that moves relative to a magnet that therefore generates a voltage that varies with movement. Generally, condenser microphones are more sensitive, but dynamic microphones have a greater dynamic range, from quiet to loud. If we had to recommend a first microphone, it would be a condenser.

❄ MONO TO STEREO

Because almost all professional microphones are monophonic, most of your audio recordings will also be monophonic. You can record from two mics into the ACID software quite easily with the right adapters (a y-adapter from two XLR connections to a stereo mini-plug). The best way to do this is by using a small mixer to pre-mix the mics before they go into your soundcard.

Microphones also have different sorts of sensitivities to the direction of incoming sounds. Directional mics come in a number of varieties. Unidirectional mics record (more or less) in only one direction (forward), are good at isolating the subject, and do not pick up peripheral noises very well. Shotgun mics for camcorders are one example of a unidirectional mic and are great general-purpose microphones that can be used from a distance if necessary. They typically don't have as good of a response range adequate for music as other microphones might. Omnidirectional mics record in a wide pattern and may be suitable for acoustic music in an isolated studio, but they are a poor choice if you need to minimize background noise. Cardioid-pattern microphones pick up noise from a broader area than a directional mic, but they are still good at eliminating unwanted environmental noise. This type of pickup pattern is a common one and is a good choice for a general-purpose microphone.

> ❄ **A CLASSIC FOR $100**
> If we had to recommend a first, general-purpose microphone, it would have to be the Shure SM58. We've used it for voiceovers recorded in a studio, as the main mic at live events, and with camcorders in the field for interviews, and it sounds great. Even better, it is fairly indestructible. Even better still, you can find it for right around $100.

If you expect to do most of your recording with a specific instrument, it may be best to buy a microphone specialized to that use. For example, when recording an acoustic guitar, you might want to use a piezoelectric pickup mic, while ribbon microphones are an excellent choice for vocalists and horn players. This is obviously a huge topic and engineers argue endlessly over the best microphone for a particular application. Suffice it to say that a quality mic doesn't need to cost a lot and is well worth the expenditure. The following site is a great place to begin your research:

http://arts.ucsc.edu/ems/music/tech_background/TE-20/teces_20.html

Consumer computer soundcards typically have a 1/8-inch stereo mini-plug input, and most microphones have an XLR output. If you are going to stick with your current soundcard and it only has a 1/8-inch plug, make sure you also get the proper adapter for your soundcard before you buy the microphone, typically an XLR-to-mini-plug adapter. Incorrect adapters can cause phasing problems that will completely cancel out the signal when mixed, so make sure you use the Down-mix Output button on the Master Bus to check for problems when you first configure your connection. Broadly speaking, you are probably making some significant compromises if you are using professional mics and your input device only has non-professional 1/8-inch stereo input jacks.

Monitoring

One of the best features of recording directly into the ACID software through your soundcard is that the application functions as a miniature studio. Once you have a good microphone and have isolated your recording environment as much as possible, the final step is figuring out how to monitor your project in the program as you record. Unlike monitoring a final mix (as discussed in Chapter 6, "Mastering the Mix"), there is really only one choice in monitoring the ACID software while recording: headphones. You can often connect headphones directly to your soundcard or even to some computer speakers. If you try to use your speakers as monitors, you will very quickly discover that feedback will make this impossible. Because monitoring simply involves playing back a project for reference while you sing or play along, the quality of the headphones is largely unimportant, although a good pair of cans would be nice. You do not need to use headphones when using electronic instruments that plug directly into your computer, because they will not generate feedback.

Recording into ACID

The ACID program is a virtual recording studio, allowing you to record original performances directly into a project. A keyboard player, for example, could use a set of jazz loops to set up a project with a bass line and drums and then record the keyboard part over it. The project could start out structured with a key progression (as discussed in Chapter 3) and have breaks and solo sections built right in. Because the process of recording is no more difficult than pressing the Record button, you can record multiple takes and choose the best one for the final mix. Better still, multiple takes give you the opportunity to select the best parts of a bunch of takes and combine them into a single flawless performance.

Recording into a Track

The basic metaphor for the ACID software is a multitrack studio. Each track in the application contains one or more media files. When recording into the software, all new parts are saved to a media file (clip) on your computer and inserted into a track on the timeline. Before you start recording, you might want to know where your recorded data is going to end up. It is a pretty good idea to set up a folder dedicated to holding your recordings instead of using the default location where the ACID software was installed. You can set the default locations of the various types of files you might record (for example, audio recordings or MIDI files) by opening the Options menu, selecting Preferences, and then clicking on the Folders tab (see Figure 5.2).

The ACID software saves the new clip to your computer and inserts a new event into the project with an event that contains the recording. Unlike conventional studios, the software is basically unlimited in the number of tracks that can be used. Further, with the right hardware and enough inputs, you can simultaneously record different parts to different tracks. To record into the application:

1. Move the timeline cursor to the position where you want to start recording.
2. From the Insert menu, select Audio Track.
3. In the Track Header, click the Arm for Record button.
4. On the Transport bar, click the Record button (or press Ctrl+R on your keyboard).
5. When you are finished recording, click the Stop button (spacebar).
6. The Recorded Files dialog opens. Click Done to finish.

The ACID software saves a media file to your computer and inserts a new event into the track. You can change the name and location of the file in the Recorded Files dialog (see Figure 5.3). If the recording was a bad take, you can click the Delete button in that dialog and start again.

Technically, you don't need to insert a track into the software before you hit the Record button. By default, the ACID program will automatically insert a new track when you press Record and immediately begin recording. The only downside to this is that you won't get much of a chance

Figure 5.2

The Folders tab in the Preferences dialog.

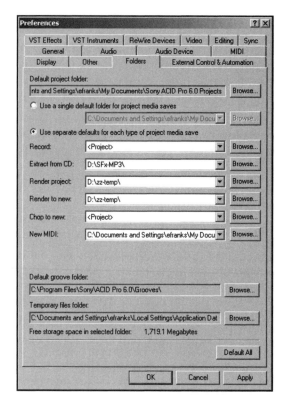

Figure 5.3

The Recorded Files dialog.

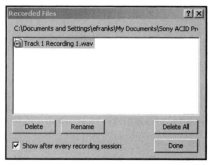

to prepare before recording begins. You can change the default behavior of the ACID software in the Preferences dialog. On the Audio tab, select a different option from Record Action When Nothing Is Armed drop-down list (see Figure 5.4).

Recorded files are automatically named and numbered according to a default scheme: Track 1 Recording 1.wav, Track 1 Recording 2.wav, and so on. Although you can change the filename in the Recorded Files dialog, the ACID software defaults back to this numbering for every take

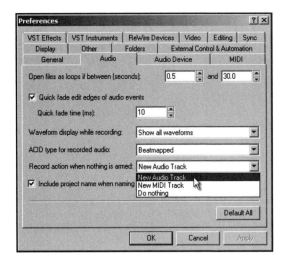

Figure 5.4

Select a different option from the Record Action When Nothing Is Armed drop-down list to change the ACID software's default behavior.

(see Figure 5.5). The events that are inserted into the timeline, however, will be named slightly differently: 1 Clip 1, 1 Clip 2, and so on. The reason for this will become apparent when we discuss the important process of recording takes a little later on.

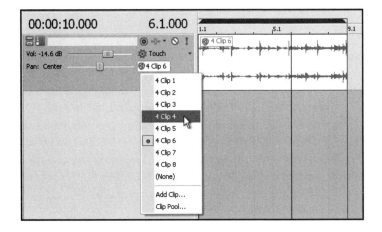

Figure 5.5

A single track with a number of recorded clips in it.

By default, performances are recorded as special ACID Beatmapped clips. This means that the media files contain extra information about the tempo of the file and where the beats fall. If you use this file in another project, the media files automatically conform to the tempo and beat of the other project. You can change this so that the software records One-Shots without tempo information on the Audio tab in the Preferences dialog.

> ❋ **MIX DOWN AND MOVE ON**
>
> It may be easiest to record short sections of a song at a time, although when you move on to the next section, you will create more takes. You might want to work on one section at a time and mix all of those takes down before moving on.

Because the ACID program defines the tempo of the project into which you are recording, adding this information into the recorded file is a straightforward process. A single audio file can have only one tempo in the application (even if the piece changes tempo in the real world) and can be set to only one key or root note (even though real songs might change key). Most popular songs do not have tempo changes, so this isn't usually a problem. Loops recorded in the ACID software will have a tempo dictated by the project tempo. Most songs do have key changes, and these can be a part of an ACID project (as discussed in Chapter 3). Because the key often changes, the root note of a recorded loop is not set in the ACID application. This means that as the key changes on the timeline, the pitch of any recorded loops will not change. Key changes in the performance are an inherent part of the performance and of course will match the project's key changes (if you want them to). If you use the loop in another project, the key may not match the project. You can set the key in the Clip Properties window on the Stretch tab. In the Root Note list, select the key of the performance. Root notes and other clip properties are discussed in more detail in Chapter 9.

Selecting an Audio Device

On most computers, you can record from your CD-audio player via an internal digital connection, from a mic jack, and also from a line-level input. On music workstations, you can often have even more inputs than that. Selecting the default audio device to record into is simply a matter of going to the Options menu and selecting Preferences. In the Preferences dialog, go to the Audio Device tab and select your preferred default audio recording device from the drop-down list. Which devices are available here depends on how your hardware and drivers are configured. There is a connection between the audio device type item and which specific channels you can record from in the default audio recording device drop-down list (see Figure 5.6). See the "Troubleshooting" section later in this chapter for a few hints on how to set that up correctly.

Figure 5.6

The Audio Device Type selection determines which channels are available on the Default audio recording device drop-down list.

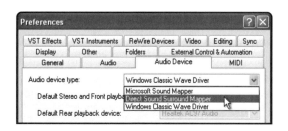

Setting the Gain

Unfortunately, it isn't entirely easy to set the gain of the recording inputs into the ACID software, primarily because of how Windows configures soundcards. While the Volume slider on the Track Header in the ACID program temptingly looks like it might also control the input gain, it does not. Instead, it only controls the volume of any clips in that track that will play back during recording. To adjust the audio mix in a soundcard (a procedure that will vary depending on your version of Windows):

1. On the taskbar in Windows, double-click the volume icon.

2. In the Play Control dialog, from the Options menu, select Properties.

3. In the Properties dialog, in the Adjust Volume For section, choose the Recording option.

4. In the Show the Following Volume Controls box, make sure the Microphone option is chosen. This controls which devices are available for mixing, not whether they are turned on.

5. Click the OK button.

6. In the Recording Control dialog (see Figure 5.7), use the sliders to adjust the gain. Close the dialog when finished.

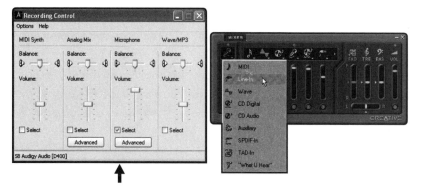

Figure 5.7

The Recording Control dialog on the left is a standard Windows feature. The mixer panel on the right is linked to an SB Live! soundcard and is really just a front end to the Windows controls (with a few extra proprietary features).

Again, unfortunately, this is a rather typically convoluted procedure to achieve the basically simple goal of turning on the microphone and adjusting its volume. You may have noticed in Step 3 that there may also be a Microphone option in the Properties dialog; there is no reason you can't use this control instead. You can also get to this same location through the Control Panel by selecting Sound and Audio Devices, clicking the Audio tab, and then choosing the Volume button under the Sound Recording section of the dialog. You can monitor the gain in real time on the meters in the Track Header of the tracks you are recording into. By switching back and forth between the soundcard's mixer panel and the Recording Control dialog, you can eventually set the gain properly.

This brings up the question of what is the proper gain for the microphone. As with the output mix in the ACID program, the primary indicator is clipping: Make sure that the maximum level on the meters never exceeds the top of the meter. Sound and data are certainly lost at this level, and distortion may occur. Beyond this basic rule, however, there is a pretty broad range of signals that you might consider strong enough. Some things to consider are:

* Correction for quiet recordings is rather easy in the ACID software, so if you are going to err, err on the side of keeping the volume low enough to prevent clipping in all situations. Meters that often jump into the red are set too high.

* Setting the gain too high can also introduce and increase unwanted background noise. Due to the environmental background noise conditions previously discussed, there is almost always some kind of background noise that becomes more and more apparent with higher gain. By keeping the gain lower, you can avoid recording this noise altogether. Once again, correcting the gain on output and using ACID filters to eliminate background noise is not difficult, but it is an extra step you may be able to avoid by setting the recording gain properly.

* Trust the meters to show you what your ears cannot hear. Meters that go all the way to the top and trigger the red Clipping Indicator are too loud, whether or not you can hear any distortion. (See Chapter 6 for more information on clipping.) Background noise that causes the meters to bounce even in the quietest recording situations reveals problems that may not be apparent to the ear.

* Finally, use your headphones. If it sounds good, it *is* good. Just because the meters are bouncing doesn't mean you are necessarily recording what you want to be recording. The meters could, in all reality, be recording pure electronic feedback, so make sure you actually monitor at least part of the performance.

RECORDING LEVELS

The meters in the Track Header also have a clipping meter that indicates that the gain on the input is too high. Click the red Clipping Indicator (see Figure 5.8) to reset it.

Figure 5.8

The meters and Clipping Indicator in the Track Header.

Clipping Indicator

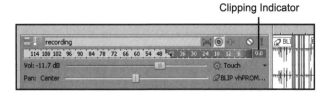

Metronome

When recording into a project with existing tracks, you can synchronize your performance by ear if you are monitoring with headphones. The ACID software also has a metronome to assist you. There are three ways to engage the metronome. First, from the Options menu, select the Metronome item. Second, you can click the Metronome button on the toolbar. The software generates the metronome beat using MIDI, and you can set its volume with the Preview fader in the Mixer window. The tempo of the metronome is, of course, determined by the tempo of the project at the position where you start recording. The sound of the metronome is not recorded along with your performance.

Troubleshooting

Figuring out how to record on your computer is not always easy. The combination of hardware, drivers, and the software-level interface makes troubleshooting a less-than-intuitive task. And while it is fairly straightforward to isolate output problems (because you can hear whether your card is working or not), you cannot always fix input and recording problems by ear. To simplify this process and avoid crashes, it is best to close all other applications while working through this process.

The first step in verifying the proper recording setup is to watch the meters in the Track Header. When everything is set up, any noises will cause the bottom of the meter to bounce up and down. If some green is moving but the levels never get very high, even when taping the microphone, then the input gain is too low, but everything is working otherwise. If no green is visible at all, then something else is wrong.

You should check to make sure your microphone is hooked up to the soundcard correctly. Most consumer-level soundcards have two 1/8-inch input jacks, one for a microphone and one for an auxiliary device (such as a Walkman or CD player). Microphones typically have a very low-level (low-impedance) output that we'll call *mic level*. CD players output a much stronger signal we'll call a *line level* output. There is some potential to damage your equipment by plugging a line-level signal into a mic-level input jack, but there is a certainty that you will know something is wrong when you do because the meters will spike all the way to the top and your speakers will scream bloody murder. Actually, both jacks may work for either type of device and may in fact be identical on some cards. Some microphones also have an on/off switch that you should check and may even have batteries.

After you have verified that you have connected everything properly, the next step is to find the mixer properties for your soundcard. The drivers that come with the card often allow you to select the type of input device(s) used for recording and set the gain. Unfortunately, these settings can be different for every soundcard. The following procedure should work for many Windows soundcards. To view the Windows Volume Control:

1. Click the Windows Start button.

2. From the Start menu, select the Settings item and then select Control Panel.

3. In the Control Panel, double-click the Multimedia item (or the Sounds and Audio Devices item). This opens the Multimedia Properties (or Sounds and Audio Devices Properties) dialog.

4. On the Audio tab (or the Volume tab), make sure the Place Volume Icon in the Taskbar option is selected (see Figure 5.9).

Figure 5.9

Check the Place Volume Icon in the Taskbar option to display a speaker icon on the taskbar.

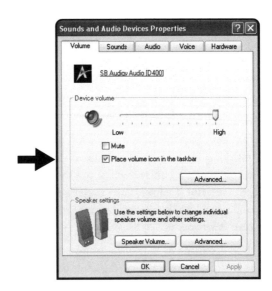

Keeping the Volume control on the taskbar is not mandatory, but it can be a convenient way to access Windows mixer controls quickly. Some soundcards add their own proprietary controls on top of Windows basic controls.

Recording Options

A number of options enable you to control recording from within the ACID software. These options are distinct from the gain/mixing options of your soundcard previously discussed. In fact, you cannot control the gain of the recording in the application at all. Keep in mind the following tips as you use these recording options:

❊ You can set the filename in the Recorded Files dialog. You can set the default location of those files on the Folders tab in the Preferences dialog. This default can be overridden to save files to the same location as your project in the Project Properties dialog.

❋ Also in the Preferences dialog on the Audio Device tab, from the Audio Device Type, if Microsoft Sound Mapper is selected, you cannot select different hardware devices (in cases where you may have two or more soundcards on one computer). Select another device besides Microsoft Sound Mapper (such as Windows Classic Wave Driver or an ASIO driver) and then, from the Default Audio Recording Device list, select the device and channel you want to record from. You can change the default input channel by right-clicking the Track Header and selecting a new input from the Record Inputs menu.

Pre-Roll

Pre-roll refers to starting the playback before the point where you want the actual recording to begin. In summary, to record using a pre-roll, you'll need to create an empty event to record into and then start playback before the empty event begins. Here's how to do it in detail.

1. Create a new track to record into (Ctrl+Q).

2. Draw a blank clip starting at the location where you want to record. Make the clip as long as you want to record.

3. Drop a marker (M) at the point you want the pre-roll to begin (typically a couple of measures before the empty event begins).

4. Select the blank event you drew in Step 2 and use Ctrl+left arrow to position the edit cursor back to the marker.

5. Click the Record button on the Transport bar to begin recording. The ACID software will not record audio until it reaches the selected empty clip, and then it will record directly into it.

You could also simply start the recording process a measure or two early and then edit the take later. The simple nature of editing takes (trimming, splitting, and so on) makes this quite effortless. Because it is difficult to begin recording and come in on measure one, beat one of a performance, it is a good idea to insert a measure or two of silence at the start of a song. If you need to insert a little time at the beginning of the project to accomplish this, from the Insert menu, select Time and enter a length of time (in measures.beats.ticks).

Working with Takes

Takes are different versions of the same performance. In a typical studio session, the engineer will record many different takes of a song or parts of a song. In the bad old days, the entire band played live into a microphone or two that was then mixed straight to tape to a single track (or a pair of stereo channels to a single track). If the drummer screwed up, the band had to go back and repeat the entire performance. With the advent of the multi-track studio, each part could be recorded to a separate track on a tape. This way, the rest of the band could go home while the drummer got his act together, recording his takes against the good takes of the rest of the band.

In movies and music recording, takes are different versions of the same section of a project. In movies, a director might film the same scene (say Scene 5) 10 times, getting 10 different takes: Scene 5, Take 1; Scene 5, Take 2; Scene 5, Take 3; and so on. In music, the "scene" is usually indicated by the measure or measures: Measures 4–16, Take 1; Measures 4–16, Take 2; and so on.

Takes in the software are handled in two different ways. The first way is simply a naming convention—that is, the ACID software automatically names the files recorded using a naming and numbering scheme that can help with take organization. The second way is to create automatically looping takes. This method allows you to use ACID looping playback to automatically play a region over and over again while continuously recording takes without a break. At the end of recording a batch of takes you'll still find a single clip, inserted into a single track. If you look in the Clip Pool window, however, you'll see something interesting: a new clip for each take. This allows you to quickly switch between the various takes to find the best ones. The primary advantage is that it allows performers to do their thing without interruption.

Recording Takes

When you record a clip into a track, the ACID program automatically inserts it as an event into the track. Each time you click the Stop button on the Transport bar, the software saves a media file (clip) into the track. When you repeat the recording procedure from the same starting location, the software will play back the first take and record a new take and a new media file (clip) just beneath the first take in a new event. The ACID application automatically names the events: 1 Clip 1, 1 Clip 2, and 1 Clip 3. The corresponding media files are Track 1 Recording 1.wav, Track 1 Recording 2.wav, and Track 1 Recording 3.wav (see Figure 5.10). When you play back the project, you will only hear the first take because that is the clip that will be on the timeline. You can access the other takes the same way you access any other clips on a track: Click the Paint Clip Selector, choose one of the other takes (clips), and paint it onto the timeline.

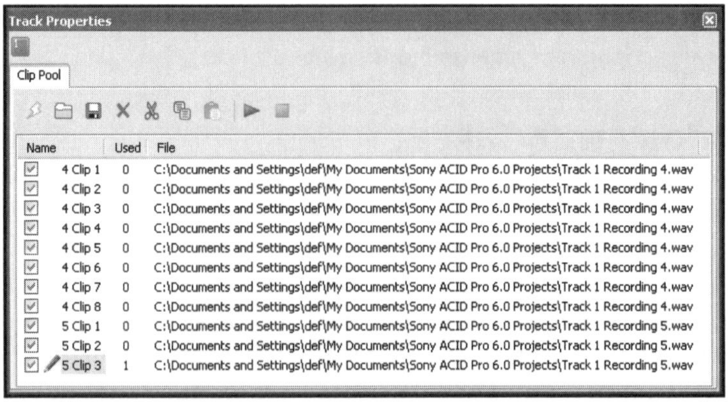

Figure 5.10

The ACID software automatically names and numbers events and clips as they are recorded.

❄ **WHERE'S MY TAKE?**

You can set the default locations of your takes by going to the Options menu, selecting Preferences, and then clicking on the Folders tab. This default can be overridden to save files to the same location as your project in the Project Properties dialog at the bottom of the Audio tab.

❄ **MUTE THAT TRACK**

After your first take, the ACID software will insert the clip into an event on the timeline. When you hit Record for another take, the software will then play back the event you just recorded. To prevent this, mute the track you are recording into (as pictured in Figure 5.11).

Figure 5.11

Click the Mute button in the track that you are recording into to prevent earlier takes from playing back.

Automatic Looping Takes

Every time you hit the spacebar to stop recording, the ACID application will begin recording a new file. Logically enough, it will be named after the track number (e.g., "Track 1") followed by the recording number (e.g., "Recording 1"). One very powerful technique is to record takes while turning on looping playback for a region.

This method lets you loop the playback to record takes continuously without interruption. This will give you and your musicians a chance to get into a rhythm and perfect a section without too many interruptions for someone to run over and stop recording and then get everyone ready for another take. All you need to do is catch your breath and go again. To create looping takes automatically:

1. Create a loop region above the timeline on the Marker bar. The loop region should probably start a few measures before the actual position where you want to begin recording to give the performers time to get ready for their cue. The metronome might be handy here as well.

2. Click the Loop button on the Transport controls.

3. Position the timeline cursor at the beginning of the loop region.

4. Click the Record button. Make sure the position in the Record From section of the dialog is correct (that is, the timeline cursor is at the beginning of the loop region).

5. Click the Start button to begin recording.

6. Playback will loop and you can continue to record takes until you are satisfied. Click the Stop button to stop.

Takes in the Clip Pool

Easy enough. When you are recording while looping playback is engaged, something very interesting (and useful) happens. Even if recording more than 10 takes into a loop region, you will only end up with one event and one clip on the timeline. Recall that recording over a take after hitting the spacebar to stop recording does indeed insert multiple events on the timeline, it's just that they are hidden under the first take. This is not the case here. Instead, if you open up the Clip Pool in the Clip Properties window, you'll see that there are in fact multiple regions listed, corresponding to your takes: 1 Clip 1, 1 Clip 2, 1 Clip 3, and so on. If you look a little closer and examine the filename for those clips, you'll notice that when I wrote "filename" it was not a slip of grammar: We only recorded one file that was then divided into separate clips (takes). This can be a little confusing at first (see Figure 5.12), but it follows what we have been doing all along. Media files on your computer are the source of the audio you play with on the timeline, but none of your editing in the application actually changes anything with your source media.

Figure 5.12

Multiple takes recorded into a single track, a single event, and a single media file (clips). The media file displayed in the Track Properties window (Clip Pool) is divided into regions.

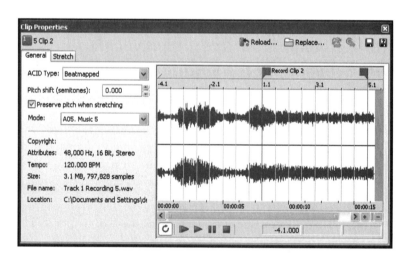

❋ **CLIP, CLIP, CLIP**

The automatic naming of takes in the ACID software as "Clip" is somewhat unfortunate, because Sony Media Software also refers to media files on your hard drive as "clips." Of course, "clipping" can also refer to having the volume or gain too high, but that coincidence is less confusing.

Takes in the Chopper

Because all of the various takes were recorded to a single file that is divided in the Clip Pool, you know there is something somewhere that is splitting these files. If you double-click any of the related clips in the Clip Pool, the Chopper will open, displaying the entire media file, with your various takes marked off as regions (see Figure 5.13). You can interact with the regions in the Chopper by clicking the various takes in the Clip Pool.

Figure 5.13
You can use the Chopper window to see the various takes in a media file as regions.

Recording MIDI

Although recording an audio source is fundamentally a different operation from recording MIDI data, the procedure for doing so is very similar. Audio is recorded as sounds and MIDI is recorded as data that you can use to recreate the performance—for example, what note was played, how hard the key was pressed, and how long the note lasted. In many ways, recording MIDI data is not unlike recording audio. In many other ways, recording MIDI data is a much more flexible option in the ACID software and has more tools to help you get a great performance. We'll deal with MIDI setup and configuration in much more detail in Chapter 10.

MIDI instruments come in many varieties, the most common being a keyboard or synthesizer, but MIDI guitars and drum machines are also popular. Many MIDI instruments have internal circuitry to produce sounds that are sometimes of very high quality. If you want to record the actual sound that comes out of a MIDI device instead of recording the MIDI data, use the procedures described previously to record any audio signal. For example, suppose you own an electronic piano with a beautiful sound to it. If you recorded MIDI data, you would lose all of that sound and instead allow your (perhaps not-so-nice) soundcard to recreate the performance. In any case, you can choose to record instruments either way. To record MIDI data:

1. Move the timeline cursor to the position where you want to start recording.

2. From the Insert menu, select MIDI Track.

3. In the Track Header, click the Arm for Record button.

4. On the Transport bar, click the Record button (or press Ctrl+R on your keyboard).

5. When you are finished recording, click the Stop button (spacebar).

6. The Recorded Files dialog opens. Click Done to finish.

As shown in Figure 5.14, the ACID software inserts a MIDI track into the project containing the MIDI data you just played. Unfortunately, although you can also use the other procedure (previously discussed) to record multiple takes as the project loops the playback, MIDI data is not saved with the additional region information that the ACID application adds to audio files. This makes it impossible to isolate takes instantly by selecting a region and limits the usefulness of this technique.

Figure 5.14

Track 2 is a MIDI track that was recorded into the ACID software.

As mentioned, the basic process of recording MIDI is similar to recording audio, but the ways that you record and configure the data are completely different. Please see Chapter 10 for a full explanation.

Chapter 5 Quiz

1. If you place your PC in a cabinet, you won't need to worry about air circulation. (T/F)

2. You determine where you want to start recording by:

    A. Positioning the timeline cursor where you want to start

    B. Entering a timeline location in the Position field in the Record From dialog

    C. Pressing Record

3. By default, the ACID software records performances as special beatmapped files (often called ACID loops). (T/F)

4. Clipping when you are recording is indicated in the ACID software by:

    A. Red clipping indicators in the Mixer window

    B. Red clipping indicators on the Track Header

    C. A small exclamation mark next to the Arm for Record button

    D. The Audio Devices tab of the Preferences dialog

5. There is no way to record with a pre-roll in the ACID software. (T/F)

6. The ACID application can record multiple takes to multiple tracks. (T/F)

7. Where would you look for multiple takes in the ACID software?

    A. In the Hot Tub

    B. In the Media Manager

    C. In the Clip Pool

    D. In the Explorer

8. Mixing various takes to a single file helps simplify your projects. (T/F)

9. Folder Tracks are a great method for:

    A. Reducing timeline track clutter and organizing your tracks

    B. Organizing your hard drive

    C. Changing the tempo of your ACID loops without changing the pitch

    D. All of the above

10. The ACID program can record audio tracks, but not MIDI tracks. (T/F)

6 } Mastering the Mix

One of the last things to do before committing a song to posterity is to adjust the final mix. Mixing is a basic and critical part of any song and was introduced in Chapter 2, "Getting Around." On the most fundamental levels, we mix to prevent clipping, which is a common mistake that happens when the volume of the project exceeds the digital maximum. This chapter discusses the more subtle and subjective aspects of mixing with Sony Media Software's ACID®-capable tools and should not be ignored. As a subjective art, however, what constitutes a good mix can be difficult for novices to judge. It is not an easy art and requires patience and practice. Perfectly good songs can be (and have been) ruined by bad mixing techniques. Whatever you do, don't let your bass player perform the final mix (just kidding).

Mixing a Master

Mixing and mastering are two related but separate concepts. The exact definition of each overlaps in that both involve adjusting the relative volumes of various tracks and so on to produce a song that sounds good. A rough mix may be performed in the studio, but typically mixing takes longer than the recording process. Mastering is more of a technical procedure. In the ACID software, you can think of mixing as what happens on the timeline and with tracks and what occurs in the Mixer window.

Home computer–based music and Internet distribution bring new elements to the mastering game. In brief, ACID projects should follow a flow from creation to mixing to rendering:

❋ Creation is where you create structure, locate media, and draw your song. This probably consumes 90 percent of your time working with the ACID program.

❋ Mixing is done concurrently with creation or shortly after a song has matured. This is where you get a song to sound good, emphasizing sounds and ideas, increasing the spatial environment, and so on. This is mostly done at the track level, and you want to maintain maximum quality (that is, the cleanest, widest dynamic range, and so on) and flexibility (leaving room for further mixing).

✳ Rendering can affect the quality of your song more than any other aspect of mixing. In this chapter, the discussion will focus on achieving the best possible quality. Some aspects of mixing can affect how a song sounds when a file is compressed and streamed over the Internet. These aspects (and rendering in general) are dealt with in Chapter 12, "Publishing."

Mastering is the last process before the final song is rendered. Modern distribution via 24-bit 48-kHz DAT or 8-bit 11-kHz streaming media has complicated this process, so you need to consider the final destination at this stage. Songs destined for the Internet may benefit from dithering and compression, while songs intended for a CD-ROM might suffer from these effects. Using higher-quality settings for mixing (such as 24-bit 48-kHz) is not a bad idea, but it is not necessary either, because you can't squeeze any additional quality out of an audio file by doing so. You will need to change these settings in the mastering phase to match the destination media.

The Studio Environment

One extremely important variable in creating a final mix is the studio environment. Equipment, speakers, speaker placement, and room acoustics all heavily influence the sound of a song. Although this book does not go into how to build a proper studio, it is important to realize that your song will sound different when it is played back on different systems. This can be frustrating on the one hand, but it can be liberating on the other. Even if you build the perfect studio, your song is still not going to be played back in an identical environment. There is a lot of variation out there, from the latest 7.1 surround systems, to tiny laptop speakers, to MP3 players with earbuds, to car stereos. It is impossible to control how the song will sound in the end.

> ✳ **THX THEATER SOUND**
> Lucas THX theater sound is an interesting example of controlling the environment. THX standards precisely define the exact placement of speakers and the ratio of the volume levels. Theaters must meet these requirements to receive THX certification. THX mixing studios are likewise standardized. By specifying the mixing and playback environments, mixing engineers can be confident that the mix they are creating will sound pretty much as they intend it to sound in any THX-certified theater.

Headphones versus Speakers

Given all these difficulties, creating a final mix can be a challenging task. Headphones are often a good choice for monitoring the mix while recording. This is especially true if you would otherwise use standard computer speakers to monitor the ACID software. Even some of the higher-end four- and five-speaker systems for computers are not particularly good for music and are really designed for gamers. This often means that the rear speakers are too loud and the bass through the subwoofer is too heavy. Although headphones are ideal (indeed, are required) for monitoring recording, they are not the best choice for mixing itself.

A good-quality pair of speakers is, therefore, essential. Many mix masters studiously avoid the use of subwoofers and surround sound. In any case, you don't need giant, expensive speakers, just good ones. Mixing speakers are called *monitors*. This is not just a fancy name for an expensive speaker, either. Reference monitors are specifically designed to have a very flat frequency response. It is very important to mix at relatively low volume levels, so reference monitors are not really designed to rock your living room. A good pair of monitors is worth the cost if you get serious about the software.

✳ **HEADPHONE CAUTION**

Headphones present all kinds of problems for mixing. For example, the effects of cupping around the ears create serious distortions in the very shape of your ear, which dramatically changes the quality of the sound. Most engineers use both headphones and monitors at different times to get the best mix.

Configuring Your System

Electronic noise can also be a problem with computers, as discussed in the previous chapter on recording. Soundcards with digital outputs can help by sending a pure digital signal to your stereo equipment. Although this can also be the perfect professional setup when sending the digital signal to a studio board and speakers, in a home studio it can add another level of complexity to the mix. The sound coming from the ACID application is mixed, then sent through the soundcard (which often has its own mixing and balancing properties), and finally out to your stereo (which also adjusts the signal). Furthermore, digital outputs sometimes do not send a 5.1 signal to your stereo, which seems odd, but that's the way it is. If you want to do 5.1 surround sound mixing, you will often need to use the analog audio outputs on your soundcard.

However you decide to work, you need to standardize your system. For this, you need a white or pink noise generator, a flat frequency response microphone (a *measurement microphone*), and a spectrum analyzer. You can buy CDs with reference tracks on them, download the files from the Internet, or even generate the noise you need yourself using your computer. Ultimately, you want to generate the white (or pink) noise through the ACID software, out of your soundcard, and out of your reference monitors. Then place your microphone where your head would be when you are mixing and make your adjustments so the spectrum analyzer matches the noise. You can buy or rent a frequency analyzer or download a software application that you can run on your computer to perform these tests. Looking at white or pink noise pumped through your system on a frequency analyzer will help you objectively set up a standard system. Human perception of sound is different than how it might be objectively measured. (For example, look up

Fletcher-Munson curves and theory on the Internet.) The whole point of this exercise is to standardize your system and make sure you are hearing what you are supposed to hear from your setup. The process is slightly more involved than what we have briefly presented here, but it isn't all that complex. And if you aren't a fanatic, you can do it once when you are building your studio and forget about it.

> ❋ **BEST GUESS**
> Unless you are a professional engineer in a well-designed studio, you are just going to have to wing your configuration. The only real test is to burn a final mix to a CD and listen to it on a couple of different systems to see how it sounds on them.

Subwoofers

With more and more home systems coming standard with subwoofers, the controversy over whether you should mix using a subwoofer is only going to heat up. Most conventional studios, however, do not use subwoofers during mixing, and most engineers mix without them. The only advice offered here is the same general advice for any mixing environment: Don't count on your listening audience to have the same equipment you do. Subwoofers can distort the bass line, making it seem stronger than it really is. Unless you are mixing for a Dolby 5.1 surround sound movie (see the "5.1 Surround Mixing" section later in this chapter), don't use your subwoofer when you mix. Even if you are mixing for a surround sound DVD, you are still going to want to make sure your mix sounds good even in stereo.

If It Sounds Good

In the end, the only way to tell whether you are mixing properly (besides going to a professional studio) is to burn a CD of your music and listen to it on your target system. Compare your mix with other CDs that you like. Is the bass all you can hear at reasonable volumes? Can people who don't know the words to your song understand the vocal parts? Pick CDs in the same genre as your music, listen to them, and set up the volume, equalization, and balance how you like it. Position a chair in the sweet spot. Listen. Pop in your CD. Listen. Ask your friends. Listen.

One word of caution, however: Just as some music is good and some bad, so some mixes on commercial CDs are good and some are bad. Don't compare your mixes to just any CD; carefully pick a few standards that you really like and stick with those. Finally, trumping everything that comes before or after this sentence in this book, remember what Duke Ellington said (and Peter Schickele often quotes): "If it sounds good, it is good."

Mixing ACID

Mixing has been briefly discussed a number of times in this book already. It is definitely a basic part of any song and project. The ACID software allows a huge amount of flexibility in mixing, far beyond most conventional hardware studio environments. In addition to simple and broadly effective volume and panning controls, the great variety of audio plug-ins and effects available in the program really enhances your mixing ability.

Workflow and Signal Path

As you already know, the ACID application is analogous to a real-world multitrack mixing environment. You can think of the entire program as a digital mixing console, something like the stylized representation of a mixer in Figure 6.1. You can see from the illustration the various parts that correspond to the ACID UI.

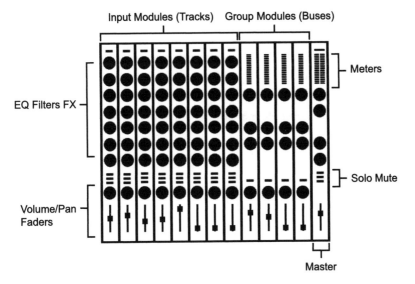

Figure 6.1

A stylized mixing console.

> ✳ **SIGNAL PATH**
>
> The official manual for the ACID software has an excellent and easy-to-follow signal path diagram. The following discussion should be considered a summary, and you should consult the official documentation to see the real complexity of what happens to a sound that enters the software as a clip and leaves the Master bus in a mix.

✳ The Input Modules on the mixer are where you plug in the various instruments and microphones. They correspond to ACID tracks, each of which also has a part of the total mix in the form of media files and clips. Along the top of each input module on a real mixer you may find a piece of masking tape with the name of the input. Of course, we can easily rename ACID tracks without a magic marker.

﹡ As with real-world mixers, each track in the ACID software has a fader that controls the volume and another for panning. ACID tracks also have an FX button for effects and EQ, Solo, and Mute buttons, just as boards in the real world often do.

﹡ The Group Modules (also called busses) on the mixer are used to group specified Input Modules together to modify and mix them as a unit. This may be done to create more manageable subgroups in a large mix or more typically to apply the same effect or EQ to a group of inputs; an example is reverb (sometimes called the Echo bus). In the ACID software, the busses in the mixer are analogous to the Group Modules and serve the same purpose. You can add FX to a bus and then assign individual tracks to that bus. You can even group busses into groups by assigning them collectively to another bus. Flexibility is what it is all about.

﹡ The Master Output controls the final volume. You can also add final equalization and FX the mix at this point (for example, a little compression). The fader on the busses in the Mixer window has two halves, one for each channel in a stereo pair, left and right.

﹡ The meters in the Mixer window let you visually monitor the volume. Real-world mixers may also have meters on every input module.

> **GET ON THE BUS**
> No auxiliary busses are visible in the ACID default configuration. To add a bus to the Mixer window, click the Insert Bus button.

Tracks and Project Structure

While the ACID software can be thought of as analogous to a traditional (and extremely expensive) sound recording studio, if that analogy doesn't work for you, you can completely drop it. In fact, if you think about the software only in terms of a mixing board in a recording studio, you are missing out on perhaps 90% of the flexibility of the application. Flexibility can lead to chaos, however, so you should understand a bit about how ACID tracks work.

A track can correspond to a single instrument or voice. In a traditional studio, you'd have a track on your mixing board for the bass, the guitar, the drums, and the vocals in a classic rock band. The ACID software can function that way if you want. But tracks are also completely flexible and can contain as many different clips as you want. To continue with the traditional studio model, you could restrict a track to only containing the lead guitar, but you could use a bunch of different clips from different takes of a single performance or even different lead guitar parts altogether. Or you could break the single-track-single-part analogy and put your bass and lead guitars in the same track. While this would make your timeline less cluttered with tracks, you cannot mix clips in a single track together (other than with a crossfade), which is a huge restriction. So while you can drop clips anywhere you want on a timeline and into any track, it is usually a good idea to pay attention to the track structure and proceed deliberately as you build your timeline.

Clipping Redux

The ACID Mixer window indicates clipping with red squares at the top of the various meters, particularly the Master meters. As mentioned in Chapter 2, clipping occurs when the volume or gain exceeds 0 dB, which in an analog or real-world system means that the system is being overdriven or is close to it. This can result in distortion or even damage to equipment. Clipping in the ACID program will not damage your equipment, but will likely result in distortion caused by lost signal above the peak (that is, it is clipped off). Some engineers recommend recording right up to the 0dB digital maximum. As previously mentioned, using lower values (perhaps from −13 to −9 dB) is perfectly acceptable and indeed gives you more room for future mixing. The only downside is the small reduction in the total dynamic range of a song. You also may want to turn the volume up a bit when playing back your songs when you compare them to other songs that have been more aggressively mixed. In a digital mix in the ACID software, clipping occurs at 0 dB and must be avoided. Bringing the levels up to 0 dB should be done only as the very last step and only if you feel it is really necessary. There is no shame in allowing your listeners to adjust the volume of their stereo as they see fit.

OLD DOGS, OLD TRICKS

Engineers who create commercials for television and radio sometimes used to cheat when setting the peak volume. Of course, the object is to get your commercial noticed, so getting the maximum playback volume (while still avoiding clipping) is critical. Advertising mixes are almost always right up to the top of the meters. The trick mixing engineers used to use was to create a reference signal (a 1-kHz tone) before the commercial that was slightly below standards. Then, when the playback engineer at the studio set up the volume for the commercial using the reference signal, the volume was actually higher than it should have been. Modern equipment and automatic gain controls make this technique irrelevant today.

Clipping means that wave amplitudes above a certain point are cut off. Clipping results in distortion, and you can see it in the waveform of media files, such as the event pictured in Figure 6.2. You can see that many of the wave peaks go all the way to the top. If you zoom in far enough, you can see the actual squaring off of individual waves. Clipping in a media file (and thus in an event on the timeline as pictured) does not result in clipping in the ACID software. You can always play back a clipped and distorted media file in the software at a lower volume. This will not fix the clipping problem, which is inherent in the media file and cannot be fixed, although some peak restoration effects and plug-ins can help. Ignoring the clipping warnings in an ACID project will result in rendered media files that are clipped, as in the file shown in Figure 6.2.

Figure 6.2

Clipping can be visually identified in the waveform of events on the timeline. In this case, clipping is an inherent part of the media file.

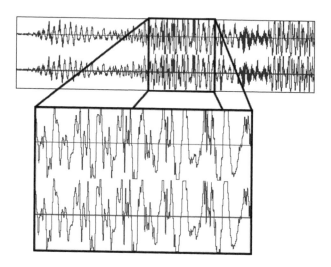

Loudness

You can monitor clipping visually by watching the peaks in the mix on the Master meter in the mixer. Although increasing the various track volumes and using other mixing techniques to make the peak volume equal to 0 dB is a rough way of maximizing the loudness without clipping, this is not the best way to make the entire mix louder. Very short bursts of sound, such as musical hits or snare drum beats, can cause peaks in loudness. You can therefore increase the overall loudness of a mix by decreasing the volume of a few of these short bursts and increasing the volume of the rest of the piece overall. One way to do this is by modifying the overall dynamics using an effect such as Graphic Dynamics or Multi-Band Dynamics. Even easier, you can use the Track Compressor plug-in on a track that is causing the highest peak. This will decrease the overall dynamics of the track, but the effect will be minimal in the overall mix.

❋ **DON'T SQUASH THE DYNAMICS**

The arms race in loudness has resulted in CDs getting louder and louder at the cost of dynamic range (the difference between the quietest and loudest sounds). Resist the urge to engage in this one-upsmanship and mix wisely. Dynamic range is exciting. Loudness is not.

The real battle here is loudness versus dynamics. No one wants to sacrifice the dynamics in a mix. Most popular music never dips below a certain threshold, except at times when there is complete silence. This lowest volume may be −40 dB or −50 dB, but whatever its value, the total range between the softest and loudest part of a song is defined as the total dynamic range. Pushing the loudness too high (and using compression to do this) lessens the total dynamic range. Leaving the peak volume at a lower level is always safe. Unfortunately, there is a very real competition among studio engineers as they try to push the edge to make sure their music is heard. This edge is different and more competitive in different genres of music, with rock-metal-dance music always catching the top of the meters and classical being much less competitive (in addition to having a much greater dynamic range). People may perceive your music as being less intense than other music in the same genre simply because the volume is lower. Obviously, this is unfair, and turning up the volume a bit on the playback system solves this problem.

As a general rule, in the ACID software, keeping the loudness down during the creation and mixing process is a good idea (perhaps from −13 to −9 dB) to give you plenty of mixing room later. The only time you may want to kick it up to 0 dB is during the final mastering, immediately before your song is immortalized to a CD. Don't feel obligated to do this, however.

Volume Envelopes

Envelopes are automated fader controls on any track. You can use envelopes to control brief spikes in an event that cause clipping or to increase the volume of a track temporarily for emphasis. Envelopes are extremely powerful and very worthwhile when used correctly. We use envelopes on every ACID project.

Volume Envelopes, when used as mixing tools, might be considered a manual form of compression in that you can reduce the gain of individual peaks in a track, thus preventing occasional clipping problems. Larger and more frequent clipping may be more easily fixed by using Track Compression, which automatically reduces peaks trackwide (as discussed later in this chapter). Volume Envelopes are especially useful in reducing one-time peaks caused by pops or clicks in the audio track that may be the result of any number of things, including dropping the microphone during recording or even by vocal plosives (such as *p*).

To use envelopes to eliminate clipping and allow you to turn up the volume of the track overall, you must first identify the places where the clipping occurs. To do this:

1. Click the Solo button on the track that is the primary culprit.

2. Press the spacebar on your keyboard to play the track.

3. As it is playing back, press the M key on your keyboard when the red Clipping Indicator above the Master meter in the mixer blinks on.

4. You will need to stop playback and then continue playback after the clipped section to reset the Clipping Indicators or quickly click the indicators to reset them. You may need to repeat this process several times.

Again, because you should use this procedure to fix only a few isolated problems, this shouldn't be too much work. If you are finding many places where clipping is occurring, it may indicate that the track is well suited to automatic adjustment with compression or that you simply need to slide the track's fader down a bit.

Once you have identified the problem sections, you can eliminate the clipping with a Volume Envelope (see Figure 6.3). To do so:

1. Press a number key along the top of your keyboard to jump to the first marker that corresponds to a problem section (as marked in the previous procedure). The actual clipping will occur somewhere just before the marker.

2. Zoom in on the project and identify the section that is causing the clipping. You will certainly need to zoom in time, giving you more precise control, but it may also be useful to change the track height so that you can see the waveform more clearly.

3. Press the V key on your keyboard to insert a Volume Envelope (or to make a preexisting Volume Envelope visible).

4. Add four nodes (key points) to the envelope: two closely spaced before the clipping and two closely spaced after. The exact position is not critical, and you can adjust it later. You can use three points for very short peaks.

5. Drag the Volume Envelope line between the points downward to decrease the volume.

Figure 6.3

A Volume Envelope used to fix momentary clipping problems in isolated sections.

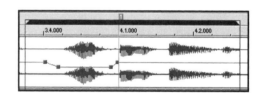

It is very useful at this point to move the loop region to include the section on which you are working. To do so, drag on the Marker bar to define the loop region, and then press L to turn looping playback on. This changes the loop region color to dark blue. Now, when you begin playback within the loop region, the section will repeatedly and continuously play back while you are making adjustments.

Remember to reset the Clipping Indicators occasionally in the Mixer window, either by stopping and restarting playback (pressing the spacebar) or by clicking the Clipping Indicators. After you have eliminated the clipping, delete the marker (right-click it and select Delete) and move on to the next section. It is best to leave the envelope between the two outside points at some angle so that the volume doesn't dip back to the baseline too suddenly. You can reverse this technique to increase the volume briefly for emphasis and also for sections that are too soft.

Busses

You can group tracks together and modify them as a unit using busses (see Figure 6.4). One reason for doing this is to control the volume of a group of tracks more easily with a single fader. Applying identical effects to groups of instruments that are supposed to sound like they originated from the same space is another excellent reason to group tracks. For those of you unfamiliar with real-world mixers, individual track outputs are physically routed through busses with cables, which is exactly analogous to how the ACID software works. Of course, the software is a lot more flexible and slightly less intuitive, but it isn't really all that hard. To insert a new bus into the Mixer window, click the Insert Bus button or right-click in the Mixer window and select Insert Bus, or, from the Insert menu—yes, you guessed it—select Insert Bus.

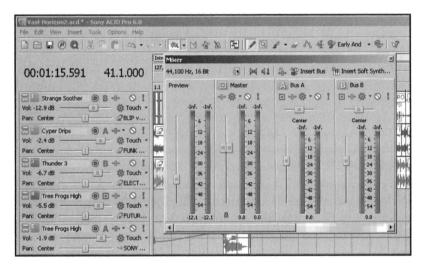

Figure 6.4

Tracks 1 and 3 are grouped to Bus A, whereas Tracks 2 and 5 are grouped to Bus B. Track 4 is not routed through any bus and, along with Bus A and B, it goes through the Master bus.

To route a track through a bus, click the Bus Assignment button in the Track Header and, from the menu, select the new bus that you want to route the track through (such as Bus A). To control the send volume from the track into the bus, use the Multipurpose fader that appears on the Track Header. Still fairly simple.

Assignable FX

Assignable FX busses can also be inserted into the Mixer window and operate very much like any other kind of bus. Assignable FX have input and output faders that let you control the mix of your signal (see Figure 6.5). Tracks use Assignable FX in a slightly different way as well. Instead of routing a track through the Assignable FX with the Bus Assignment button, you'll use the new fader that appears on the Track Header of all tracks in the project to control the mix of the effect into the track. This Multipurpose fader can also control the mix into the various busses as well.

Figure 6.5

Regular busses lack the input/output controls that an Assignable FX bus has.

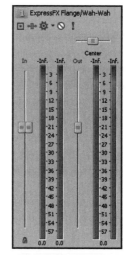

Bus   Assignable FX

Okay, if this all makes sense to you now, you should probably stop reading. The ACID software is extremely flexible. Not only can you route the Assignable FX bus through any other bus by clicking the Bus Assignment button, but you can also route busses through other busses. In other words, that wonderfully complex Signal Flow Diagram that Sony Media Software's official documentation presents is not merely a geeky excess: it's exactly how the software works. Fortunately, the mixing of your project does not necessarily need to route tracks through Assignable FX busses, through regular busses that have effects chains that are routed through other busses, if you don't want. In other words, if your project gets hopelessly complex with virtual signal path spaghetti connections, it's your own fault.

Folder Tracks and Busses

Folder Tracks are structural elements of the ACID timeline that help you organize your tracks visually and have no impact on the mix of a project. You cannot apply effects to a Folder Track and you cannot route a Folder Track through a bus. The only controls on a Folder Track that alter the mix at all are the Mute and Solo buttons.

Bus Tracks

Bus Tracks are simply tracks that appear on the main timeline that let you visualize bus levels over time. To make the Bus Tracks visible, from the View menu, select Bus Tracks or press B on your keyboard at any time. Bus Tracks look a bit like regular tracks at first, except they hang out at the bottom of the timeline. The other radical difference is that you cannot draw or paint events into the Bus Tracks. But you can insert envelopes, which you'll recall are how you automate control of the volume or panning or effects over time. Let's take a simple example. Suppose you are scoring a television show. You have your narrator's voiceover and you have a song you have composed. The song is a simple one, but it spans 20 or so tracks. To duck each one of those tracks down under the VO, you'd have to make the Volume Envelopes of 20 tracks visible, create 80 or so nodes, and duck the volume down in a process that would take an hour. Or, you could route all of the music tracks through a bus and use one Volume Envelope, four nodes, and about 15 seconds of work to duck them all down at the same time (see Figure 6.6).

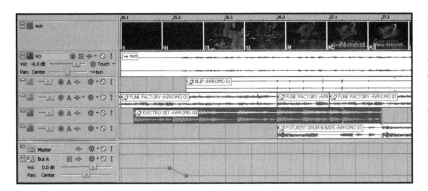

Figure 6.6
The music tracks here are all routed through Bus A, which then has a Volume Envelope on it to duck the volume of all the tracks down under the narrator's VO, which is in Track 1.

Space and Panning

Space or the spatial sense of a song describes the perceived environment in which the song is being performed. From a small coffee shop with a folk musician to a mystical flute played in the Taj Mahal, space is a very important part of the mix. How the listener's mind perceives space in a mix is another topic that could fill an entire book. In the context of mixing, space is most easily created by panning tracks left or right to create the illusion that, for example, the drummer is in the back and center with a trumpet solo up front, while the bass player is hanging off to the right and the piano player is off to the left. It is easy to overdo panning, so you need some restraint when adjusting it. Panning can also solve some volume and clipping problems in the ACID software: The volume might not be too high, but all of the tracks bunched up in the center might cause clipping. Panning is not the only way to add perceived space to a mix. In particular, see Chapter 8, "FX Dictionary," for more information on reverb and space, where we'll discuss some additional ideas.

Panning to Create Space

Panning individual parts of a song is a primary method of creating a feeling of space and realism in a mix. The Pan fader is directly below the Volume fader for stereo projects. 5.1 surround sound projects use a different Surround Panner and do not have a stereo Pan fader. Listen to music of the genre you are mixing and note which instruments and parts are where. Also, listen to different genres and see how these vary as well. Broadly speaking, pop and rock tend to bunch up in the center because most parts in these songs are coming out of amplifiers and are not localized with the performers. Jazz, on the other hand, has instruments that are very easy to localize in space on a recording. Drums tend to be in the center. Pianos tend to be off to one side or another. Vocals tend to be in the center. The bass part is a special case, where the bass itself is usually off to one side, but because of the nature of how we perceive low-frequency sounds, the bass is usually balanced in the center. In classical music, instrument position is more or less rigidly defined by the orchestra, whereas electronic music is completely unshackled by any conventions. If you pan beyond 30 percent left or right you must be careful, because this can give the mix an artificial feel.

Unlike Volume Envelopes, Panning Envelopes are not particularly useful in natural-sounding mixes. It is a rare recording indeed where the piano is wheeled about on the stage. Instead, Panning Envelopes are most useful in electronic and dance music and should be considered an effects tool rather than a mixing tool.

Panning to Solve Volume Problems

Sometimes bunching up the entire mix in the center can cause volume problems. By moving instruments and parts to the left or right, you not only can solve loudness and clipping problems, but you can also increase the distinctiveness of a mix. You can control panning using the fader on the various tracks: Click the Multipurpose Fade Mode button to switch the function to a Pan fader.

FX and Space

There are many other sometimes surprising ways to create space in a song. Many of these are available through plug-ins and effects (FX) that you can add to a track or to a final mix. The following list contains a few ideas, with more information on each contained in the relevant sections in Chapter 8:

* **Reverb.** Reverb is an all-purpose space-generating machine widely used in many mixes. Reverb simulates the bouncing of sound off of the walls of a room. Indeed, the presets available in the Reverb FX plug-ins in the ACID software allow you to select the particular room size and brightness from a list. Reverb can be carefully used at the track level, but it might result in a rather strange mix if the singer sounds like he is in a small room and the piano player sounds like she is in a cavern. More typically, you'll add a hint of reverb to the Master bus in the Mixer window as one of the final modifiers in a song.

* **Amplitude modulation.** This varies the volume of a sound or track rapidly and periodically over time and can make a track sound bigger. Again, subtlety is a virtue here.

* **Chorus.** You can use chorus to make a track or instrument sound fuller by adding additional voices to it. Each of these additional voices is delayed a bit, which has the side effect of creating an illusion of space.

- ❋ **Delay.** The Delay plug-ins are the most straightforward and easy to understand FX when creating space. Delay can be thought of as an echo effect as sound bounces off of distant walls or canyons.

- ❋ **Equalization.** Increasing the prominence of the higher-frequency ranges in a mix can simulate perceived depth or make a song sound as if it were recorded in a larger room.

There are additional creative ways to create space in a song, including the very cool Acoustic Mirror plug-in, which can be purchased from Sony Media Software and used in the ACID software.

5.1 Surround Mixing

So far, this chapter has been about mixing two stereo channels, but the Pro version of the ACID software also lets you create surround sound projects. Everything that we've covered also applies to 5.1 surround sound mixing, except that instead of two channels, 5.1 mixes have six: two front, two rear, a center channel, and a subwoofer. This is not simply a problem of addition, and 5.1 surround mixing is a full magnitude harder than stereo mixing. It is harder to configure an appropriate mixing environment, it will add new tracks to your project, and, most complicated of all, 5.1 mixing is incredibly challenging artistically. If you thought creating a good stereo mix was tough, wait until you try surround. Surround mixing is incredibly fun, however, and with the pragmatic tips we'll cover in the next few pages, you should be able to pull off some clever surround tricks for your movies.

> ❋ **SURROUND ENCODING**
> Surround sound mixing is relatively easy, and most modern computers can do it. But there is one very serious problem you need to address before you start: How will you encode and distribute your surround sound mix? If you can't answer that question now, read on, but don't start working on a serious project until you can answer both parts of that question. Otherwise, you are just mixing for fun—and there's nothing wrong with that!

Distribution

Your first consideration for any surround project is distribution: How is your audience going to listen to your music or sound track? For example, DVD-Audio discs may become more popular as more audiophiles buy DVD-Audio-compatible players, but my speculation is that the format will never catch on—the age of discs and physical distribution for music is at an end. The most common distribution method today is to use a DVD-Video player or to send digital files over the Internet. Besides considering distribution, you are also going to need to consider your audience's equipment. Not everyone who has a DVD player is going to have it hooked up to a 5.1 surround system. This means that you also need to make sure your mix sounds good in stereo as well. For that matter, experienced mixers must make sure their audio sounds good out of one monophonic speaker.

> ❄ **DVD-VIDEO FOR YOUR AUDIO**
>
> Because DVD-Audio disc players are relatively rare but nearly everyone has a DVD-Video player, you can create pseudo-DVD-Audio discs with minimal video tracks (perhaps even just blank video) and a 5.1 surround audio track.

The final consideration for creating Dolby AC3 5.1 surround mixes is that it is a licensed technology. In other words, it is not free (not even close to free, really). AC3 5.1 surround mixes need to be encoded into a specially formatted file, and the encoder costs money. You can purchase Sony Media Software's 5.1 Surround Plug-In Pack to do this for you or use Vegas+DVD. If you already own an AC3 5.1 encoder, you can output the six channels from the ACID software and do your processing with that application.

Configuring ACID for 5.1

Okay, so you know how you are going to distribute your project (for example, on DVD-Video disc) and you own an AC3 5.1 surround sound encoder: What else do you need? First of all, you'll need an appropriate 5.1 surround soundcard. Fortunately, 5.1 soundcards have been available for a few years now and are relatively common and inexpensive. You can even find 7.1 surround hardware, but this is currently a gimmick more than anything else. In many situations, you will not need to configure anything because the ACID software will use your compatible soundcard's Windows Classic Wave Driver or DirectSound Surround Mapper defaults. The default surround settings can be changed and manually specified if you use your soundcard's ASIO drivers:

1. From the Options menu, select Preferences and go to the Audio Device tab.
2. From the Audio Device Type drop-down list, select your soundcard's ASIO driver. For example, for Creative Labs products, this will be the Creative ASIO driver.
3. From the Default Stereo and Front Playback Device drop-down list, select Front L/R.
4. From the Default Rear Playback Device drop-down list, select Rear L/R.
5. From the Default Center and LFE Playback Device drop-down list, select Center/LFE.
6. Click OK.

To change your project to the appropriate sample rate:

1. From the File menu, select Properties and go to the Audio tab.

2. From the Master Bus Mode drop-down list, select 5.1 Surround.

3. From the Sample Rate (Hz) drop-down list, select 48,000 Hz.

4. Click OK.

Now check out the Mixer window (press Alt+3). You'll see a whole new rack of faders corresponding to your new channels (see Figure 6.7).

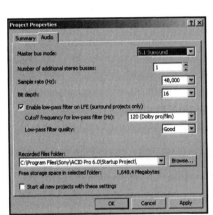
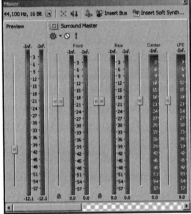

Figure 6.7

5.1 surround sound project properties and the Mixer window with surround channels.

5.1 OUT

You will also have to configure your soundcard to output to 5.1 speakers. This might mean using three stereo mini-plugs output to six speakers or a digital coax or optical connection. Driver-wise, you'll need to go into the Sound and Audio Devices Properties Control Panel in Windows and adjust your speaker settings.

Fundamentals of 5.1 Surround Mixing

Although we've spent most of this chapter on stereo mixing, we are going to cover surround mixing only at its most basic level. Let's start by simply setting up all of the necessary tracks in an exaggerated way to test whether we have configured everything successfully. To test your surround setup:

1. Drag an audio file to the timeline from the Explorer window to create a new track.

2. Draw an event onto the timeline.

3. Create a loop region, click the Loop Playback button, and play your project.

4. Double-click the Surround Pan panel on the Track Header of the new track.

5. In the Surround Panner, click and drag the orange panning diamond around in the Surround Panner window and listen to the results.

You should now be having a ton of fun (see Figure 6.8). As you move the diamond around, you should be able to move the sound around four of your speakers: front-left, front-right, rear-left, and rear-right. Watch the Mixer window to see the various meters jumping about as you do. You'll notice that the center channel is silent and the meters are not moving, however. You can add a stereo downmix of your track to the center channel with the Center slider. The center channel can be a completely independent track or it can be a part of the combined front stereo channels.

❄ **DIALOGUE TO THE CENTER**

The center channel is typically dedicated to dialogue in movies and vocal and solo tracks in music. This doesn't mean that those are the only audio elements that get mixed into the center or that those parts don't spill over into other channels, but it is usually the explicit purpose of the center channel.

Figure 6.8

5.1 surround sound mixing.

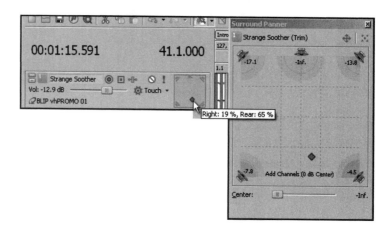

Dialogue on a DVD is typically sent to the center channel. The LFE (low-frequency effects) channel is the subwoofer and is a special case. It is commonly used for explosions and rumbles in movies. You can also use it to emphasize a bass line in a song. Because it is felt more than it is heard, one pragmatic tip that you might find useful is to create a decent bass track for the main mix and then duplicate that track and assign it to the LFE:

1. Add a bass track to your project.

2. Right-click the Track Header and select Duplicate Track.

3. Right-click the Surround Pan panel and select LFE Only.

The Surround Pan panel now displays LFE, and the track's Volume slider now controls only the subwoofer output (see Figure 6.9). You can now play with this a bit to see the results. LFE audio is quite unique and you will need to find media that is appropriate for the application. One fun way that we've used it is to create an almost inaudible rumble that comes in behind the mix to create tension. Subwoofer mixing is very tricky, so be careful not to overdo it.

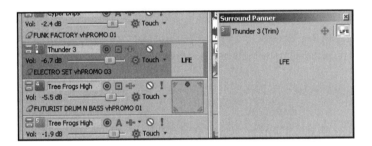

Figure 6.9

The LFE (low-frequency effects) channel or subwoofer output.

One tremendous way to waste an afternoon is to automate a surround mix and simply imagine what you can do and maybe even how you can make some money with this new skill. For fun, at least, find a helicopter sound effect and see if you can't make it "fly" around the room. To animate and automate a surround mix:

1. Select Automation Write (Touch) from the Automation Settings button in the Track Header.

2. Click the Automation Settings button to enable automation.

3. Open the Surround Panning window by double-clicking the Surround Pan panel on the Track Header to see a larger control.

4. Move the timeline cursor to a position and then move the orange panning diamond. Notice that a blue keyframe diamond has appeared under the event on the timeline.

5. Click the Play button on the Transport bar.

6. Move the Surround Pan indicator around as the project plays back.

7. Click the Stop button.

8. Play back the project to see your automation in action.

Now you'll also see a track appear in the Surround Panner window (see Figure 6.10). This represents the path of your sound through time. The Smoothness slider controls the amount of

Figure 6.10

Automating a 5.1 surround sound mix.

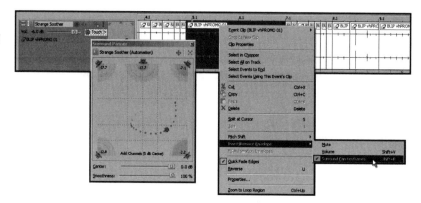

curve that the path will take between keyframes. Play back the project and see how it sounds. You can find more information on automating effects and keyframes in Chapter 7.

Rendering a 5.1 Surround Mix

We will discuss two possible ways to distribute your 5.1 surround mix. Ultimately, however, you need to encode it using a surround sound encoder. If you already have an encoder, you can output the six individual channels from the ACID software into six monophonic files that the encoder will recombine into a mixed file. In principle, this is a straightforward and simple process, provided you have six tracks for the six channels. This is not the normal way the software works, however, and many (if not most) tracks are stereo, containing left and right channels.

The easiest way to produce the six files necessary for an external encoder is in the Render As dialog:

1. From the File menu, select Render As.
2. In the Render As dialog, make sure the Save Each Channel as a Separate File option near the bottom of the dialog is selected. (If you don't have the AC3 encoder plug-in, it is automatically selected and cannot be unselected.)

This will automatically create a "family" of files and label them with the appropriate speaker/ channel tag. To encode your surround mix for distribution manually:

1. In the Mixer window, click the Unlock Fader Channels button under the slider channels you want (in this case, Front).
2. Slide the channel slider you don't want all the way down (for this current example, you would thus slide the right channel down).

3. From the File menu, select Render As and output a WAV file. Click the Custom button and set the sample rate to 48,000 Hz and the channels to Mono (leaving the bit depth at 16).

4. Name the file something appropriate (such as front-left.wav) and save the file.

Now you need to repeat this process for the remaining channels. After you have your six files, you can import them into your encoder to output your 5.1 surround file (such as an AC3 file for a DVD). Besides standalone encoders, you might find surround sound AC3 encoders in a video editing application (such as Sony Media Software's Vegas) or in a DVD-authoring application. Note the following caution about DVD-authoring apps and marketing: Apps that tout AC3 support are not the same as apps that include an AC3 encoder. Also, be sure you determine whether any included encoder is a stereo encoder (which is common) or a 5.1 encoder (which is more rare and expensive). Again, the reason for this is that AC3 is a licensed technology from Dolby and it costs money.

Obviously, using Sony Media Software's AC3 encoding plug-in is easier, with the only downside being that it costs money and is available only for the ACID Pro software. Right now, the plug-in only supports DVD-Video standards, but this is not really an issue, because very few people currently own DVD-Audio players. To encode a surround mix:

1. From the File menu, select Render As.

2. In the Render As dialog, on the Save as Type list, select Dolby Digital AC-3 (*.ac3).

3. From the Template list, select 5.1 Surround DVD.

This file is now ready to be inserted into most midrange DVD-authoring applications that support AC3 audio as an audio track.

If you haven't gotten the point by now, 5.1 surround is primarily a tool for DVD movies today. In the workflow, surround mixing the soundtrack to a movie would be one of the very last tasks before you burn the movie to DVD. You would first completely edit your movie and then bring it into the ACID software for scoring. Now you can precisely synchronize the soundtrack with the video. When you are ready to output, you (typically) won't use the ACID software to render the video. Instead, you would output an AC3 file and then insert the video and audio separately into your DVD-authoring app and let that program do your rendering and burning. The software is a great scoring tool, however, so check out Chapter 11, "Video," for more information.

Surround encoding is relatively new to Internet video formats (such as DivX or Windows Media 9), but the process of encoding is much easier for these formats, primarily because the encoders are inexpensive and included with your software. For example, when you select the Windows Media Audio format in the Render As dialog, you will notice that the template choice has been set to Audio: 256 Kbps, 44,100 Hz, 5.1 Surround by default. This will render a WMA surround file.

Track FX

Sound effects (FX) and plug-ins have two entire chapters (7 and 8) devoted to them, but there are three effects that are particularly important to mixing that we'd like to highlight here: compression, gating, and equalization (EQ). Track compression is a very powerful effect that can really bring out a track in a mix, especially in recordings that have sections that are too quiet. Track gating (i.e., Noise Gate) is a general-purpose tool for eliminating low-level background hums and static and can fix problems introduced by compression effects. Sony Media Software track EQ is automatically inserted into every track by default, although the levels are flat so no changes are made to a track. Together, these effects move beyond the simple Volume faders on the tracks to more advanced mixing.

Track FX plug-ins generally consists of simpler versions of some of the other effects available from Sony Media Software, such as the XFX series of plug-ins. Some types of effects work better on a project level, such as using reverb to create a room atmosphere for an entire song. Some effects are best used at the track level, such as using a Noise Gate to remove the hum of a camera motor in the soundtrack of a video clip. Track FX plug-ins are optimized for ease of use on tracks, but can be used at the bus and project level as well, although they might cause problems on slower computers. Likewise, there is no reason not to use ExpressFX or other effects on the track level either.

Compression

Track compression is another excellent way to emphasize a track in a song, but it differs significantly from equalization. You can use equalization and compression in concert to improve the sound of a track. Compression is extremely widely used and is a primary tool in any engineer's toolbox, especially in popular music. Almost all popular music you hear has had some compression applied to it, most commonly at the track level. Many people feel that compression is overused nowadays. In reality, it is bad compression that is overused. Compression is a powerful and useful tool that should be intelligently used where needed. For example, you can help out musicians who typically have difficulty controlling their own dynamics in relation to an entire mix. After all, musicians play, engineers mix. Compression is an excellent effect to use early in a chain of plug-ins (see Chapter 7).

> ❄ **DON'T SQUEEZE ME**
> Be cautious about using compression because it takes away some of the dynamic range. By making the loud parts softer, the total expressive range of the track is more limited. While this can (and is) used to bring a part out, it can also negatively impact the overall quality of the track. Compression may not be useful on most high-quality commercial loops, which are professionally recorded and mixed files.

Compression is an automated way to adjust the volume or consistency of the level of a track variably, raising all valleys or diminishing all peaks. Either adjustment results in a smaller dynamic range for the track overall. Figure 6.11 shows a voiceover narration that was not recorded particularly well, with the narrator perhaps turning away from the microphone at a number of points, resulting in sections of the file being too quiet. (Notice especially the middle part of the top event.) Simply increasing the volume of the track would not work because this would also raise the volume of the parts that are loud enough, making them too loud and possibly causing clipping. By applying compression to the track, you can reduce the peaks and then raise the overall volume without problems.

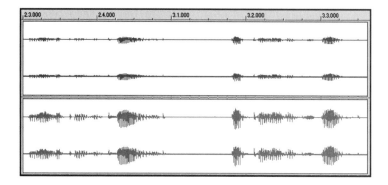

Figure 6.11

An uneven narration before and after applying compression. By reducing the peaks (and thus reducing the overall dynamic range), you can increase the gain on the track (to bring out softer parts) without causing clipping.

The best place to use compression in the ACID software is at the track level. The danger of squashing a song into dynamic oblivion increases greatly when you use compression at the bus or project level. The Sony Media Software Track Compressor is the simplest of the compression plug-ins. Using it usually increases a track's loudness, although this isn't necessarily the case. To apply the Track Compressor:

1. Click the Solo button on the track to isolate it.

2. Click the Track FX button. This opens the Audio Plug-In dialog.

3. In the Audio Plug-In dialog, click the Edit Chain button. This opens the Plug-In Chooser dialog.

4. In the Audio FX folder, open the Sony Media Software subfolder and double-click the Sony Track Compressor item (or select it and click the Add button).

5. Click the OK button. This closes the Plug-in Chooser dialog and returns you to the Audio Plug-In dialog with the Track Compressor selected (see Figure 6.12).

6. In the Track Compressor dialog, adjust the effect (see the following section).

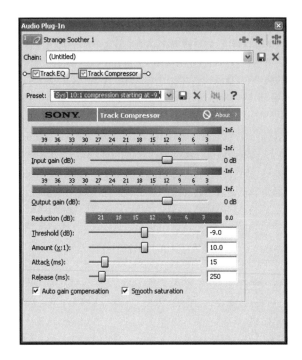

Figure 6.12

The Sony Media Software Track Compressor dialog.

To fix a voiceover narration that is too quiet in some places, you first need to reduce (compress) the peaks and then raise the Output gain (the volume) of the track as a whole. Click the Solo button on the track and play it back while adjusting the compression, all the while monitoring the Master meter in the Mixer window as follows:

❋ The Input/Output gain faders and meters control the signal into and out of the effect. Typically, you'll want to increase the Output gain to increase the loudness of the track.

❋ The Reduction meter measures how much the peaks are reduced (if they are reduced at all). Right-click the Peak decibel indicator on the right side of the meter to set the range to a more sensitive range, such as −12 to −0 dB.

❋ The Threshold slider sets the level where the compression begins to take effect (see Figure 6.13). When you're trying to bring a track out of the mix and increase the loudness overall (a typical use for compression), set the threshold to a lower value, but keep it above the level of the parts of the track that are too quiet. After all, you don't want to reduce those sections.

❋ The amount of compression can be set fairly higher in the voiceover narration example. Too much will result in a very dynamically flat sound, but you don't usually want a large dynamic range in a voiceover narration. Compression is expressed in a ratio, such as 10:1. This means that for peaks that rise above the threshold, what was originally (Input) a 10-dB jump in the meter would only result in a 1-dB increase (Output). Because it is a ratio, the louder the peak (the higher above the threshold), the more it is compressed. Setting the amount to Inf completely flattens all peaks above the threshold, which can be surprisingly useful at times and is certainly better than clipping, which would simply cut out all of this information.

❄ The Attack and Release parameters set how quickly the plug-in responds to peaks. A quick attack (so that the plug-in starts immediately) and a slow release are typical. Too fast of a release can result in the gain being turned up very loudly very suddenly in very quiet sections (even silent sections), resulting in background noise becoming audible. This is often called a breathing or pumping effect. The Smooth Saturation item can also help with making the compression seem more natural.

❄ The Auto Gain Compensation feature is a very important part of this plug-in and is very useful in normalizing a voiceover narration.

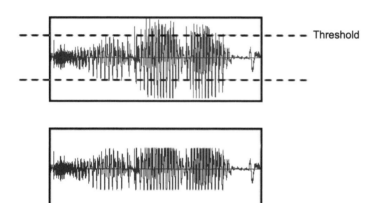

Threshold

Figure 6.13
The Threshold slider sets the level above which compression occurs. Waves that peak below the threshold remain unaffected. The lower waveform shows the results of applying compression.

Sony Media Software also has two more capable and flexible FX that you can use for compression. See Chapter 7 for more information on the Graphics Dynamics and Multi-Band Dynamics plug-ins. Consider taking the time to go though a track and use Volume Envelopes to adjust individual peaks and valleys to solve small problems. Although this may be a lot of work, the results can be worth it. This can be especially worthwhile in improving voiceovers in video narration or the lead vocals in a song, which are always critical aspects of any project.

Compression tends to increase background noise, especially during periods of silence. The Attack and Release controls can help eliminate this noise, but many times the only solution is to use a Noise Gate plug-in just after the compression plug-in in the FX chain.

Noise Gate

Noise Gate is a simple method of eliminating background noise from a track by setting the threshold for the minimum level of sound that is audible. The Track Noise Gate plug-in is especially useful in reducing the intensity of background hums caused by computer equipment or camera motors in the recording environment, hisses or static, and even people talking far in the background. You'll add the Noise Gate plug-in to a track in the same way you add any other plug-in (as previously described), and it often is found before compression in an FX chain.

The basic procedure is first to click the Solo button on the track so you can concentrate on it, play back the project to listen to the track (looping playback of a short section often helps), and gradually increase the threshold (see Figure 6.14) until the background noise is gone. It might not be possible to eliminate the noise completely without creating problems in the audio that you want to keep. A short attack and a longer release will improve the smoothness of the effect and prevent sharp jumps and drops in gain. See Chapter 7 for more information about Noise Gates.

Figure 6.14

The Threshold slider sets the level below which the audio is silenced and would be applied to both stereo channels in the waveform.

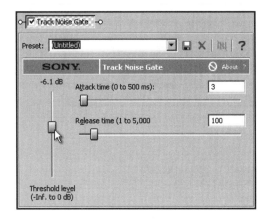

Equalization

Equalization is the next level in mixing after you have eliminated clipping from a song. Remember that clipping is the result of the volume peaking too high in a song, cutting off some parts of the song. (See the section "Clipping Redux" earlier in this chapter for more detailed information.) Roughly speaking, this means that the volume is too high overall, but clipping can occur at what seems to be lower volumes. Trust the clipping meters in the ACID software, not your ears. Sometimes a mix can be very bass-heavy, causing clipping at lower frequencies. Lowering the volume of higher-frequency tracks will not solve these problems. Clipping is, therefore, only an indication of problems, and identifying (and fixing) the actual cause can be more complex.

Equalization should be used to balance the song overall or, on the track level, to color and distinguish instruments. Configuring your monitoring environment is important if you want to use equalization effectively. (See the section "Configuring Your System" earlier in this chapter.) Equalization can be done at the track level with individual loops, to groups of tracks assigned to a bus, and as a final step to the project as a whole. Several different equalization plug-ins are available from Sony Media Software:

- ❋ Track EQ
- ❋ ExpressFX Equalization
- ❋ Graphic EQ
- ❋ Paragraphic EQ
- ❋ Parametric EQ

All do basically the same thing, with the difference being in the level of control and how that control is achieved through the effect's dialog. Each of the effects can be applied to any of the levels (track, grouped tracks, and project) as discussed in the following subsections.

Track EQ

Every track has its own default equalization plug-in that can be used to enhance the sound of an individual loop. To equalize a track:

1. Click the Solo button on the track to isolate it.

2. Click the Track FX button.

3. In the Audio Plug-In dialog, click the Track EQ button.

4. Without closing the Track EQ dialog, click the timeline to shift the application's focus to the timeline.

5. Press the spacebar to begin playback (or click the Play button on the Transport bar).

6. Go back to the Track EQ dialog and adjust the equalization. (See the following section.)

The default Track EQ plug-in is more than adequate for most purposes. It is divided into four frequency bands: Low Shelf, Band 2, Band 3, and High Shelf. The easiest way to adjust the equalization is to drag the various band indicators around on the graphic display (see Figure 6.15). Dragging a number up increases the gain, and dropping the number down decreases the gain. Dragging the number left and right changes the central frequency for Bands 2 and 3, and adjusting the Bandwidth slider on Bands 2 and 3 controls the width of the band. The Rolloff in Bands 1 and 4 sets the steepness for the rolloff curve. The number on the graphic display for these bands marks the beginning of the rolloff. While the Track EQ plug-in is the default, any of Sony Media Software's EQ FX can be used at the track level. It would be redundant and of questionable value to use two or more EQ FX in the same FX chain.

Figure 6.15

A basic track EQ plug-in.

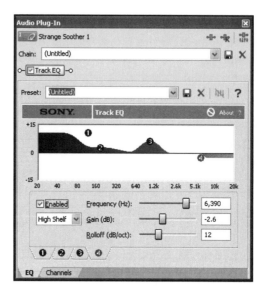

Track EQ might be best implemented across a number of different tracks individually. In other words, instead of only boosting the frequencies between 1,000 Hz and 4,000 Hz on a vocal line to bring it out more, you might also want to decrease that same range in a few other tracks that might interfere. This is more subtle and effective than simply adjusting the volume of the two competing tracks, although it is more difficult to perform.

Group Track EQ (Bus EQ)

You can group tracks to apply equalization to them together as a unit. To do so, you group individual tracks to a bus and then apply an assignable FX to the bus. To equalize a group of tracks:

1. Click the Insert Bus button in the Mixer window.

2. In the new Bus *X* monitor (where *X* is the letter of the bus), click the Bus FX button.

3. In the Plug-In Chooser dialog, locate and double-click the Track EQ plug-in. If an FX has already been added, click the Edit Chain button to open the Plug-In Chooser dialog.

4. Click the OK button. The Audio Plug-In dialog opens with the Track EQ controls (and the Plug-In Chooser dialog closes).

5. In the Track Header, click the Bus Assignment button on the tracks you want to equalize as a group (one at a time) and, from the menu, select the bus that has the equalization assigned to it.

6. Click the Solo button on the bus to isolate it.

7. Without closing the Track EQ dialog, click the timeline to shift the application's focus to the timeline. Press the spacebar to begin playback (or click the Play button on the Transport bar).

8. Go back to the Track EQ dialog and adjust the equalization (as previously described).

Applying FX to a bus is a very effective way to apply unified effects quickly and is dealt with in more detail in Chapter 7.

Project EQ

Project-level equalization as a last step is a very useful and highly recommended procedure. Once again, you can choose from a number of different equalization plug-ins. In this example, the Track EQ is used again because of its simplicity. To equalize a project:

1. Click the Master FX button on the Master bus in the Mixer window.

2. In the Plug-In Chooser dialog, locate and double-click the Track EQ plug-in. If an FX has already been added, click the Edit Chain button to open the Plug-In Chooser dialog.

3. Click the OK button. The Audio Plug-In dialog opens with the Track EQ controls (and the Plug-In Chooser dialog closes).

4. Without closing the Track EQ dialog, click the timeline to shift the application's focus to the timeline. Press the spacebar to begin playback (or click the Play button on the Transport bar).

5. Go back to the Track EQ dialog and adjust the equalization (as previously described).

> ❄ **TOGGLING FX**
> To toggle the effect of the equalization plug-in (or any plug-in), clear and check the small box on the plug-in's button in the Audio Plug-In dialog. After tweaking for a while, you can easily forget what the original track sounded like and might find that you were better off before you started messing around with all the toys. Toggle, listen, and then toggle again.

Equalization can also be used to influence many other subtle aspects of a song. For example, you can alter the higher-frequency ranges to simulate perceived depth or make a song sound as if it were recorded in a larger room. Although adding reverb would be a more direct way to do this, you shouldn't underestimate the power of using an EQ plug-in at the project level at the end of a project.

FX Chains

You can use more than one FX at a time on a single track, bus, or project. FX plug-ins are applied in a particular order in an FX chain (see Figure 6.16). The order of plug-ins can be important in the final sound. Some FX plug-ins belong very late in the chain (such as EQ and reverb) and some earlier (such as compression). Others should be used in a particular order. Track FX plug-ins are often applied in this order: Noise Gate, EQ, and finally Compression. This is not a hard-and-fast rule, and there might be creative reasons for altering this sequence. FX chains and ordering are discussed in more detail in Chapter 7.

Figure 6.16

Three effects applied in a chain to a track in the Audio Plug-In dialog.

Chapter 6 Quiz

1. The sound of your song will be influenced by your:

   A. Speaker placement

   B. Room acoustics

   C. Equipment selection

   D. All of the above

2. You can send white or pink noise through your audio system and then look at it on a frequency analyzer in order to:

   A. Color-coordinate your studio

   B. Set the volume for your monitors

   C. Standardize your system

   D. Keep the noise level of your equipment to a minimum

3. Panning more than 30 percent left or right can sound artificial. (T/F)

4. If the mixer meters indicate a signal is clipping, that means the signal is below 0 dB. (T/F)

5. Clipping means that the amplitude waves:

   A. Are sine waves

   B. Are square waves

   C. Are sawtooth waves

   D. Are cut off

6. Volume Envelopes can be used to control brief signal spikes. (T/F)

7. Panning can be used to create a sense of realism and space in your mix. (T/F)

8. The difference between the loudest and softest part of a song is called the:

   A. Dynamic range

   B. Signal to noise ratio

   C. Verse

   D. Chorus

9. To configure the ACID software for surround, you'll need an audio interface with enough outputs to accommodate your surround channels. (T/F)

10. Surround encoders are free and included with all versions of the ACID software. (T/F)

7 } Grooves and FX

We're going to tackle two topics in this chapter that are completely different and unrelated, yet unified by both their great potential for sophisticated subtlety or outright mayhem. Sony Media Software's ACID® software includes groove modification tools to give your computer-generated music swing and audio FX that give your sound complexity and depth. Groove modification is the process of swinging the tempo of your audio out of the realm of computer perfection. Audio FX are processes that modify your sound in a myriad of remarkable ways and can fix bad audio, sweeten good audio, and warp great audio in unimaginably bizarre ways. Together, grooves and FX give you amazing creative control over the final sound of your project.

> ❈ **MIXING FX**
> Mixing is a more fundamental topic than grooves or FX, so it appears a chapter earlier than this one in the book. In your workflow, however, you would certainly go back to mixing as a final step after working with your audio FX.

Grooving

The Groove tools in the ACID software (available in the Pro version only) are subtle, but remarkable. There are a few reasons you might want to groove in the ACID application. First, you might need to fix problems with a recorded performance that was good but not perfect. Second, and more commonly, you might want to use a loop recorded in a certain style in a completely different musical genre. Finally, you might want to take a straight-ahead and artificially perfect computer-generated pattern (such as a MIDI clip) and give it a little swing (because you know it don't mean a thing, if it ain't got that).

The effects might be subtle at first, but the Groove Pool adds an important element of interest to your tracks. For example, suppose that you are using a straight 4/4 drum kit track for a rock song. There is a monotonous and regular precision as the sticks fall on the beat. Let's say you want to reuse this loop in a salsa project. You might be able to use the Groove tools to add a lilt to the track and give it that salsa flavor you desire. Essentially, the Groove tools are variations on the time stretch effects and the core of the ACID software that allow you to use loops recorded at various tempos together in the same project of a different tempo. The difference is that groove quantization allows you to stretch (and compress) your audio over multiple short periods of time automatically at the beat level.

> **LOOPS, ONE-SHOTS, AND MIDI**
> The Groove tools work properly only on Loop and One-Shot clips. Perhaps most interestingly, grooves can also be applied to MIDI clips.

In reality, using the Groove tools is rarely that simple or straightforward. Groove quantization is not a magical process, but it is effective. Let's start by looking at the Groove Pool, which you can open from the View menu by selecting Groove Pool or by pressing the three-fingered keyboard shortcut Ctrl+Alt+2. As you can see in Figure 7.1, the Groove Pool window is pretty simple, with a browser with a bunch of preset groove templates with descriptive names. The Groove Editor at the bottom of the window lets you adjust just how groovy you are going to get.

Figure 7.1

The Groove Pool window with its browser on top and the Groove Editor at the bottom.

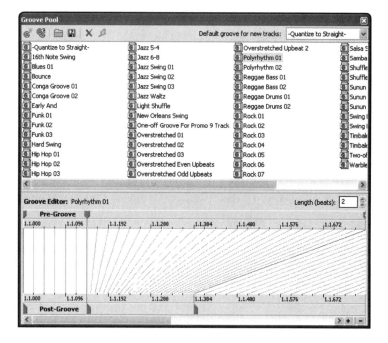

Painting a Groove

There are a number of ways to groove your project and, as with so many other effects in the ACID software, the method you choose depends on where in your project you want to apply the effect:

❋ To groove an entire track, select a template from the top of the Groove Pool and drag it to the track (either directly or to the Track Header). When you do, you'll see the extended groove event appear below the entire track. You can remove the groove by right-clicking in the Track Header and selecting Remove Groove from Track.

❋ To groove more selectively at the equivalent of the event level, click the Groove Tool button on the toolbar and then paint the selected groove into the track over the events that you want to modify (see Figure 7.2). The Groove Tool button also displays a drop-down list where you can more quickly select the groove you want to use. Click the Groove Erase tool to erase portions of a groove selectively by painting on the track.

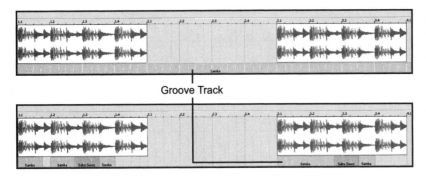

Groove Track

Figure 7.2

The groove track appears below the events on the timeline. Applying a groove at the track level merely draws a groove the length of the track.

Now that you know how to apply a groove, we'd strongly recommend that you give it a try to hear what the heck it is we are talking about:

1. Find a simple 4/4 drum track and paint it into a track on the timeline. Country 1.wav from Essential Sounds II is a good example and about as straight as you can get.

2. Set a loop region, hit play, and listen to the beat.

3. From the Groove Pool, drag the Hard Swing groove to the event on the timeline. The groove will automatically be painted across the entire duration of the track.

4. Try some other grooves, such as Jazz Waltz, or get really strange with some of the Over-stretched and Polyrhythm grooves.

Editing a Groove

The Groove Editor at the bottom of the Groove Pool is where you will create and modify the details of your groove. Figure 7.3 shows how a groove works to alter the pace of a measure over time. First, click the New Groove button to start out with a fresh template. In the top part of the figure, you can see that the Groove Editor timeline displays a measure from 1.1.000 to 2.1.000. Four markers are present, each on one of the beats in the measure. You can drop additional markers by pressing M on your keyboard. Each marker is actually two markers: a blue one at the top (Pre-Groove) and a pinkish one at the bottom (Post-Groove). Suppose that you want to swing Beat 3 to hesitate and come in a bit late and syncopated. To do this, you drag the Post-Groove marker at the bottom to the right, as you can see in the bottom part of Figure 7.3. As soon as you drag the marker, the vertical lines around the beat begin to shift, stretching to the left and compressing to the right. The blue Pre-Groove marker at the top of the timeline also acquires a white asterisk or star to indicate that it is now officially grooved. The farther you drag a particular beat, the greater the stretch. In Figure 7.3, we've dragged the marker an entire half of a beat (to 1.3.384), which is significant. As with all of the time-stretching prowess of the ACID software, the process has limits, but sometimes the crazy effects are pretty cool.

Figure 7.3

The original measure with no quantization is on top. In the bottom image, Beat 3 has been delayed by half a beat.

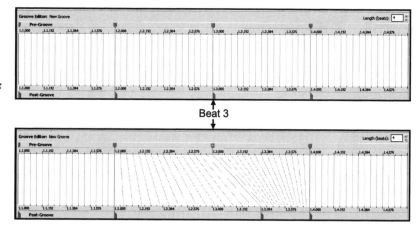

Groovy Advice

The Groove tools are clearly quite advanced in function as well as in how they are implemented by the artist. How you use these tools also depends on whether you are trying to fix mistakes or, more commonly, trying to put a little swing into fairly perfect professional loops. Here's a little advice on how you too can get up for the down stroke:

❋ It is often easiest to hear groove quantization on drum loops. Select a simple 4/4 straight-ahead rock loop to experiment with as you learn. You probably noticed that most of the groove templates in the Groove Pool are percussion-related.

❋ You can use multiple different groove events over the duration of a track.

❋ To create a groove based on a loop in a project automatically, right-click the Track Header, select Paint Clip and then select Add to Groove Pool. This new groove is added to the Groove Pool and is named after the track's name (which is the name of the loop by default). This is a very cool feature, but it isn't magical: You can't create an exotic Cuban guajira son groove by analyzing a loop you grabbed from a classic Tito Puente song.

❋ Although it might be pragmatic to use a drum loop to groove, the easiest way to understand just about any idea is to carry it to its logical extreme. Try importing a vocal track (especially something with words) into the ACID software and then go crazy and groove it until it screams. You'll very quickly find that you can hear the effects of groove stretching even at tiny variations of 100ms.

ACID FX

Special effects are audio processes that change and modify a basic sound. We use FX for three reasons. First, we use FX to clean up audio files that have problems. Second, we adjust, tweak, and sweeten a mix to perfection, livening it up or adding depth and texture. Finally, we use FX to perform crazy transmutations and distortions. Effects are used in very nearly every ACID project in one of these three ways and can be completely unnoticed by the listener. After all, most of us want our music, not our effects, to move our audiences. FX are ubiquitous in music: Every CD you listen to has been modified with some kind of processing. Even the equalization on your home stereo is an effect of sorts, because it modifies the original sound. In the ACID software, FX are powerful and often fun tools for turning a good basic mix into a truly professional auditory treat. One word of caution, however: Effects are most effectively used sparingly and with a specific purpose in mind. Nothing ruins a project or muddies a mix quicker than a wash of indiscriminate effects.

Audio effects are called FX throughout the ACID user interface. The actual FX software, however, may also be referred to as plug-ins. Plug-ins are small but sophisticated computer programs that are designed to work within another larger program. FX become available in the ACID software when you install audio effects plug-ins. Sony Media Software and a number of other companies sell DirectX and VST audio plug-ins for use with any compatible program, such as the ACID software.

> ❄ **REWIRE**
> There are a lot of really neat software effects modules and audio applications that compliment the ACID program, but don't necessarily plug-in like most DirectX and VST effects do. Some support a software interface called ReWire. See the chapter on MIDI for more information on ReWire devices.

There are a few different ways that we could sort FX in the software. In a very broad way, we'll divide them into FX that process and sweeten audio and FX that are used in more special and creative ways. There is quite a lot of overlap between these two categories, but it is still a useful distinction nonetheless.

Process	Creative
Dither	Amplitude Modulation
Graphic Dynamics	Chorus
Graphic EQ	Distortion
Multi-Band Dynamics	Flange/Wah-Wah
Noise Gate	Gapper/Snipper
Paragraphic EQ	Multi-Tap Delay
Parametric EQ	Resonant Filter
Pitch Shift	Reverb
Smooth/Enhance	Simple Delay
Time Stretch	Vibrato
Track Compressor	
Track EQ	
Track Noise Gate	
Wave Hammer	

Again, just because an effect is in the Process column doesn't mean it can't be used in interesting and creative ways. For example, we'll most often use the Time Stretch plug-in to change the duration of an audio file without noticeably distorting it otherwise. Beyond a certain point, however, stretching (or compressing) a file in time will do funky things to it, but that might be exactly what you're looking for. And just because we've chosen to put an effect in the Creative column doesn't mean it can't be used in very subtle and natural-sounding ways. The Reverb plug-in is a great example because it is widely used in music to improve the spatial aspects of a recording. It doesn't usually sound like an artificial effect, but instead imitates a natural environment or room. Here are some other ways we might categorize ACID FX. Notice that many plug-ins end up being included in more than one category.

Category	Effect
Delay/Chorus	Chorus, Flange/Wah-Wah, Multi-Tap Delay, Simple Delay, Reverb
Modulated	Amplitude Modulation, Flange/Wah-Wah, Vibrato, Gapper/Snipper
Dynamic	Noise Gate, Track Compressor, Distortion, Graphic Dynamics, Multi-Band Dynamics
Equalization	Smooth/Enhance, Track EQ, Graphic EQ, Paragraphic EQ, Parametric EQ
Pitch	Vibrato, Pitch Shift, Chorus, Flange/Wah-Wah
Special	Dither, Time Stretch

INCLUDED EFFECTS
While the ACID Pro software comes with all of the plug-ins discussed in this chapter, not all versions of the ACID software do. See the Sony Media Software Web site for more information about your version and the availability of upgrades and additional plug-in packages.

FX in Action

You can add FX to a project anywhere you see a green FX button, as shown in Figure 7.4. (See the section "Where Should FX Go?" later in this chapter.) To view the FX installed on your computer, click the FX button, which opens the Plug-In Chooser dialog (see Figure 7.5). At the top of the dialog, you'll find a folder selector that allows you to move around and sort the various plug-ins folders. You might have a few or a lot of plug-ins. This is where the ACID software puts all of the DirectX-compatible and VST audio plug-ins it scanned for and detected when you installed the software. The program automatically detects new plug-ins as they are installed every time you run it.

Figure 7.4

Various places you can add FX in the ACID software.

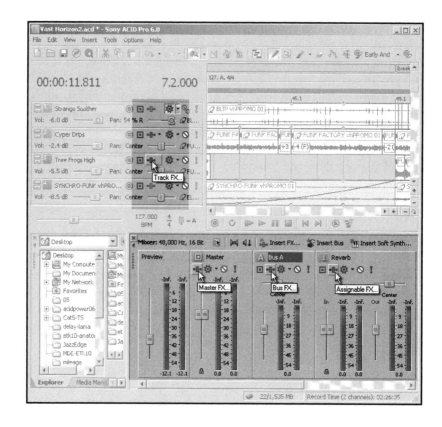

Figure 7.5

The Plug-In Chooser dialog opens the first time you press an FX button or when you press the Edit Chain button in the Audio Plug-In window.

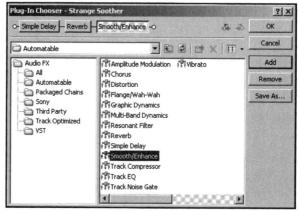

> ❉ **FREE FX**
>
> If you are using only the few FX that come with the ACID software, you should go online and do a search for DirectX and VST plug-ins in your favorite search engine. Hundreds of effects that are compatible with the software are available, many of them for free.

To add an effect, click the FX button to open the Plug-In Chooser dialog. Then select the plug-in you want to use from the list and click the Add button. This places a button with the effect's name on it at the top of the dialog. When you use multiple plug-ins simultaneously, they are lined up in a chain across this top area. When you are finished, click the OK button. The Plug-In Chooser dialog closes and the Audio Plug-In dialog opens with the last plug-in inserted active, meaning that the button in the chain at the top of the dialog is pressed and the controls for the plug-in are visible. There's more information about chaining effects a little later in this chapter.

Click the "X" in the top-right corner of the dialog to close the Audio Plug-In dialog. This dialog can also remain on the workspace or docked in the Window Docking Area at the bottom of the program, just like any other window in the ACID software. Subsequent FX button presses anywhere in the software will open the Audio Plug-In dialog or update the dialog to an existing chain if it is already open.

Bypassing FX

The check box on a plug-in button means that it is actively modifying the audio signal passing through the chain. Deselecting (or unchecking) the box prevents the effect from modifying the signal (bypassing it) without removing it from the chain. To remove a plug-in from the chain, right-click the effect's button at the top of the Audio Plug-In dialog and, from the context menu, choose Remove.

FX Button Colors

In most situations, the FX button is green wherever it occurs in the ACID software. In some situations, it may turn yellow, however. This caution signal merely indicates that the waveform of the audio drawn in the event may not be in sync with the audio signal coming out of the plug-in because the plug-in is changing the timing of the audio. Any plug-in effect that shifts the timing of a clip will do this—for example, the Time Stretch plug-in.

Experimenting

Every effect has its own array of controls that you'll use to modify the parameters of the plug-in. We'll discuss the details later in the chapter, but some general procedures will allow you to audition and modify any effect. You can modify effects as the project is playing back, which means that you can change the effects' variables in real time while you listen to the results. With the Audio Plug-In dialog open to the plug-in that you want to work on, click on the timeline (or press Alt+0) to set the focus to the timeline, then press Play. It is often useful to use a looped playback of a shorter section of a project to hear the results of an effect. At this stage, it would be very difficult to tweak FX subtly within the complexity of an entire project, so it is necessary to isolate the output of the project so you can hear what you are doing. To tweak your FX:

1. Isolate the target of the FX (either a track or a bus) by clicking the Solo button.

2. Isolate the specific effect in a chain of effects by unchecking all of the other effects in the chain.

3. Reduce the gain of the Dry slider while working with an effect to hear the processed signal more clearly.

The ultimate goal is to get an effect to mesh perfectly with a project. As you experiment, gradually reverse each of the above and fine-tune the effect. Start by increasing the gain on the Dry signal and mix the effect itself with the unprocessed signal. Then add the other effects in the chain back in. Finally, click the Solo button again so that the track or bus is no longer isolated and then adjust the effect in relation to the final mix. In the end, the entire project will be mixed together—events, tracks, busses, and effects.

BETTER ONE OR BETTER TWO?
When working with effects, you should make a point of periodically bypassing the effect and then listening to the result. You might think an effect is getting better and better, only to discover that the original is really closer to what you need, and that you have really only mucked things up with your processing.

Saving your project is especially important when working with effects. It is extremely easy to get carried away and forget what the original source sounded like or even what you intended to achieve with your effects. And in the course of a few minutes, it is possible to make so many changes that it is difficult to get back to the original sound. One simple idea is to do a Save As and save the project to a new name. This guarantees you can always get back to the original.

Where Should FX Go?

There are two places where you can add FX to the processing chain: into a track or into the Mixer window. Within the Mixer window, however, there are three places where FX might go: into an Assignable FX, into a preexisting bus, or into the Master bus (see Figure 7.4).

Track-Level FX

Track FX apply only to a single track and thus only to a single audio file or loop. Click the Track FX button to add an effect at this level. Although you can use any effect at any location, some effects work better at particular levels. The FX that work well on the track level might be ones that are used to process and sweeten a media file. For example, a Noise Gate would be perfect at the track level for a media file that has a background hum. Using a Noise Gate at the project level would be overkill and would likely negatively alter a project. Compression is great at the track level to punch up your drums, bass, and vocals. Track-level equalization is ideal for isolating instruments in their own frequency ranges. As another example, you should use caution when using a reverb effect at the track level. Because we use reverb to place music in a spatial environment, it would seem strange to have your sax solo track in a cavernous hall and your piano track in a virtual bathroom. Then again, maybe you want a strange effect.

Bus-Level FX (Multiple Tracks)

Busses have two distinct purposes—to group tracks and to route tracks to hardware devices. Within the context of tracks, you would most commonly use bus FX to group tracks and apply the same effect to all of them with identical settings. One example would be to apply equalization to a group of tracks to bring them out of the mix as a unit. This is also a more appropriate location for a reverb effect, where the grouping of the tracks guarantees that the instruments sound like they are in the same virtual space. Another example might be to send the entire song into a slow flange, while your trance diva soars clearly above the mix. It would be very tedious to add the same flange (with the same parameters) over and over again to all of the tracks in the project when you could just assign them to a bus and modify the effect there.

To use effects at the bus level, you must first insert a bus into the project by clicking the Insert Bus button in the Mixer window. Then you'll assign specific tracks to the bus by clicking the Bus button (initially concentric squares and assigned to Microsoft Sound Mapper) in each track and assigning it to the bus (for example, Bus A). You can use multiple selection techniques to assign multiple tracks to a bus at a time: Hold down the Shift key and click on the first and last Track Header in a range, or hold down the Ctrl key as you click on various tracks, click one of the Bus buttons, and then select a bus. Finally, click the FX button on the bus in the Mixer window and select a plug-in.

Assignable FX

Assignable FX (added to the Mixer window) are the most powerful and effective way to add effects in the ACID software for many reasons. For one, you can route individual tracks through an Assignable FX and into the final mix. You can also send multiple tracks through an Assignable FX bus, which makes Assignable FX a convenient way to reuse an effect and group tracks efficiently. The most powerful advantage to using effects this way is that you can use envelopes on the timeline to modify them, much like Volume or Pan Envelopes (although you can also animate track-level effects this way). Using envelopes, you can fade effects in and out and otherwise animate the level of the effect over time. Assignable FX busses in the mixer have two sets of faders that control the input gain of the effect and the final output.

WET OR DRY?

You must right-click the Multipurpose Fader Mode button and select Pre Volume to use the Volume and FX faders to adjust the Dry/Wet mix.

To use Assignable FX, click the Insert Assignable FX button in the Mixer window. Then select an effect from the Plug-In window that automatically opens. Paradoxically, you do not need to assign tracks to the Assignable FX bus the way you would a hardware or group bus. Instead, the Assignable FX is available to all tracks, and you need only click the Multipurpose Fader Mode button and select the FX from the list to adjust the volume of the effect in a particular track.

The main track Volume fader and the FX fader can operate as another set of Dry/Wet faders to control the mix of the effect. By default, Assignable FX are applied after the track volume is set (Post Volume), which means that if the track volume is set to –Inf., nothing leaves the track to be processed by the Assignable FX. Right-click the Multipurpose Fader Mode button and select Pre Volume to change when the Assignable FX is processed.

ONE MORE TIME

You must right-click the Multipurpose Fader Mode button and select Pre Volume to use the Volume and FX faders to adjust the Dry/Wet mix. Yes, this note is the same as the previous one, but it is easy to forget, and the FX fader and FX Envelopes won't work unless you do this.

To use envelopes to animate the mix of the effect over time, right-click a blank portion of the timeline in the track in which you want to use envelopes and select the Assignable FX (such as FX1) from the list. Double-click the envelope to add a node and then drag the node up or down to adjust the gain. The ACID software will mix the plug-in effect with the volume setting, so use a Volume Envelope to adjust the total mix further.

Project-Level FX (Master Bus)

You can also add effects to the Master bus in the Mixer window. These effects will then modify the entire audio signal as it is passed out of the software and to your soundcard. Some plug-ins are better than others for use at this stage; you should carefully consider which FX you use here because you can quickly degrade an entire project with one simple effect. A good example of a potential project-level effect is compression, which reduces the dynamic range of an audio signal with the eventual goal of increasing the loudness. Applying compression at the project level risks squashing a song and reducing its liveliness. A much better idea is to use compression more intelligently and selectively on individual tracks that you want to bring out in a mix. On the other hand, the Master bus is the perfect place to apply ambience to a mix with the Reverb effect.

Some FX are better used at the track level and some are better used in the Mixer window, but all options are possible for maximum flexibility. We'll give specific recommendations in the descriptions of the actual plug-ins later in this chapter.

FX Chains

You can add more than one effect to a track or the Mixer window at a time. The specific order is critical to the final sound, and some hierarchies work better than others (see the next section). To create an FX chain, simply add multiple plug-ins in the Plug-In Chooser dialog or click the Edit Chain button in the Audio Plug-In window. After you have added some effects, they appear as buttons in a row at the top of the Audio Plug-In window. To change the order of the effects, drag the buttons to a new location in the chain. To bypass or disable a plug-in in the chain temporarily, uncheck the box on that plug-in's button (see Figure 7.6).

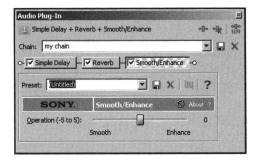

Figure 7.6
A plug-in chain in the Audio Plug-In window.

In addition to the order of the FX being important to the final sound, the way tracks are mixed together is also important. For example, you could apply a flange to Track 1 and the same flange to Track 2. The flange will modify each effect, and then the ACID software will mix the two tracks. A different method is to use the flange as an Assignable FX and then assign the two tracks to the Assignable FX in the Mixer window. In this case, the program will first mix the two tracks and then apply the flange. Sometimes this can make a dramatic difference in the final sound. One thing to consider is that if you use an Assignable FX, you have only one effect to modify. If you went with two-track FX, on the other hand, you would have more control and could isolate the tracks individually as you adjust the effect. The flange is a good example. Because this effect often varies over time, if you used it in two different tracks, they could easily get out of sync.

Recommendations on FX Placement

The order of effects in a chain is important to the final sound. The following sections offer some suggestions about where in the ACID software you might typically put an effect. Keep in mind that the total effects package in the application runs through a full, complex signal flow, from input through to the final mix. Therefore, the first effect on the Master bus will also be the first effect after the last track effect. In other words, an early Master bus effect might actually be late in the overall signal flow. We make the following recommendations assuming you are trying to achieve a more traditional or natural sound to your mix. Electronic genres (such as techno, dub, and jungle) and many other types of music may benefit from radical effects ordering, but the explanations that follow will help you understand why the effects are placed in this order (and why you might want to ignore that order anyway).

Because you can use effects in three different places in the ACID software, deciding where to use an effect is not always a simple matter. You must also consider the order of the effects in the chain as well as in the entire signal flow (see the software's online help for a great signal flow diagram), because FX added at the Master bus level will be the final effects in a long overall chain. Following are some recommendations as to where you might best use FX: early, middle, or late in a sequence. You must consider the total sequence of plug-ins together. For example, a single chain on a track with Effects A, B, and C would be the same as having Effect A on a track routed through an Assignable FX B, which was then routed through a bus with Effect C. Depending on the purpose, some plug-ins are useful in multiple places on a single project. For example, you might use a Noise Gate to eliminate background noise on a problematic track and then use it again at the project level after applying compression to an entire project. These recommendations are not written large or in stone, however, and should serve only as guidelines to understanding how effects work in the ACID program.

> ❋ **NO STRICT HIERARCHY**
> It would be impossible to arrange all of the Sony Media Software plug-ins in a strict hierarchical list from 1 to 30, but doing so really wouldn't make much sense anyway. Instead, the following is a just a rough guide, with similar plug-ins grouped into paragraphs.

Early

The first effects in a chain are typically the ones used to correct tracks with problems (such as background noise) or to clean up a sound to prepare it for later effects. The Track Compression plug-in is frequently the first effect in a chain and it might then be quickly followed by a Noise Gate to remove any artifacts caused by the compression. On the other hand, it is often better to use the Noise Gate first to remove problems before they become prominent because of compression. Ultimately, you'll probably try both methods before you determine the correct order for the situation you are in. These are both effects that modify the level and dynamics of a sound, so you would also use related effects at this stage: Graphic Dynamics and Multi-Band Dynamics.

The next class of effects that might follow the dynamics plug-ins consists of the equalization (EQ) filters. These include the Graphic EQ, Paragraphic EQ, Parametric EQ, and Track EQ, as well as the Smooth/Enhance plug-in. Many mixes sound muddy and end up being too busy from having too many sounds and instruments. Cleaning up individual tracks with equalization early in the mix allows you to emphasize parts by removing unwanted frequencies and generally create a cleaner and brighter mix. Track EQ is a default plug-in on every track. Equalization may also be useful at the project level, very late in the effects chain, as a final touch up.

Pitch Shift and especially Time Stretch are special plug-ins that are not usually found in a traditional studio effects chain. These should definitely be the first effects in just about any chain.

Middle

After you clean up the signal with dynamics and equalization, you might want to apply some of the more special effects. Distortion on a guitar part would come immediately after the previous early effects. You might follow this with one of the pitch effects, such as Vibrato or the Gapper/Snipper effect. Next in line would be the modulation-type effects, such as Amplitude Modulation or Flange/Wah-Wah. This would also be the time to add delay effects, such as Chorus, Multi-Tap Delay, or Simple Delay.

Late

The last effects in a chain are best used at the project level as Master bus FX. For example, you might want to throw in a Reverb effect as the last effect in a chain. Reverb is also a delay-type effect and adds space to a mix, simulating various room types and environments. Use caution when applying reverb at the track level, unless you want your various tracks to sound like they come from different rooms. Sometimes, however, an engineer will use reverb on the drums or vocals to bring these parts out of a mix. You can also use EQ filters effectively at the project level to polish a mix in the final stages. It is still a good idea to take the time and use EQ more precisely at the track level to highlight individual parts and instruments, even if you are using EQ at the end as well.

The Dither effect is a special plug-in that is particular to computer music and digital processing. We use it to fix problems caused by rendering a project at a lower bit depth from the source media. For example, when using media from a DAT at 24 bits and creating a final song for the Internet at 8 bits, dithering, as the last step, can eliminate some compression artifacts. Some projects contain a mix of different types of media, perhaps using commercial loops at a 16-bit depth with recorded tracks at 24 bits. In these cases, the Dither plug-in is most efficiently used as the last effect only in the tracks that have a higher bit depth than the project's bit depth. Avoid using dithering twice at both the track and the project level because it always affects the fidelity of the audio.

Summary of Sony Media Software FX

Sony Media Software has developed a wide range of effects for use with its flagship Sound Forge editing tool. These effects comply with DirectX standards and work with any application that supports DirectX audio plug-ins, including the ACID software. The ACID Pro package ships with the full complement of basic FX from Sony Media Software. Other versions of the ACID software come with other plug-in sets that differ from the Pro set. Sony Media Software makes a couple of other more advanced plug-ins that are not included (notably Noise Reduction and Acoustic Mirror), but the effects that are included are formidable, varied, and capable.

> ❋ **ACID SOFTWARE VARIATIONS**
> Several different versions of the ACID software are available from Sony Media Software, from free promotional versions, to inexpensive novice versions, to the Pro version. Not all versions have all of the FX, although the Pro version comes with the most.

Track FX

All Track FX are included with all versions of the ACID software. These basic effects are some of the most important and fundamental filters that you need when sweetening and cleaning up a mix. Although they are optimized for the track level, there is no reason these FX cannot be used at the bus or project level. Track FX are specifically discussed at the end of Chapter 6, "Mastering the Mix."

Track FX are not the same as Track Optimized FX, which are a subset of plug-ins that Sony Media Software recommends for use at the track level and are contained in a separate folder in the Plug-In Chooser dialog. These are a subset of all of the FX available from Sony Media Software. You can use any FX at the track level, not just the Track Optimized FX. Likewise, you can use Track FX at any level, but they can sometimes cause problems on slower machines when used at the project level.

ExpressFX

ExpressFX are all simplified versions of the professional XFX plug-ins from Sony Media Software, but are also included with the ACID Pro program. These FX are certainly capable, are very high quality, and are more than adequate for many operations. If you have purchased a version of the ACID software that did not include the full set of XFX plug-ins, the ExpressFX are an economical alternative to purchasing more expensive plug-ins. Besides, they are often much easier to use.

> ❋ **EXPRESS YOURSELF**
> It is important to note that while the control and flexibility of the ExpressFX plug-ins are more limited compared to that of XFX, the quality is not.

VST and DirectX Audio Plug-Ins

The effects audio plug-ins from Sony Media Software are all DirectX-compliant. Any compatible VST and DirectX audio plug-in from another company or developer should also work in the ACID software. The terms "VST" and "DirectX" compatibility mean that the plug-ins follow a strict set of programming guidelines that result in a standardized plug-in architecture. This allows other companies (such as Twelve Tone Systems) to create effects for the ACID software. This also allows Sony Media Software to create effects for use in other programs (such as SONAR).

General FX Concepts

Many effects share a core set of controls that are the same for every plug-in. The following section details many of these controls and how they are used. Each plug-in also has its own set of controls that are particular to that plug-in. These controls are detailed in the description of the specific plug-ins later in the chapter.

Presets

At the top of every plug-in dialog is a preset drop-down list. This unassuming little feature might not jump out at you as the first thing that you would want to play with in these dialogs, but it really should. The first reason is that it contains a list of settings that were created by the audio professionals at Sony Media Software and are specifically designed to show off the effect in a wide variety of situations. These presets can also serve as great jumping-off points for creating your own customized effects. One of the best things about the presets is that they autoposition the effect's controls, allowing you to see what settings are required to produce a specific effect. This is the first step to learning how to create interesting effect settings.

Which brings us to the second reason the preset list is vital: You can save your own custom presets to the list.

❋ To save your own presets, first type a name for your preset and then click the Save button to the right of the list.

❋ To modify one of your own presets, select it from the list, modify the parameters in the dialog, and then click the Save button.

❋ To delete one of your own presets, select it from the list and click the Delete button to the right of the Save button.

The presets from Sony Media Software are protected and cannot be saved with modifications or deleted, but you can start with a Sony Media Software preset and save it to a new name.

Dry/Wet

A pure pre-effect signal that is routed through a processor or effect but is not modified by it is considered to be Dry. Wet, therefore, refers to the signal after it has been modified. You can control the strength or prominence of the effect by adjusting the Wet (with effect) and Dry (without effect) mix. Many of the effects have Dry and Wet sliders that you can use to control this mix, although sometimes the Wet slider is named after the plug-in; for example, the Chorus effect slider that controls the Wet signal is called Chorus Out. Some other effects control the Wet/Dry mix with a single slider labeled with the name of the effect (Wet) on one end and Original (Dry) at the other, with the center of the slider being a 50/50 mix. FX that you add as Assignable FX can also be controlled with the Multipurpose fader to set the Dry/Wet mix of the FX. Make sure to right-click the Multipurpose fader and select Pre Volume to use the fader in this way. Figure 7.7 displays many of the different ways you can adjust the Dry/Wet mix.

Figure 7.7

The various forms that the basic Dry/Wet mix faders can take.

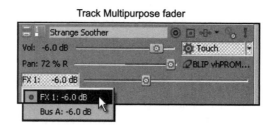

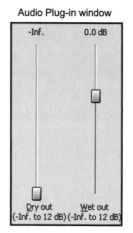

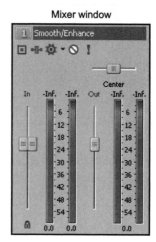

Assignable FX also let you use FX envelopes, which automate the gain over time of the FX in exactly the same way that the Multipurpose fader allows you to set the gain. Using both volume and FX envelopes, you can animate the Dry/Wet mix over time, letting you fade an effect in and out of a mix.

The In and Out faders in the Mixer window of an Assignable FX bus are not the same as the Wet/Dry controls within the effects dialog itself. Instead, the Volume control on the track and the In slider of the Assignable FX in the Mixer window both control the Input gain as it is fed into the plug-in, much like a pre-amp. Setting the gain on the Dry mix to 0 percent or –Inf. results in a signal that is 100 percent modified by the effect with none of the original signal in the mix. Setting the gain to –Inf. on the In slider of an Assignable FX results in no sound being fed into the effect at all. Setting the gain to –Inf. on the Volume control of a track results in no sound coming from the track to go to the Assignable FX when the Multipurpose fader is set to Post Volume. (Right-click the Multipurpose fader to change this setting.) Some effects also have Input sliders that control the level of the signal coming into the plug-in.

CAN YOU HEAR ME NOW?

By turning up the gain on the Wet/Out slider, you can hear more clearly the results of changes made in the Audio Plug-In dialog. After you get a sound you like, mix the Dry signal back in for a subtler, more realistic and natural sound.

Rate and Hertz (Hz)

Many effects are modulated and vary periodically over time. The period of this variation is measured in cycles per second or Hertz (Hz) and is the measurement used in the ACID software for the rate controls on the plug-ins. For example, 1 Hz is one cycle per second, 10 Hz is 10 cycles per second, and 0.1 Hz is one cycle every 10 seconds. This is a very logical and easy way to talk about periodic variation, and it is very easy to instantly see that 2 Hz is twice per second and 7 Hz is seven times per second, but it is less intuitive once the period drops below once per second. In this case, the smaller the fraction, the slower the period. You can quickly calculate the proper rate to set by dividing one by the period you want. So, to get a period of once every seven seconds, you would divide one by seven (1/7) and get a rate of 0.143 Hz. The rate range in the ACID software is from 20 times a second (20 Hz) to once every 1,000 seconds (almost 17 minutes: 0.001 Hz). You can use the following table to calculate the proper rate:

Period in Seconds	Hertz (Hz)
1	1.000
2	0.500
3	0.333
4	0.250
5	0.200
6	0.167
7	0.143
8	0.125
9	0.111
10	0.100
20	0.050

> ❄ **FX DICTIONARY**
>
> A number of the effects that vary over time have much more convenient controls to set the period of the effect in terms of seconds, measures, and tempo (at least in the ACID Pro software). These tempo-based DirectX effects include Amplitude Modulation, Chorus, Flange/Wah-Wah, and Simple Delay. You can find more information in the section detailing each plug-in found in Chapter 8, "FX Dictionary."

Calculating Rates

Many of the effects that modulate or cycle over time (such as Delay and Flange/Wah-Wah) can easily and effectively be synchronized to the beat of a song even if they are not the new tempo-based effects. The rates for these effects are measured in cycles per second and the project tempo is set to beats per minute (BPM), so divide 60 seconds in a minute by the number of beats per minute to get the delay in seconds. By default, ACID projects are 120 BPM, so:

60 seconds / 120 BPM = 0.500 seconds between beats

Next, you need to convert this into cycles per second:

1 second / 0.500 seconds for one beat = 2.000 Hz

So, if you wanted a "wah" on every beat, you would need a rate of 2.000 Hz or two cycles per second. For a 140-BPM project, we get 2.331 Hz, and for 100 BPM, we get a rate of 1.667 Hz. Flanges often have much longer cycles that you might want to synchronize in terms of measures. Because tempo is often annotated in terms of a quarter note as one beat and, by default, the ACID application has four beats in a measure, you only have to multiply the number of seconds by four and convert to Hertz:

60 seconds / 155 BPM = 0.387 seconds for one beat * 4 beats a measure = 0.774 seconds for one measure

You can convert this to cycles per second:

1 cycle / 0.774 seconds = 1.292 Hz

For multiple-measure flanges, multiply the seconds per measure by the number of measures that you want the flange to occur over (often 4, 8, 12, or 16 measures):

1 cycle / (0.774 sec. * 16 measure flange) = 0.161 Hz

See Chapter 3, "Composition," for more information on measures and phrasing.

Frequency (Pitch)

All of the equalization effects operate on the frequency of the sound. Frequency is a strict definition of the pitch or key in terms of the number of waves of sound per second, measured from peak to peak in a pure tone. A peak-to-peak cycle per second is a Hertz (Hz).

The note A is used as the foundation of the Western scale (not C). It was defined to be 440 cycles per second (440 Hz) and lands somewhere around the middle of a piano. Obviously, music and instruments (and pianos, for that matter) had existed long before oscilloscopes and Mr. Hertz, so people have been tuning instruments by ear for millennia. In 1939, the International Standards Association (ISA), along with scientists and musicians, arbitrarily decided that exactly 440 Hz was A, and this has been the standard ever since. This decision wasn't completely arbitrary, however: Before 1939, A was closer to 435 Hz, but this was very close to a nice, even number and standardization is important. It's not entirely unlike sensibly setting the freezing point of water to 0°C and the boiling point to 100°C.

An octave in a Western scale is, by definition, either one-half the frequency or double the frequency of the note from which you started. So one octave up from middle A (440 Hz) is 880 Hz. This relationship is very simply displayed in the frequency graphs on the EQ plug-ins or on the equalizer on your stereo. Figure 7.8 has a line much like the scale on the graphs in the EQ plug-ins. Notice that the frequencies don't increase linearly. If they did, the scale numbers would read 20, 40, 60, 80, 100, and so on. Instead, the scale doubles at every point and marks octave intervals. Each horizontal hash mark on an EQ graph or fader is twice as much as the previous one, indicating a doubling in the frequency equal to one octave. The keyboard below the scale in Figure 7.8 is a standard 88-key piano keyboard, and the lines represent the standard tuning of a six-string guitar. This should give you some idea of what the various frequencies sound like in the real world.

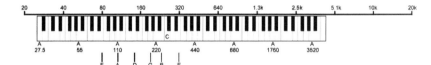

Figure 7.8

The scale from an EQ frequency graph compared to an 88-key keyboard and a six-string guitar. All frequencies are in Hertz (Hz).

FX Automation

One of the most powerful features of the Pro version of ACID software effects is that they can be automated (animated) over time. The process and results are exactly like using Volume or Pan Envelopes. In the simplest case, we can apply a Volume Envelope to a track to fade the volume of an event in (or out) gradually. Likewise, with an effect, we could start with an event playing normally with no effect present and then gradually strengthen the presence of the effect in the mix. The ACID Pro software includes more than a dozen effects that you can animate, each with dozens of parameters that you can vary over time. Clearly, there's a lot of flexibility here.

Not all effects can be automated. This isn't arbitrary: It makes sense to animate some effects (such as Reverb) and not others (such as Dither). When you open the Plug-In Chooser dialog on a track, you'll notice that the effects have a few different types of icons. The Sony Media Software plug-ins that have three orange miniature sliders on the bottom of the icon (see Figure 7.9) can be animated.

Figure 7.9

Plug-ins that can be auto-mated (animated) have three miniature sliders on the bottom of the icon.

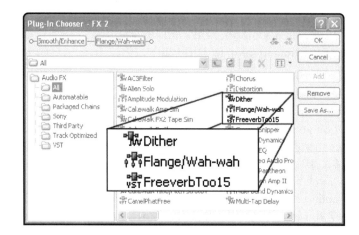

Here is a list of automatable and non-automatable plug-ins:

Automatable	Non-Automatable
Amplitude Modulation	Dither
Chorus	Gapper/Snipper
Distortion	Graphic EQ
Flange/Wah-Wah	Multi-Tap Delay
Graphic Dynamics	Noise Gate
Multi-Band Dynamics	Paragraphic EQ
Resonant Filter	Parametric EQ
Reverb	Pitch Shift
Simple Delay	Time Stretch
Smooth/Enhance	
Track Compressor	
Track EQ	
Track Noise Gate	
Vibrato	

Let's start by adding an automatable effect to a track. In the upper-right corner of the Audio Plug-In window, you see an icon for the automatable effect. If you click it, you see a list of parameters that can be animated. Select the ones you want and click OK. You can also select these parameters by clicking the small triangle next to the FX button on the track and selecting FX Automation from the drop-down list. After you have selected a parameter (or as many as you want), right-click on the track and move your mouse over the FX Automation Envelopes item. From the submenu that appears, select the parameter you want to automate. Each of the parameters you select will have an automation envelope associated with it. You can modify this envelope the same way you would any other track envelope: Double-click on the envelope to add a node and then drag it to change the level of the effect parameter at that point in time. Use pairs of envelopes to make sure previous levels remain unchanged and drag on the line itself to move the entire line up and down between two nodes.

Clearly, with all of these effects, parameters, automation options, envelopes, and nodes, you can get pretty crazy (Figure 7.10), so here's a little advice on using this powerful feature:

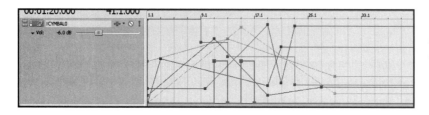

Figure 7.10
Modern art or too many FX automation envelopes?

❋ Open up the Audio Plug-In window as you work with FX automation and notice how the various parameters change as you adjust the FX envelopes. Alternatively, you can adjust a parameter in an effect and modify an envelope that way.

❋ Set the Automation Write to Touch and enable automation to record fader movements on the fly as your project plays back. Right-click the envelope and select Reset All to delete all of the recorded envelope points, and then try again.

❋ Move your mouse over an envelope to see the name of the parameter, then move your mouse over the node to see the value of that parameter (see Figure 7.11).

❋ You can alter the shape of the line between two nodes from a perfectly straight line (linear) to something smoother. Right-click the line and select from the context menu one of the shapes: Linear Fade, Fast Fade, Slow Fade, Smooth Fade, Sharp Fade, or Hold (a horizontal line with no change). Figure 7.12 shows an example of these shapes.

Figure 7.11

Move your mouse over envelopes and nodes to see the name and value of a parameter.

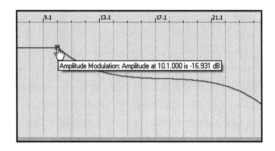

Figure 7.12

Envelopes can have subtle curves.

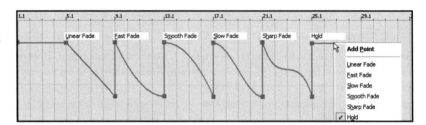

❋ Not all parameters work well when automated or even make sense to automate, even though the software allows you to do so. For example, we can't really think of a reason why you would want to turn the Tempo Sync item on and off over time. Then again, maybe you can, so we're glad the option is there.

❋ Some items are either on or off, such as a Bypass option. In this case, the envelope line has only two discrete positions: the top or bottom of the track. You can add nodes, but there is no in-between state for the parameter, and the envelope makes strictly 90-degree angles in what looks like a square-wave pattern. When the line runs across the top, the Bypass is true, which means that Bypass is on and the effect is off. (Confused?) This lets you turn the effect on and off whenever you want.

❋ Some automatable parameters have a number of discrete choices beyond on and off. For example, the Flange/Wah-Wah effect has an Effect parameter that can be set to Flange, Phaser, or Wah-Wah. The automation envelope also has three positions: top (Flange), center (Phaser), and bottom (Wah-Wah). Again, there is no half-flange/half-phaser position, so the envelope has only right-angle lines.

❋ Some parameters are clearly more useful than others. For example, parameters that control the strength of the effect over time are important to fade an effect in and out gradually. Dry/Wet and Output gain are examples.

❄ Frequency sweeps can produce some very interesting and perhaps surprising results. Try sweeping a frequency envelope from bottom to top in a gradual slope in the Resonant Filter, for example.

❄ You can set the colors of the various envelopes on the Display tab in the Preferences dialog. Pragmatically, there are too many parameters and millions of colors, so it probably isn't the best use of your time to set the colors yourself. Instead, when you find parameters that you frequently like to automate, set only those.

Chapter 7 Quiz

1. Which of the following is not an ACID effect?

   A. Noise Gate

   B. Flange/Wah-Wah

   C. Paragraphic EQ

   D. All are effects in the ACID software

2. To add an effect:

   A. Click the Envelope tool over an event

   B. Click the FX button to open the Plug-In Chooser dialog

   C. Click the Get Media button

   D. Click the Enable Snapping button

3. It is not possible to get carried away with ACID effects. (T/F)

4. Which of the following effects placements does the ACID software allow you to choose?

   A. Track-level FX

   B. Bus-level FX

   C. Assignable FX

   D. All of the above

5. The ACID software lets you add more than one effect to a track or Mixer window at a time. (T/F)

6. The order of effects in an effects chain makes no difference to the final sound. (T/F)

7. ExpressFX are:

    A. Effects that process audio faster than other effects

    B. An economical version of Sony Media Software's professional plug-ins

    C. Effects with smaller graphic interfaces

    D. All of the above

8. The ACID program is compatible with DirectX plug-ins. (T/F)

9. Effects in the ACID application cannot be automated. (T/F)

10. There are some effects parameters for which automation would not make sense. (T/F)

❉ ❉ ❉

8 } FX Dictionary

This chapter is devoted to a thorough explanation of the various effects that come with the ACID® Pro software. Not all of these effects are included in all versions of the software, and many other effects are available from Sony Media Software and other developers. These explanations are intended to be concise and helpful, but the only way to really understand what is going on is to use your ears and experiment with these effects yourself in the ACID software.

Amplitude Modulation

Amplitude is the volume (gain) of a sound. The Amplitude Modulation effect, not surprisingly, periodically varies (modulates) the volume of a sound at specific user-selected frequencies. The effect has traditionally been used to create a tremolo sound in electric guitars—for example, the cool surf guitar sound or the spacey guitar parts in grand 1960s instrumentals. It is also common for organ parts in rock music and can be used to change the spatial characteristics of a sound. Tremolo is, by definition, a modulation of the volume, which is not to be confused with vibrato (although it often is), which is a modulation of the pitch. Amplitude refers to the peaks of the waves in a sound. You can see these peaks in the waveform of events on the timeline: The larger the peak, the larger the amplitude and the louder the sound (see Figure 8.1).

Amplitude Modulation's controls and settings include the following:

* The **Amplitude slider** sets the level of the minimum gain in the effect. In other words, setting the Amplitude slider to the lowest level (–Inf.) results in the largest variation in amplitude and the greatest effect. If you set the slider to the highest level (0 dB), the lowest point will not be low at all, and the plug-in will have very little effect.

* Use the **graph** to set the shape of the modulation curve. Set the overall frequency of the modulation—for example, 1 Hz (once a second)—and then use the graph to shape how the modulation actually occurs within that single cycle. Click the line on the graph to add a square envelope point (in other words, node or keyframe) and drag the node to a new

position. Try a few of the presets to see a few graphs set up by the audio professionals at Sony Media Software. You'll use the **Blend Graph Edges** check box to smooth the transition from the end of the graph back to the beginning of the next cycle.

* The **Tempo Sync** check box is a cool way to synchronize the period of the effect with the actual tempo of the project, without going through all of the crazy calculations we outlined previously in Chapter 7. The **Modulation Period** can be set in terms of measures or beats. This feature is only available in the Pro version of the ACID software.

* The **Mod. Freq.** is the rate or period of the gain modulation in cycles per second (Hz) as it is applied to the input signal. This controls the speed of the tremolo, just like the Tempo Sync feature does. However, working with Mod. Freq. isn't as easy as working with Tempo Sync.

* The **Stereo pan** controls whether the modulation also pans back and forth across the two stereo channels of a file. Using this control, you can roughly simulate a rotating speaker effect used in some classic real-world organs (such as the Hammond B2) and speakers (such as the Leslies in the B2). Try a Mod. Freq. of at least 2 Hz, set the amplitude very low, and set the Stereo pan to a higher percentage to simulate this effect.

* Use a **Low-Pass Start Freq.** filter to tone down the higher frequencies, which an Amplitude effect can sometimes seem to emphasize.

Figure 8.1

The top waveform is the original loop file, and the bottom one is the same waveform modified by the Amplitude Modulation plug-in, using the Wacky preset.

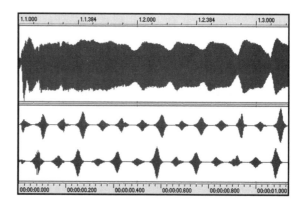

Low-Tech Modulation

One of the earliest amplitude modulation effects (from early in the last century) was created by mechanically spinning or rotating a speaker, most famously in Hammond organs using Leslie speakers. The apparent volume decreases as the speaker points away from the listener and increases as it points toward the listener. In other words, the amplitude modulates. The physical movement of the speaker also produced tonal changes (vibrato) as a result of a Doppler shift, increasing the pitch slightly as the speaker spun toward the listener and decreasing the pitch as it spun away.

Calculating Rates

It is very useful to synchronize the Amplitude Modulation effect with the tempo and beat of a project, even if you don't have the Tempo sync feature in your version of the ACID software. Amplitude Modulation is a faster-period effect that may occur on the beat (or multiple times for each beat). See the section "Calculating Rates" in Chapter 7 for information about how to calculate and synchronize this effect with a project.

Chorus

A chorus is, by definition, composed of more than one member. The Chorus effect in the software can make a single instrument or voice sound like multiple instruments or voices. No matter how much skill or practice a group of performers has, however, they will still not play or sing in perfect unison. If the Chorus effect simply added more voices with perfect computer precision, it would only result in a louder output. Instead, the Chorus effect allows you to control how much out of sync the various parts are (delay) and how much they vary over time (modulation).

The Chorus effect is the foundation of a number of other effects. For example, a chorus can be two voices, with the original first and the chorused voice following. If you add a long enough delay, you have a Delay effect. Add another voice and you get a Multitap Delay. Change the modulation rate and depth and add a little feedback and you get a Phaser, a Flange, or a Wah-Wah. The Chorus is, indeed, a very powerful and flexible effect with possibilities far beyond the simple presentation of multiple voices.

The following table details some of the possible differences between these variations, although the flexibility of the ACID program means that most of these parameters have much greater range:

Effect	Typical Delay	Notes
Chorus	More than 20ms but less than 50ms	Although the delay itself is not noticeable as a separate delay, you can distinctly hear another voice.
Delay	Greater than 50ms (often much more)	This is a simple Chorus effect with a longer and clearly noticeable delay or echo effect. Delay effects are not modulated.
Flange/Wah-Wah/Phaser	Between 0.1 and 20ms	The delay is not heard as a delay or echo because it is too short. These

Effect	Typical Delay	Notes
		effects are made distinct with the addition of distortion or feedback, and a noticeable sweeping modulation that varies from a few times a second to once every dozen seconds or so. These effects usually use only one additional voice.

Although the Chorus effect is the foundation of many other effects, it is not always easy to derive these other specialized effects from the Chorus plug-in. For example, the additional controls that are specific to the Wah-Wah plug-in give you more flexibility when dealing with that particular effect. For flanges, on the other hand, the Chorus plug-in has additional controls that allow you to set the delay and control the all-important feedback, which sometimes makes the Chorus a more powerful flange than the actual Flange plug-in. Some of the presets in the Chorus effect do produce very nice flanges, phasers, and wah-wahs, so don't underestimate this plug-in as a simple tool used only to add additional voices and richness to a track.

Here are some other tips for using Chorus:

* Select the **Invert the Chorus Phase** item to set the phase of the wave peaks to be 180 degrees out of phase with the original. The **Dry Out** slider, which mixes the original signal with the processed signal, must be set higher for the phase to be heard. **Invert the Feedback Phase** does the same thing, but only to the feedback, so the **Feedback** slider must be set at a higher level for this to be noticeable.

* The **Chorus Size** determines the number of additional voices added, from one to three.

* Use the **Tempo Sync** check box to synchronize the period of the effect with the actual tempo of the project, without going through all of the calculations outlined in Chapter 7. The **Modulation Period** can be set in terms of measures or beats. This feature is available only in the Pro version of the ACID software.

* The **Modulation Rate** is a manual way of setting the **Modulation Period** in Hertz and is not nearly as easy or fun to use, although the results are identical.

* The **Modulation Depth** controls the strength of the modulation. Set the depth to higher levels to vary further from the delay setting (as a percentage of the total delay). The modulation can be heard most clearly when the depth is greater. Flange-type effects often require larger depth settings.

- ✳ **Feedback** is an important element for flange-type effects. It is also a way to increase the number of apparent voices by adding subtle echoes to the signal.
- ✳ The **Chorus Out Delay** is simply the delay of the voices.
- ✳ Check the **Attenuate High Frequencies Above (Hz)** option to mute or soften the higher frequencies that can come to dominate some applications of the Chorus plug-in. This is also called a low-pass filter in some other plug-ins, because it allows everything below the selected frequency to pass through it.

Compressor (Track)

Compression is an automated way to adjust the volume of a track variably, ultimately raising all valleys and diminishing all peaks. By doing so, you can increase the overall loudness of a track without causing clipping in places where the volume is already high. This effect is very widely used in popular music production and results in a loss of dynamic range in a song. This might be fine in full-speed-ahead pop music, but you should exercise caution when using compression in other genres where dynamics are important, such as all thoughtful and worthwhile forms of music (including good pop music).

That being said, compression can be a lifesaver when working with a track that must be made louder to stand out in a mix or when fixing a recording with uneven levels. As the name suggests, the Track Compressor is best used intelligently at the track level, although technically you could use it at the project level as well. See the discussion about the Graphic Dynamics plug-in later in this chapter or Chapter 6 for a much more detailed explanation on how to use compression properly in a mix. Compression is not all work and no play, however. More creative uses of compression can cause very interesting and effective distortions, especially in guitar parts, creating awesomely chunky guitars.

Distortion

You can accidentally cause distortion by turning up the volume too loud, which can cause clipping in a digital environment or can drive an amplifier or speakers beyond their specifications. An intentional distortion effect has been successfully used, especially in noisy or dirty electric rock guitar parts, to create fuzzy or raspy sounds. Originally, distortion was caused by overdriving the analog tube-based amplifiers and speakers used for electric guitars. Modern distortion boxes and plug-ins can simulate these old-fashioned devices (more or less), and some of the presets in the Distortion plug-in refer to transistors and tubes. Of course, distortion has many other applications beyond guitar parts. Perhaps surprisingly, the Distortion effect plug-in can be used to create space or even to remove noise below a certain threshold, much like a Noise Gate filter. Because distortion affects the signal above a certain level, it is sometimes useful to apply compression just before distortion in an effects chain to boost some of the quieter parts of the signal.

Here are some tips for using the Distortion plug-in:

* **The graph** controls the level of the effect in terms of input versus output. Click the line on the graph to add envelope points (in other words, nodes or keyframes) and drag them up or down. Try some of the presets to get an idea of what some typical distortion settings look like on the graph. A diagonal line from the bottom-left to the top-right indicates that the input and the output are equal, meaning that no distortion occurs.

* **The Graph Polarity Edit mode** sets the behavior of the effect: The setting Individual only affects the graphs as seen; Synchronize matches the X/Y values to the graph and tends to yield a raspy sound; and Mirror X, Mirror Y, and Mirror X/Y sets these values to the opposite (or mirror) of the graph. The **Positive/Negative** button determines which of the two graphs (lines) you are editing, with the line displayed on the button being the one that is black, and the opposite graph displayed as a dashed line in the background. Positive is the part of the wave in a waveform that is above the –Inf. center line, and Negative is the part of the wave that is below that line.

* **The Slew Rate (1 to 100)** in the real world is a measure of an amplifier's ability to follow the input signal. Higher numbers are better if you want your amplifier to produce a pure sound with little distortion, with 100 resulting in no change. With distortion being a goal here, however, lowering the slew rate simulates an analog distortion that is not keeping up with changes in amplitude in the signal, and results in a characteristic type of noise in the output signal.

* Check the **Low-Pass Start Freq. (Hz)** box to attenuate or soften the higher frequencies. As the name implies, this filter allows everything below the selected frequency to pass and filters everything above it. You could also call this **Attenuate High Frequencies Above (Hz)**, and, indeed, some other plug-ins call it exactly that.

Dither

Dithering is the process of smoothing rough edges in digital media. An analog signal is a continuous signal, but when we record a sound on a computer, it must be recorded in a digital format. This digital format is necessarily composed of individual discrete parts, or quanta. The more pieces (quanta) into which we break up the sound, the greater the fidelity and quality of the digitization. The number of parts is expressed in terms of the sample rate, measured in the number of samples per second. Each part in turn can be measured by the quantity of computer bits that are used to describe it, with more being better. This can be expressed in terms of the resolution or depth (bit depth) of the recording.

For our source recordings, we always try to record at the highest-quality settings that we can. When we distribute our music, we often have to reduce the digital quality somewhat to comply with a particular format (such as 16 bits per sample for CD or DVD) or to reduce the file size for the Internet. Sometimes the process of moving from a higher bit-depth recording to a lower one can result in the addition of noisy artifacts in the signal. For example, when down-converting from a 24-bit DAT source to a 16-bit CD-audio disc, you necessarily lose some information. In this case, the information lost is likely to be minor, perhaps even inaudible, but the situation becomes more serious if you are down-converting all the way to 8 bits per sample for a small file destined for the Internet. Down-converting can sometimes be heard as a tinny echo in spoken-word recordings, a static crackle after percussion beats, or a distortion in low-level (volume) signals.

WHAT ABOUT SAMPLE RATE?
The Dither plug-in does nothing to remove artifacts introduced by down-sampling.

The Dither plug-in smoothes the sharp noise that sometimes results from such a conversion by adding a random hiss to the down-conversion artifacts and then changing the frequency of this noise so that it can no longer be heard or is at least less noticeable to human perception. This comes at the minor price of adding background hiss, but it allows more of the original low-level signal to be maintained in the down-converted sound. The effect of the Dither plug-in can be very difficult to hear because it is not designed to change a sound or song audibly, but is instead used to preserve the original sound as much as possible through the conversion process to a lower bit depth. Although you can set the audio characteristics when you render the final song, you will not be able to preview the effects of the Dither plug-in on your project unless you set the Project Properties to the target audio format. Simple drum and percussion parts with silence between the beats can reveal the dithering most clearly; individual beats are strongly affected by decreasing the bit depth and can be surrounded by static-like clicks and distortion, which can be easily masked by the random hiss added by the Dither plug-in. In the end, as with all plug-ins and effects, if it sounds better with a dither, you should use it. This is definitely one plug-in that you want to try out whenever you are having problems getting a high-quality yet highly compressed file for streaming over the Internet. Keep in mind, though, that dithering does nothing for problems caused by lowering the sample rate (44 kHz to 22 kHz). Also, do not confuse bit depth with the Internet/streaming/data transfer–specific term *bit rate* (expressed in kilobits per second, or Kbps), which is unaffected by dithering. The Dither plug-in controls are straightforward:

❊ Select the bit depth to which you are converting with the **Quantization Depth** control. For example, if you are converting an audio track from a 24-bit source to a 16-bit track for an audio CD, you would set the Quantization depth to 16 bits (the default setting). Dithering is more important when down-converting to 8 bits.

❊ The **Dither Type** sets resolution of the dithering, so 1/2 bit results in a smoother dither.

- ❋ **Noise Shape Type** sets the type of noise reduction that is used in combination with the dithering to remove the hiss that is added as a part of the dithering process. Use caution when using noise shaping on files with lower sample rates, such as 22 kHz, because this ends up pushing the noise into very noticeable frequencies.

Dithering can be used on individual tracks, especially if only some tracks will be down-converted. Dithering is more typically used on the entire project as the very last plug-in, especially when you are down-converting for the Internet. You should definitely avoid using dithering at two stages: at the track level and at the project level.

Flange/Wah-Wah

The Flange/Wah-Wah effect is really three related plug-ins in one: Flange, Wah-Wah, and Phaser. You can select the specific effect by choosing the radio button that corresponds to the one you want to use. Wah-Wah and Phaser periodically shift or modulate the frequencies that are dominant in the output. Flanging is also a periodic effect, but works by modulating the delay of a chorus of parts. This is probably one of the most fun plug-ins of the bunch, and you should definitely click through the three radio buttons and try out the presets to hear the difference between these three effects.

The Flange plug-in is difficult to describe, but it is an instantly recognizable sweeping sound that smoothly enhances different frequencies in a sound periodically. The Flange's effect is actually a variation of the Phaser, but you'll notice that the Flange effect doesn't use the Center Frequency or Resonance Control. It sounds a bit like singing a long ooo sound and gradually transitioning to a long eee and back. Flanging is widely used in techno and other electronic music. Surprisingly, flanging is also similar to a Chorus effect, except that the effect is varied periodically over time and the delay used is usually less than 10ms, too short for humans to perceive as a delay. (See the "Chorus" section for important details.) Because it is varied by shortening and lengthening the delayed signal, flanging creates a periodic shift in pitch. (Shortening the delayed signal causes an increased pitch.) The controls for the Flange plug-in are as follows:

- ❋ The **Rate** is the number of cycles per second (Hz) of the effect. Flanges tend to have slower rates, perhaps measured in seconds, and produce a pronounced sweeping effect.

- ❋ The **Depth** determines the range in the amount of the delay. You cannot use the Flange plug-in to control the delay (see the section "Chorus").

- ❋ Use the **Tempo Sync** check box to synchronize the period of the effect with the actual tempo of the project without going through all of the calculations outlined in Chapter 7. You can set the **Modulation Period** in measures or beats. This feature is available only in the Pro version of the ACID software.

Wah-Wah is an onomatopoetic effect often used in electric funk guitar. It creates an almost vocal effect on guitar (and other instrument) parts, almost as if one were singing "wah-wah-wah." Although this is not a hard and fast rule by any means, flanging usually takes place over a longer period of time, whereas classic wah-wah and phasing take place over shorter periods of time. In the ACID application, this is completely irrelevant because we can use any period we want for all of these effects.

Phaser effects refer not to *Star Trek,* but to the waves in a sound. Sound waves, as with waves of water, have peaks and troughs. The distance between two troughs is the frequency of the sound, which defines the tone or pitch. By chorusing the original sound, you can play two instances of the same sound together. When the waves are moving together, they are in phase, whereas waves that peak while others are in a trough are said to be out of phase by 180 degrees. The Phaser plug-in periodically reinforces some parts of a sound and weakens others by moving them in and out of phase. Two more controls are available in the Audio Plug-In window when you select either the Wah-Wah or Phaser effect:

※ The **Center Frequency** is the tonal center of the sweeping effect. Slide this setting around to achieve either a more intense or a more subtle effect.

※ **Resonance** is when two sounds work together to reinforce each other, making the total louder or more intense than the sum of the parts. The slider in this plug-in controls the phase of the multiple voices in this effect, with higher percentages keeping the sounds more in phase, resulting in more reinforcement and a more intense sound. For a Wah-Wah effect, resonance controls the amount of band-pass filtering. For a Phaser effect, it controls the amount of phase shifting.

Calculating Rates

You can easily and effectively synchronize Phaser and Wah-Wah effects to the beat of a song. See the section "Calculating Rates" in Chapter 7 for information about how to calculate and synchronize this effect with a project.

Gapper/Snipper

The Gapper/Snipper plug-in works by inserting silence (Gapper) or by cutting material out (Snipper) periodically. At higher rates, you get a tremolo-like effect by modulation of volume. In practice, given the same settings in the Audio Plug-In window, the Gapper produces a slightly harsher and more clearly delineated stutter (because there are distinct areas of silence), whereas the Snipper produces a softer, more continuous sound. Figure 8.2 graphically displays the effects of the Gapper and the Snipper on the waveform of an audio file. The media file is a spoken-word file that will help you to visualize the results of this plug-in and is not meant as an example of a typical usage. You can see that the Gapper event has silence inserted, but no material from the original is lost; it is pushed down the timeline, making the event longer. The Snipper, on the other hand, removes material, moves it left to be flush with the start of the cut, leaves no sections of silence, and results in a shorter event. The controls of the Gapper/Snipper plug-in are as follows:

※ **Freq. to Gap/Snip Events** sets the period (frequency) of the stuttering in Hertz (Hz or cycles per second). "Events" here refers to a gap inserted or a snip removed, not to ACID events on the timeline.

※ **Length of One Event** sets the duration of the gap inserted or the section removed.

※ **Fade Edges of Each Event** prevents the slight clicking or popping sound that can occur from sharp edges created by the effect as a percentage of the length of the gap or snip.

※ **Percent of Original** shows how the frequency and length combine to affect the original audio. The Gapper expresses this in terms of +100 percent (because it is inserting silence), making the event longer, whereas the Snipper uses percentages of less than 100 percent (because the resulting event is shorter than the original).

Figure 8.2

The effects of the Gapper/ Snipper on a spoken-word media file.

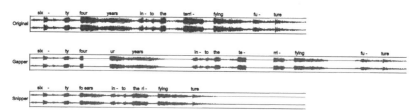

Calculating Rates

It is very useful to synchronize the Gapper/Snipper effect with the tempo and beat of a project. The Gapper/Snipper effect is a faster-period effect that may occur on the beat or often multiple times each beat. See the "Calculating Rates" section in Chapter 7 for information about how to calculate and synchronize this effect with a project.

Graphic Dynamics

The Graphic Dynamics plug-in is the first of a number of dynamics plug-ins that you can use for precisely controlling compression, limiting, and expansion of a sound in the ACID software. The specific tool you use to adjust the dynamics is largely a matter of personal preference, although some plug-ins are tailored to particular uses (such as Compression and Noise Gate). The Graphic Dynamics plug-in is particularly well suited to perform detailed compression across all frequencies in a track and is similar to, but more flexible than, the Track Compressor. Compression is the process of lowering peaks in a signal and raising valleys, with the ultimate goal of increasing the loudness of a track overall. Expansion is the opposite and adds dynamic range to a track: Low-level (volume) signals are lowered, and high-level signals are raised. Limiting is hard/absolute compression and is a way to make sure the peaks in a waveform never rise above a certain level.

This effect is yet another way you can increase the overall loudness of the track without causing clipping. See Chapter 6 for more information on effective use of compression.

The Graphics Dynamics and Multi-Band Dynamics plug-ins are probably the two most difficult plug-ins to understand because of the large number of controls each contains. They are also difficult to use because of the subtle but important ways they modify an audio signal. One suggestion is to try out the various presets on a track, noticing the various types of graphs that the engineers at Sony Media Software have created and listening to the results on your music. One difficulty with exploring this and other correction plug-ins in the ACID software is that media files and loops from commercial vendors are recorded and engineered by professionals who have already (one would expect) optimized the dynamics and equalization.

Controls for the Graphics Dynamics plug-in include the following:

❋   The **Output Gain** sets the volume of the processed signal. The usual goal of applying compression is to increase the overall loudness, and you can do that with this fader.

❋   The **Auto Gain Compensation** is a very important part of this plug-in and is very useful in normalizing a signal. This automatically raises the gain on the quiet parts, resulting in a smoother compression overall. More than likely, you'll also want to increase manually the Output gain slightly whether this option is checked or not.

❋   The **Sync Stereo Gain** means that the compression/limiting is applied to both stereo channels equally. If one channel is peaking out and the other is fine, make sure that you do *not* select this option. Compression will then be applied to both channels independently.

❋   The **graph** is the heart of this effect. When you first start, the line on the graph runs from the bottom-left to the top-right. This zero line indicates that you are not changing the dynamics of the signal, because the vertical Out is equal to the horizontal In. To add an envelope point (in other words, node or keyframe) on the line, click on the line and drag it to a new position. To delete a node, double-click it. You'll notice that the line already has one node on it at the −24, −24 dB position. This node is the threshold in this plug-in, and it is a standard place where you might want to ease into the compression slowly. If you look at a few of the presets, you'll see that although this node moves up and down in volume (gain), it is always at the X=Y position. The compression presets start on the zero line and then angle to the right and below the line. This is what compression looks like graphically. Noise Gating is the process of eliminating unwanted low-level background noise. In this case, you want to add a node at a low gain and then drag the line down and away, again decreasing the output gain. See Figure 8.3.

The graph allows you to do both compression and Noise Gating at the same time. A good example of where you might want to use both is when working with a spoken-word recording using the microphone on a camcorder. Using a camcorder's on-camera mic is rarely a good idea, but sometimes you have no choice. Because the subject is talking into the camera from a distance and the microphone usually isn't of the highest quality, you might get some very uneven recording levels, especially if the camera operator is also talking, creating sections that are much louder. To increase the gain for the quieter parts, you first need to reduce the gain of the really loud parts and then increase the whole thing together. The final result will have much less dynamic range (difference between the quiet and loud parts). Most consumer camcorders have an automatic gain circuit that tries to increase the gain for quieter sections. Onboard camcorder microphones also usually introduce annoying background motor noise into a recording. Such noise can become especially prominent when you turn up the gain. So, at the same time you are working with some compression on the graph, you might also want to use a Noise Gate to get rid of the hum. Figure 8.3 shows what the graph might look like to solve this problem. In the figure, the relatively steep slope of the Noise Gate starting at −60 dB indicates that the noise is cut out fairly quickly and sharply. The compression slope is more gradual and results in an easing in of the compression at −24 dB as the gain increases. By the time the gain in the input hits 0 dB, it is being compressed by −12 dB. This compression slope is typical, because low-level sounds are harder to hear and Noise Gating is frequently a vertical line at a particular gain (a hard gate). If you wanted to do a hard limit (compression that doesn't slope at all), you would create a horizontal line at some upper limit. Expansion would involve dragging the graph line above the zero line, but this is rarely done.

Figure 8.3

Compression and Noise Gating in the Graphic Dynamics plug-in.

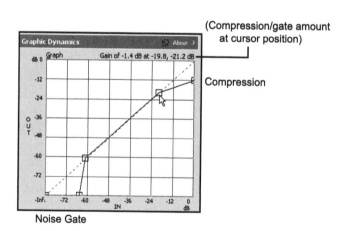

* The **Attack** and **Release** parameters set how quickly the plug-in responds to peaks. A quick attack (so that the plug-in starts immediately) and a slow release are typical. If a release is too fast, very quiet sections (even silence) can result in the gain suddenly being turned up very loud, and thus background noise becomes audible. This results in a breathing or pumping effect.

✳ **The Threshold** sets the level where the compression begins to take effect. This slider moves the default threshold node on the graph line up and down while maintaining the relative X:Y ratio.

✳ **The Ratio** slider sets the slope of the compression line, raising and lowering the final node on the graph. The zero line is at a ratio of 1:1, resulting in no compression. A 2:0 ratio above −24 dB indicates that for every 2-dB increase in gain above −24 dB, the gain will be reduced 1dB. So a −22-dB signal input will decrease to −23 dB output, −12 dB in to −18 dB out, and 0 dB in to −12 dB out.

Graphic EQ

The Graphic EQ is the first of a number of equalization plug-ins that you can use to adjust the overall tonal qualities of your audio. The specific type of equalization that you use is largely a matter of personal preference, although you might find some EQ plug-ins easier to use than others in specific instances. (Some suggestions are given within the plug-in definitions.)

> ✳ **MULTI-EQ**
>
> It is not highly recommended that you use multiple EQ plug-ins in the total effects chain. At most, you might want to use EQ at the track level to fix a few problems and maybe also on the Master bus in the Mixer to polish off a project, but you should think very carefully about whether you can find a better way to do the same thing more efficiently. This is actually good advice for all plug-ins.

The Graphic EQ actually is a very nice blend of simplicity and power. All three tabs in the plug-in window control the same parameters. When you move a slider on one, the sliders and envelope nodes on the others move with it. On the 10 Band tab, you can quickly set up a rough EQ curve, then on the 20 Band tab, you can make a few more minor adjustments, and finally on the Envelope tab, you will find the greatest level of control. Figure 8.4 shows an exploded view of all three tabs and how they look with exactly the same settings. Each slider on the 10 Band corresponds to a pair of sliders on the 20 Band. Initially the number of nodes on the envelope line corresponds to the complexity and variation in the sliders (for example, a flat line needs only two nodes), but you can add additional nodes by clicking and dragging the envelope line. You can delete nodes by double-clicking or right-clicking them. Dragging nodes (or sliders) up and down (vertically) controls the gain at any specific frequency. You can also drag nodes left and right (horizontally) to fine-tune the exact frequency of the node. The Output Gain fader enables you to control the overall volume of the signal leaving the plug-in.

Figure 8.4

The Graphic EQ plug-in tabs from the top: 10 Band (the most coarse level of control), 20 Band, and Envelope (the finest level of control).

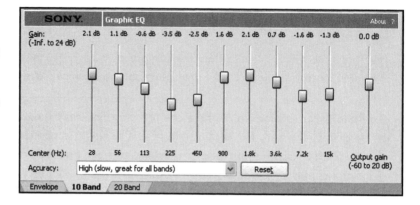

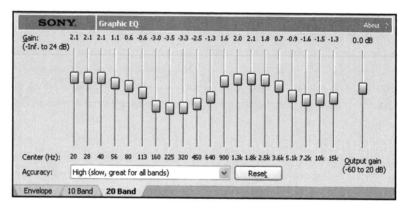

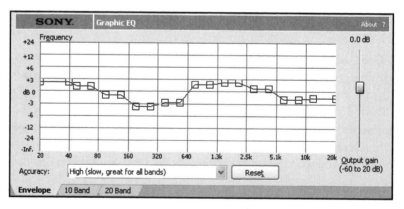

The Accuracy list is where you adjust the quality of the plug-in. Higher-quality settings will force your computer to work harder. If you have a slower machine (such as a 500-MHz CPU) or if your project is particularly complex (that is, it uses a lot of tracks and effects), you might want to use the Medium or Low settings. As you'll notice from the list, higher bands are easier to process, so you can get away with using the lower Accuracy items when applying EQ only to the upper frequencies. These settings only affect timeline playback of the project in real time. You should definitely use High settings whenever you render, because the computer will take as much time as it needs to create the final output.

You can use equalization to bring a track or part out of a mix, or you can use it at the track level to clean up the sound of a track. This is especially useful if you are using a loop or media file that has a number of different instruments and you want to focus on one in particular. The trick is to figure out which frequencies to boost (see Figure 8.4). To give you a rough idea of the range of frequencies of a typical 88-key piano keyboard, you can see frequencies from about 27 Hz to 4,200 Hz, with middle C at about 262 Hz, which can serve as an arbitrary divider between high and low frequencies. It would be impossible to make recommendations about which frequencies to boost for the human voice because it covers such a large range (four or five octaves). By playing back a section of a project (within a loop region and with looping turned on) with a track soloed (click the Solo button on the track) and adjusting the sliders on the 10 Band tab one by one, you can hear which ones emphasize the part you want to bring out. Then you can move on to the other tabs for greater accuracy (see Figure 8.4). When trying to eliminate a particular frequency, it is often easier first to boost the frequencies you suspect are causing the unwanted noise to figure out what makes the sound the loudest, then drag the sliders back down to get rid of the sound.

You can also use equalization very effectively at the project and bus levels. In these cases, you wouldn't want to solo the track while trying to bring a part out of the overall mix, but the procedure would be the same. Another use of EQ is to bring brightness back to a mix or track that has been compressed or otherwise muddied. Surprisingly, a gentle boosting of the high-frequency band can also add a greater spatial sense to a mix. This is because very low frequencies are very nondirectional (in smaller spaces), while with higher frequencies identifying the location of the sound is easier. The higher frequencies are, therefore, more important to the perceived spatial aspects of a mix. Finally, you can use EQ to minimize constant-frequency background noises, whether low-frequency hums or high-frequency hisses. The Notch frequencies around 450 Hz are an example of a preset that might be used for such a purpose. You can also use EQ to hide pops and crackles as well, just as long as the frequency of these artifacts remains constant.

Multi-Band Dynamics

The Multi-Band Dynamics plug-in takes compression one step further by allowing you to apply compression at specific frequencies instead of broadly across the entire spectrum. (See the explanations of compression in the "Graphic Dynamics" section and in Chapter 6.) This kind of custom tailoring can allow you to target your effect more precisely, potentially avoiding some of the pitfalls that plague compression. This customizing is not necessarily easy, but in some cases it is very important. Any time you can identify clear peaks or spikes in a signal, either by ear or by looking for very sharp and narrow spikes in the waveform, you should consider this plug-in instead of squashing the entire track with one of the broader effects. This is especially true with pops and clicks or when a speaker spits a p into the microphone. In all of these cases, the sound probably occupies a fairly narrow frequency range that is different from the material you want to keep, which often occupies a much broader frequency. The tricky part is figuring out the frequency of the noise that you want to compress. You cannot perform Noise Gating with this plug-in.

First, you can apply compression (or limit where the Amount slider is set to 50:1) to four individual bands: two on the first page of the plug-in and two on the other. You can use one or all four bands when you are done, but you'll definitely want to work with one band at a time by selecting the Solo option on the band you are modifying. To activate a band, uncheck the Band # Bypass option at the bottom of the dialog.

Next, identify the section of the event that has a typical example of something that you want to compress, such as a p in the microphone. On the timeline, create a loop region around one section that is causing problems, turn looping playback on, and click the Play button. As with all plug-ins, you'll want to preview the soloed track while you make adjustments. Click the Preset list and select Reduce Loud Plosives. This is a great place to start, and it sets the threshold to −15 dB, which is the point above which the compression begins. For this preset, the compression slope is fairly sharp with an amount of 32:1. If we used the Graphic Dynamics plug-in, it would look like Figure 8.5.

Figure 8.5

Compression applied to all signals of all frequencies above −15 dB at a 32:1 ratio in the Graphic Dynamics plug-in.

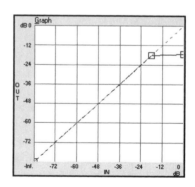

Using the Multi-Band Dynamics plug-in, however, the compression will apply to only a limited range of frequencies. The type of band, in this case, is a low-shelf, which means that all frequencies below the one specified by the Frequency slider will be compressed—in this example, 500 Hz. In summary, all sounds between the lowest sound possible (20 Hz) and 500 Hz will be compressed (almost limited at 32:1) when they rise above −15 dB. This compression should catch those nasty plosives. The next time you record, you can coach your talent on how to use a microphone properly so you don't have to go through this again.

A trickier example is a harsh s sound, which is caused by air blown directly into a microphone with certain consonants. Sibilants typically occur at completely different frequencies from the plosives. From the Preset list, select the Reduce Loud Sibilants item. This preset only changes Band 1, so you cannot use the presets on two separate bands, one for sibilants and one for plosives. This time, the type is band-notch and the center of the frequency that will be compressed is at 5,000 Hz with a width of 1.0 octave. The threshold is set very low at –30 dB with a 25:1 compression. Figure 8.6 shows what the low-shelf and the band-notch might look like in the Track EQ plug-in, with the low-shelf being identified on the left with a 1 and the one octave band-notch at 5,000 Hz identified by the 2. Finally, there is a preset named Reduce Plosives and Sibilants that works on both and is a great place to start if your talent ate the microphone.

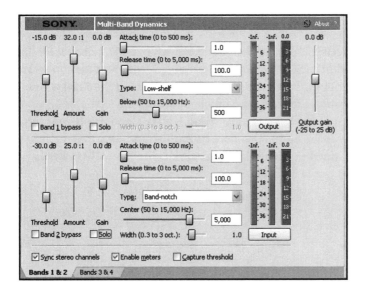

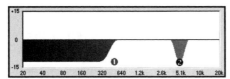

Figure 8.6

Top: The settings used in Band 1 to eliminate plosives and in Band 2 to eliminate sibilants. Bottom: What these two frequencies might look like in the Track EQ plug-in.

Starting with a preset is a great idea, but presets are usually just that: starting points. Make sure the Enable Meters item at the bottom of the window is checked and the button below the meters on the band you are working on is set to Output. Then, while the loop region is playing back on the timeline, move the Center slider back and forth to try to zero in on the exact frequency of the s or whatever noise you want to compress. You should also adjust the Width slider to try to minimize the range of frequencies that you are compressing. There is no magic way to do this, and it takes time, practice, and a good ear to get it right. You can probably eliminate a few scattered s sounds with this technique, but eliminating wind in the microphone will be tough (if not impossible) to do. Once again, next time coach your talent to keep the mic close, but not directly in front of their mouth, and get a windsock the next time you are shooting video on the beach.

The attack and release operate in exactly the same way they do in the Graphic Dynamics plug-in, usually with a fast attack and a slower release. The Sync Stereo Channels item at the bottom of the window is the same as well. Deselect this default option if you are having problems in only one channel.

The final item is one of the most important. You should select the Capture Threshold check box when you want to find automatically the highest peak(s) to compress. To do this, select the Capture Threshold option and then play back the section of the track that has the problem. The Threshold slider becomes disabled, and the labels around it turn red. Now, when a peak occurs, the Threshold slider automatically adjusts to that level. Now you can drag the Threshold slider down slightly to make sure you compress these peaks. To the left of the main meters is a third red meter. This is the compression meter, and it operates from the top down, allowing you to see when compression is occurring and by how much. If the meter is not moving, you are not hitting your target. If it is constantly bouncing all the way to the bottom, you are probably squashing the track too much or you have really poor source audio that cannot be fixed. Don't worry, you'll probably hear this with your ears well before you get to this point.

CAPTURE THRESHOLD

When the Capture Threshold check box is selected, the Threshold slider is disabled. If you try to drag the slider up and down, it will simply jump back to the position at which it detected the peak.

Multi-Tap Delay

Multi-Tap Delay is a more complicated version of the Simple Delay effect. Both essentially create echoes from a signal, simulating audio waves bouncing off of surfaces and returning to the listener a bit later. You can use this plug-in to create perceived space in a song, but it is more commonly used as an interesting special effect. (Reverb is a more natural way to create space with delays.) Instead of a single echo (as created in the Simple Delay effect), the Multi-Tap Delay creates multiple echoes. You can use this effect to simulate canyon walls at different distances or more complex spaces where echoes return at different times. Quite a few other controls are available that can subtly modify the delayed signal. As with the Simple Delay plug-in, Multi-Tap Delay is most effective with solo voices or instrument parts that can clearly show the effect of the delay. The delay can continue well after the event on the timeline ends.

The controls of the Multi-Tap Delay plug-in include the following:

❋ **The Input Gain** sets the level of the signal coming into the effect. It is set to 0.0 dB by default, which represents no change in gain. Anything less will diminish the volume.

❋ **The Dry Out and Wet Out faders** are usually used to mix the original signal with the processed signal, but it is a slightly different situation in this effect. With some effects (such as dynamics and equalization), you might want to turn the Dry fader all the way down to –Inf. for maximum effect. With this effect, you need to hear the Dry Out (original) signal; otherwise, the echo won't make any sense. Hearing only the echo and not the sound that caused it would be odd indeed. Usually, the Wet Out fader gain is the same as, or lower than, the Dry Out gain. These controls set the gain for the entire effect; you can also set the gain of individual taps using other sliders.

❋ **The Number of Taps** sets the number of delayed signals that are returned as echoes. As you move the slider to add more taps, the numbers on the **Current Tap list** become active one by one. All of the controls below this list apply to whichever current tap is selected; to modify the third tap, for example, make sure at least three taps are available and then select the radio button before the 3. Taps appear on the graph as vertical lines, with the active tap colored red.

❋ **The Tap Gain** sets the initial volume of the processed signal for each tap. One reasonable way to determine a naturalistic gain for each tap is to make sure that taps with greater delay times also have lower volumes. You can see the gain of each tap represented on the graph: Taller tap lines are louder. The tap gain can be set to +/−100 percent, with negative values being 180 degrees out of phase; this means that the peaks of negative and positive waves occur at different times. These differing peaks can be important in any delay effect (such as Chorus) because waves that occur in sync reinforce each other and sound like a unison signal. In other words, an earlier and louder delay can mask a later delay if the two are completely in phase. Altering the tap gain +/− from tap to tap can solve this problem and add space to the effect.

❋ **The graph** visually represents the gain and the delay (see Figure 8.7). You cannot change anything on the graph directly. The **Graph Resolution** allows you to view more or less detail on the graph (zoom in and out). To determine the total length of the graph, set the time from 500ms to 5,000ms.

❋ **The Delay** sets the time of the echo return in milliseconds. Hold down the Ctrl key while dragging the slider to position the delay more accurately. (This also works for many controls in the ACID software.) The line on the graph moves in response to the slider's movements. Each tap can be at any delay setting, but for most users it simply makes sense if the shortest delay is Tap 1, the next one is Tap 2, and so on.

✳ The **Pan control** allows you to set the stereo panning of the delays. This is important because you are using the Multi-Tap Delay effect to simulate multiple echoes coming from walls at different distances, and probably different directions, from the listener. It might help to think about a room or location and the position of the listener in the room as you adjust the plug-in. You can think of each tap as modifying the echo from a single wall.

✳ The **Mod. Rate** sets the modulation in the pitch of the individual delays. This creates a more realistic effect, in contrast with a relentlessly perfect computer delay. Subtle manipulation allows you to differentiate the delayed signals more easily from the Dry Out signal. The **Mod. Depth** setting determines the strength of the modulation.

✳ The **Feedback control** can also set up additional delay-type effects by running the delays through the filter again.

✳ The **Low-Pass Start Freq. control** allows you to add a filter that cuts out some of the higher frequencies (and lets lower frequencies pass through). The frequency set here determines where the filter starts, with everything above this level being filtered. High-frequency sounds are important in our perception of depth, and filtering out these frequencies can create a warmer and less harsh effect.

Figure 8.7

The graph displays the information about the fourth tap in the effect, which is represented by a red line. The other taps are displayed on both sides of the Gain line in gray.

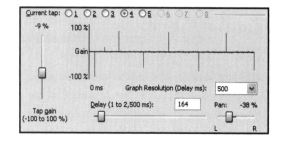

Calculating Rates

It is very useful to synchronize the Multi-Tap Delay effect with the tempo and beat of a project. See the section "Calculating Rates" in Chapter 7 for information about how to calculate and synchronize this effect with a project.

Noise Gate

Noise Gate primarily eliminates low-level background noise from a sound and is a special case of a dynamics plug-in. See Figure 8.8 for a comparison of what the same settings in the Noise Gate plug-in might look like in the Graphic Dynamics plug-in. You can see in the example that the threshold in both is −32 dB. Sounds below this threshold are silence to −Inf. The line in the graph is vertical, which means that everything is cut off, with no rolloff. Noise Gates are especially useful in eliminating constant low-level noises, from electronic hums to video camera motor noises that become apparent during sections where there is no program audio and therefore should be silent. The Noise Gate Help file shows two events with waveforms that display a low-level hum that could be eliminated with a Noise Gate.

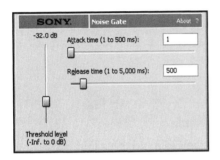
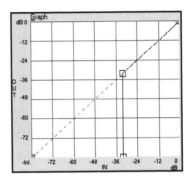

Figure 8.8
What the Noise Gate plug-in might look like, as expressed on the graph in the Graphic Dynamics plug-in.

The following are Noise Gate's controls:

* ❋ The **Threshold** sets the minimum level that a sound must reach to pass through the filter. All sounds below the threshold are silenced.

* ❋ The **Attack** and **Release** parameters set how quickly the plug-in responds to peaks. A quick attack (so that the effect starts immediately) and a slow release (so that the effect wears off imperceptibly) are typical.

Paragraphic EQ

Paragraphic EQ is another visual or graphic equalization plug-in that allows you to see the various frequencies and how they are modified. It is actually very similar to the Track EQ plug-in (they even share many of the same presets) except that it has two additional bands. Figure 8.9 shows some of the similarities. The plug-in automatically calculates smooth curves between the various nodes, resulting in smoother transitions, which is something that the graph on the Graphic EQ does not do.

Like the Track EQ effect, the Paragraphic EQ has bands that you can customize and adjust individually, although Paragraphic EQ has a total of six: four distinct main areas plus a low- and high-shelf (see Figure 8.9). In the Track EQ plug-in, the various controls span four different tabs. In the Paragraphic EQ effect, all of the controls are on a single page, which can make the plug-in look intimidating. Four bands are just below the graph, whereas the low- and high-shelf bands are at the bottom of the window. (These are called shelves because of the flat ends to the equalization curves.)

Figure 8.9

The same settings in both the Track EQ and Paragraphic EQ plug-ins.

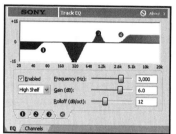
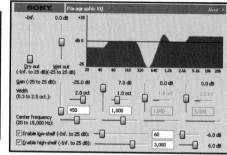

Here are Paragraphic EQ's controls:

❋ The only additional control that the Paragraphic EQ has are **Dry/Wet Mix faders,** which control the mix of the original signal with the processed signal.

❋ The four bands below the graph are gray until you move the **Gain fader** for that band. In other words, until you move a slider, the bands are not modifying the audio.

❋ The bands default to a **Center frequency** of 100 Hz, 300 Hz, 1,000 Hz, and 5,000 Hz. After adjusting the gain to make a band active, drag the slider to change the Center frequency. Although they default from lowest to highest, left to right, there is no reason to leave them that way. The second band could just as easily center at 9,000 Hz if you desire. As with most sliders in the ACID software, hold the Ctrl key while dragging a slider to make it more sensitive and move it in smaller increments. You can use the slider to sweep up and down the frequency range conveniently while playing the track back so that you can quickly target what you need.

❋ The **Width** is set by the middle slider (see Figure 8.10) and is measured in terms of octaves.

❋ Select the **Enable Low-Shelf** or **Enable High-Shelf options** to use these bands as well. The first slider controls the frequency at which the shelf rolloff begins, and the last smaller slider controls the gain.

Figure 8.10

The band controls on the Paragraphic EQ plug-in.

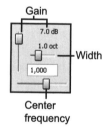

As with many other effects, the best way to work with this plug-in is to click the Solo button on the track on which you are using the plug-in, create a loop region on the timeline, and play back the project while you modify the various parameters. For example, imagine you want to get rid of an annoying hum. (This plug-in is well suited to this use.) There are two ways to figure out the frequency of the hum. In both cases, to isolate the noise, you pick a section of the event that has no content and that is as silent as possible. Then, while that section is repeatedly looping, you increase the gain on one of the bands and then slide the Center frequency slider back and forth until you make the sound as loud as possible. Or, you could reduce the gain to –Inf. and see whether you can make the sound disappear, but some people find this more challenging. After identifying the frequency as accurately as possible, adjust the width of the band and lower the gain. Then, go back to the track and preview the EQ settings on a section of the track with content. More than likely, the plug-in will have a negative impact on the sound you want to keep as well, so you will need to play a balancing game to get rid of as much of the problem as possible without damaging the rest of the track.

Parametric EQ

The Parametric EQ is another reconfiguration of the same controls found in the Graphic Dynamics, Paragraphic, and Track EQ plug-ins. It has a slightly higher range (up to 22,050 Hz) and an in-line Output Gain control, but otherwise it has Low-Shelf, Band 1, Band 2, and High-Shelf that are almost identical to those in the Track EQ. The difference is that this plug-in is specialized to apply only one specific filter discretely to a track, either to boost a specific band or to attenuate it. As with all ACID effects, the presets offer several examples that you might try out to get a feel for the plug-in. Again, the basic controls are similar to the other EQ plug-ins:

* ❋ The **Output Gain** controls the volume of the processed signal as it leaves the plug-in.

* ❋ The **Amount fader** is the same as the gain sliders in the other EQs and sets the level at which the selected frequencies are attenuated or boosted.

* ❋ The **Filter Style list** is unique to this effect. You can choose from four types of curves. The **Low-** and **High-Frequency Shelf** items are like the shelves in the other two plug-ins and create a flat adjustment of the signal below or above the selected **Cutoff frequency**, with a small rolloff. This rolloff is set with the Width slider, specifically the **Transition Width slider** in these two cases. The **Band-Pass filter** boosts everything outside of the selected **Center frequency** of the **Band Width** selected and can isolate and remove a sound. This filter, by default, produces a louder output because it boosts most of the frequencies. The **Band-Notch/Boost filter** works by isolating a specific frequency and then boosts the gain on that frequency alone, leaving the rest of the frequencies unchanged.

* ❋ The **graph** is simply a picture that represents the filter style and does not reflect any of the control settings.

* The **Accuracy list** adjusts the quality of the plug-in. Choosing higher quality requires your computer to work harder. Almost all newer machines (+700-MHz CPU) should use the High setting unless you have a particularly complex project with a lot of effects. Problems will only crop up during timeline playback of the project in real time. You should definitely choose the High setting whenever you render because the computer takes as much time as it needs to create the final output.

Pitch Shift

The ACID software handles pitch shifting very easily, automatically, and effectively (see Chapter 4), even without a dedicated plug-in effect. The advantages to using the Pitch Shift plug-in rather than the native timeline pitch shifting is that the plug-in gives you explicit control over how the shifting takes place. Here are its controls:

* **Semitones to Shift Pitch By** sets how much the effect shifts the pitch up or down. By default, the shifting also changes the duration of the media file, although events on the timeline or in the waveform will not reflect these changes. You can shift the pitch by +/−50 semitones (half-steps) when the duration is not preserved. (See the following discussion of Preserve Duration.) You can make smaller changes with the **Cents to Shift Pitch By slider**. Logically enough, there are 100 cents in a semitone, which also defines the range of this control.

* The **Accuracy list** simply adjusts the quality of the plug-in. Selecting higher quality requires your computer to work harder. This additional processing potentially only causes problems for timeline playback of the project in real time. You should definitely use High setting whenever you render because the computer will take as much time as it needs to create the final output. If you are experiencing problems with playback, you might want to use the High setting and render to a new track (from the Tools menu) and create a new media file with the Pitch Shift settings.

* Select the **Apply an Anti-Alias Filter during Pitch Shift option** to smooth out the effects of this filter when pitch shifting up, especially if you are using the Preserve Duration option. This filter requires more processing power and may deaden the sound a bit, but can be important in removing some annoying artifacts.

* Select the **Preserve Duration option** to keep the length of the media file the same as the original. This option requires quite a bit more computational power to do well and is not effective beyond +/−12 semitones (one octave). The Semitones slider label changes to reflect this limit. The **Mode list** allows you to select how the plug-in functions and what additional filters are applied. The only way to choose the correct mode is first to guess which one matches your requirements most closely and then listen and experiment.

❋ The bottom of the window has two labels that display information about the shift. The **Musical Equivalent** shows the name of the musical interval (for example, 12 semitones = one octave; see Chapter 4) in relation to the shift in semitones, while the **Transposition Ratio** shows the ratio of the actual frequency change (2.0000 is 2:1, or twice the original frequency).

❋ The initial time is always 00:01:00.000 because the ACID software cannot determine the duration of a media file from Windows. Because of this limitation, you need to enter the length of the file, which you can determine by right-clicking the file in the ACID Explorer window and selecting Properties. After you do so, the Final Time label accurately displays the change in duration of the file as it is used in the application. To use and view these features, you must not select the Preserve Duration option.

Resonant Filter

The Resonant Filter effect is a hybrid of an Equalization filter with a Flange/Wah-Wah. It lets you zero in on a target frequency and isolate it so that the periodic modulation of the effect is more accurate. This plug-in's effect is in many ways more precise than that of the Flange/Wah-Wah plug-in, but it is also not as flexible. This filter has a large number of fun and descriptive presets that you will enjoy playing with as you learn how the effect works. This is a truly awesome filter to use with FX Automation, sweeping the frequency across the band to produce deep flange effects. The plug-in's controls are as follows:

❋ Use the **Frequency slider** (20–20,000 Hz) with the **Filter Type radio buttons** to isolate the effects of this filter. The most obvious choice is to use the **Band Pass Filter type,** which lets the frequencies you have selected with the slider through to the effect. Selecting **Low Pass** lets everything below your selected frequency through, whereas **High Pass** lets everything above your selected frequency through to the effect.

❋ The **Resonance fader** (0.0–100.0 percent) simply sets the strength of the effect.

❋ The **Wet/Dry fader** (0.0–100.0 percent) controls the mix of the original signal with the processed signal.

❋ The **Filter Order** sets strength of the resonant output of the filter. (Order here refers to strength, not the chronology of the effect in a plug-in chain.) Fourth-Order sets the gain on the octaves twice as high as Second-Order.

One of the best ways to get a grip on this effect is to select the Band Pass option, set the Resonance fader all the way up, set ACID playback into loop mode, and then drag the Frequency slider up and down.

Reverb

Reverb is one of the most widely used effects and is a common control on everything from guitar amplifiers to mixing boards. The main goal of reverb is subtly to add a sense of space or depth to a recording. This is especially useful on recording done with close-miking techniques in a studio environment, which produce extremely clean recordings that are devoid of any background sounds or room characteristics. It is certainly easier to start with a clean recording than to have to clean it up later. Almost all of the commercially available loops are extremely clean, with the notable exception of many of the ambient, drone, and electronica music loops that have reverb as a part of the digital genre. Reverb, therefore, is particularly effective in making songs created in the ACID software sound more alive, with a more realistic sense of space.

Reverb is a delay-type effect and is similar in many ways to the Simple Delay and Multi-Tap Delay effects. You can immediately see from the plug-in window that Reverb has many more controls to adjust the delay subtly and potentially make it sound more natural. On the track level, you can use Reverb to bring a part out of the mix, although you should use it cautiously and with restraint.

Here are the controls for Reverb:

* The **Reverberation Mode list** is another set of presets that alter many background characteristics of the effect. None of the parameters that are modified by the selections on this list is available for manual adjustment in the plug-in window. The Preset list at the top of the window is a good place to start exploring pre-engineered settings for many of the other settings that you can adjust manually in this complex and important effect.

* The **Dry Out/Reverb Out fader** controls the mix of the original signal with the processed signal. Reverb Out is the main part of the effect and is heard as a delay or echo.

* The **Early Out fader** sets the gain for the first and fastest reflection or echo in the effect. You can hear it most clearly if you turn the Dry Out fader all the way down to –Inf.

* The **Early Reflection Style list** has 10 modes that allow you to set the bright and very quick reflection that occurs before the main reverb. Again, you can hear this most clearly by turning down the Dry Out and Reverb Out sliders.

* **Decay Time** defines how quickly the reverb fades out. It modifies only the reverb, not the Early Reflection. The Decay Time attribute can produce a sustained effect on notes that some real-world rooms produce acoustically.

* The **Pre-delay** determines the main reverb delay or echo and provides the first clue as to the size of the virtual space you are simulating. This slider also modifies only the reverb, not the early reflection.

❊ Select the **Attenuate Bass Freqs. Below option** to set a filter that diminishes everything below the frequency set with the corresponding slider. This control is similar to the low-shelf filter in the EQ plug-ins.

❊ Likewise, select the **Attenuate High Freqs. Above option** to set a filter for all frequencies above the one selected with the corresponding slider. This control is like the high-shelf filter in some of the EQ plug-ins. You should be careful when filtering the higher frequencies, because these are the exact frequencies that are most important to the spatial sense of a sound.

Although you probably want to use reverb on the Master bus at the end of a project to keep all of the tracks in the same virtual space, you might want to click the Solo button on one of the primary tracks and adjust the reverb while listening to it alone. Reverb is more clearly heard in solo instrument and voice parts. Before you settle on a final effect setting, you will need to fine-tune the reverb for the whole project.

Simple Delay

The Simple Delay effect is a variation of the Multi-Tap Delay and has exactly the same results, except that you are limited to only one delay or echo. (In the Pro version of the ACID software, the Simple Delay can also be synchronized with the tempo of a project, which is a powerful automatic feature not found in the Multi-Tap Delay effect.) The plug-in simulates the reflection of sound off of a surface and what it sounds like as it returns. The farther away the surface, the longer the delay before the return of the echo. By creating a delayed signal in this effect, you can create the illusion of perceived depth or simulate that the recording took place in a large room. This effect is not particularly subtle: Reverb is better suited to simulating smaller spaces more realistically. Even so, the Simple Delay effect can add some interesting ambience to a track or project. Adding this effect to a single, clear track is probably the best way to focus on the effects of this plug-in. Media files that contain solo instruments and voices with even brief moments of silence are good candidates. Keep in mind that adding a delay to a sax solo track in a song might sound very nice and can bring that part out of the mix more, but it is not very realistic to have one instrument playing in a large hall and the rest in a small studio. Try out a few of the presets to get you started with this (and any) plug-in.

Here are Simple Delay's controls:

❊ The **Dry Out** and **Delay Out faders** are usually used to mix the original signal with the processed signal, but it is a slightly different situation in this effect. With some FX (such as dynamics or equalization), you might want to turn the Dry fader all the way down to –Inf. for maximum effect. With this effect, you need to hear the Dry Out (original) signal; otherwise, the echo won't make any sense. Hearing only the echo and not the sound that caused it would be odd indeed. Usually, the Delay Out fader gain is lower than the Dry Out gain.

❋ You can set the **Delay Time** in terms of time or tempo. Set the **Time** of the delay in seconds. The greater the delay, the larger the virtual room size. In more basic versions of the ACID software, this is a simple slider control.

❋ Use **Tempo Sync Delay** check box to synchronize the delay with the actual tempo of the project. The tempo can be set in terms of beats, which you can assign to notes of any value. This feature is available only in the Pro version of the software.

❋ When the Multiple Delay box is selected, the **Decay Time options** become available. These control how quickly the echoes fade. Long decays make the simulated space sound more alive and bright, while shorter decays simulate a space where the walls absorb the sound more quickly (although the original echo is still strong). You can set the decay time in terms of time or tempo, just as you can the main delay. In more basic versions of the ACID program, this is a simple slider control.

❋ The **Multiple Delays (Feedback)** check box sets up the echoes to bounce repeatedly around the simulated space. This option can produce some very strange and interesting, if artificial, effects. The delay can continue well after the event on the timeline ends. The feedback of this effect is very different from that of the effects of the Multi-Tap Delay plug-in.

Calculating Rates

It is very useful to synchronize the Simple Delay effect with the tempo and beat of a project. See the section "Calculating Rates" in Chapter 7 for information about how to calculate and synchronize this effect with a project if you do not have the Pro version of the ACID software.

Smooth/Enhance

The Smooth/Enhance plug-in creates a very special equalization effect that is carefully tuned to eliminate (smooth) some of the artifacts caused by other processes and effects or by problems with the source audio. The other use is to brighten up (enhance) a track quickly, especially one that has been softened with any number of other effects. One example might be a track that you have compressed to make it a bit louder in a mix. Such compression can sometimes result in a flatter and less lively sound. Another notable example is when down-sampling. Down-sampling is the process of changing the sample rate from, for example, an audio CD at 44,100 Hz to a Web page–friendly 11,025 Hz. Samples are the discrete digital elements that make up a sound on a computer or audio CD, and the sample rate is measured in samples per second or Hertz (Hz). More samples per second yield a better quality, but also a larger, file. Sample rate is distinct from the bit depth, which is discussed along with the Dither plug-in.

The Smooth/Enhance plug-in has one simple Operation slider that controls the effect.

Time Stretch

Time Stretch is a sophisticated plug-in with many excellent presets that allow you to make a media file shorter or longer without pitch shifting it. Of course, there are limits to how much you should change a file's duration; the less you alter the time, the better the results you will get, although you'll be amazed at what you can get away with. Some types of audio, such as vocal tracks, do not stand up to the rigors of time stretching as well as other less familiar sounds. You can set the time stretch in terms of percentage, absolute time, or tempo. The Time Stretch plug-in's controls include the following:

* ❊ The **Mode drop-down list** is a preset list that targets specific applications of the plug-in. Several artifacts and problems can crop up when you alter the duration of a file, and you should first match the type of file you are stretching with some close approximation from the list. Then preview the results and select a different item from the list that looks like it might address the problem.

* ❊ The **Final Percentage slider** determines the stretching or shrinking, from 50 percent to 500 percent. You can also enter a value manually in the text box. You can also use this slider in terms of tempo or time (Final Tempo or Final Time) by changing the input format.

* ❊ Set the **Input format** to **Time** (*hr.mn.sc.xxx*) to specify a desired length of time for the final file and thus the amount of time stretching. The **Initial Time** and the **Final Time** are equivalent at first, because the plug-in is not stretching the media. Adjust the Final Time slider to set the stretching.

* ❊ You can also change the tempo of the file (as it appears in the ACID software) by selecting **Tempo (bpm)**. As with the Time option, you'll need to enter the both the **Initial Tempo** (the default initial tempo is always 120 BPM, but you can figure out the initial tempo from the Track Properties window) and the **Final Tempo**. This option is ideal when you need to match the tempo of a project with a file that doesn't have beat information or when a file just isn't sounding right in a project. In most cases, the ACID software automatically handles these adjustments very well, but you might need to try some of the Mode options with this plug-in if you are having problems.

You can also lengthen and shorten loops very quickly and easily using the Track Properties dialog to modify the beats and change the length of an event, although the Time Stretch FX gives you more flexibility. See Chapter 9 for more information.

> ❄ **WAVE MISMATCH**
> The waveform of events on tracks that have been time stretched will no longer match the audio output from the track. You can mix the track down to a new track to see the proper waveforms (and to free up processor cycles by not having to use the plug-in anymore).

Track Compressor

See the "Compressor (Track)" section earlier in this chapter and the discussion of compression in the mixing process at the end of Chapter 6.

Track EQ

Every track has its own default equalization plug-in that can be used to enhance the sound of an individual loop. To equalize a track:

1. Click the Solo button on the track to isolate it.

2. Click the Track FX button.

3. In the Audio Plug-In dialog, click the Track EQ button.

4. Without closing the Track EQ dialog, click the timeline to shift the application's focus to the timeline. You can also press Ctrl+spacebar at any time, from any window, to play back the timeline.

5. Press the spacebar to begin playback (or click the Play button on the Transport bar).

6. Go back to the Track EQ dialog and adjust the equalization. (See the following paragraph.)

The default Track EQ plug-in is more than adequate for most purposes. It is divided into four frequency bands: (1) Low Shelf, (2) Band 2, (3) Band 3, and (4) High Shelf. The easiest way to adjust the equalization is to drag the various band indicators on the graphic display (see Figure 8.11). Dragging a number up increases the gain, whereas dragging down decreases the gain. Dragging the number left and right changes the center frequency for Bands 2 and 3, and you can control the width of the band by adjusting the Bandwidth slider on Bands 2 and 3. The rolloff in Bands 1 and 4 sets the steepness for the rolloff curve. The number on the graphic display for these bands marks the beginning of the rolloff. Although the Track EQ plug-in is the default, any of Sony Media Software's EQ FX can be used at the track level. It would be redundant and of questionable value to use two or more EQ FX in the same FX chain.

Track Noise Gate

See the "Noise Gate" section and the discussion of gating in the mixing process in Chapter 6.

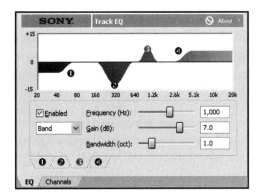

Figure 8.11
The basic Track EQ plug-in.

Vibrato

Vibrato is a technique used by musicians and singers to modulate or oscillate the pitch of a note between the original note and a slightly lower tone. Artists use vibrato to embellish and make a note more expressive. Vibrato is distinct from tremolo, which is a modulation based on a change in loudness (amplitude). The effect is probably best used on individual tracks (such as an organ solo), not at the project level.

The Vibrato plug-in's controls are as follows:

❄ The **Output gain** sets the volume of the processed effect.

❄ The **Semitones fader** sets the range or resolution of the graph, which sets the possible range of the effect. It does not determine the actual range of the vibrato, however. As you drag the fader up and down, watch the labels at the top and bottom of the graph. After an envelope (as discussed in the following description of the graph control) has been drawn on the graph, it does not change shape in relation to the graph, but its range changes as you adjust the Semitone fader.

❄ The **graph** is where you draw the curve of the vibrato over the period of time set with the Modulation Freq. slider. Initially, the envelope line runs from 0 to 0 across the center and is hard to see. Click and drag the centerline to add a node and reposition it. You can delete nodes by double-clicking or right-clicking them. Explore a few of the presets to get an idea of the graph's purposes. Nodes dragged above the centerline increase the pitch, and nodes dragged below the line decrease the pitch.

❄ You can select the **Blend Graph Edges option** if the start and end nodes on the graph do not line up.

❄ The **Modulation Freq.** sets the rate or speed of the vibrato in cycles per second or Hertz. See the "Rate and Hertz (Hz)" section in Chapter 7 for a more detailed explanation.

Although it can be fairly time-consuming, you can add vibrato to individual notes in an event by using Vibrato as an Assignable FX. Assign a track to the FX bus and then use envelopes to isolate and apply Vibrato to each note you want to effect. Singers often use vibrato to emphasize particular notes, and you can use the Vibrato effect almost in the same way.

Calculating Rates

It is very useful to synchronize the Vibrato effect with the tempo and beat of a project. Vibrato is a faster-period effect that might occur on the beat or even multiple times for each beat. See the "Calculating Rates" section in Chapter 7 for information about how to calculate and synchronize this effect with a project.

Chapter 8 Quiz

1. The Amplitude Modulation plug-in varies the volume of a signal over time. (T/F)

2. Which parameter is not part of the Chorus plug-in?

   A. Tempo Sync

   B. Mod. Freq.

   C. Modulation Rate

   D. Feedback

3. Dither smoothes out rough edges in digital media. (T/F)

4. The Compressor (Track) adjusts the volume of a track:

   A. Absolutely

   B. Softly

   C. Dynamically

   D. None of the above

5. The Gapper/Snipper inserts silence or cuts material periodically. (T/F)

6. You will want to use multiple EQs on the same track. (T/F)

7. Which of the following are parameters included in the Graphic Dynamics plug-in?

   A. Sync Stereo Gain

   B. Auto Gain Compensation

   C. Threshold

   D. All of the above

8. Multi-band compression allows you to compress specific frequencies. (T/F)

9. The Multi-Tap Delay has a maximum of how many taps?

    A. 8

    B. 7

    C. 6

    D. 5

10. Reverb is used to create a sense of space in a recording. (T/F)

9 Loops

Up until this point, we've used the word "loop" in a very general and rather lazy way, referring to any audio file in Sony Media Software's ACID® software as a loop. A loop was originally a physical loop of audiotape that had the two ends spliced together to create an infinitely repeating audio clip. In much the same way, the archetypal loop file on a computer is a short file that plays back seamlessly end to end. Most commercial loop files are designed to work this way. But the definition has definitely expanded to include material that will not endlessly and seamlessly loop, and many "loops" don't actually loop. After all, we still "dial" telephone numbers, so this isn't really such an unusual link in linguistic evolution.

ACID loops are more than they might seem at first glance. As you've probably noticed by now, an amazingly large variety of loops are available for many different genres, and they sound pretty good together when mixed in the ACID software straight out of the box. This compatibility isn't because the audio files were carefully recorded to match one another, but is instead the result of background beatmatching and pitch adjustments. This chapter will reveal all of the many facets of loops—from Sony Media Software, from other commercial loop libraries, and from your own creative talents.

Media Files and Clips

There are three broad types of media files that you can use in the ACID software: audio files, MIDI files, and video files. Although all three might have an audio component to them, only audio files can truly be considered to be proper loops. MIDI files are not composed of actual audio data, but instead contain instructions to tell your computer how to create sound. A MIDI event may very well loop, but that's not what we're going to discuss here. Video files may contain an audio track and, although you can use only the video portion of one video track in a project at a time, you can use the audio part of a movie file just like any other audio file. Theoretically, the audio portion of the file could even loop and work like any other loop in the software.

Media files are simply files on your computer that contain audio or video content. Within the ACID program, media files are often referred to as *clips*. Of course, the origin of the word "clip" is itself one that comes from the ancient analog world of tape recorders and razorblades.

Clip Types

The different media categories behave differently when we start inserting clips into the timeline. Video clips go into a single video track. MIDI clips go into MIDI tracks. Audio clips go into audio tracks. Audio clips, however, can be further subdivided into three subcategories of clip types: Loop, One-Shot, and Beatmapped. You can recognize each of the three types of tracks with a glance at the Track Header, which contains an icon identifying the ACID Type, as shown in Figure 9.1. The three audio clip types are each easily identified by icons in the upper-left part of any events inserted into the timeline (also as seen in Figure 9.1).

Figure 9.1

The three various types of tracks in the ACID software and three audio events with iconic markers indicating Loop, One-Shot, and Beatmapped loops.

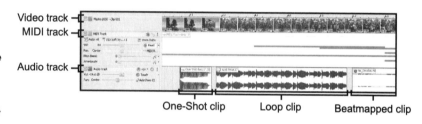

Video track
MIDI track
Audio track

One-Shot clip　　Loop clip　　Beatmapped clip

❄ **CLIP TYPE = ACID TYPE**

The type of clip—Loop, One-Shot, or Beatmapped—can be changed using an interface item labeled "ACID Type" in the Clip Properties dialog. Therefore, the generic "clip type" is equivalent to "ACID Type" in the context of this book.

Audio Loops

Video files are obviously not proper loops, so we won't call them that here. As an important media component of the ACID software, we have a chapter devoted to video later. We also aren't going to be talking about MIDI in this chapter, although you can certainly design short MIDI files that act much like audio loops. Instead, the rest of this chapter is going to discuss audio files, which might informally all be called loops, whether they loop or not. The most popular format for audio files used as loops on Windows machines is the Windows *.wav file format. To Windows or another audio application, the *.wav files that go into an ACID project all look the same. That is, although the software has three different types of audio clips, Windows sees these as all the same. The special ACIDized information in the header of these audio files is simply ignored by most Windows applications. The information that the ACID software uses to separate these types is proprietary to the application, although the popularity of the program means that other programs might also use this information. Even Apple's GarageBand can read and use ACID loops.

ACID Loops

So what makes a loop an ACID loop? ACID loops are simply audio files, available from Sony Media Software and many other vendors, that have had beat, pitch, and tempo information added to them. As mentioned, this information is only useful to the ACID software and compatible applications. Information about a media file as it pertains to the software can be found in the ACID Explorer window, in the Clip Properties window, and in the Media Manager, as shown in Figure 9.2.

Do not construe the previous discussion to mean that you cannot use another company's loop files and libraries in the ACID program. You can use almost any audio file in any of a large number of popular formats in the ACID software. These files will not necessarily have the beat, pitch, or tempo information inherent in an ACID loop, so the software will not automatically adjust them to match the project, but they will certainly work as well as any other audio file. In fact, ACIDized loops might be a characteristic to look for when you are shopping for additions to your loop library. Even if an audio file does not have ACID information in it, you can make the ACID application take a guess as to tempo and beat information, and it will frequently get it right. The program cannot detect pitch information, however. You can add all of this information manually, as you'll find out later in this chapter.

Because the tempo, beat, and pitch ACID properties of a clip are not an inherent part of the clip itself, you can change and edit that information in the Clip Properties window. To view the Clip Properties window, from the View menu, select Clip Properties or press Ctrl+Alt+3. To see a specific clip's properties, click a clip when the window is open. The Clip Properties window displays, and lets you change, the type of clip information for that media file. Again, keep in mind that this does not actually affect any of the data in the media file. Just because you change the root note of a clip does not mean you actually change the pitch of the media file in any applications outside of the ACID software.

RIGHT-CLICK > CLIP PROPERTIES
I usually get to the Clip Properties window by right-clicking an event on the timeline (or in the Clip Pool) and selecting Clip Properties. Actually, I get to a lot of features with a right-click: It's always worth a try!

Loops

Now we get to the most specific and proper definition of a loop in the ACID software. Most (but not all) loops are fairly short, with durations measured in seconds, and are designed to repeat, often seamlessly. You can identify Loop clips by the loop icon in the upper-left part of a loop event on the timeline.

Figure 9.2

Information about a media file (type, duration, tempo, sample rate, bit depth, channels, and compression) can be found in the Explorer window, the Media Manager, and the Clip Properties window.

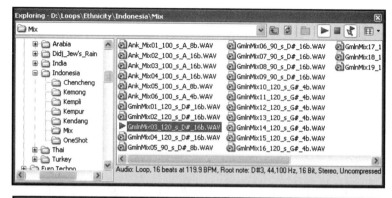

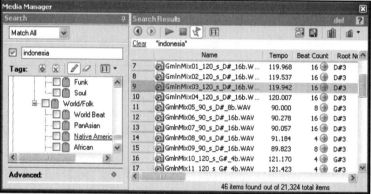

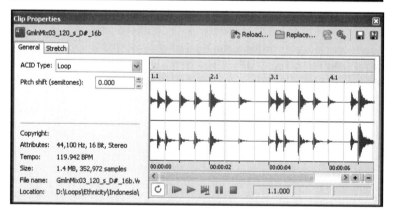

Loop clips and the Sony Media Software media files that they contain have beat, pitch, tempo, and type information saved with the file. The ACID software assumes that any audio file shorter than about 30 seconds long is a loop and inserts it as a Loop clip, with the program taking its best guess about the beats and tempo. Pitch information will not be included, although pitch is an important aspect of a Loop clip because these clips can be pitch shifted automatically or manually. The Stretch tab in the Clip Properties dialog controls this information. Although most loop files contain pitch information, such information is not really necessary for loops that are not primarily tonal, such as drum and percussion parts. Most percussion loops are inserted as Loop clips and can have pitch information added, but do not have a root note selected on the Stretch tab by default.

One of the most obvious aspects of a loop is the fact that it can repeat over and over. You can identify this looping on the timeline by the notches in an event that mark each repetition. When the ACID Type of a loop is changed to something else (e.g., One-Shot), the ACID software no longer automatically repeats the media file in the event in a looping manner with notched events (see Figure 9.3).

For commercial loops from Sony Media Software, a small bit of information is saved with the media file that tells the ACID software what type of loop the file is and, therefore the ACID Type that should be used. For media files that do not have this information, the program follows a few default rules:

❊ Files with durations less than 0.5 seconds are inserted as One-Shot clips.

❊ Files with durations greater than 0.5 seconds, but less than 30 seconds, are inserted as Loop clips.

❊ Files with durations greater than 30 seconds can be inserted as Beatmapped clips.

To change this behavior, select Preferences from the Options menu, and, on the Audio tab, change the Open Files as Loops if Between (Seconds) item.

One-Shots

One-Shots are nonlooping files that are not intended to be looped repeatedly, primarily because the end of the file does not blend seamlessly back into the beginning of the file. A One-Shot might be a spoken-word vocal performance, an instrumental solo, or a single snare drum beat, for example. As you can see from the Clip Properties window, One-Shots do not have a Stretch tab, and the ACID software does not adjust them to match the key of a project. This can be especially important with vocal performances that might sound bizarre if pitch shifted too much or with the audio part of a video file, in which you might need to synchronize the audio and video. One-Shot clips do not change pitch or key as the project changes key either. When you record a solo part into an ACID project that changes key with key markers, you respond to the key changes. That performance is inserted into the software as a One-Shot, so your original performance changes key as you played it, but does not change key according to the key markers in the project.

Again, the type of track into which the file is inserted is not an inherent part of the Windows *.wav file format, but is instead a part of ACID loop files. You can change One-Shot clips into Loop clips by selecting Loop from the ACID Type list. This selection changes how the ACID software treats the original media file in the current project, but does not alter the file on your hard disk. By changing the ACID Type to Loop, you can add pitch information to the track (by selecting a root note on the Stretch tab) so that a One-Shot can respond to key changes in a project.

❄ **DROP ONE-SHOTS ON THE FLY**

You can lay down One-Shot clips on the fly as the ACID software plays your project back. First, copy the One-Shot to the Clipboard (right-click it and select Copy or press Ctrl+C). Then play your project and press Shift+Y to drop events at the Play cursor (Paste at Play Cursor command on the Edit menu, although that is hard to execute on the fly).

Finally, events created from One-Shot clips do not loop. To repeat a One-Shot over and over, you need to create multiple individual events, because each event in a One-Shot clip contains only one occurrence of a media file. Changing the ACID Type between Loop and One-Shot does more than just change how events occur in a track, because it also alters whether tempo information is used. When you insert a One-Shot clip into a project, the ACID application ignores the tempo information and plays back the media file at the rate inherent in the media file without modification. When you change the ACID Type to Loop, the software uses the tempo information and the duration of the media file in the project changes. In Figure 9.3, the top track has a One-Shot clip that is exactly the same duration as the original media file. The bottom track in the figure has a clip created from the same file, but the Clip Properties were changed to Loop. You can see the loop point where the clip repeats and starts again. You can also see that the single occurrence of the media file in the One-Shot clip is considerably longer than a single repetition in the Loop clip, which indicates that the file is played back much more quickly. This can result in distortion, although the program does its best to prevent this.

Figure 9.3

The same media file inserted into a track as a One-Shot clip (top) and inserted as a Loop clip.

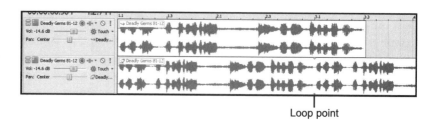

Loop point

Beatmapped Clips

Beatmapped clips are usually much longer media files, perhaps tens of seconds or even minutes long. These files might even be entire songs that have beat and tempo characteristics. The word *beatmapping* comes from the technique DJs use when mixing two songs seamlessly together. They need to match the beat of an outgoing song to an incoming one in a process known as *beatmatching.* To mix two songs together in a truly seamless way, a DJ also needs both songs to be playing at the same tempo (speed). Obviously, songs are recorded at many different tempos, so special turntables (and now CD players and software) are used that can adjust the speed of playback. The DJ then monitors the mix through headphones (the audience cannot hear this) and matches the beat of the new song with that of the currently playing tune. Once this is done, the DJ can make a perfect transition by gradually fading one song out while fading the other in. Beatmatching during a live mix is not nearly as easy as it sounds and takes quite a bit of practice.

Beatmapping in the ACID software serves a similar purpose, but it is much easier. You can easily insert entire songs into the program and synchronize them to a project's tempo and beat if they are beatmapped. Most song-length media files are probably either *.mp3 files on your computer or perhaps media files that you have recorded for yourself in a *.wav format, so you will need to do almost all of the beatmapping yourself when you insert the media file in a project. When you insert a longer file into the ACID software, the Beatmapper Wizard automatically opens to guide you through the process of beatmapping the media file as it occurs in the project. To start the Beatmapper Wizard, simply insert a longer media file into an ACID project. You can override this automatic behavior by deselecting the Automatically Start the Beatmapper Wizard for Long Files option in the first page of the Wizard. By default, files that are less than 30 seconds long are opened as loops. To change this behavior, select Preferences from the Options menu and, on the Audio tab, change the Open Files as Loops if Between (Seconds) item. This item sets a range, with files longer than the range being opened as Beatmapped and files shorter than the range (0.5 seconds) being opened as One-Shots (typically a single drum beat). You can also start the Beatmapper Wizard manually by clicking the Beatmapper Wizard button on the Stretch tab in the Clip Properties window for Beatmap-type clips. If a longer file is initially inserted into a One-Shot clip, you need to change it to a Beatmapped clip to use the Beatmapper Wizard. To use the Beatmapper Wizard:

1. Step 1 in the Wizard is to determine the first downbeat. A downbeat can be the "one" as you count through a song: one, two, three, four. The ACID software takes its best guess based on short, sharp peaks in the waveform, which usually indicate percussion parts. The first downbeat is labeled with a timeline cursor in the dialog tagged Downbeat. Use the Play button to verify that this is the first downbeat and drag the Downbeat marker to change the position if it is not. The marker and cursor position should be aligned with the very beginning of the first beat. If the song fades in or has some type of introduction that makes it difficult to find the first downbeat, move the Downbeat marker farther in on the song to the earliest place where the beat is clear. The first downbeat is used to determine the beginning of the media file in events, so moving this marker trims all material before the first downbeat. You can move the first downbeat back to the beginning of the song in Step 3 if you need to correct this. Use the Zoom In and Out buttons (+ and −) on the scroll bar to increase the accuracy of your adjustments. Click the Next button when you are finished. You can also

adjust the first downbeat in the Stretch tab of the Clip Properties window. Click the Next button to move to Step 2.

2. Step 2 sets the tempo by guessing the length of a single measure. The loop region at the top of the dialog is the ACID software's estimate of one measure. Click the Play button to listen to the measure. The metronome is very useful, and you should listen to see whether it counts out the one, two, three, four of the song. You can also use the waveform and metronome beat lines to check whether the measure is lined up correctly. Dragging the left edge of the loop region moves the initial downbeat's location and lengthens the measure. Dragging the right edge of the loop region only lengthens the measure. As the measure is shortened or lengthened, the beats, which evenly divide the measure, also move. Click the Next button to move to Step 3.

3. Step 3 allows you manually to make any final adjustments as the single measure in Step 2 is extrapolated to beatmap the entire song. Initially, the dialog highlights the single measure isolated in Step 2, and that measure continues to serve as a loop region. Any inaccuracies will become more obvious over time and result in a drift away from the correct tempo. Use the Measure slider to move to and inspect other measures in the song. The beginning of each measure is marked with an orange marker, which you can drag to correct errors. Dragging one marker repositions all markers in the song and cannot be used to compensate for variation in individual measures caused by tempo variations or beats. The first downbeat in a measure is audibly indicated by a higher-toned metronome beat. It is not practical or necessarily useful to check every single measure; use the slider to examine a few measures here and there along the entire duration of the file. Click the Next button to move to the last step. You can also change the position of the measure markers in the Stretch tab of the Clip Properties window.

4. In the last page of the Wizard, you have three options. Click the Finish button after you have selected the options you want to use:

   ※ The Change the Project Tempo to Match the Beatmapped Clip option automatically adjusts the project's tempo after you click the Next button. This is a good idea if the Beatmapped media file is a major or important part of your project and prevents the file from being distorted by being stretched.

   ※ The Preserve Pitch of Beatmapped Clip When Tempo Changes option is related to the previous option. When the project's tempo is different from the tempo of the Beatmapped file or when the tempo changes in the project, this item prevents the pitch of the file from changing.

   ※ Select the Save Beatmapper Information with File option to add a small amount of data to the file and allow it to be used in other ACID projects as a Beatmapped file. If you do not select this option, the media file is beatmapped only in the current project. Clicking the Save button in the Clip Properties window does the same thing.

Outside of the Beatmapper Wizard (see Figure 9.4), the beatmapping of a media file (as it is inserted into a track) can be adjusted in the Clip Properties window on the Stretch tab. You can adjust the first downbeat and individual measures while you are playing back the main project to align the media in the Beatmapped clip with the project. Use a simple drumbeat to compare the project tempo and beat with the Beatmapped clip, because this window does not include a metronome. There is, however, a metronome in the ACID software that can help.

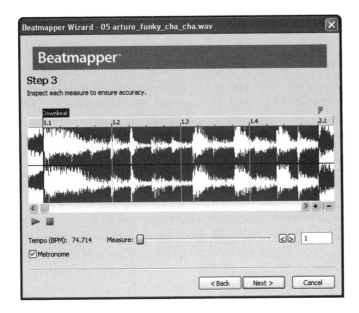

Figure 9.4
The Beatmapper Wizard automatically sets up the tempo and beat of a file that you can modify manually in the Clip Properties window.

Using much longer media files in a project is a special use of the ACID application that must be carefully considered. Perhaps the most obvious use for longer media files is to create your own mix sets, using the software to beatmap and then mix songs together to form a continuous mix set. This is not what the software is really good at, but it can be done and it can be done very well. Because the ACID program is an original, loop-based composition tool, the use of longer copyrighted material presents a problem—if not a legal one, then at least an ethical one. However, unless you are making big money, this problem probably isn't a pragmatic concern. When you buy a commercial loop library, you are also buying a license to use these loops in your own projects. When you sample your own loops from other artists' songs, you almost certainly do not have the legal right to use this material in commercial productions. Sampling a beat or riff of short duration is usually not a problem, but the longer the sample, the bigger the problem. There is no set duration (for example, 10 seconds is fine but 11 seconds is too long), and use may also be based on distinctiveness of the sound. One common misconception is that if you cite the original artist in your credits, then it is legal. While this might be flattering and might keep you out of trouble with the original artist if he takes it that way, it is also a clear admission of guilt. You obviously knew the clip was copyrighted or you wouldn't have cited the original performer.

Another potential use for longer media files inserted into Beatmapped clips is to use the file as a template for your own project. This is not a bad idea, especially when you are getting used to the concepts of song structure and composition. Take a song you like, insert it into the ACID software, and then mark out the structure of the song using markers (such as Intro, Verse 1, Refrain, Break, and so on) and use that as an outline for your own piece. There is nothing wrong and no shame in copying the structure from a songwriter you respect.

※ **LOAD IT IN RAM**

Loop clips (and media files) are loaded into your computer's active memory (*random access memory*, or *RAM*) from your hard disk drive (HDD) when inserted into a project. One-Shot and Beatmapped clips are not. If you change a large (long) One-Shot or Beatmapped clip into a Loop clip, it might take up significant amounts of RAM and can hurt performance.

Finally, you may want to use beatmapping when inserting longer original media files that you have recorded in your studio. Of course, this avoids all legal and ethical issues you might otherwise face, but it can also be less of a technical issue in the ACID software as well. If you want to use media that you have recorded in the distant past, long before you purchased the software, you can beatmap the file as previously outlined. Otherwise, all tracks that are recorded into the application are automatically beatmapped and saved with tempo information by default. These files are not saved with pitch information and, as with all Beatmapped clips, will not change key as the project does. If you set the root note in the Stretch tab of the Clip Properties window to something other than Don't Transpose, it will change key along with the project. You can change the default ACID Type for recorded files from Beatmapped to One-Shot or Loop on the Audio tab in the Preferences dialog.

Clip Properties

As mentioned in the previous section, loop files from Sony Media Software (or any audio files that are compatible with the ACID software) have some information about pitch, beat, and tempo saved with the file. This information becomes relevant when you use the loop in a track in an ACID project. Although you can change both the loop's properties and its associated track's properties independently, changes to a loop's properties are permanent and are saved to the media file on your hard disk, whereas changes to a track's properties are saved only to the current project.

Many of a loop's properties are displayed in the Explorer window in the Summary view area (click the View button to view or hide this feature) when a media file is selected (see Figure 9.2).

Modifying Existing Loops

You can modify the properties of a loop as it occurs in the ACID software through the Clip Properties window. To view a loop's properties after inserting it into a project (track), select Clip Properties from the View menu. Click on a track to change the focus of the program to that track and view its properties in the Clip Properties window. Although a clip's initial properties are inherited from the information saved with the media file, the clip is still independent and can be changed. The specific properties that are available depend on the clip type, as previously discussed. MIDI and video files do not have counterparts that are compatible with the program. MIDI and video tracks are discussed in their own chapters.

SAVE THOSE PROPERTIES

The Save File button at the top of the Clip Properties window saves any changes in a loop's properties to the media file on your computer. These properties are only informational and do not change the audio data of the media file. They are analogous to a caption on a picture. You can also save a new version of the file with the new information by clicking the Save File As button.

The top of the Clip Properties window has six buttons. The Reload button copies the media file back into the project from your hard disk and allows you to discard any changes you have made to the loop's properties. You can think of this as a type of reset button. The second button is the Replace button. This is useful if you have created a track that has been carefully adjusted with audio FX and envelopes, but you want to change the particular media file that is being used in that track. Click the Replace button and then browse for the new file that you want to use. This can be especially useful when you want to duplicate a key change sequence (pitch shifting events) with a different instrument. First, duplicate the track and then replace the media file associated with it. The Edit button enables you to open and edit the project from which the file was originally created. This is only available if the file was originally rendered using the Save Project as Path Reference in Rendered Media option in the Render As dialog. The next button is the Groove Pool button, which was covered in Chapter 7.

The last two buttons are the Save File and Save File As buttons, which are used to save the loop's properties to the media file on your hard disk. This information does not alter any of the audio data in the media file and is useful only in the ACID software and compatible applications. The information that can be saved to a file or changed includes everything that can be altered in the Clip Properties window. This information is saved in the header portion of a media file and not in any of the areas that contain actual audio data.

General Tab

The General tab in the Clip Properties window serves a number of basic purposes: It sets the ACID Type, displays the loop's properties, and allows you to add media file–level markers and regions (see Figure 9.5).

Figure 9.5
The General tab determines the ACID Type and has a timeline similar to the main timeline in the ACID software.

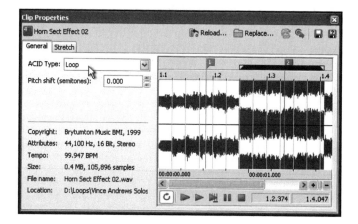

The General tab's controls include the following:

* **ACID Type** sets the type of the track for audio files: Loop, One-Shot, or Beatmapped. Video tracks and MIDI tracks cannot be changed.

* **Pitch Shift** sets the change in key or pitch of the entire track. You can adjust this parameter by pressing the + and − keys on the number pad on your keyboard after first clicking on the Track Header of a track.

* **Preserve Pitch When Stretching** (available for Beatmapped clips only) tells the ACID software to make sure the pitch of a Beatmapped media file does not change when the project's tempo is different from the media file's tempo, which causes stretching and potential distortion. You must select this option to access the Pitch Shift control in a Beatmapped clip.

* **Mode** (Beatmapped clips only) determines how the pitch is preserved when stretching. Select one of the presets from the drop-down list that most closely matches your source audio.

* **Summary of Properties** displays some of the properties of the media file.

* **Transport Controls** allow you to play back the media file. The Loop button repeats the loop region over and over.

* **Timeline** is very similar to the timeline in the main program workspace. You can add markers and regions to a media file that will be saved with the file when you click the Save button at the top of the Clip Properties window. Again, this control doesn't change the actual audio

data. See Chapter 3, "Composition," for more information on using markers and regions in the ACID application.

Stretch Tab

The Stretch tab controls how a media file (or a part of it) is stretched (or compressed) in time to accommodate a project's tempo. One-Shot clips and files do not have this tab because it is generally a bad idea to stretch One-Shot media, but this tab provides a lot of information for Loop and Beatmapped clips.

Root Note

The root note is the key of a loop. You can change the root note on the Stretch tab in the Clip Properties window of Loop and Beatmapped clips. The root note allows a track to be automatically pitch shifted to match a project's key or to follow key changes that occur in a project as a result of key change markers. Setting the root note to Don't Transpose prevents this automatic pitch shift. Any time you want to protect a loop from key changes, you should select Don't Transpose. You'll notice that most percussion and drum loops, as well as some vocal and spoken-word loops, have Don't Transpose set for a root note.

Another place where you will most likely want to use a root note of Don't Transpose is for your own recorded material, which is automatically inserted into Beatmapped clips. When you record parts into a song with key changes, your performance changes key to match the song. If you then further modified this performance by adding key change markers in the ACID software, the file will not match the original recording. This is why tracks that you record in the program do not have key or pitch information saved with them.

Stretch Tab - Loops

The Stretch tab for Loop clips and files sets how the ACID software adjusts the loop when in a project. It controls the tempo and where the beats fall. For loop files, the software stretches and compresses smaller subdivisions in the file to force the beat to match the project. This means that the playback of a loop file may vary over time. The tab includes the following controls:

❋ **Number of Beats** is based on how many beats are in the media file, which in turn is based the number of beats in a measure times the number of measures in the file. Most commercial loops are based on four beats in a measure, so most loops have 4, 8, 12, or 16 beats. This property is critical in determining how the loop matches the tempo of a project. Try changing the tempo on a melodic commercial loop that already has a Number of Beats property. If the original number of beats is 8 and you change it to 16, the loop plays back at half its normal speed. Changing the number of beats to 4 doubles its speed. Although you usually want to leave the number of beats at its default value, sometimes you can record a loop in a different time signature (such as 6/8) to fit in an ACID project that is in 4/4. (See Chapter 3 for more information.) Doubling the speed temporarily is a good transition technique between sections of a song.

✳ **Stretching Method** determines how the media file is stretched to fit the beat and tempo of a project. You can choose from three different methods, each of which is suited to a different purpose. When a track is distorted because of too much stretching or compression, experiment by trying all three methods to try to solve the problem. The default method, **Looping Segments**, is a good general-purpose choice for most types of loops. **Nonlooping Segments** is better for longer and smoother audio files, such as pads and ambient background loops. **Pitch Shift Segments** allows the audio to be pitch shifted as it is stretched. This can prevent artificial-sounding artifacts, echoes, and flanging-type noises associated with stretching, but the event may fall out of tune with the rest of the project.

✳ **Transient Sensitivity** sets up how many beat and stretch markers are positioned on the timeline. A higher percentage means more markers, which gives you more control over stretching and grooving, but also adds complexity to the project.

✳ **Timing Tightness** lets you fine-tune how the ACID software matches the beats in the file to the beats in the project. For example, set the divisions to quarter notes and move the beat markers on the timeline to every beat in a 4/4 loop. By default, the beat markers are spaced equidistant. Of course, the beat in a project is evenly divided, so by changing the beat markers on a loop, you cause the application automatically to stretch the segment of the loop between the two beats to match the project. Sixty-fourth notes give you the greatest degree of control.

✳ **Stretch Spacing** determines the accuracy of the orange stretch markers at the bottom of the timeline. Select Whole Notes from the drop-down to get a few stretch markers. Sixty-fourth-note triplets adds a whole bunch more markers. Again, this won't affect the groove, but it will give you more control.

✳ **Transport Controls** control playback and looping, just like any other ACID Transport controls. You might notice an unusual play button here: Play Quantized. This play button stretches individual beats to match a groove, as defined by the stretching you perform in this dialog with the various markers.

✳ **Timeline** has markers on the top and bottom. The top-most blue markers are beat anchors. The green markers at the top are beat markers, which can be repositioned relative to the beat anchors by dragging them. The orange markers at the bottom are stretch markers. Double-click a stretch marker to move it away from the green beat. Right-click the Marker bar and select Reset All to undo all of your changes.

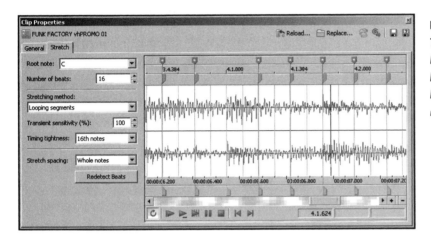

The orange stretch markers are very important in fine-tuning stretching in the ACID software (see Figure 9.6) relative to the green beat markers at the top of the timeline and relative to the blue beat anchors. The ACID software does not simply stretch a media file uniformly, but instead uses these beat markers as reference points and attempts to line these up with the beat of a project. Save any changes you make to these markers by clicking the Save File or Save File As button at the top of the Clip Properties window.

Figure 9.6
The Stretch tab of the Clip Properties window for a loop file. Zoom in to get a better look at the various markers.

Stretch Tab - Beatmapped

The Stretch tab for Beatmapped clips provides a manual way to modify the characteristics that you can set using the Beatmapper Wizard (see Figure 9.4). The controls include the following:

- ❋ **Original Tempo** sets the tempo of the loop as it was recorded or as you set it in the Beatmapper Wizard. Increasing this value speeds up the media file, whereas decreasing this value slows down the loop as it occurs in a project. Notice that changing the tempo value also has the effect of changing the relative spacing of all the measure markers on the timeline.

- ❋ **Downbeat Offset** is a numerical representation of the position of the first Downbeat marker. You can drag the Downbeat marker to reposition it or you can enter a number in the box.

- ❋ **Beatmapper Wizard** button starts the Beatmapper Wizard as previously described.

- ❋ **Transport Controls** control the playback of the media file.

- ❋ **Timeline** sets the orange markers that divide measures in the loop. Dragging any of the measure markers resizes all the measure divisions in the media file. This can have the effect of changing the speed of the file in a project, just as changing the Original Tempo does. In fact, the tempo changes as you drag these markers, and vice versa. The Downbeat marker sets the first downbeat and sets where in a media file an event will start.

Creating Your Own Loops

Literally hundreds of gigabytes of loops are available in professional loop libraries from Sony Media Software and other companies. The quality of these loops is typically very high and the variety is immense. Still, nothing is better than creating your own loops. The source for these loops could be your own vocal or instrumental recordings (see Chapter 6, "Mastering the Mix"), or you could record audio samples from just about any source. Some excellent sources are audio CDs, movies, television shows, or politicians from the nightly news. Beats, bass lines, main instrumental refrains, and even solos can make for interesting source material. The samples can be radically split and mixed into completely new forms or distorted beyond recognition with audio effects plug-ins. Rap, hip-hop, and electronica have been major users of sampled material and are good places to find examples of the effective use of samples in music. Perhaps the most interesting result of using popular music for samples is that the new song also has a very familiar feel to it, yet is completely different. This is often the most surprising and interesting when the samples come from one genre (jazz or classical) and are then used in another (trip-hop or drum and bass). Remember the television game show *Name That Tune*? You'd be surprised how short of a sample you can use to create an instantly recognizable riff. Perhaps the most recognizable sample ever is a single "ha" from Mr. James Brown.

Legal and Ethical Issues

This book is not a legal tome and doesn't pretend to offer any advice on whether sampling loops from your CDs is legal. Our opinion is that sampled material of a short duration is probably okay to use without getting explicit permission from the artist. As a matter of fact, copyright is the only right in the body of the United States Constitution itself and is very clearly designed to both protect the author and to encourage creative derivatives "[t]o promote the progress of science and useful art." The Constitution does this through granting a copyright "for limited times." Whether our ACID songs are "useful arts" is something we could debate.

❋ **THE LAW OF THE LAND**
U.S. Constitution, Article I, Section 7:

"To promote the progress of science and useful arts, by securing for limited times to authors and inventors the exclusive right to their respective writings and discoveries."

Fair use is a concept pretty well defined through legal precedent and statutes (but not in the Constitution) for printed material, but is widely misunderstood in common parlance. Fair use describes how much material you can quote in printed material and for what purposes. For news stories and research, this concept is important, but does fair use apply to fiction? Poetry? You can see that the issue becomes more complex when you talk about art. In music, fair use depends on a number of gray areas: uniqueness of the sample, originality of your piece, citation of work sampled, where your work will be used, fame of the sampled artist, and genre. Using material for educational or illustrative purposes is also permitted. As a rule, however, the law is simple: Everything is copyrighted and, unless you have a specific right to copy, you cannot use another person's material. Not an hour of it, not a minute of it, and not even a second of it.

The modern world has gotten really crazy, however. Not only has the definition of "limited time" been stretched many decades, but even thinking about using a sample is probably against the law according to the DMCA (*Digital Millennium Copyright Act*). Furthermore, the MPAA (*Motion Picture Association of America*), the RIAA (*Recording Industry and Artists of America*), and, most importantly, the FBI (*Federal Bureau of Investigation*) are getting serious in their antipiracy campaign. They are not primarily concerned with ACID artists and sampling, but legally, they could be. Whether you make money commercially is completely irrelevant to the law, but, pragmatically speaking, whether you get sued largely depends on whether you are worth suing.

Another question to ask: Is the sample so unique that it is a signature of the artist? You would be wise not to try to sell a commercial song using Intel's ubiquitous four tones, even though they only last a second. This is a branded and explicitly copyrighted sound, and you'll have cease-and-desist e-mail before your AMD Athlon CPU gets to its next clock cycle. Likewise, many products and artists have very unique and distinctive trademarks (registered or not) that are sure to invite trouble if used in your music. This isn't even copyright territory, but it is about corporate branding and identity. The concept of originality is another gray area. A song that is 50 percent a single sample is clearly not original, yet legislating a percentage, much less measuring that percentage, is not feasible.

As with publishing an article, citation is important and is certainly ethical. Make sure you credit the source of your samples: artist, song, composer, and album. Credits and attributions can be in the liner notes of a CD, posted with the song on ACIDplanet, or saved in the header data area of the song in a few formats, such as *.mp3, *.rm, and *.wma. All three formats allow you to save extended information about a song with the file. In the ACID software, select Render As from the File menu and choose one of these formats. Then, in the Render As dialog, click the Custom button. Click the Summary tab (*.rm and *.wma) or the ID3 tab (*.mp3) and enter any information you need to credit properly in the Copyright or Comments tab of any samples used. Again, citation is not a legal issue, but an ethical one. Simply crediting your sources will not protect you from any legal actions and, in fact, any copyright attorney worth her salt will use your citations against you to prove that you were intentionally and knowingly using copyrighted material. Isn't this game fun?

Where and how your music is used is also important. If you are producing music for a commercial advertisement, the restrictions are certainly much higher—so high, in fact, that you probably cannot use sampled material at all in a commercial. You might be able to get away with this in a small market (and you have probably seen violations of this on TV), but that doesn't make it any more legal. If you are pressing a commercial CD, the standards are higher than if you are distributing on the Internet. You should attempt to contact the record company or artist and ask for permission through ASCAP, BMI, or SESAC. Unfortunately, although most fellow musicians would likely be flattered that you are sampling a bit of their work and would appreciate you asking, record companies will not be as friendly. One major anecdotal exception to this is when creating soundtracks to films for the purpose of entering contests and festivals: Getting permissions for very limited showings is often surprisingly easy.

This brings us full circle to how recognizable a sample is. The Material Girl is going to be much more tense about you using her material than a relatively unknown band in your area. How the sample is used is important as well, because using a sample as a tribute to your favorite artist is going to be received quite differently from a parody or satire, although parody is protected speech and therefore is legal, ironically enough.

Genre is very important in this discussion as well. Some genres of music are more inclined to tolerate sampling (for example, hip-hop) than others. Some types of music rely on sampling, such as techno and most electronica forms. Interestingly, we cross into another gray area here between sampling and remixing. When are you sampling to create an original piece and when are you remixing a song? Again, there isn't much legal precedent here, but dropping a percussion loop on a Cincinnati Pops Orchestra performance and calling it your own is probably going to raise the ire of Erich Kunzel and dozens of musicians who have spent a lifetime on their art. Remixing in a live performance won't often get you into hot water, but remixing and selling a song definitely requires the original artist's permission.

If you do receive a cease-and-desist order, you probably should. And, if you work for ACME MegaCorp and your ad just appeared during the Super Bowl, you'd better call your lawyer. The heading for this section is "Legal and Ethical Issues": Just because you think you can get away with it without anyone noticing or suing you doesn't make it right. Finally, turnabout is fair play. When using samples from other artists, imagine that you have worked for years nurturing your talent and suffering for your art, when suddenly, the latest Top 40 tune selling millions of copies prominently features a riff from one of your songs. If that would make you angry, you better not use samples you don't own explicit copyright to at all. Although this whole discussion is very gray in legal terms, ethically and artistically it is not.

COMMUNITY STANDARDS
One excellent place to explore this issue more fully is on ACIDplanet (http://www.acidplanet.com) in the Community section. One warning: On ethical and, more importantly, artistic grounds, most ACID-planeteers vehemently oppose the use of sampled material from CDs. Don your asbestos suit and prepare for flames if you disagree.

Recording and Editing

Technically speaking, recording your own loops is not difficult and falls into three basic steps: acquiring the source material, editing the source into a loop, and making the loop compatible with the ACID software. Again, loop (with a lowercase l) is a general term used to describe audio files used in the application to create songs. The material you sample may ultimately be used as One-Shot, Loop, or Beatmapped files. No matter how you acquire loop material, you will ultimately want to use the ACID software to edit it.

Acquiring Source Material

Source material can come from anything that can make a noise or produce an audio signal. Analog instruments, voices, and anything you can record with a microphone are valid, using the techniques discussed in Chapter 5, "Recording Vocals and Instruments." Or you could use any auxiliary analog source, such as a Walkman, a VCR, or an MP3 player. Using the appropriate connector cables, you can output the audio from these sources into your soundcard. Very likely, this will involve a 1/8-inch-to-1/8-inch (male-to-male) connector for a Walkman or a stereo RCA Y cable from a VCR to the 1/8-inch jack on your soundcard. In any case, connecting an analog source to a soundcard is the same as hooking up a microphone, as long as you watch your levels into the appropriate input: mic or line level. Setting the gain on the input and getting a good, quiet signal without any electronic hum is critical. You can record samples straight into a track in the project on which you are working. Precise timing is not important because you can edit later. See Chapter 5 for more information.

Acquiring material from a digital source is easier, because the levels are automatically adjusted. Digital sources might be FireWire sources such as DV camcorders, coaxial and optical digital connections, and, most commonly, CD-ROM drives in your computer. When sampling from a digital source, you might need to use special software that interfaces with your device, but we will not deal with the specifics here. Getting digital audio data from an audio CD also requires special software. Fortunately, the name of that software in this case is ACID:

1. Insert an audio CD into your CD-ROM drive.
2. From the File menu, select Extract Audio from CD.
3. In the Extract Audio from CD dialog, select from the list the CD (or DVD) drive that has the audio CD in it (if you have multiple disk drives).
4. Click on the CD track (or tracks) that you want to extract (see Figure 9.7).
5. Click the OK button.

This process extracts or rips the entire song from the CD to your hard disk drive (HDD) in an uncompressed format. It takes roughly 10 to 20 seconds for every minute of audio, depending

Figure 9.7

*Select multiple tracks to
extract by holding down
the Ctrl key while clicking
on CD tracks.*

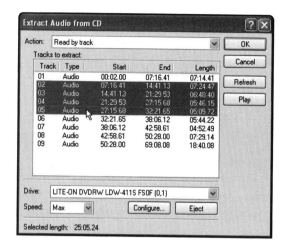

on the speed of your disk drive. The final file size will be about 10 MB per minute of audio. The file is automatically named and saved, by default, to <C:\Documents and Settings\[user name]\ My Documents\Sony ACID Pro 6.0 Projects\>, although you can change this default behavior in the Preferences dialog. An additional file called a peak file (*.sfk) is also saved in the same directory as the file. This small file contains a picture of the waveform of the file that helps the ACID software display the waveform more quickly on the timeline. You can delete this file if you want, but if you do, the program spends a small amount of time recreating it every time you use this media file in a project.

The new media file is automatically inserted into a track in your project, and the Beatmapper Wizard starts (by default) the process of making the media file compatible with the ACID software. (See the section "Beatmapped Clips" earlier in this chapter.) Copyright restricts you from using the entire song in your project, but you can trim events using the software to get what you want. You can trim events directly on the timeline or by using the Chopper. The Chopper is probably more useful in this case because you can create multiple regions yielding multiple separate samples (loops) from the same media file. Remember that the application is a nondestructive editor that does not alter the original media file on your computer. See the next section for more on editing media files using the ACID software.

Editing Sampled Material

After recording or extracting the raw source material, you need to trim the file into a shorter sample and then use the ACID software on it. You can do this in any audio editing application (for example, Sony Media Software's Sound Forge), but unless you have very special needs or just love working with your sound editor, you might as well use the ACID software to create the new loop files. The reason for this is that you can edit and render new loop files all at once with the program.

The basic techniques of using the ACID software to isolate short samples from a much longer piece are discussed in Chapter 1, "A Song Is Born." Specifically, see the sections on editing and trimming, as well as the "Chopper Window" section. Chapter 4, "Polishing Up," has more information on the Chopper window and how to use regions to isolate sections of a media file. Remember that you can easily copy, paste, and duplicate events on the timeline to use a loop repeatedly. All of these actions are completely nondestructive and do not alter the original media file. The downside to this is that the larger media file continues to take up space on your hard drive. The other problem is that edits made to events in a project are not available to other projects unless you render out the project. On the upside, you can isolate different loops from different parts of the file. But then again, on the downside, because you are not saving the project as separate media files, you cannot make adjustments to the looped sections or make them compatible with the software, as detailed in the rest of this chapter.

If you have an external sound editing application, you can use it to edit the media file and thus save disk space on your computer. (You can also use the ACID software; see the following section.) Right-click the track that the media file is in, the Clip Properties window, or the media file itself in the Explorer window, then select Edit in *X*, where *X* is the name of your preferred sound editor. To specify the sound editors that appear on this menu (you can select as many as three), select Preferences from the Options menu, then click the Editing tab. Then browse for the applications you want to use in the Editing application boxes. After editing a file and saving it to a new name, you must insert the new media file into the project. The ACID software automatically updates any changes to a loop file in the project. This updating can result in some events not matching the media file or the project if the duration of the original media file was changed. Press F5 on your keyboard in the ACID application's Explorer window if you cannot see the new file. Even if you use an external editor to trim and adjust your loop files, in the end you need to use the ACID software to add tempo and key information.

Using ACID as a Loop Editor

The ACID software is not primarily a media file trimmer or editing program, but it is an extremely capable and flexible media file editing environment nonetheless. By creating an event, splitting it, trimming it, modifying it with effects, and then rendering the event, you can very effectively change a loop in myriad ways. To create a new loop file:

1. Click the Solo button on the track with the source media file in it.

2. Create a loop region to define the new loop.

3. From the File menu, select Render As and check the Render Loop Region Only option.

4. Type in a name for the new loop and click Save.

Remember, the ACID software is a nondestructive editor, and you cannot create a file of the same name in the same location as any file used in your project. You must delete, rename, or overwrite the file manually in Windows Explorer. If you are editing a media file that is already in a mature project with carefully placed events, finely tuned effects, and delicately curved envelopes, you can always replace the source media file for the track with the newly edited media file using a different name by clicking the Reload button in the Clip Properties window.

Loop Editing Techniques

Editing and trimming media files are not difficult or complex tasks and simply require practice. Creating media files that loop seamlessly and naturally is more involved. (In this discussion, *loop* refers to a formal loop that is intended to repeat over and over.) One of the best ways to learn how to create such a loop is to examine some simple drum tracks in which the waveform is clearly visible and see how the media file is constructed. As you can see in Figure 9.8, you should start with first things first: Beat 1 should fall immediately at the beginning of the media file. Be careful not to cut anything off from Beat 1, but make sure it falls at the beginning. The end of the media file is not just after Beat 4, but is instead just before (but not including) Beat 1 of the next measure. When you are starting with longer source material, the initial ACID Type is likely to be a One-Shot or Beatmapped clip. In many ways, a One-Shot is simpler and less error-prone, but a Beatmapped clip gives you more control.

Figure 9.8

An event that reveals a few measures from a larger media file. This event will be used as the basis of the loop to be created.

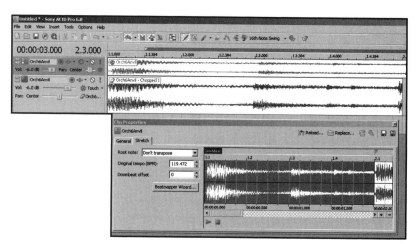

There really isn't much magic to creating a loop, with trial and error being the only real way to get it right. Here are a few bits of advice that might help:

❋ Save a number of slightly different trimmed files with different names to see which ones work best.

❋ Play with the tempo (see the next section) when making a media file compatible with the ACID software to get it to fit.

❊ Use the ACID software to edit an event based on the media file, and then duplicate the event to see how it works as a loop. Then render a single occurrence of the event, using a loop region, as a new loop.

❊ Watch out for pops and clicks that can sometimes occur at the edges of sharply edited media files. Use the Quick Fade Audio Event Edges option in the Preferences dialog to prevent these sorts of problems.

As you can see, using the ACID program as your primary loop audio editor has significant advantages. Although it isn't formally an audio editing environment, you can still use the ACID software to trim loops. Trimming ACID events is a simple process, and you can listen to the media file and future loop against the destination project. The ACID software can also determine the all-important tempo of the loop.

Making ACID Loops

Adding a small bit of information to the header of an audio file tells the ACID software the type of file (One-Shot, Loop, or Beatmapped), the pitch, the tempo, and the beat structure of the file. Some other information also may be added, such as markers, regions, and copyright information, but these properties are all secondary to the main goal of creating effective loops. The Explorer window and the Clip Properties window display the information that is saved with a file that's compatible with the software. You can change many characteristics of a loop (such as the root note) in the Clip Properties window and save the changes to the media file by clicking the Save button at the top of the window.

❊ **FRESH LOOPS**

By far the best and easiest way to create new loops with ACID beat, tempo, and key information automatically is to click the Solo button on a track and then render a loop region straight out of the ACID software to a new media file. Make sure to select the Render Loop Region Only option in the Render As dialog.

Beatmapping to Make a File Compatible with ACID

No matter whether you want to create a Loop or a Beatmapped final media file, the Beatmapper Wizard is a good tool to use to determine the tempo:

1. Insert the original media file into a project and change the ACID Type to Beatmapped on the General tab in the Clip Properties window.

2. Click the Beatmapper Wizard button on the Stretch tab in the Clip Properties window.

3. Determine the downbeat in Step 1. This doesn't need to be the first downbeat in the media file because you are creating a shorter loop file, not an entire Beatmapped file. It might even

be easier to start the downbeat at the beginning of the section that contains the loop you want. Then, when you draw an event on the timeline, the event will begin at the downbeat. Click Next to go to Step 2 of the Wizard.

4. Use the metronome to listen and set the tempo as closely as possible to the media file's natural tempo. Drag the Downbeat marker to move the metronome beats more in line with the media file and adjust the length of a measure to adjust the tempo. The duration of the measure not only sets the tempo, but will also probably be the basis of the loop itself. Click the Next button.

5. Step 3 of the Wizard is important in making sure the beats line up through the whole file. Because you need to determine the tempo for only a short loop section, this step is not as important here. Just make sure that the section you want to use as a loop is perfect. Click Next.

6. Select Change Project Tempo to Match Beatmapped Clip or, from the main timeline, right-click the Track Header and select Use Original Tempo to set the project tempo to the tempo of the loop. This guarantees that the ACID software will not stretch or distort the new media loop rendered from the project. You don't need to save the beatmapped information with the file because the final goal is to create a new loop file.

7. Create an event that spans the duration of the loop you want to create.

8. Test the looping of the event by duplicating it (by holding down Ctrl while dragging the event with the mouse) and repeating it on the timeline. Listen to it and see if it works. Insert a simple drum loop and see how your loop matches the beat. Go back to the Clip Properties window and adjust the downbeat and the measure size.

9. Click the Solo button on the track, create a loop region around the area from which you want to create a loop, and render the new loop file. In the Render As dialog, make sure the Render Loop Region Only option is selected.

The ACID software saves the new loop file to your hard disk with the name you selected. Remember to press F5 in the ACID Explorer window to refresh the window and see any new files. The newly rendered loop will have a tempo that is equal to the project's tempo in beats per minute and will automatically be a Loop clip if its length is between the default durations of 0.5 seconds and 30 seconds. The number of beats on the Stretch tab will be four times the number of measures of the loop region in the project (four beats per measure). The root note will be the project's default key, but this will have no bearing on the actual key of the media file itself.

In Step 8, you can make many final adjustments to the tempo and downbeat. Moving the Downbeat marker around in the Clip Properties dialog will reposition the entire media file in the event and will help you set up the loop to begin on Beat 1. You can also adjust the tempo either manually or by dragging the orange measure markers, using a simple drum track as the metronome. Make sure that after you adjust the tempo, you again right-click the Track Header and select Use Original Tempo to set the project tempo to the new tempo of the loop.

As long as the project tempo is the same as the tempo assigned to the media file, there is no loss of quality. It doesn't matter if you randomly guess at the tempo in the Beatmapper Wizard or Clip Properties window; as long as tempo assigned to the project and media files is the same, the ACID software will not stretch the file.

One-Shots to Make a File Compatible with ACID

Between all of the tempo changes and then matching the project tempo and then adjusting the downbeat, the previous procedure can get frustrating when used on media files that do not have a very constant tempo or a non-distinctive beat. Another way to set the tempo is by first changing the track to a One-Shot. In many ways, this is easier and less prone to error because One-Shot clips are always played back without distortion. Recall that One-Shot clips do not have tempo or beat information, so they always play back at their default speed. By placing a simple drumbeat loop in another track and then adjusting the tempo of the entire project, you can perhaps more easily figure out the tempo of a media file. And, because the eventual goal is to create a short loop file from the original, it doesn't matter that no beat information is saved with the original. Press F8 to turn snapping off while dragging the event back and forth to line the beats in the media file up with the drum beat.

SLIP TRIM

Slip trimming may be useful here: Hold down the Alt key while dragging the middle of an event. This slides the media around inside the event without moving the event or its edges.

Finally, when the beats are synchronized between the media file and the drum track, mute the drum track (or click the Solo button on the track with the loop material) and render the new loop file, making sure that the Render Loop Region Only option is selected. Figure 9.9 shows a long One-Shot clip that has been carefully lined up to match the simple beat in the track below it. The tempo of the project was carefully adjusted to match the One-Shot. To make such an adjustment, you would need to listen to the beat in the other track, which changed tempo with the project while the One-Shot clip did not. Notice also that you do not need to trim the event because the loop region will determine which material will be rendered to the new media file.

In summary, when creating new looped media files using One-Shot clips, the technique is to modify the tempo of the entire project to match the tempo of the original media file and then render the loop, which will be made compatible with the ACID software automatically based on the project.

Once you have determined the tempo, you might want to change the track back to a Beatmapped clip armed with this new tempo knowledge, which you can add to the Stretch tab in the Clip

Properties window. Click the Save button in that window to save the tempo information with the file.

Figure 9.9

Determining the tempo of a One-Shot clip by altering the project tempo and comparing it to the media file. The simple drum loop acts as a metronome.

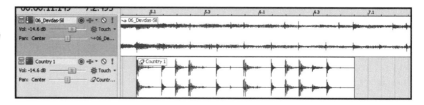

Tempo, Beats, and Loops

Loop clips do not technically have a tempo adjustment, but the Number of Beats item on the Stretch tab in the Clip Properties window can control the speed of playback in a rough way. Loop media files are recorded at a set tempo, however, and, as with other media files that are compatible with the ACID software, this information is saved with the file. The Save button in the Clip Properties window does not save beat or tempo information for loop files.

Tempo information in a file needs to be saved in a different way for loops. Because the Clip Properties window for Loop clips does not have a tempo item, there is no way to change a loop's tempo. Changing the ACID Type to Beatmapped, changing the tempo, and clicking the Save button saves the tempo information, but only as long as the media file is used in a Beatmapped clip. As soon as you change the ACID Type to Loop, the original tempo of the loop will be used. This can allow you to have two separate tempos associated with a media file, one for the Beatmapped version and one for the Loop.

Loop tempo is saved only with a newly rendered file in which the project tempo determines the loop tempo. If you wanted to change the default tempo in the media file, you would need to render the loop to a new media file from a project with the tempo you want to use.

As previously mentioned, the Number of Beats item can adjust the tempo of a loop in an indirect and rough way. The default number of beats is saved to the media file of a loop when the loop is rendered out of the ACID application. It is simply the number of measures times four. In a project with a tempo of 150 bpm, a loop that is created from a loop region of four measures will have a Number of Beats entry of 16. If you change this to 8, the software plays the file as if it only had eight beats and at twice the rate. If you used this media file in a project that had a tempo of 75 bpm (half of the original tempo) and you changed the Number of Beats entry to 8 (playback at twice the speed), it would play back at the original rate it was created. Figure 9.10 shows the same media file used in three different tracks. Track 1 uses the default number of beats (8) for a two-measure loop file. In the duplicated Track 2 (right-click the Track Header and select Duplicate Track), the Number of Beats entry was changed to 4. One occurrence of the loop now occupies only one measure, and the file plays back twice as fast. Track 3 is another duplicate of Track 1, but the Number of Beats entry is 16 in this case.

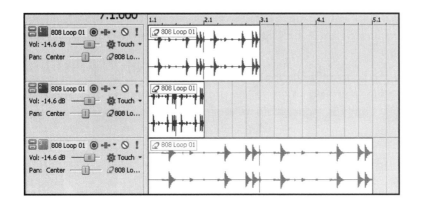

Figure 9.10

The same media file is used in all three tracks, with the Number of Beats entry in the Clip Properties window being the only difference.

There is one special use for the Number of Beats item, and that is when matching media files recorded in differing time signatures. Although most commercial loop files are recorded in 4/4 time—that is, four beats in every measure (4/1) with a quarter note (1/4) getting a single beat—some loops are recorded in different time signatures. If you ever find the perfect loop but find that it was recorded in 6/8, you might be able to force it to fit by changing the Number of Beats entry. For example, in the loop 6-8_Cowbell.wav, the default Number of Beats entry is 8. In a project composed of mostly 4/4 media files, the cowbell will not fall on the beat. If you change the Number of Beats entry to 6 in the cowbell track, the beat will align with a 4/4 project. This setting squeezes the media file and causes some distortion, although the distortion might not be audible. Figure 9.11 shows this more clearly.

6/8 native clip
default 4 beats

with 6 beats

with 8 beats

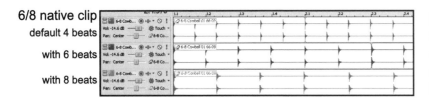

Figure 9.11

The top track contains a 4/4 reference file, with a drum hit on every beat. Tracks 2 and 3 are the same media file, with different Number of Beats properties.

Determining the Key

Unless you have perfect pitch, there is no easy way to determine the key of a media file. If you recorded your own performance, you may already know the key. If you used a piece of sheet music, it is possible to figure out the key from the key signature. The guitar is one of the more natural instruments to use to identify key because the chords played on the guitar are expressed in keys. Keep in mind that longer media files and recorded materials frequently have a number of key changes, which makes for interesting listening but defeats the purpose of setting a key for a media file. In this case, you would want to make sure the media file is inserted into a One-Shot clip or that the root note on the Stretch tab in the Clip Properties window of Loop or Beatmapped clips is set to Don't Transpose.

The purpose of setting the key of a Loop or Beatmapped file is to enable the ACID software to pitch shift the track automatically to fit the project key or follow project key changes (see Chapter 4). This feature is convenient, but it depends on accurate determination of the key as saved to a media file.

IT'S NOT MAGIC

As with tempo information, key information is extra user-entered data and is not determined in any way by the inherent audio characteristics of the file, which the ACID software cannot detect automatically. A file that was recorded of you playing the guitar at 100 bpm in the key of G can be made compatible with the application at 160 bpm in the key of D#. When you insert the project into ACID projects, the result is likely to be bizarre.

If you don't know the key of a performance or a sampled media file and you are sure it is short and doesn't contain any key changes, there are at least two ways you can determine the key of a loop with minimal trial-and-error stumbling. Keep in mind that while the root note of a loop and the key of the loop are similar in concept, the root note does not actually need to occur in the loop. You could write an entire symphony in the key of D and never play the actual note D at any time.

The first way to determine the key requires an ear that is not tone deaf and an instrument that can play a clean tone. An electronic instrument is best because these are already in tune. Determine the key of the loop by playing a note on the instrument while the media file is playing back and take a guess at the key. This isn't hard, but it does require some practice. Unfortunately, there aren't any magic secrets to getting it right.

The other way to determine the key is to find a few simple loops with clear tonal qualities that have key information saved with them. Simple solo parts without complex harmonies work best. Insert a loop that's compatible with the ACID software, most likely a loop from Sony Media Software, into a project. Change the project's key to be the same as the media file's key. The media file's key can be seen in the Summary region at the bottom of the Explorer window or as the root note in the Clip Properties window. The number after the key (such as A3) should represent the octave of the note, but it always seems to be either octave 3 or 4 in the ACID software, from the lowest sub-bass to the highest piccolo, so we're not entirely sure that Sony Media Software or loop authors pay a whole lot of attention to this key number. Figure 9.12 shows the various octaves. A3 might be called A4 if the first octave were numbered octave 1 (instead of 0), as it sometimes is.

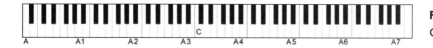

Figure 9.12

Octave numbers on a standard keyboard.

After changing the project to match the reference media file, insert into the project the file for which you want to determine the key, then create an event. Create a loop region and play back the project continuously over the section of the event you want to use as a loop. Now adjust the pitch of the reference event or track up and down using the + and – arrows on the number pad. You will not have to move more than 11 semitones up or down. When the tones match, you have determined the key. This requires a pretty good ear, and several harmonies may not match exactly but still sound quite good. After matching the key, add or subtract the number of half-steps (semi-tones) from the project key to calculate the actual key. For example, if the project is in A and you need to pitch shift the reference loop +5, then the key of the unknown loop is D. Use the Project Key pop-up menu to count this out visually if necessary. You could change the project to this key and then render the loop to save the key information to the media file, but, unlike changing the tempo, saving key information to a loop is simply a matter of changing the root note and then clicking the Save button at the top of the Clip Properties window. For user-created loops, the octave is always 3, as in A3.

Loop Limitations

All of this automatic pitch shifting and tempo adjusting by the ACID software is transparent to most users, as it should be; you don't really need to be thinking about these technicalities when you are in a creative groove. However, the application is making powerful calculations to ensure that, as the tempo of a project accelerates and the various loops keep up with the beat, the loops don't end up sounding like a chipmunk band. This process of changing the tempo without changing the pitch is a foundational technology that makes the ACID software work. In a similar way, you can change the pitch or key of a loop without changing the tempo.

Limiting the Limitations

As the heading to this section suggests, the magic of loops has some real-world limits. All pitch and tempo changes, beyond the original key and tempo of an audio file, result in some distortion to the audio. For small changes and in most typical ACID projects, this distortion is completely inaudible. At some point, however, the effects of changing the tempo without changing the pitch become noticeable. Beyond this point, the damage becomes intolerable. In the end, it is a sub-jective call as to what is unacceptable, but there are some general guidelines:

* The ACID software has a hard limit of +/−24 semitones (half-steps) for pitch shifting. This is a four-octave range, which is about the range of the very best singers in the world. Because you can use a pitch shift on a project, track, and event simultaneously, and these changes are all additive, technically you can pitch shift in a range of more than eight octaves, but only your dog will care about this ability.

* ACID projects are limited to a tempo range from 70 bpm to 200 bpm by default. Again, this is a huge range, suitable for most music genres. To change this to an even greater range (or to limit it even more), select Preferences from the Options menu. Then, on the Editing tab, change the project tempo range.

* The type of music or audio is important. Vocals are especially good at revealing distortion caused by stretching or pitch shifting. Clear and simple solo instruments without complex harmonics (such as a flute) also do not tolerate large changes in tempo while the ACID software tries to maintain the pitch.

What does this distortion sound like? Distortion from pitch shifting is most obvious and therefore least likely to be troublesome, because you usually start getting an artificial sound from the pitch shift itself (that is, chipmunk sounds) before the distortions from maintaining the tempo become obvious. Adjusting the tempo without causing pitch shifting must be approached more cautiously. The negative effects can range from simply sounding a little false, to stuttering, to emitting strange echoes and flanging effects.

On the Other Hand...

Chipmunks are kind of fun. In most normal situations, you will not want to change the pitch and the tempo at the same time, but that would happen if the ACID software did not compensate for one or the other during processing. By disabling these features, you can transform Loop and especially Beatmapped files into cartoonish songs performed by chipmunks. This is good for about a 10-minute diversion when you could be spending valuable time watching television, so you should definitely go ahead and try it:

1. Insert a song recorded from a CD or a Beatmapped file into a track.

2. If the file has not already been beatmapped, you can quickly run through the Beatmapper Wizard to get a rough tempo, although because the Wizard is usually used to prevent the pitch shifting that you are about to create, it isn't particularly important to get this 100-percent correct.

3. In the Clip Properties window, change the tempo to one-half of the original tempo and play back the track.

Loop Management

Loop libraries are typically sold on CD-ROM discs, but DVDs are becoming more common, especially for collections. Although it is perfectly acceptable to leave the loop files on the original discs, CD-ROM drives are much slower than hard disk drives (HDD). In addition, switching CDs in and out of the CD drive is not a very convenient way to access your loops. For these reasons, we highly recommend that you transfer all of your loop files from CD-ROM to your hard disk. Multimedia files take up a large amount of space, however, so this could be a strain on your limited resources. The advantages are significant, however, and with drive prices falling to well under 50 cents a gigabyte on sale (usually after rebate), buying an additional HDD is an easy and inexpensive upgrade. And, as with your basement or garage, you can never have too much space.

Reorganizing the loops on your HDD is also a good idea. A typical loop CD from Sony Media Software might be organized such that loop files are buried a level or two into the folder tree. For example, a library named Techno Basics might have loops organized like this:

CD:\Loops\Bass\Bass01.wav.

On your HDD, you might want to create a Loops folder (D:\Loops\) and then organize individual libraries by name:

D:\Loops\Techno_Basics\Loops\Bass\Bass01.wav.

As you can see, the Loops subfolder below the Techno_Basics folder is redundant: You already know this is a loops folder. This redundancy is not a big deal, but you can save yourself a mouse click by moving all of the loops from the Loops folder and into the root for that particular library, as shown in Figure 9.13. It may seem that this saves you only a single click, which is true, but when multiplied by the hundreds and hundreds of times you will browse through your loops, the time savings are significant.

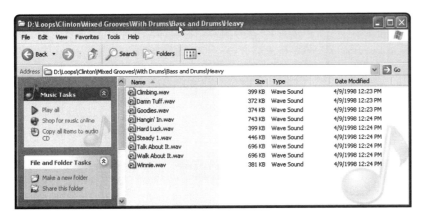

Figure 9.13
Renaming folders for loop libraries on your hard drive can save time because path names can be long and convoluted.

Media Manager

The Media Manager is a powerful database tool that uses the Microsoft SQL Server Desktop to organize the thousands of loop files that will clutter your hard disk no matter how carefully you organize them in Windows file folders. Although setting up the Media Manager can be a some-what tedious task at first, the benefits will quickly become apparent, especially to advanced users and professionals. For example, suppose that you are looking for a melodic ambient pad to lay down under a techno track you are creating. You know that your orchestral loops collection includes some great pads, and you remember a few good ones in that trance library you pur-chased last year. Using the Explorer window, you would normally go to your orchestral folder, start browsing around and previewing files, and then go back up the folder tree and back down into the trance folders. This browsing process is not difficult, but it does interrupt your workflow and, perhaps more importantly, it interrupts your creative momentum.

Setting Up the Media Manager

Before you can use the Media Manager, you'll need to point it to your loop library on your hard disk and let it compile a database. This process is (or at least can be) automatic (see Figure 9.14). To compile a database with Media Manager:

1. Open the Media Manager (from the View menu, select Media Manager, or press Alt+5).

2. Click the Add Files to Media Library button.

3. Browse for the root folder where you store your loops and click OK.

4. In the Add Files to Media Library dialog, select the Use File and Folder Names to Apply Tags Automatically option.

Figure 9.14

The Media Manager Options dialog with the Sony Sound Series Loops and Samples reference library.

If you have organized your folders at least somewhat logically, using the existing folder structure as a starting point for your database will help. Depending on how many files you have, this process takes some time to scan all of the files and create the new database. We found that it took about a minute for every gigabyte of audio files we had on a relatively fast 7,200-rpm hard disk, or about 15 minutes for 20,000 loops. This is a good time to take a break, make a sandwich, or check your e-mail. As you purchase more loop libraries and individual audio files or create more of your own loops, you can periodically update the database, scanning only for newer files. This is a much faster process.

The automatic process is not perfect because the Media Manager initially searches for folder and filenames to prime the data. For example, in our search for orchestral pads, our initial database places any file in a folder with the word "pad" in it into the Pads subfolder of the Orchestral folder in the Media Manager's tree. This subfolder will include all of the loops in the Futurist Drum n Bass library's \keys\pads\ folder, for example, which isn't exactly the same as the orchestral pads we were looking for in our example (see Figure 9.15).

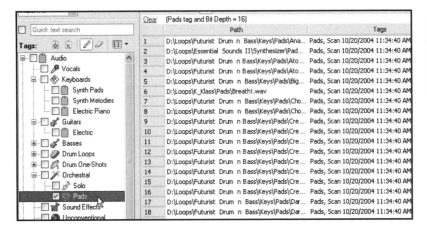

Figure 9.15
An Orchestral > Pads search (left side) turns up Drum n Bass loops in the Search pane.

Remember, the Media Manager is only as good as the data it has to work with. There are two approaches to dealing with this, so let's continue with the reasonable real-world example of the existing 20,000-loop library. First, you could scrap the library and start from scratch, manually adding your loop libraries one at a time and identifying problems as you do. Second, you could use the automatic database and fix the tags as you work. When you start out, you can have multiple databases: Click the Media Library Actions button (in the upper-right corner of the Media Manager window) and select New Media Library. Although you can continue to use multiple databases, we recommend that you eventually settle on one after some experimentation because loading and unloading databases takes time. Ultimately, your database will be very valuable to you, so make sure you back it up: Click the Media Library Actions button and select Back Up Media Library.

Using the Media Manager

After you have created a database, you can begin exploring your files and organizing how you access them. Because the database contains only pointers to your files, you can change any information you like without altering the original files on your drive. Although the Media Manager might seem cumbersome at first, continued use and the addition of more information will make it increasingly useful over time. Eventually, the Media Manager will be like your microwave oven: You'll wonder how you ever got by without it.

In its simplest form, the Media Manager can operate like a more flexible Explorer window. You can browse around, select files, and preview them. To add a loop to a project, double-click it or drag and drop it onto the timeline. The Media Manager is strongest, however, when you are using its search features.

AUDITIONING MULTIPLE FILES

If you select multiple files in the Media Manager, the ACID software will automatically audition each for a second or so and then move to the next one to give you an automatic preview.

The Interface

The main database portion of the Media Manager, dominating the right side of the window, is a database application much like any other. As we're sure you've noticed by now, the database has a huge number of fields; a dual-monitor setup is really useful for any multimedia work, but would be especially helpful here. The columns along the top represent the various fields:

* You can reorder columns by clicking and dragging them.
* Add or remove columns by right-clicking the column header and selecting the appropriate menu item. Columns that are removed are really only hidden, and you can display them again by clicking the Column Chooser item.
* You can sort items in the database by clicking the column header. Sorting is more useful on some columns than others. For example, alphabetizing by name is useful, but sorting the Copyright column might be less so.

NO UNDO WITH DATABASES

Unfortunately, as you will quickly discover, there is no such thing as Undo in the realm of database design, sorting, and searching. The Previous Search and Next Search buttons do act somewhat like undo and redo for searching and sorting, however.

Tags

The most important part of the Media Manager and your database are the tags. Initially, we sorted all of our 20,000 media files automatically, and our tags (or keywords) were generated based on the folder paths and filenames. In our first orchestral pads search example, we didn't get quite what we wanted. We selected the Pads item under the Orchestral item in the Search pane. As you can see in Figure 9.15, this gave us dance synthesizer pads as well as orchestral pads because the ACID software automatically tagged all of them as pads. To create a more effective search:

❄ To add a tag, simply drag a tag item from the Search pane to the media file you want to tag. You can select multiple files at a time by holding down the Shift key and selecting a range, or do noncontiguous selections by holding the Ctrl key and clicking various loops, and then drop a tag to the selections.

❄ To remove a tag, right-click a media file entry (or a selection of entries) and select Remove Tag. Then, from the Remove Tag dialog, select the tag you want to delete and click OK.

So, we've started the process of retagging entries (files) to make the Search pane more useful. (You can also use the Add and Remove Tag mode buttons at the top of the Search pane.) As you work with the ACID software, you can continually add new tags (and delete old ones) to make your database more useful. Figure 9.16 highlights a loop and shows all of the various tags associated with it in the database.

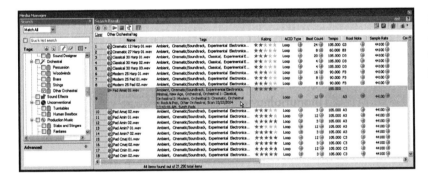

Figure 9.16
All of the tags associated with "Pad Amaj 01.wav" in the database.

❄ **QUICK SEARCH AND TAG**
As you might have guessed, the initial automatic tagging by the ACID software may not be entirely accurate. Use the Quick Text Search box to search the actual filenames and folders to find more files. Then retag the results to make your data more accurate.

Advanced

The Advanced options below the Tags pane contain three additional search filters, by default (see Figure 9.17). To use one of the filters, check the check box to the left of the filter you want.

❋ **ACID Type** filters your search by clip type: Loop, One-Shot, or Beatmapped.

❋ **Tempo** sets the range of tempos in bpm that the search will return. Click the minimum to maximum tempo items to adjust the range of allowed tempos.

❋ **Beat Count** basically allows you to limit your search by the number of beats in a loop file. Essentially, this lets you filter out loops by limiting the durations. Click the minimum to maximum number of beats items to adjust the range of allowed tempos.

These are just the three filters that are available by default the first time you run the ACID software. You can remove items from the Advanced Filter list by clicking the delete button (X) to the right of the filter. To add additional filters to the list, click the add (+) button at the top of the pane or drag the term you want to the pane. This opens the Search Criteria Chooser, which you'll see has a lot of filters you can use, many of which will be useful for media outside of the ACID application (for example, in video projects in Vegas). Double-click a filter term to add it to the Advanced Filter pane. The filter will not become active until you select it with the check box in the pane.

Figure 9.17

The Advanced Filter pane and the Search Criteria Chooser.

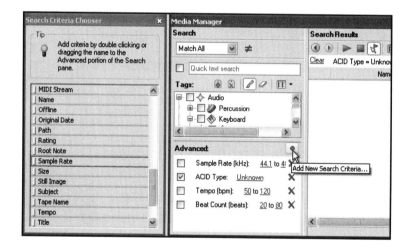

Search Pane

Tags work well only with the Search pane, which is the colorful folder tree list on the left side of the Media Manager. This tree list simply consists of search terms that are coordinated with the tags associated with the media files in your database. You can expand and minimize the hierarchical tree structure by clicking the plus and minus tree items. You can search for tags by clicking the check box next to one of the items (a green check mark appears in the box). Essentially, these check boxes act as a filter on your database, returning only the items that match your search parameters. You can search for multiple tags with an AND operator by checking multiple boxes. You can also use the Quick Text Search box at the top of the dialog, although, ironically, this option tends to not be very quick at all because it searches the Path field for matches. After you have sorted your data, a "clear" item appears at the top of the window. Click it to unfilter your search and start again (see Figure 9.18).

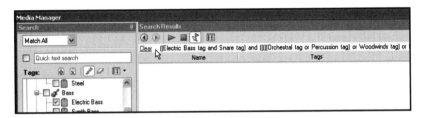

Figure 9.18
Click the Clear item to reset the tag criteria and start a new search.

A few engineers at Sony Media Software have set up a basic organizational hierarchy that you might find useful. You should certainly not feel restricted by their choices and you should configure the Media Manager to make it the most efficient tool for how you work. Let's take a look at how you can customize the Search pane, continuing to work through our pads example. First, the ACID software automatically tagged our files based on the folder or filenames of anything that had "pad" associated with them. This search got us 157 files initially. What we wanted was orchestral pads, but we also got synth pads in the bargain because all were tagged as pads. Then we retagged a bunch of techno pads as synth pads using the tag we found under the Keyboards item. Suppose that we use pads all of the time and having them scattered under two headings (Keyboards and, incorrectly in our opinion, Orchestral) is not really useful to us. Fine: It's our database and it's our opinion that matters, after all. To reorganize this database:

1. Drag the Pads tag out from under Orchestral and put it at the highest level under Audio. With a click in the Search pane, you can now see all of your pads.

2. Add a new Orchestral Pads subsearch to the Pads search: Right-click the Pads item and select Add. This creates a new tag based on the date. Rename this tag "Orchestral Pads" and drag it under the Pads item to create a hierarchy.

3. Finally, multiple-select (hold down the Shift key and click a range) all of your orchestral pads (which are listed consecutively because they are found in the same folder) and drag your new tag to the selected entries.

Now we're getting somewhere. In Figure 9.19, you can see the results of all of this tagging and reorganizing. Getting used to all of this database work requires a little thought about organization and hierarchy, but it is ultimately up to you to find an organization and structure that fits your needs. For example, you should not duplicate tag names. (If you do, it will mess up your searches.)

So, in our example, it isn't really a good idea to have both a Pads > Synth Pads hierarchy and a Keyboards > Synth Pads hierarchy because both will add a synth pads tag to the media file's field. You could use slightly different names to convey the same information, but it all depends on how you want to work. Although it is logical enough to put some pads under the Keyboards item, perhaps that's not where you would ever look for them yourself; go ahead and delete that item. This is just one example, and we want to be clear that we are not suggesting that this is a preferred or even a particularly good organization, but you clearly have a great deal of flexibility and power with this tool.

Figure 9.19

The results of our retagging example for a Pads category with types of pads the next level down.

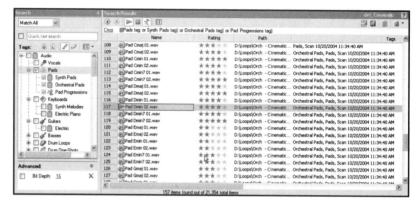

 DATABASE DESIGN

Ultimately, the Media Manager is only as useful as the database that you design.

Customizing and Rating

Customizing the tags and the Search pane is easy and fun:

* Drag search items around to create new hierarchies.

* Rename tags by clicking and typing. Be careful, however, because this renaming does not change the tags that you have already added to the media files in your database. After you rename a tag, you will also be unable to remove the old tag from files (without first renaming the tag back to the original name).

* Use the colorful icons to identify your search tags visually by double-clicking the tag icon and selecting a new icon from the dialog.

* As you preview loops, click Ratings stars for every loop you listen to. You can change these ratings effortlessly at any later time, so there is no disadvantage to rating your favorites now. (You'll have to double-click to lower star ratings later.)

- ❄ The Comments field is also useful, but probably not for describing all 20,000 loops in your collection. Instead, you might want to use it to identify the song in which you've used the loop so you don't overuse it later, for example. The field is purely for your own convenience.

- ❄ You can always add new columns as you see fit: Right-click the column header, select Custom Columns, and click the Add New Column item (the green plus sign).

Loop Relationships

By default, the ACID software learns from how you use loops in projects and automatically adds data to your Media Manager database. (Make sure Save Media-Usage Relationships in Active Media Library is selected on the General tab of the Preferences dialog.) When you find loops that work together (however you personally define that) and include them in the same project, the database adds an entry that will help you find related files in the future. When a loop you have used before appears in the Search pane, right-click it and select the Find Related Items option. Then select a relationship—for example, Used With—to find all other media files that were used in other projects with that file. This won't work retroactively on old projects, but it will become more useful the more you use the application.

More Loops!

There are literally dozens of places where you can get more media files to use as loops. This section is devoted to various sources for more loops, both commercial loops for sale and loops available for free on the Web. In all cases, you need to read the license agreements carefully to determine whether you can use the loops legally in your own projects. In almost all cases, when you purchase loops from a loop library, you are also purchasing the rights to use these loops as well. This is often described as *royalty-free* or *buyout*, which means you can use them without paying additional royalties. It might be more difficult to assess the licensing and royalty situation of loops that are available for download from the Web. Although none of the sources presented here are guaranteed, and inclusion on this list does not imply an endorsement, at the time of this writing the sites mentioned were well maintained and appeared to offer high-quality loops. Likewise, this list is not comprehensive, but only a list of a handful of loop sources to get you started. Like any favorites list on the Internet, it is only of limited temporary value, and you should try typing "loop, sample, audio sample, library" into your favorite search engine to find more.

http://www.sonymediasoftware.com/loop_libraries/default.asp

http://www.acidplanet.com

http://apocalypse-sound.com

http://www.digimpro.com/music.aspx

http://www.djsamples.com/DJSamples

http://www.flashkit.com/loops

http://www.fruityloops.com

http://www.groundloops.com

http://www.looperman.com

http://www.modarchive.com/waveworld

http://pocketfuel.com

http://wavesamples.cjb.net

Chapter 9 Quiz

1. ACID loops are:

    A. Audio files with beat, pitch, and tempo information added to them

    B. MIDI files with MIDI channel, note, and velocity information added to them

    C. Video files with frame rate and color information added to them

    D. None of the above

2. ACID loops are usually used to repeat over and over. (T/F)

3. One-Shot ACID loops are loops that:

    A. Contain one very loud volume peak

    B. Do not repeat

    C. You can only add one time to your project

    D. None of the above

4. By default, files less than 30 seconds long are opened as loops. (T/F)

5. You can modify the properties of a loop through the Clip Properties window. (T/F)

6. The General tab's controls include the following:

    A. Timeline

    B. Pitch Shift

    C. Both A and B

    D. Neither A nor B

7. The Stretch tab controls how a media file is pitch shifted. (T/F)

8. Root note refers to:

   A. Where on the timeline a loop plays

   B. The volume of a loop

   C. The key of a loop

   D. The tempo of a loop

9. You can legally use samples from Madonna songs in your projects if you make sure they are shorter than three seconds. (T/F)

10. The ACID software cannot be used as a loop editor. (T/F)

10 The Secret Life of ACID MIDI

The ACID® software did not start out life as a MIDI application. The most recent version, however, brings a formidable arsenal of new MIDI tools to the table. Whether you will be integrating MIDI files into your project, performing on MIDI instruments, or starting from scratch and composing by inputting MIDI parameters directly into the application, you'll find exceptional tools to meet your needs. The surprising thing about all of this, especially considering the complexity of MIDI, is that the simplicity of the ACID software remains.

MIDI

MIDI stands for *Music Instrument Digital Interface*. This relatively simple and universal computer communications standard allows synthesizers, sequencers, drum machines, electronic instruments, controllers, and computers to talk to one another. MIDI data is not audio data that can be used to create noise out of a speaker, unlike .wav or other media files with audio data. Instead, it is a set of instructions that tells a MIDI instrument how to play. In the case of your computer, your soundcard might be that MIDI instrument or device. Although MIDI is a fairly simple standard, the huge variety of devices and possible configurations can rapidly lead to confusion.

It is very important to understand the distinction between a MIDI device that creates sound out of your speakers and the actual source of the MIDI data itself. One of the easiest ways to identify this difference is to look at the size of a MIDI file compared to the size of an audio file. Thirty seconds of MIDI data is only a very small fraction of the size of 30 seconds of audio data, no matter how highly compressed the audio data is. A simple example of a MIDI device is a MIDI keyboard plugged into your computer. The most simple MIDI keyboards are only "dummy" devices that output MIDI data, such as the note played and how long the key is pressed. The keyboard does not actually make any music by itself, but sends this MIDI data to the soundcard, which interprets and then outputs the data to your speakers. Ultimately, the quality of the sound depends on the quality of the device that interprets the MIDI data, not on the device that generated it. Some keyboards do make sounds by themselves without being plugged into your computer.

These synthesizers and pianos are really two MIDI devices in one—one to generate the MIDI data, and one to interpret this data and the output sounds. Often these devices have two or more outputs—one that outputs MIDI data, and one that outputs an audio signal. The sound that comes straight out of the keyboard into an amplifier is quite different from the MIDI data as interpreted by your soundcard.

In the ACID software, MIDI means MIDI data, not the sound produced by your MIDI instrument. If you have a high-quality keyboard with excellent audio output, such as a high-end digital piano, you might want to record the audio signal into the application, just as you would record any real-world audio source (see Chapter 5, "Recording Vocals and Instruments"). MIDI files, MIDI tracks, and the recording of MIDI data in the ACID software are MIDI data issues and thus are topics of this chapter.

MIDI Standard

The first version of the MIDI standard was released in 1983 as a way to ensure that all electronic instruments (and now home computers) would speak the same language. Although the protocol has been modified and extended a number of times in the intervening years, the basics remain the same.

MIDI Data

The stream of MIDI data from a MIDI keyboard or a MIDI file in the ACID software contains information about the music to be produced by the MIDI playback device (for example, the soundcard synthesizer). For a single note, this information includes (among other things) the key of the note, how long it is played (duration), the instrument used (voice, patch), how loud the note is played (velocity), whether it is sustained with a sustain pedal, how it fades after it is released, modulation, volume, and panning. As one example of MIDI data, the key or pitch of a note can be expressed as a numerical value from 000–127. This gives MIDI a total range of 128 semitones or half-steps, which is considerably more than a standard 88-key piano keyboard. Figure 10.1 shows this range against a piano keyboard. The frequency of the sound is marked in Hertz (Hz) along the top of the diagram.

Figure 10.1

The total range of possible MIDI notes extends well beyond a standard keyboard and well below the threshold of human hearing.

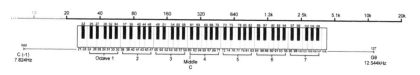

General MIDI

General MIDI (GM) is the basic repertoire of 128 instrument sounds and specifies how those sounds are assigned to the various patch numbers. There are 128 instrument sounds (patches) in the MIDI standard. These may be numbered 1–128 or 0–127. These sounds can be broken up into 16 family groups.

Piano	Bass	Reed	Synth FX
1. Piano	33. Acoustic	65. Soprano Sax	97. Rain
2. Bright Piano	34. Fingered	66. Alto Sax	98. Soundtrack
3. Grand Piano	35. Picked	67. Tenor Sax	99. Crystal
4. Honky Tonk	36. Fretless	68. Baritone Sax	100. Atmosphere
5. Electric 1	37. Slap 1	69. Oboe	101. Brightness
6. Electric 2	38. Slap 2	70. English Horn	102. Goblins
7. Harpsichord	39. Synth Bass 1	71. Bassoon	103. Echoes
8. Clavichord	40. Synth Bass 2	72. Clarinet	104. Sci-Fi
Chromatic Percussion	Strings	Pipe	Ethnic
9. Celesta	41. Violin	73. Piccolo	105. Sitar
10. Glockenspiel	42. Viola	74. Flute	106. Banjo
11. Music Box	43. Cello	75. Recorder	107. Shamisen
12. Vibraphone	44. Contrabass	76. Pan Flute	108. Koto
13. Marimba	45. Tremolo Strings	77. Blown Bottle	109. Kalimba
14. Xylophone	46. Pizzicato Strings	78. Shakuhachi	110. Bagpipe
15. Tubular Bells	47. Harp	79. Whistle	111. Fiddle
16. Dulcimer	48. Timpani	80. Ocarina	112. Shenai
Organ	Ensemble	Synth Lead	Percussive
17. Drawbar	49. Strings	81. Square Wave	113. Tinker Bell
18. Percussive	50. Slow Strings	82. Sawtooth Wave	114. Agogo
19. Rock	51. Synth Strings 1	83. Calliope	115. Steel Drums
20. Church	52. Synth Strings 2	84. Chiff	116. Woodblock
21. Reed	53. Choir Aahs	85. Charang	117. Taiko
22. Accordion	54. Voice Oohs	86. Solo Vox	118. Melodic Toms
23. Harmonica	55. Synth Vox	87. Fifths (Sawtooth)	119. Synth Drums
24. Tango Accordion	56. Orchestral Hit	88. Bass + Lead	120. Reverse Cymbal

(continued)

Guitar	Brass	Pads	FX
25. Nylon	57. Trumpet	89. New Age	121. Guitar Fret
26. Steel	58. Trombone	90. Warm	122. Breathe
27. Jazz	59. Tuba	91. Polysynth	123. Seashore
28. Electric	60. Muted Trumpet	92. Choir (Vox)	124. Bird Tweet
29. Muted Electric	61. French Horns	93. Bowed Glass	125. Telephone
30. Overdriven	62. Brass	94. Metallic	126. Helicopter
31. Distorted	63. Synth Brass 1	95. Halo	127. Applause
32. Harmonic	64. Synth Brass 2	96. Sweep	128. Gunshot

The General MIDI Standard was created so that generic standard MIDI files generated on a sequencer or notation application can be played back on another device while preserving the integrity of the original selection. Another part of this standard is a separate set of percussion instrument sounds, usually assigned to Channel 10. This is a special instrument (patch) because each note on the keyboard can be assigned to a different instrument (for example, C = snare, D = woodblock, and E = cymbal).

Different companies have expanded on the basic GM standard over the years. For example, Roland uses what they call GS (*General Standard*) and Yamaha uses XG, but each of these manufacturers' standards produces instruments that basically function the same way and are largely compatible. All of these standards specify only how the instruments are organized and do not have anything to do with the quality of the sound or the type of sound synthesis, which is ultimately device-dependent.

Controller Maps

There are many different ways the basic MIDI sounds can be laid out on different synthesizers by default. The list of voices and which banks they are stored in is called a *Controller Map*. It is simple enough to switch to any number of popular synthesizer Controller Maps in the ACID software:

1. Right-click a MIDI Track Header and select Properties.

2. On the Output Settings tab, select Controller Maps from the top drop-down list.

3. Click the Load button and select your synthesizer from the list (see Figure 10.2).

This loads a simple data file that contains the appropriate names and bank information into the ACID software, but it does not load any of the actual sounds.

Basic MIDI Synthesis

The most important issue in soundcard quality as it relates to MIDI is synthesis of the data into sound. Until this point, the quality of your soundcard has not mattered much when working with

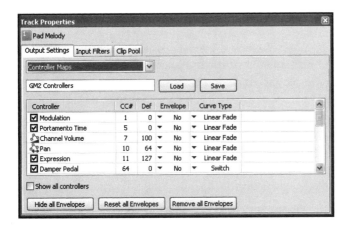

Figure 10.2

You can switch to many popular synthesizer Controller Maps in the software.

the ACID application because (beyond a certain basic level) all soundcards play back and output audio files with fairly high fidelity. Of course, there might be important differences in the quality of the card itself, such as whether it outputs analog or digital signals and how electronically quiet it is, but essentially all cards play back media files the same way, and even consumer-level hardware outputs very high-quality sound. MIDI is a totally different story.

FM Synthesis

The quality of your soundcard's MIDI is very important if you use it to synthesize your MIDI data, as most ACID users do. At the lowest-quality levels, MIDI data can be interpreted by the FM synthesizer on your soundcard. This device sounds a lot like a video game. Unless you are going for a Casio sound (as Trio famously did with "Da Da Da" back in the early 1980s) or you only want artificial electronic-sounding instruments (perfect for techno and other electronica genres), FM synthesis is limited. Most soundcards come with some sort of hardware-based FM synthesizer that may even be the default MIDI playback device. Because this synthesizer is usually on the soundcard itself, your computer does not need to process any information when playing back MIDI files; it only needs to send the MIDI data to the soundcard. This advantageously frees up your CPU for more important tasks. Many older games use the hardware FM synthesizer on your soundcard for just this reason.

Wavetable Synthesis

A step up in quality from FM synthesis is wavetable synthesis, which interprets MIDI data and then plays back this data using actual samples from real instruments. If you think this sounds like playing back loops in the ACID software, you're right. Wavetable synthesis is a huge improvement over a basic FM synthesizer and may be all you ever need. Keep in mind that the quality of the sound from wavetable synthesis depends on the quality of the samples, so wavetable is not a magic way to get perfect MIDI. On a soundcard that costs less than $100, the samples are unlikely to be of the highest quality. On the high end, for example, professional-level digital pianos often have extremely high-quality samples from real instruments that most of us would not be allowed to touch in real life.

Wavetable synthesis on a soundcard is sometimes hardware-based. This means that the MIDI instructions are sent to the card and are played back and mixed on the card, which is where the instrument samples (wavetable) are stored. Generally, this means the samples that make up the wavetable do not take up any random access memory (RAM) on your computer. Many popular soundcards load the wavetable into RAM, which can hurt the performance of your computer. Some soundcards allow you to replace the samples on the wavetable with other samples, either of your own creation or as created by professionals. Two examples of this are SoundFonts and the more general DLS (Downloadable Sounds) standard.

Wavetable samples are similar to ACID loops and fall very near one another on a musical continuum. Samples typically used for MIDI applications are shorter in duration than most ACID loops and are frequently only a single note. With the right software, such as Sound Forge and Creative Labs Vienna, you can use .wav files as loops in the ACID software from SoundFont samples or convert ACID loops into SoundFont samples.

Software Synthesis

So far, the discussion of synthesis has focused on your soundcard and what it can do in terms of MIDI. In the past, soundcards have been a critical part of the MIDI equation because computer memory (RAM) and CPU speed were at a premium and needed to be optimized. It was very important for the soundcard to take care of as much MIDI processing as it could to free up the rest of your computer for other tasks. Although we would all like to maximize our computer's performance, freeing up RAM or CPU cycles is no longer that important. Modern multimedia machines in the twenty-first century are quite powerful and are loaded with RAM, and this has led to the possibility of using a software synthesizer to interpret MIDI data. As with any software on your computer, software synths get loaded into RAM and use your CPU to generate music. Perhaps surprisingly, many of the most popular soundcards with wavetable synthesis actually load the wavetable samples into RAM anyway, although the actual wavetable synthesizer is on the soundcard itself. The great advantage to this is that you do not need to be limited to your soundcard's hardware. Most soundcards also come with some sort of software synthesizer. If you have a decent soundcard but are unhappy with the MIDI playback, you might consider purchasing a good-quality software MIDI synthesizer instead of buying new hardware.

> ❋ **WHAT YOU HEAR**
> Perhaps the most powerful reason to use DLS or VSTi soft synths (besides the fact that a huge variety of them are available) is that what you hear in the ACID software is what is rendered to your output file. This is not the case with synthesizers that are external to the application, including the ones on your soundcard.

A wide range of software-based synthesizers are available, including software emulation of FM synthesis, ancient pipe organs, classic old arena-rock synthesizers, some of the best modern synthesizers from famous manufacturers, and wavetable synthesis. Software synths for the ACID software come in three varieties: DLS, VSTi, and ReWire.

❊ **CONVERT DLS**

DLS sets are similar in many ways to the proprietary SoundFonts from Creative Labs and Ensoniq. With the right software (for example, Audio Compositor or Awave Studio), you can convert SoundFonts to the DLS format, although you might lose some quality because many SoundFonts use audio filters (such as compression or low-pass filters) to make the various notes in a set more uniform.

VSTi Soft Synths

The VSTi (*Virtual Studio Technology instrument*) synth is a very popular example of a software synth, and, although the other soft synths are slightly different, they all do the same thing in the end. One difference is that you can organize VSTi synths somewhat in the Preferences dialog (choose Preferences from the Options menu). Another special difference is that VSTi synths can have multiple ports that show up in the Mixer window. Right-click on the main bus for the VSTi in the Mixer window to see all of the various ports (see Figure 10.3).

To insert a VSTi soft synth into a project:

1. In the Mixer window, click Insert Soft Synth.

2. In the Soft Synth Chooser dialog that opens, select a synth to use from the list and click OK.

3. The Soft Synth Properties window opens, and a soft synth bus is inserted into the Mixer window.

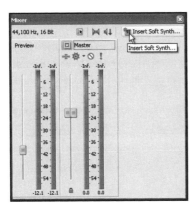

Figure 10.3
Getting a soft synth into a project.

4. Now insert a MIDI track into a project. You can either use the Insert menu or select a pre-existing MIDI file (.mid) on your computer using the ACID Explorer window.

5. Click the Device Selection button in the Track Header and, from the pop-up menu, select the soft synth you inserted into the project in Step 1.

You can open the Soft Synth Chooser dialog to change the particular instrument from the Mixer window. You can open the Soft Synth Properties window by double-clicking the bus number of the soft synth in the Mixer window or selecting Soft Synth Properties from the View menu. You can also press the shortcut key Alt+8.

ReWire

ReWire is a sophisticated software interface (supported by the ACID Pro software) that allows compatible applications to talk to one another, exchange information, and ultimately synchronize their performances at the sample level, either for studio recording or for live concerts.

ReWire is a bit like creating MIDI masters and slaves (ReWire hosts and clients). ReWire is more flexible and sophisticated, however. All you need are two apps that support the standard. Suppose, for example, that SONAR is your favorite MIDI app. Although the ACID software has some good MIDI tools, they aren't as good as SONAR's, so you would really like to dump your very cool South Asian percussion groove from the ACID application (client) into SONAR (host), where you'll use your synth to compose the MIDI parts of the soundtrack. All apps have their own strengths. The ACID software can also be used as a ReWire mixer (a host), which is one of the software's specialties. ReWire control is implemented through the soft synth interface. Here's how you'd set up the ACID software (host) to send audio to a Reason software synthesizer module (client) that is installed on the computer:

1. Insert a MIDI track into an ACID project.

2. Click the Device Selection button in the Track Header of the new MIDI track and select Insert Soft Synth from the menu.

3. In the Soft Synth Chooser dialog that opens, click the ReWire Devices tab and select a ReWire device application. In this example, we'll select a Reason synth (see Figure 10.4). Click OK.

4. In the Soft Synth Properties dialog (Alt+8), click the Open ReWire Panel Application button.

5. In the ReWire app that just ran (Reason), open a project and configure your channels.

6. Back in the ACID software, insert a MIDI file into your MIDI track (or compose one yourself using the piano roll, or record a MIDI file with a MIDI keyboard) and hit play. The ReWire device should immediately start playing back in exact synchronization with the ACID software.

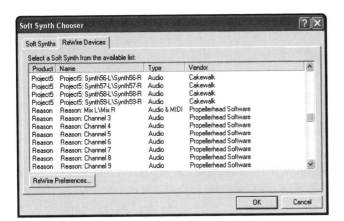

Figure 10.4
Configuring the ACID software to use an external Reason software synthesizer module for playback of an ACID MIDI track.

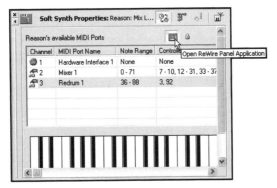

This is just one example of how you might configure the ACID software to work with a ReWire app. In this case, we took advantage of the program as our composition and recording tool and used the Reason soft synth because of its excellent sound, which is certainly much better than a simple on-the-motherboard soundcard and its FM synthesizer. Because of the large number of ReWire devices you can control (and, not in small measure, due to their sometimes cryptic inter-faces), it is difficult to say that this explanation is enough, but it should get you started. The ACID Help file has a number of additional examples, including entries for Ableton Live, Cubase, Nuendo, Orion, ProTools, and SONAR.

Configuring MIDI in ACID

As mentioned, the quality of the MIDI output from the ACID software does not depend on the software itself, but instead depends on your soundcard (or the quality of your software synth). Configuring the application to use the correct MIDI device can be complicated. Because wavetable synthesis is often the highest-quality synthesis on a soundcard, getting the ACID software to output wavetable samples is important. Unfortunately, wavetable synthesizers often use some of the same circuitry that the soundcard needs to play back regular media files, and this can cause conflict. This section discusses how to configure ACID MIDI tracks to get the highest quality and talks about some workarounds for a few potential problems.

Preferences Dialog

To begin configuring the ACID software for MIDI, choose Preferences from the Options menu. In the Preferences dialog, click the MIDI tab. The list at the top of the tab contains all of the possible MIDI devices that are currently available on your system. This list is identical to the devices listed in the Windows Multimedia Properties dialog, which you can access by clicking the Start button on the taskbar and selecting Control Panel. Then, in the Control Panel, double-click the Multimedia item and click the MIDI tab. You can add new instruments to the list in this dialog, but that is usually an automatic action when you install the software for a new device. You can configure the list of instruments in the ACID software to be a subset of all instruments by selecting only preferred instruments (see Figure 10.5).

Figure 10.5

Select a subset of devices in the ACID software to make available for playback and MIDI Clock generation.

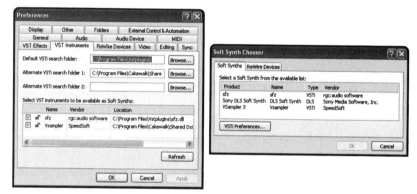

Working with MIDI

The ACID software deftly handles MIDI data, going beyond simply allowing you to include MIDI in your project. You can also record MIDI from a live performance on a MIDI instrument, step edit a song on the Piano Roll and timeline, or even edit individual MIDI events completely by hand in the List Editor.

Adding MIDI to ACID

Adding MIDI files (and thus MIDI data) to a project is as simple as adding any other type of media file to the ACID software, although the data itself is fundamentally different. To add a MIDI file (.mid, .smf, or .rmi) to the ACID program, use the Explorer window to locate and preview the file, then double-click it or drag it to the timeline. The software inserts a number of MIDI tracks into the timeline based on the different parts that the MIDI file contains (see Figure 10.6). All of the tracks in that file are grouped into a Folder Track that contains them and is named for the MIDI file you inserted. When you are not editing the MIDI tracks, simply click the minimize button on the Folder Track to collapse them and get them out of the way.

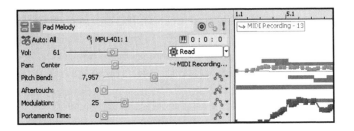

Figure 10.6

MIDI tracks and events as inserted into an ACID project from a single MIDI file.

MIDI tracks and events behave much the same as other tracks and events in the ACID software. The Track Header contains Mute and Solo buttons as well as a multipurpose slider to control panning and volume, in addition to a number of other possible sliders that correspond to other MIDI data (see Figure 10.7). You can pitch shift tracks and events by right-clicking the Track Header or by pressing the + or − keys on your keyboard's number pad. MIDI tracks cannot use FX or FX envelopes. Many MIDI data parameters, however, such as modulation or pitch bend, can be varied over time using envelopes.

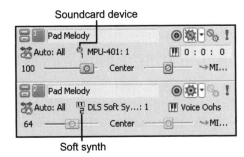

Figure 10.7

The Track Header for a MIDI track can have a number of controls that regular audio tracks do not.

MIDI events do not display waveform information as audio events do because MIDI files are not composed of audio data. Instead, the short horizontal lines in the event correspond to the duration of individual notes, whereas the vertical position roughly indicates the tone or pitch of the notes. These lines are only meant to serve as visual cues that correspond to the contents of the event and, like waveforms, they are very useful when you are eyeballing alignment of events in the ACID software. As with other types of files, the ACID program uses the tempo and beat information inherent in the files to synchronize the MIDI data with the project and with other media in the project. Key (pitch) information is not a separate part of a MIDI file, but you can set a root note for a MIDI file and it will be detected by the ACID software, allowing the MIDI track to follow key changes in the ACID project.

Because MIDI files are often longer than just a few seconds, MIDI events are not usually looped, although they will loop if the events are made long enough. (Look for the notches in the events.) When you begin drawing a MIDI event on the timeline, no matter where you begin, the event will start drawing at the beginning of the file (as it will with all events). This can make finding short sections in the middle of a five-minute MIDI file difficult. One way to deal with this is to draw out the entire event to locate the parts you want, and then split the event where needed (press S on your keyboard). Also, try using the Slip Trim technique, which enables you to move the media around within the event without changing the event boundaries. To use this technique, press and hold down the Alt key while dragging inside of an event.

MIDI Track Properties

As with standard audio files in the ACID software, you can change several variables in the Track Properties dialog for MIDI files. The MIDI Track Properties dialog contains three tabs: Output Settings, Input Filters, and Clip Pool. In summary, the Output Settings apply to playback, the Input Filters are for recording, and the Clip Pool, which exists on all types of tracks, lets you specify which media file is going to be painted into a track. To open the Track Properties window for a MIDI track:

1. Right-click on the Track Header and, from the context menu, select Track Properties.

2. Double-click the Track Number button on the Track Header.

3. If the Track Properties window is already visible, simply click the Track Header.

4. If the Track Properties window is not visible, from the View menu, select Track Properties.

Output Settings Tab

The Output Settings tab might seem a bit intimidating at first glance, and, indeed, it contains a lot of raw MIDI data that you can manually modify. Fundamentally, this is where you will control the sound of the output. The Output Settings tab actually has three separate sets of controls that are somewhat hidden, but are easy enough to access using the first drop-down at the top of the dialog:

※ **Controller Maps.** This lets you configure what MIDI data is sent to your MIDI device, whether that device is a software synthesizer on your computer or an external hardware device. You can also manually modify the outgoing parameters in some detail here.

※ **Program Change.** This is where you can view the voices (instruments, patches) and groups that are used to play back the MIDI data.

※ **Drum Map.** This lets you quickly switch entire sets of drums.

Controller Maps

The Controller Maps item sets up the Output Settings tab with everything you need to interact with your software synths and external hardware (see Figure 10.8). You can change the controller mapping to match your MIDI device, and you can select what kind of MIDI data is sent to the device.

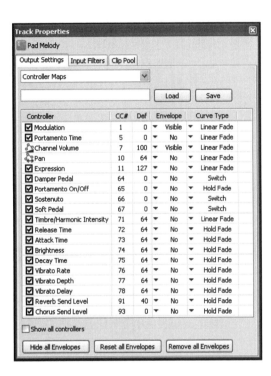

Figure 10.8
The various options available for the controllers.

Program Change

One of the most fundamental modifications you can make to a MIDI clip is to change the voice, patch, or instrument used to play back the note data. For example, you can change the melody line from a piano to a guitar or a glockenspiel. The easiest way to change the voice of a clip in a particular track is to click the Program button on the Track Header and follow through the voice groups to the submenu that has the particular voice you want to use (see Figure 10.9).

You can also change the voice on the Output Settings tab in the Track Properties dialog for a MIDI track. Select the Program Change item to see the various options (see Figure 10.10).

Figure 10.9

Click the Program button and follow the menus to change the voice for a track.

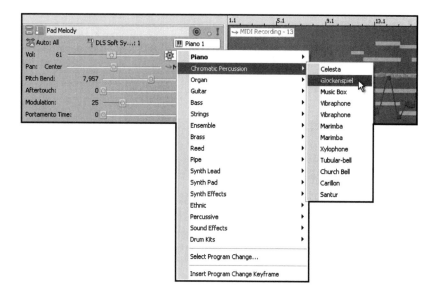

Figure 10.10

The Program Change option lets you see the instrument used to play back clips in a MIDI track.

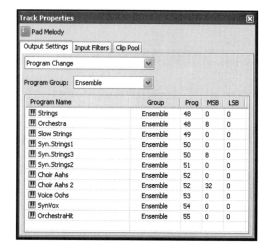

To change the voice used for a particular clip:

1. Select the Program Change option from the top drop-down list.

2. Select a program group from the next drop-down.

3. Select a program name from the Patch list.

Besides selecting a new patch, none of the other data on this list can be edited. The patches that are available on the list depend on the synthesizer you are using for playback, coordinated by loading the matching Controller Map so that the right patch names are listed.

Drum Map

The Drum Map options are not unlike the Voice options in function, although they are specialized for percussion instruments. While most voices and instruments have a range of tonal frequencies, many drums have (more or less) a single tone. Of course some drums, especially hand drums, have a whole range of tones that can be produced, but the limited tones of many drums means that you don't need an entire 88-key keyboard to express a snare drum, for example. Therefore, it is possible to have an entire drum kit spread across a range of keys on a keyboard, with the kick drum in the lower register, the toms a little higher, the snares above that, and then maybe the various cymbals. It's slightly more complex than that in reality, but that's the general idea. The Drum Map options in the ACID software let you quickly select a particular drum kit from the MIDI Drum Map Template list (see Figure 10.11). This list will vary, depending on the kits you have installed and which ones you have selected from the MIDI Device list.

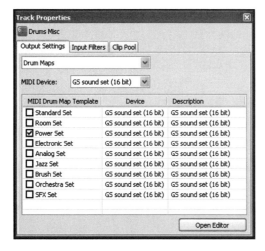

Figure 10.11
Select a MIDI drum template from the list to change the drum kit for a clip.

To work with the Drum Map options:

1. Right-click the Track Header of a MIDI track with drums (typically MIDI channel 10) and select Properties.

2. From the first drop-down list at the top of the Track Properties dialog, select Drum Maps.

3. Click the Open Editor button at the bottom of the dialog.

4. Click the Copy button in the toolbar in the dialog to copy a default Drum Map so you can alter it.

The original sets are locked, but you can create a new custom drum set that can be modified however you like using the controls found in the Drum Map Editor dialog box (see Figure 10.12). You can change how the various percussion instruments are laid out for a particular copy of a drum set and save your changes.

Figure 10.12

The Drum Map Editor dialog lets you create your own custom drum maps.

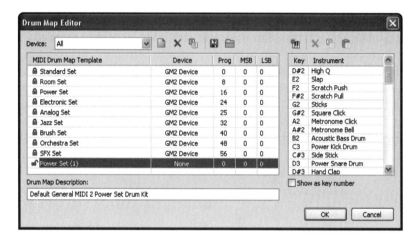

1. Select a MIDI drum map template from the list that you want to modify.

2. Click the Copy button. A new MIDI drum map template is created at the bottom of the list, based on the template you selected in Step 1.

3. On the right side of the dialog, you can now manually enter new key values and instrument (patch) names.

4. When you are finished, click the Save As button to save the new map to an XML data file.

Input Filters Tab

The Input Filters tab (see Figure 10.13) lets you control what MIDI data is recorded into the ACID software, depending, of course, on what types of data your instrument is capable of sending. For example, any MIDI keyboard is capable of sending pitch and duration data, but many also send variable note velocity (loudness), attack and release parameters, pitch blending, sustain pedals, and so on. To accurately record the automation of MIDI parameters, you'll want to record all of this data into the ACID application, but there might be reasons why you want to limit (filter out) some data to make editing easier later. One example of where you might want to do this is if you are primarily a composer and not much of a performer in real life. By filtering out your inconsistently input velocity and only saving pitch and duration data, you can sometimes make fine adjustments later to note velocity more easily if that data does not already exist.

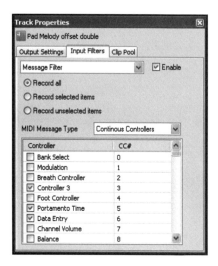

Figure 10.13
The three input filter groups in the dialog let you record (automate) different parameters.

There are three sets of input filter parameters that you can select from in the dialog (see Figure 10.13). Like the Output Settings tab, each of these sets of controls is accessed by selecting it from the drop-down list at the top of the dialog box. Check the Enable box next to the drop-down to enable recording of the particular automation parameters.

❈ **Message filters** include the note, bank selection changes, sustain pedals, and dozens of other possible inputs. The MIDI Message Type list has four additional subcategories of data that you can chose from.

❈ **Velocity** controls the expressive loudness of a note. Velocity-sensitive keyboards play keys that are physically struck harder as louder notes and play softly struck keys more quietly. You record start and release velocity data or you can set up ranges or flat responses.

❈ **Quantize** will allow you to control the timing and duration of when notes fall, essentially snapping them to a time grid. This can allow you to record more precisely synchronized performances, even if you are not a keyboard virtuoso. There are also options here to add a little swing to vary the computer-perfected performance. The Quantize tools are strongly related to the Groove tools in the ACID software.

Editing MIDI

There are a couple of ways you can edit and create new MIDI data in the ACID software by actually painting notes into events. We'll talk about the Piano Roll Editor in the next section, but the easiest and most fun way to edit MIDI in the application is directly on the timeline. To do this, click the Enable Inline MIDI Editing button on the main toolbar. This will create a large piano roll-type interface right on the main timeline (see Figure 10.14).

Figure 10.14

The main timeline in Inline MIDI Editing mode.

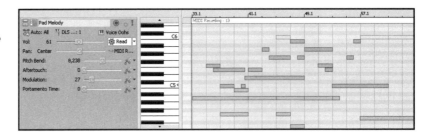

Use the Draw tool to draw notes directly onto the timeline. The vertical position represents the tone of the note, as indicated by the piano keyboard along the left side of the track. The duration of the notes is represented by the horizontal length of the notes you draw, which is pretty much how any other event works in the ACID software.

Editing Velocity Data

The velocity, or loudness, of a note is a little trickier, because we've already used up our two onscreen dimensions. To see and edit note velocities, from the View menu select Show Inline MIDI Editing > Note-On Velocities. Or you can just press the F key on your keyboard. Now you can change the velocity data for a note by dragging the diamond-shaped node on the vertical bar up or down (see Figure 10.15), keeping in mind that there very well may be multiple notes starting at any point in time. You can also view and edit Note-Off velocities (which have a different-shaped node on the top), although this parameter is often simply zero in many MIDI recordings.

Figure 10.15

Editable Note-On and Note-Off velocity data on the main timeline in Inline MIDI Editing mode.

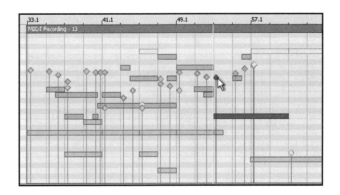

As you edit your MIDI files, you can save changes when you save the project. As a matter of fact, the MIDI data is saved with the project, because MIDI files have a relatively small amount of data associated with them. If you started out by referencing a preexisting MIDI file on your computer, after you save your project, you will not need to reference that file again because the MIDI data will be saved to the project. When you change MIDI data for a clip in the project, the MIDI data will change for all instances (events) of that clip in the project.

SAVING MIDI
When you save your project, any changes you have made to any MIDI files are also saved to the project.

Drum Grids and Piano Rolls

The piano keyboard that runs vertically along the left side of a MIDI track in Inline MIDI Editing mode and in the Piano Roll Editor has piano keys that help you visually identify the pitch or tone of the notes you are working with in the ACID software. For drums, the piano keyboard is not so much divided up into various pitches as it is divided into different sorts of percussion instruments across the span of the keyboard. Drum tracks are somewhat special in that they are often assigned to MIDI Channel 10, although this isn't always strictly necessary. When a drum track is expanded in Inline MIDI Editing mode or on a Piano Roll, you'll notice that the piano keyboard is replaced by the Drum Grid (see Figure 10.16), which lists all of the various instruments. Other than that, editing a Drum Grid is basically no different than any other kind of MIDI editing.

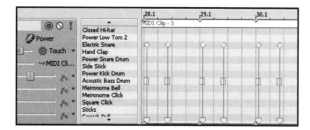

Figure 10.16
The Drum Grid on the main timeline in Inline MIDI Editing mode. Notice the velocity bars at the bottom of the grid.

MIDI Clip Properties

The Clip Properties dialog has some fairly serious composition tools for creating new MIDI parts from scratch or modifying existing MIDI compositions, perhaps to tweak a performance you just recorded. To open the Clip Properties dialog, right-click on a MIDI event on the timeline or in the Clip Pool for a track.

Piano Roll Editor Tab

The Piano Roll Editor tab graphically and colorfully displays the MIDI data, with a prominent keyboard on the left side as a reference. You can actually edit and compose on this tab, but it is best suited to light MIDI duty, not serious composition. The MIDI timeline graphically displays the

MIDI information. Individual horizontal lines represent MIDI note information, which can be assigned to an instrument or patch. The length of the line shows the duration of individual notes. The vertical position of the line corresponds to the pitch of the note. You can create markers and regions on the timeline, but you cannot save them with the MIDI file by clicking the Save button at the top of the window. Instead, you must save this information with the project. As the toolbar on this tab suggests, this is a mini-application within the ACID software. You can find standard copy, cut, and paste tools as well as drawing and painting tools that you may recognize from the ACID main window. The two tools unique to this window are the Enable Snapping Notes to a Specified Scale tool and the Quantize tool:

* The **Enable Snapping Notes to Specified Scale tool** works like a temporal snap tool, except it pops drawn (or painted) notes to a specific subset of notes within a specific key as defined by a specific scale. Click the drop-down list and select Root Note and Scale (see Figure 10.17). This ultra-cool tool enables you to create amazing jazz improvisations without memorizing scales. After you figure out the root note and scale, there are no wrong notes. Oscar Peterson will be so jealous.

* The **Quantize tool** is simpler in function and brings your notes in line with the beat and tempo. If you record a MIDI track into the ACID software, you can open the Piano Roll Editor, select a group of MIDI events (or even the entire performance), and then use the Quantize tool. You can also quantize notes created with the Draw and Paint tools.

* The bottom of the window has a **graph** that typically displays the velocity (volume) values of the MIDI data over time. You can quickly alter this data by clicking and dragging your mouse across the graph. Click the Velocity item to reveal a whole host of possible variables to display on the graph, depending on the data in the MIDI file.

Changes made to clips in the Piano Roll Editor will show up on the events on the timeline in both regular editing modes and Inline MIDI Editing mode.

Editing Velocity Data

At the bottom of the Piano Roll Editor is another small timeline that has a bunch of bars on it corresponding to the notes that are visible on the roll above. The height of each of these bars is a visual representation of the velocity (loudness) data, by default. Simply click and use your mouse to change the velocity of any note (see Figure 10.18). You'll notice that the scale on the left side of the timeline ranges from 0–127, which is the numeric range of MIDI velocity data. The Velocity drop-down list lets you list other kinds of MIDI data here for editing as well—for example, pitch bending, which is particularly well-suited to graphical manipulation.

List Editor Tab

The List Editor tab is for hard-core MIDI editing at the program level. Although you can edit this list manually, several tools along the top of the dialog can assist you with your editing. For

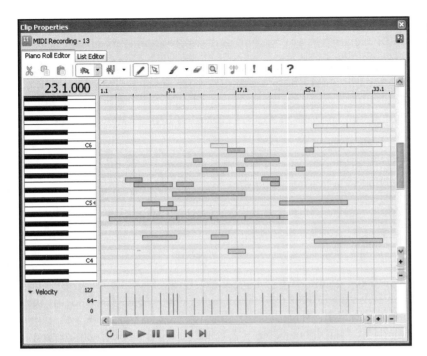

Figure 10.17
The Piano Roll Editor.

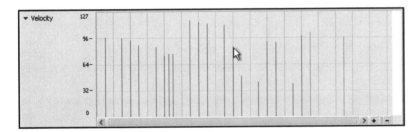

Figure 10.18
Changing velocity data on the Piano Roll Editor.

example, the Event Filter button can help you find the particular type of data you need. Another useful tool is the Edit Event button, which displays a context-sensitive dialog related to the event you selected before you clicked it. This then tells you what kinds of options are valid for the type of event and makes editing easier.

Recording MIDI

Just as you can record a sonic performance into an audio track in the ACID software, you can also record a performance from a MIDI device into a MIDI track. In this case, MIDI data is recorded (note, duration, instrument, and velocity, for example), not audio data. This distinction is important because audio data takes up much more space on your computer but can also be manipulated in different ways. For example, you can modify audio data with envelopes and route it through auxiliary busses, whereas MIDI data allows you to change the voices and instruments used.

Recording the performance data from a MIDI instrument live while a project is playing back is perhaps simpler than recording audio data. The procedure is much the same (see Chapter 6), but you don't have to worry about the many problems surrounding recording audio through a microphone, such as ambient noise and recording levels. To record MIDI data from a performance while an ACID project plays back:

1. Insert a MIDI track into your project.

2. Click the Arm for Record button in the Track Header.

3. Move the timeline cursor to the position where you want to start recording.

4. On the Transport bar, click the Record button or press Ctrl+R.

5. Click the Stop button to end the recording.

The MIDI data is recorded into a clip on the ACID timeline. MIDI data takes up relatively little storage space on your computer, so the data is actually saved in your project file (*.acd). The MIDI clip in the track will automatically be named "MIDI Recording" and subsequent clips will be numbered "MIDI Recording -1," "MIDI Recording – 2," and so on. If you turn on looping while recording, you can record multiple takes for the same section, each being recorded to another clip in succession. To paint these other clips on the timeline, use the Paint Clip Selector on the Track Header (see Figure 10.19).

EXPORT MIDI DATA

If you want to export the MIDI data in an ACID project as a MIDI file (*.mid), from the File menu, select Export MIDI.

Monitoring MIDI Performances

When recording MIDI data, the ACID software is not recording audio data. Although it wouldn't make much sense to work this way, if you haven't configured a playback device on your computer, it is possible to record the MIDI data from an external keyboard without actually hearing anything. This obviously makes recording difficult, so you need to select a device to monitor your performance. From the Options menu, select Preferences, and then in the Preferences dialog, go to the MIDI tab. On the MIDI Thru option, select a MIDI device. Only devices that are selected on the list at the top of the tab are available, as shown in Figure 10.20. When recording with some software synths, latency issues make accurate monitoring impossible due to the delayed audio. In any case, what you hear is not what is being recorded: MIDI data is being recorded, so the actual device used to monitor the performance is simply a matter of personal preference.

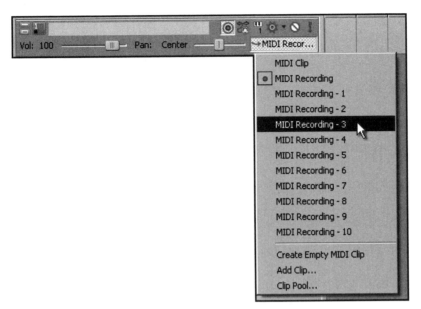

Figure 10.19
The Paint Clip Selector lets you choose the recorded MIDI file you want to paint on the timeline.

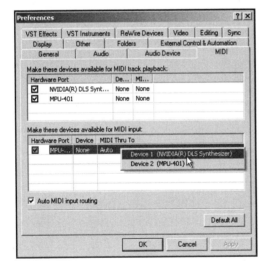

Figure 10.20
The MIDI Thru option is used to monitor MIDI performances.

Although you can turn the volume up too loud on a MIDI track and cause clipping in the final mix, it is not possible to cause clipping when recording MIDI data.

MIDI Step Recording

For those of us who are better composers than we are performers, there's a great little mode you can use called *MIDI Step Recording*. When you use this mode, the ACID software will step ahead one note (or so—it's configurable) at a time and wait for you to press a key on your MIDI keyboard. It will record that note and then step ahead to the next beat, and so on. This is a really wonderful way to compose by ear, without needing to keep up with the tempo of a song or worry about hitting wrong notes at the wrong time. To record in MIDI Step Recording mode:

1. Create a new MIDI track on the timeline (Insert menu > MIDI track [Ctrl+Alt+Q]).

2. Click the Arm for Record button in the track.

3. Click the MIDI Step Record button on the timeline Transport bar (see Figure 10.21).

4. In the MIDI Step Record dialog, set up the step size and the duration of the notes.

5. Play the note (or notes) on your MIDI keyboard. These will be recorded to the MIDI clip event on the timeline.

6. The ACID software steps forward one unit (as specified in Step 3). Play the next note (or notes) and continue.

7. When you are finished recording, click the Stop button.

Figure 10.21

The MIDI Step Record and MIDI Merge Record buttons and the MIDI Step Record dialog box.

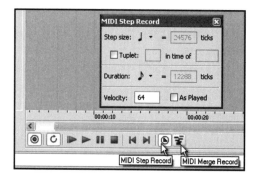

MIDI Merge Recording

You can add MIDI notes to an already recorded MIDI file without overwriting what is already there using MIDI Merge Recording. Click the MIDI Merge Record button on the Transport bar to use this feature.

1. Create a new MIDI track on the timeline (Insert menu > MIDI track [Ctrl+Alt+Q]).

2. Click the MIDI Merge Record button on the timeline Transport bar (see Figure 10.21).

3. Click the Arm Track button on the track you want to record into.

4. Create a loop region above the timeline and click the Loop Playback button on the Transport bar.

5. Click the Record button on the Transport bar. Each time the recording loops, you will hear the notes you have already recorded and be able to add more notes.

6. When you are finished recording, click the Stop button.

MIDI Triggers and Time Code

The ACID software can act as a MIDI device in a studio setup, both outputting MIDI Timecode (MTC) to other devices and accepting MIDI triggers from other devices and applications. The purpose of this is to synchronize the ACID application with your MIDI setup by allowing other devices to start ACID playback or to start and synchronize other devices from within the ACID application when you start playback of a project. The MIDI device or software application must be capable of sending and/or receiving MTC, so simple dummy keyboards will not work, but more complex synthesizers with sequencers often have this capability. Professional MIDI studios often have a small box dedicated to generating timecode and synchronization, sometimes called a *controller* or a *sync unit*.

MTC is a standard way of measuring time in MIDI and is not the same as a MIDI Clock. MIDI Clock is based on musical beats from the start of a song, played at a specific tempo, and is therefore relative to time in the real world. You can use MTC to trigger the ACID software, and the software can generate both MTC and MIDI Clock data to trigger other devices and applications. MTC is not the same as timecode used in video, although the two can be set to measure time the same way. For clarity, in this book, the term *timecode* is used to refer to the various types of SMPTE (*Society of Motion Picture and Television Engineers*, pronounced "simpty") video timecode, and MIDI code is referred to as MTC or MIDI Timecode (also a standard from SMPTE) as it is in the ACID program. This convention is not widely followed, however. In this discussion, a master device is the device or application that generates the MTC or MIDI Clock that is used to control the slave device, which is triggered by and synchronized with the master.

MTC or MIDI Clock?

Whether you choose MTC or MIDI Clock is largely a matter of what the slave application wants to use. In some situations—for example, when your project has tempo changes—the MIDI Clock might work better. The MIDI Clock is also a better choice for MIDI-exclusive applications, such as MIDI editors and sequencers. MTC, on the other hand, is more broadly targeted and can be used with everything from tape machines to video production equipment. In the end, the right choice is the one that works.

Generate or Trigger?

Should you generate MTC or trigger applications and devices from MTC in the ACID software? (You cannot trigger them from the MIDI Clock.) In other words, should the ACID software be the master device or the slave? Very broadly speaking, the ACID application seems to be better in the role of master, generating MTC or MIDI Clock to trigger and sync a slave application. Because of the ACID software's primary role as a multitrack mixing application, this is often the most logical workflow anyhow, with the ACID application as the general project master device triggering specialized slave devices, such as synthesizers and sequencers.

Generating MTC and MIDI Clock from ACID

You can configure the ACID software to output or generate MTC to trigger and synchronize compliant external hardware devices and other MIDI software applications on your computer. Any ACID project can generate MTC regardless of whether you are using MIDI in the project.

Configuring MTC Generation

MTC and MIDI Clock data are generated in the ACID software using a MIDI device on your computer. Configuring the software to generate code is a matter of selecting a device to use, much the same as you select a MIDI device for MIDI playback at the track level. To set up the ACID software to generate MTC:

1. From the Options menu, select Preferences.

2. Click the Sync tab (see Figure 10.22).

3. Under the Generate MIDI Timecode Settings option, select an output device. Choose the MIDI device, hardware or software, that is on your soundcard.

4. From the Frame Rate list, select the format you want to use to measure time.

Figure 10.22
The Sync tab of the Preferences dialog.

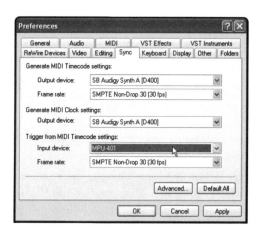

The frame rate does not speed up or slow down time, but rather determines how it is measured. The listed frame rates are all various standards that have been used for different purposes over the years. For example, movies are 24 frames per second (fps), whereas color television in the United States is 29.97 fps. In audio, 30 fps is probably the most frequently used standard. More important than which particular standard you choose is for both of your devices (in other words, the ACID software and the other application) to use the same standard. MTC and other relevant timecodes are measured in hours, minutes, seconds, and frames (*hh:mm:ss:ff*), with the number of frames in a second being the only difference.

Triggering another Device with ACID

After you set up the ACID software as the master device to generate the appropriate MTC, the next step is to configure the slave device that the data will trigger and synchronize. For software applications, this step involves selecting a port from which to listen for MTC and making sure the frame rates are the same. The process is similar to setting up the ACID program to listen for MTC, so see the following section for more information on that process. To configure the device:

1. Cue the slave device or application to listen for MTC.

2. In the ACID software, from the Options menu, go to the Timecode item and select Generate MIDI Timecode, or press F7.

3. Right-click the time display above the Track list and select MIDI Timecode Out from the context menu.

4. Play back the ACID project.

The ACID software immediately begins playback and generates the MTC at the same time, using the output device or port specified in the Preferences dialog. You use the Transport controls (for example, Play and Stop) to control the external devices. Because many types of devices, both hardware and software, can listen for and be triggered by MTC, it is not possible to tell you how to set up your specific device. Another software application, however, is likely to listen for MTC much as the ACID software does; for more information, see the next section on how to trigger ACID playback using an external MTC device.

WAIT FOR IT…

Although playback begins almost immediately and is perfectly synchronized, there can be a 1–3 second delay between when you press Stop in the ACID software and when the slave device stops.

The time display at the upper-left of the timeline can display the MTC and MIDI Clock that the ACID software is sending from the chosen device. To view the MTC that is being generated by the software, right-click the time display and select MIDI Timecode Out from the context menu (see Figure 10.23).

As you have noticed, configuring and generating MIDI Clock is a similar process. As with MTC, you need to select an output device, but MIDI Clock is measured in terms of tempo, measures, and beats, so it is not necessary to select a format. A shared device used for playback can generate MIDI Clock.

Figure 10.23

You can view the MTC that the ACID software generates on the time display. Notice that you can also enable MTC generation here as well.

Triggering ACID with MTC

You can also use the ACID application as the slave device, receiving MTC from a master device and using that to cue project playback and synchronize with a master device. The master device might be another software application on your computer or an external sequencer or a dedicated MTC generator. The process is basically the reverse of that described in the preceding section: Configure the ACID software, enable (arm) the program to listen for MTC, then begin playback or generation of MTC from the master device. To configure the ACID software to accept MTC:

1. From the Options menu, select Preferences.

2. Click the Sync tab.

3. Under the Trigger from MIDI Timecode Settings option, select an input device. Choose the MIDI device, hardware or software, that is on your soundcard.

Most consumer-level soundcards have only one hardware MIDI port and therefore only one default driver for MIDI input. Two applications running at the same time can share this input driver, so you can trigger and synchronize playback from two applications at the same time. It is not possible to use this port to enable communications between two software applications, but you can install a software-based Virtual MIDI Router (VMR) to create another MIDI input port so you can use another software application to trigger the ACID software if you don't have hardware support. After configuring the master device to generate MTC, make sure the frame rate of the device and the ACID application match. Then, to complete the configuration of the ACID software as the slave device:

1. Ready the master device for playback and generation of MTC.

2. In the ACID software, from the Options menu, go to the Timecode item and select Trigger from MIDI Timecode, or press Ctrl+F7.

3. Right-click the time display and select MIDI Timecode In. The display shows a MIDI Timecode In - Waiting message to verify that the software is listening for MTC.

4. Begin generation of MTC from the external device or start playback of the master device.

When the ACID software is chasing MTC, the time display message is MIDI Timecode In - Locked, and all controls within the program are disabled. Although the ACID application can generate MTC and MIDI Clock data with this setup, only MTC can trigger the application. Such a setup is not unusual; you might find that many devices can accept MIDI Clock data from another device, but the data cannot trigger the devices.

Advanced Sync Preferences

There are a number of advanced MTC generation and triggering options. You can access these advanced options by clicking the Advanced button on the Sync tab in the Preferences dialog. This opens the Advanced Sync Preferences dialog with three potential tabs, one for each of the three sync options. If you have not selected a device in the Preferences dialog, the corresponding tab will not be visible in this dialog. Many of these options will only need to be adjusted when you are having problems with devices interacting incorrectly with the ACID software, perhaps not responding quickly enough.

The MTC Input tab corresponds to the Trigger from MIDI Timecode Settings item and allows the ACID software to compensate for breaks, delays, and other irregularities that may occur when you are listening to MTC generated by a master device. After being triggered and synchronized, the application can continue at the same rate and stay roughly in sync without any additional input. If the program is responding to trigger messages but is falling out of sync, these options might help. You can keep the Free-Wheel for Timecode Loss option selected in almost all situations. If the ACID software remains waiting (listening) and is not triggered by the master device, these options will not solve the problem.

The MTC Output tab corresponds to the Generate MIDI Timecode Settings item and allows you to configure which messages are sent to the slave device. In most situations, it will only be necessary to generate Full-Frame Messages: On Start and Stop of Playback and Record.

The MIDI Clock Output tab corresponds to the Generate MIDI Clock settings (see Figure 10.24). This tab configures the Song Position Pointer (SSP) and is specifically used to synchronize the timeline cursor. You can select the optional item at the top of the tab always to send a start signal when playing back, even if playback starts mid-song. This option makes the slave device always start at the beginning of the song. If you do not select this option and you begin playback in the ACID software mid-song, the slave device begins playback from the current cursor position in the application, allowing you to stop and play the ACID software and maintain control of the slave.

Figure 10.24

The MIDI Clock Output tab.

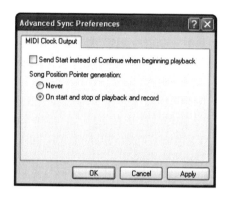

Syncing Example: SONAR to ACID

All of this talk of MTC, syncing, and virtual routing can seem rather complicated, which it is considering all of the potential devices that you can hook together. As one example, the following procedure shows you how to use the ACID software to trigger and synchronize Cakewalk SONAR using MIDI Clock. In this case, the ACID software is the master device and SONAR is the slave. If you have a choice, this setup seems to work better than the other way around. And, because SONAR is the primary MIDI application, in this example the ACID program generates MIDI Clock, which SONAR also seems to prefer. To use the ACID application to trigger and synchronize SONAR using MIDI Clock:

1. Run both the ACID software and SONAR.

2. Configure the ACID software to output MIDI Clock using your soundcard as an output device for the Generate MIDI Clock settings on the Sync tab of the Preferences dialog.

3. Right-click the time display and select MIDI Clock Out to view the generated clock. Press Shift+F7 to enable (arm) the ACID application. The time display reads MIDI Clock Out - Enabled.

4. In SONAR, from the Options menu, select MIDI Devices. In the MIDI Ports dialog, select from the Input Ports list the corresponding audio device (single-click it to highlight it) and click the OK button.

5. From the View menu, select Toolbars and make sure the Sync toolbar is selected and visible. Click the MIDI button and press Play. A message appears in the lower-left corner of the workspace reading Press <Esc> to Cancel: Waiting for MIDI Sync.

6. Press Play in the ACID software. The ACID application begins playing, and SONAR immediately follows.

Every time you stop playback in the ACID software, you will need to re-arm SONAR to listen for MIDI Clock. SONAR automatically synchronizes playback beginning at any point in your ACID project.

SONAR THE SLAVE
SONAR seems to work better as the slave, with the ACID software as the master.

FX and MIDI Tracks

One of the most common criticisms about MIDI is that it sounds very unnatural. This flaw is to be expected, given that MIDI sound is computer-generated, but advances in MIDI technology have made it sound more and more realistic. Perhaps the greatest advance in recent years has been the widespread use of wavetable synthesis, which uses real instruments to create the sound. MIDI-authoring tools have also gotten better and better, even allowing the composer to add imperfections in timing to individual notes, simulating human performers. Of course, controlling the quality of samples and the details of MIDI authoring are all well outside the domain of the ACID software.

MIDI files using even the best wavetable synthesis also tend to sound very clean and flat. This is because authors need to create samples to be used in the widest variety of situations. Almost all samples are therefore completely devoid of any sense of space or ambience. ACID FX plug-ins can be useful in making an artificially perfect and balanced MIDI file sound more natural by enabling you to add this sort of space to the track.

NO MIDI FX
The ACID software's audio FX cannot be applied to MIDI clips and events. You can, however, apply effects to the Soft Synth bus in the Mixer. Another (less flexible) option is to create an audio file from the MIDI data and then apply audio FX to that.

The best plug-in for creating space is probably the Reverb FX. To add the Reverb plug-in to a MIDI track:

1. Make sure the MIDI track is using the master device for playback.

2. Click the FX button on the MIDI Instrument bus in the Mixer window.

3. In the Audio Plug-In window, click the Edit Chain button.

4. In the Plug-In Chooser dialog, select the Reverb plug-in and click the Add button, then click the OK button.

5. The controls for the Reverb plug-in are visible in the Audio Plug-In window. Click the Solo button on the MIDI track and adjust the reverb. Then unsolo the track and finish adjusting the FX in relation to the project.

Chapter 7 includes detailed information on using FX in general, and in Chapter 8 you can also find a detailed examination of the Reverb plug-ins. Be careful not to overdo the Reverb effect, which is easy to do because more space generally sounds more interesting. At some point, however, the reverb begins to sound very artificial. You also need to try to match the sense of space in the MIDI track carefully with the other media files used in the project. Although it is not technically an FX, panning individual voices 10–20 percent left or right on a MIDI track can do wonders for a sense of space. MIDI files often bunch up all of the various voices in the middle, which adds to the artificial sound of the files.

Equalization plug-ins can be especially useful in improving the quality of MIDI in the ACID software. You can use any of these to bring out the specific voices you want to emphasize. Keep in mind, though, that you can also do this by increasing the volume of individual voices in the Track Properties dialog. Boosting the bass frequencies a little can often add richness to MIDI tracks.

Chapter 10 Quiz

1. MIDI is:

   A. A communications standard for musical instruments

   B. A computer software language

   C. An exclusive feature of the ACID software

   D. Not relevant to the ACID software

2. A software synthesizer:

   A. Synthesizes multiple software applications together

   B. Is a synthesizer application on your PC that accepts MIDI data and generates audio from the MIDI data

   C. Is a hardware synthesizer that has been programmed at a factory

   D. All of the above

3. The ACID software is not compatible with VST instruments. (T/F)

4. You can use the ReWire protocol to send the output of the ACID 6 software to a sequencer, such as SONAR or Cubase SX. (T/F)

5. For creating and editing MIDI:

    A. The ACID software offers extensive MIDI editing and creation tools

    B. The ACID software offers no MIDI support at all

    C. The ACID software is primarily a MIDI composition tool

    D. None of the above

6. You cannot pitch shift MIDI tracks in the ACID software. (T/F)

7. You cannot record MIDI in the ACID software. (T/F)

8. The ACID software can generate the following synchronization formats:

    A. MTC

    B. MIDI Clock

    C. SMPTE

    D. A and B

9. The ACID software can act as either MTC master or MTC slave. (T/F)

10. You would never want to add effects to MIDI tracks. (T/F)

11 } Video

Sony Media Software's ACID® software is an excellent tool for scoring a soundtrack or music video. Although it is emphatically *not* a tool for editing video, audio is half of the experience of watching a movie, and the ACID software plays an important role here. This might surprise you, but nearly all of the audio you hear in a movie was not recorded with microphones at the shoot, but was instead added to the movie after production. Of course, the music is added later, but sound effects and even dialogue are typically redubbed in post-production. The ACID program is an excellent tool for soundtrack creation and, of course, for scoring a film. Because of the powerful background tempo adjustments (without pitch shifting) that it offers, the program can precisely sync music to the video content effortlessly. Advanced 5.1 surround sound mixing tools make the ACID software ideal for DVD authoring.

TELL THE STORY WITH SOUND

By manipulating what you hear and how you hear it–and what other things you don't hear–you can not only help tell the story, you can help the audience get into the mind of the character.

–Walter Murch

Working with Video

The ACID software is not a video-editing application, but is instead a soundtrack and scoring tool. Because of this, its video features are robust, but basic. This section will show you how to add video to ACID projects and how to use some of the more complex features, precisely synchronizing video to audio, lining up action to tempo, and matching an audio sample to the video frame.

Adding Video

Adding video to the ACID software is much the same as adding audio or MIDI files. First, browse for video media using the ACID Explorer window and add a video track, either by a drag-and-drop operation or by simply double-clicking the video file. Unlike with audio media files, you cannot preview the video part of files as you browse for them in the Explorer window, although you can hear the audio. To listen to this audio:

1. Browse for video media using the Explorer window.

2. In the Explorer window, single-click on the video file that you want to use. Only the audio will be previewed. Turn on automatic previewing by clicking the Auto Preview button on the Explorer window toolbar.

3. Double-click files to add the video to the timeline or drag the file to the timeline. Although it will initially appear that you can add the video file anywhere, the video will automatically be placed in the top track, unnumbered. The audio from the file will be added where you drop the clip.

The video file is inserted into a video track at the top of the timeline with an event that automatically spans the entire duration of the file. If you double-clicked the file to add it, the audio is added just below the video track as a One-Shot clip (see Figure 11.1). This track contains an event that contains the audio from the video file, if one exists. Because the video files used in the ACID software typically span the entire project (indeed, they often define the project), the audio track can be quite long. This means that you will likely have to wait a few seconds while a peak file (.sfk) is built. Peak files are graphical representations of the waveform of events on the timeline. As discussed in Chapter 9, "Loops," One-Shot clips are not loaded into RAM, so the audio track is always accessed from the hard disk (as is the video itself).

Figure 11.1

A video track and its associated audio in a project.

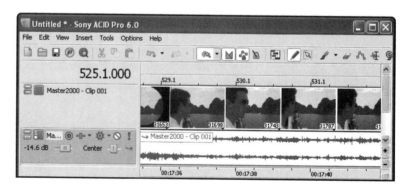

The audio track is just like any other audio track in the ACID software. Usually you will want the audio component of the video file to remain in sync with the video, so you probably won't want to change the Clip Properties to Loop or Beatmapped. Remember, if the tempo of the project changes, the duration of Beatmapped and Loop events also changes, but One-Shot events do not change. Tempo changes do not affect the video track.

To remove a video track, right-click the video track and select Remove Video. This does not remove the corresponding audio track. You can also hide the video track from view, so you have more room for your audio, without removing it from the project. Right-click the video track and select Hide Video. The track disappears, leaving the corresponding audio track untouched, but the video remains a part of the project and you can still preview it in the Video window. The Show Video Track option on the View menu restores the video track to the timeline.

Previewing Video

The Video Preview window is the simplest window in the ACID software, with only a couple of buttons. The window is used only to preview the video from the timeline and cannot be used to preview video from the Explorer window. You can view the Video window from the View menu by clicking Video or by pressing Alt+4. You can resize the Video Preview window to any size by dragging the edges of the window. The video inside of the window is locked into specific aspect ratios of the original source video to prevent distortion (and improve playback performance). The top of the window has a simple toolbar that displays the name of the media file, a Copy button to grab a de-interlaced screen capture of the video, and an External Monitor button (explained in the following section). The bottom of the window can display a status bar (right-click the View Preview window and select Show Status Bar) that shows the dimensions and frame rate of the original source media file, as well as the displayed dimensions of the video (as it appears in the Video Preview window) and the displayed frame rate (as displayed by your computer). A few other options are available on the context menu, which you can display by right-clicking anywhere in the window (see Figure 11.2). Selecting Display at Media Size sets the display size to the size of the original file, which can result in only a portion of the video being visible if the Video Preview window is smaller than the frame size of the media file.

External Monitor

As of the year 2006, most television monitors are fundamentally different from computer monitors. When color television was initially developed in the mid- to late-1950s, a number of technical problems needed to be resolved. One issue was that it was difficult with then-current technology to achieve a frame rate that was fast enough to prevent visible flickering of the image. The solution was to divide every frame into two fields: one composed of all of the odd lines in the picture, and another composed of all of the even-numbered lines. These two fields were then combined or interlaced into a frame of video. So video at 30 frames per second (fps) would really be displayed at 60 fps. Due to problems with interference with the 60-Hz electric standard (among other things), the NTSC video standard in the United States is now 29.97 fps and is interlaced. Color computer monitors developed only in the last 20 or so years are not interlaced and are referred to as

Figure 11.2

The Video Preview window and its associated context menu.

progressive scanning monitors. In addition, computer monitors typically display video using tens of millions of colors, whereas televisions are realistically limited to about two million. As more and more people buy LCD and plasma technology televisions, the old NTSC television standard will gradually give way to the new ATSC standard, and progressively scanned television will be more common. Despite the congressional mandates that push this transition, most Americans don't seem to be all that excited about spending $1,000 or more on a television, so the conversion is happening very slowly.

A significant problem with creating video for interlaced television is that you cannot be sure that what you see on a computer monitor is what your movie will look like on a television. Because any potential problems will have been introduced into the video in your primary video-editing program and not in the ACID software, a full discussion of this problem is beyond the scope of this book. However, the External Monitor option allows you to preview video on your television, via an OHCI-compliant IEEE-1394 DV (FireWire) card and Mini DV camcorder. This can be a good way to preview video because it frees up valuable screen real estate. Whether you can use an external monitor depends on your hardware and Mini DV camcorder. This setup can be troublesome, but Sony Media Software has a number of documents online to assist you with getting this feature to work. In short, to set up a camcorder to preview video on your television:

1. Connect your camcorder to your FireWire card and turn the camera on in playback mode (VTR).

2. Connect the video out (RCA or S-video jack) from the camcorder to your television. You do not need to connect the audio cables because audio is not sent through the DV card for preview purposes.

3. In the ACID Video Preview window, click the External Monitor button.

After a short pause, the video should appear on your television. You can hide or minimize the Video Preview window in the ACID software to regain workspace area and use the television exclusively for previewing. Figure 11.3 summarizes the configuration.

Figure 11.3

Previewing video using your television, via a Mini DV camcorder and a FireWire connection.

IEEE-1394 cable
(FireWire)

RCA/S-VHS
Video Out

From the Options menu, select Preferences, and then, in the Preferences dialog, go to the Video tab. From the External Monitor device list, select the device that you want to use. Usually, only one DV device is listed as OHCI-compliant IEEE 1394/DV (see Figure 11.4). Because this feature is hardware-dependent, only DV cards that meet this standard will work, but the vast majority of modern FireWire ports comply. When your camcorder is not connected and powered up, the Details section in the dialog displays the message "Device Unavailable." If you use source media files that are not DV files, the ACID software attempts to convert these to DV on the fly for previewing purposes. The speed of your computer, the complexity of your project, and the particular format of the video file will determine how successful the ACID application is at converting these files.

✳ **COMPRESSION CRANKINESS**

MPEG-2 (DVD standard) and MPEG-4 (such as DivX and WMV9) video make the ACID software (and most editing applications) particularly cranky, causing playback problems on all but the fastest of computers.

In some cases, because of hardware issues, the video on the external monitor might not be synchronized with the audio. This potential problem can become quite critical in the ACID software. If you notice that the video in the Video window in the ACID application is precisely synchronized

Figure 11.4

Selecting your particular FireWire hardware and the External Monitor button in the Preview window.

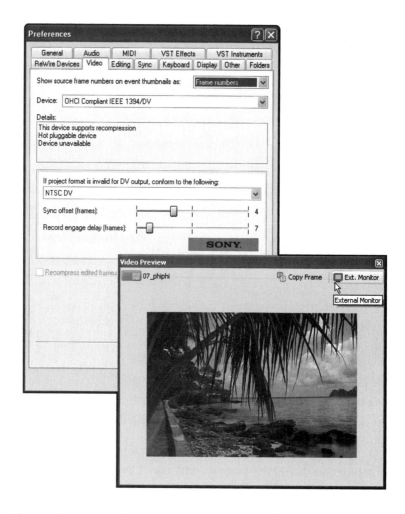

with your audio, but the video on the external monitor is not, you can adjust the sync offset to bring the video back in line.

Adding Flash Movies

You can add finished Macromedia Flash movies to the ACID timeline the same way you add any other sort of video, even though it is a fundamentally different media format. Simply browse for your Flash file (.swf) using the ACID software's Explorer window, and then drag the file to the timeline (or just double-click it). Once the movie is on the timeline it behaves in much the same way as any other video file: You can have only one video track (Flash or otherwise) and you can trim and reposition the file, but you can't otherwise edit it. One important difference is that any existing audio from a Flash movie will not be imported into an ACID project. The ACID software can have problems with some older Flash movies and will not play them back correctly, but most files authored in the last few years seem to be largely compatible. The video from Flash movies will preview to an external DV device (see the previous section), but the frames will need to be recompressed to do so (just like any other non-DV video source). This is a nice feature that will allow you to see your Flash movies on your television set.

Video Tracks

Only one video track and one video event are allowed in the ACID software. The track is always the first one in the project. Unlike with other tracks, you cannot alter the color or change the name of the track. You can change the size (height) of the track, however. You cannot split the single video event, but you can trim it from either end and you can move it back and forth on the timeline. When you render the final video media file, areas of the project at the beginning or end that only have audio content appear black in the video.

THERE CAN BE ONLY ONE
You can only use one video track in the ACID software at a time and you cannot split the single event.

Video events on the timeline do not have any properties you can alter. None of the audio controls (Volume slider, Mute button, and so on) on audio and MIDI tracks is available (or needed, for that matter) on a video track, and neither are any audio envelopes.

Video Events

The single video event that spans the duration of the media file can be dragged on the timeline and trimmed, but you cannot split or change it as you can with other events. The event displays some information about the file on it (see Figure 11.5). The pictures (thumbnails) in the video event derive from individual frames in the video, with the small triangles below the pictures marking the location of the frame on the timeline and the numbers on the picture identifying the frame number. You can change the exact format of the numbers displayed to match the time ruler or to match the format of the media file, or you can simply hide the numbers by going to the Video tab in the Preferences dialog.

Because of the many different types of media that you can use in the ACID software, there is a wide variety of ways that you can measure time. The right half of the time display always shows the measures.beats.milliseconds, as does the ruler at the top of the timeline. You can customize the left side of the time display to fit your preferences. For example, when using Mini DV footage or creating video projects for broadcast in the United States, you would want to use the NTSC video standard, which is SMPTE Drop (29.97 fps, video). To change the format displayed, right-click the time display or the time ruler below the timeline and, from the context menu, choose Time at Cursor Format and select the format. If the time ruler at the bottom of the timeline is not visible, select Time Ruler from the View menu and then select the Show Time Ruler option.

Figure 11.5

Video events display numerical values identifying frame numbers in several formats.

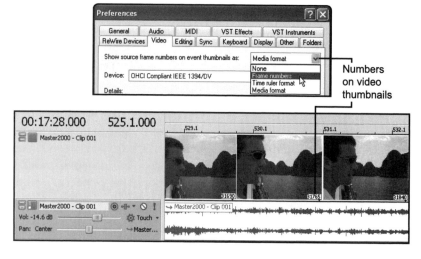

Numbers on video thumbnails

Scrubbing

Scrubbing is the term for shuttling back and forth over a video event to preview the contents of the file. This gives you more control over positioning the cursor for editing purposes. Scrubbing is not particularly important for audio work, but is highly useful in quickly finding particular frames of video. Use the left and right arrow keys to move the timeline cursor and scrub the video. The Video Preview window always displays the contents of the video at the cursor position, but the picture in the video event on the timeline also displays the contents of the video at the cursor position. As you move the cursor back and forth, notice that the triangle and frame number move with the cursor inside the picture in the event, and the contents of the frame change constantly. The amount of movement with each press of the arrow keys depends on the zoom level on the project. When zoomed out, each press might move a number of frames at a time, whereas at higher zoom levels, each press might advance or retreat one frame (or less).

 ONE FRAME AT A TIME
To move the cursor one frame at a time regardless of zoom level, press the Alt key while using the right and left arrow keys.

Zooming

The frame numbers and triangles beneath the pictorial representation of frames change with the zoom level in the project. Zooming in further reveals more detail, and eventually, at higher zoom levels, individual frames are marked by lines between the numbered frames. At even higher zoom levels, every frame is represented by a picture in the event and a frame number. As you can see in Figure 11.6, the time ruler matches the frame marks in the event if the time format selected is the same as that of the source video. Zooming thus serves as a quick way to convert absolute frame numbers into the more complex time formats if the event starts at time zero in the project. A mouse wheel is useful for quickly zooming in and out, something that you might do even more often when working with video.

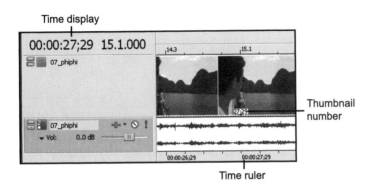

Time display

Thumbnail number

Time ruler

Figure 11.6

The time display, time ruler, and frame numbers on the event thumbnails can be set to match.

Video events snap to the grid marks in a project, which demarcate measures and beats. At higher zoom levels, when individual frames can be resolved, video events also snap to frame boundaries. You can toggle this behavior on and off by pressing F8.

Synchronizing Audio and Video

The whole purpose of bringing video into the ACID software is to synchronize audio events with the action in the video. There are a number of different situations in which you might want to do this more or less carefully. For example, synching a song's tempo with the action in a video is not particularly hard, but synching footfall sound FX with the actual steps of your actors requires much more diligence and care. Synchronizing re-recorded dialogue to the actors' lip movements in a video is an art all by itself, and while the ACID application certainly has the tools to do the trick, there isn't anything really magical that will make the job any less tedious.

Re-Synching Audio

If the natural soundtrack of the video file becomes out of sync with the video due to trimming or movement of the video event, right-click the audio event and select Synchronize with Video from the context menu. This works only for the audio from the video file. If the file has remained a One-Shot clip (as it probably should), this option moves the file back into sync. If the audio track type has been changed to Beatmapped and the project tempo has changed, the audio file moves back in sync and the tempo changes to one that allows the audio to be exactly synchronized with the video for its duration, which is the original tempo of the project when the video event was inserted.

Although the video event must remain whole, the audio event associated with the video can be split, trimmed, moved, and otherwise processed (for example, with envelopes and effects), just as any other One-Shot clip can. You can move each individual event independently and can therefore move one out of sync. You can move these individual events back into sync individually by right-clicking and selecting Synchronize with Video.

Marking Video Frames with Hit Markers

Synchronizing sound effects with video first requires that you figure out where on the timeline a video action (for example, a footstep) occurs. Video is composed of discrete frames, so the exact time when a frame begins is marked with a triangle below the image representing the frame in the event. Lining up audio events with frame boundaries can be fairly important and is not all that hard to do. The problem is that at most reasonable zoom levels for working with audio, individual frames of video are not visible, so finding the exact two frames that divide one scene from another can be tricky. Markers are very useful here, and you might want to zoom in first and find the critical junctures in the video event, mark the frame boundaries with hit markers (a.k.a. time markers; press H on your keyboard), and then zoom out to work on the audio. Hit markers are purple and appear on their own track at the bottom of the timeline. As Figure 11.7 shows, when zoomed in far enough, individual frames are visible and numbered (all frame numbers increment by one). The cut between the two scenes is clearly visible, but because the zoom level is so high, working with the audio is difficult. Notice that in the top image, the entire timeline encompasses only a few frames and spans only a fraction of a second (as you can see from the numbers on the time ruler at the bottom of the timelines). The bottom image is zoomed out to a level at which beats and measures are visible.

Figure 11.7

Individual frames are numbered in the top example, whereas the bottom example is zoomed out further.

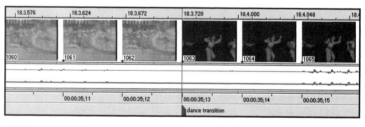

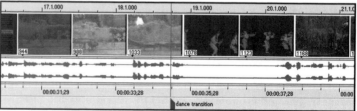

✴ **THUMBNAILS VARY**

When dropping a marker on an exact frame boundary at a high zoom level, you might notice that it does not seem to be at the boundary after you zoom back out. Trust the marker and not the thumbnail representations on the video.

The time marker that defines the exact position of the cut between the two scenes no longer appears to fall between the two scenes, but it does. Trust the marker in this situation, not the thumbnail representations of the contents of the event. Watch the Video Preview window to verify this because it always displays the exact frame at the cursor position. The arrow keys are very useful in this situation for moving back and forth in the project a frame or so at a time.

In terms of timing, sounds effects should often be placed just slightly before actual visual action occurs. You'll need to zoom in to the individual frame level on your timeline to find the exact moment. Then drop the sound clip so that it starts a few frames before. It is often tricky to find the exact frame visually, so this is as much of an art as anything and requires a lot of practice. Ultimately, if you do your job right, no one will even notice all of your hard work. After all, when is the last time you went to a movie and noticed that the gunshots, car doors closing, or footsteps were out of sync? Yet they were almost certainly all recreated in post.

Matching Project Tempo to Video

Matching tempo to the action in a video can be very important. If you look at the top image in Figure 11.8, you'll notice that the marker does not fall exactly on the beat, but occurs just before Beat 4 of Measure 18 (18.4). This may or may not be close enough for your purposes, but suppose that you really wanted the cut between those two scenes to fall exactly on Beat 1 of Measure 19 (19.1) or even Measure 20 (20.1). Recall that changing the project tempo changes the duration of the project and thus shifts the timing of every event as it relates to the video, which acts as a One-Shot and does not stretch or compress as a result of tempo variations.

To adjust the tempo to the exact value that you need to move that marker to 20.1, follow this procedure exactly. Any extraneous mouse clicks will mess up this process, so be careful and get ready to press Ctrl+Z (Undo) and start again. To match project tempo to video:

1. Drop a time marker (a.k.a. hit marker) at the scene change (as shown in Figure 11.8) by pressing H on your keyboard. Notice that the project tempo is 120.000 bpm.

2. Click the marker to move the timeline cursor to the marker's position.

3. Drag the marker to the place on the timeline where you want the scene change to take place. For this example, drag the marker to the 20.1.000 position. Leave snapping turned on so that the marker instantly snaps to the 20.1 grid marker. Note that the timeline cursor remains at the marker's original position and did not move with it as it was dragged.

4. Right-click the marker and, from the context menu, select Adjust Tempo to Match Cursor to Marker.

Figure 11.8

Adjusting the tempo of a project to match the action in the video.

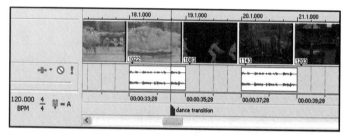

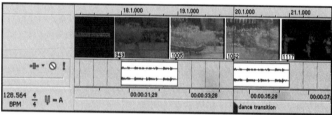

❄ **MARKERS AND HIT MARKERS**

The preceding procedure also works with regular markers. (Press M to drop an orange marker at the top of the timeline.) These markers move with the project, however, so for video (which has an unchanging tempo, so to speak), hit markers are a better choice because they move with the video in absolute time.

The entire project shifts relative to the absolute and unchanging tempo of the video (and any other One-Shot clip, such as the audio from the video file) as a result of a change in tempo. In this example, the tempo speeds up to 128.564 bpm, as you can see in Figure 11.8. If you zoom in on the marker position, it remains exactly where it was before in the video and thus at exactly the same position relative to time in the real world. In relation to the project and existing Beatmapped and Loop clips, however, it is in a completely different position. The tempo difference from 120 to 128.564 is not that great, but it is noticeable in the context of video synchronization, even though the ACID software ensures that the pitch of the events does not shift. Here we moved only a little more than a measure in a project that lasts almost four minutes, but the change in tempo was still fairly significant. It is important to have the video and audio as closely synchronized as you can get it before using this process to make final adjustments. Although this example used a cut in the video as the synchronizing event, this process is also very useful when synchronizing the project audio with the audio track from a video file.

Use this process in conjunction with tempo markers (press T to drop a blue tempo marker at the top of the timeline) to repeatedly change the tempo to sync up with the video. When you perform the Adjust Tempo to Match Cursor to Marker procedure, it only adjusts the tempo of the previous tempo marker on the timeline. (If there aren't any, it adjusts the entire project.)

Audio Tracks

The audio tracks that a videographer or filmmaker adds to a project will typically look very different from the audio tracks laid down by a composer when creating a song. Although the timeline for a song or a musical score will look very similar, video projects have a lot of specialized types of audio that need to be considered. For example, ambiences and backgrounds will run for very long stretches of time, certainly as long as a particular scene. This type of audio actually holds the scene together, letting the audience know that we are still in the same space. Sound effects typically last for a very short length of time, perhaps a second or less. Music beds are going to be much longer. Voiceover tracks are going to look different from dialogue tracks. Project organization for video can be very different from the organization you'd see for pure music. The following conversation suggests a workflow and organization that you might find useful.

Dialogue Tracks and the Clip Pool

Redubbed dialogue tracks can get very messy and complex. The ACID software is a great environment to re-record dialogue tracks in the studio, especially because an actor can sit at the computer and loop playback and record multiple takes until the dialogue is just right. Once the recording is done and you have figured out which takes you are going to keep and which you are going to discard, you will still likely be left with dozens, if not hundreds, of individual clips for even a single character. Because it is a very rare film indeed that has the same character talking at the same time as herself, you really don't need to mix dialogue from the same character together. In other words, it really isn't necessary to stack various lines up horizontally on the timeline in a bunch of different tracks. One very effective technique is to pile a single character's dialogue into a single track and then use the Clip Pool as your primary organizational tool. Then you can drop individual lines of dialogue for a character into a single track on the timeline. Life never turns out to be quite that simple, so I often end up with a handful of tracks for a single character, but that is certainly better than a few hundred tracks. It is also easy enough to organize the half a dozen character tracks into a nested Folder Track structure.

Sound Effects and Folder Tracks

Unlike dialogue tracks, sound effects are usually richly mixed and layered on the timeline and require multiple tracks. There's the waterfall in the background, the birds in the trees, the crunch of leaves underfoot, the rustle of clothing, the opening of a bag of candy, and so on. Multiple track problems like this are most easily handled by using the nested Folder Track structure in the ACID software. From the Insert menu, select Folder Track and then drag related audio tracks onto it to organize them. In a classic example, you could use a single track for a single character's footsteps, with left and right footfalls from different clips. The character's walking partner would get his own track, with two clips for left and right footsteps. The two would then be combined into a Folder Track you named "Footsteps," or they could be a part of a larger sound effect Folder Track called "Character Effects." Although it might be best to have this structure in mind when you start a project, I often find that the final structure actually emerges as the project matures. Fortunately, the tools in the ACID program are flexible enough to accommodate a number of different workflows and layouts.

One other special consideration for sound effects is how they are routed through busses. It is important to keep the sounds in the scene space you are working in. So, for example, if a scene is taking place in a cavernous warehouse, you could set up a delay or echo effect on a bus and route all of the character sound effects through a single plug-in chain. The dialogue would probably not go through that chain, but you would likewise route all of the dialogue from characters in the same space in a room through the same effects mix.

Ambiences and Crossfades

Ambiences are another important category of sound in a video and are quite different to work with from anything we have so far discussed. Because ambiences are relatively static throughout a scene (for example, the background sounds of a cityscape), these clips and events also tend to be longer. Ambiences are not always long enough to cover a scene and are rarely seamlessly loopable, however. It is often necessary to use an ambience over a few times, and you will also usually need to overlap the ends to make the transition inaudible. The easiest way to do this is to use the automatic crossfade feature and simply drag one event over another in the same track. To turn this feature on, from the Options menu, select Automatic Crossfades.

Native Soundtrack

Modern video cameras and shooting techniques mean that it isn't uncommon to work with the natural soundtrack recorded in the field. This is clearly a concern for documentaries and news gathering, but it is also often the first instinct for beginners and sometimes a requirement due to the budgetary and time constraints of a project. Native sound (nat sound) tracks from a video file require some special consideration in the ACID software. They are not loops and should not be stretched or altered. They usually aren't beatmapped, often for the same reason. They often are the longest audio events in the project and, as discussed previously, they often need to remain in sync with the video.

As with all audio (and video for that matter), the most important factors in getting good-quality audio happen well before you get to post-production in the ACID software. Camcorder microphones are very high on the list of microphones that you want to avoid using to record audio. Any decent external microphone will eliminate a host of background noise problems, but you need to do some research to get the right microphone for your application and camcorder. One common example is a shotgun mic, which you can find for less than $150 U.S. Lapel mics are even cheaper and are great for interviews. Be careful with wireless mics, however, because they can be unpredictable and might receive interference depending on your location. If your subjects are going to remain very close to the camcorder, a wired lapel mic is more reliable and cheaper. In any case, when using an external microphone (which not all camcorders accept), get a pair of headphones to monitor the recording session. If possible (and it is not on most camcorders), turn off the automatic audio gain control, especially in interview situations, and adjust the gain yourself with a sound check before recording.

When recording a live concert, it is best to avoid the entire microphone issue all together. In this case, bring along an additional recording device and hook it directly into the soundboard or mixer. Camcorder microphones are perfect for recording ambient crowd noise to mix into the ACID software later, but the sound from the band is of the highest quality through the mixer. Small DAT recorders are ideal for this purpose, but any device that records digitally (such as an MD recorder or even a spare DV camcorder) will work.

✳ **MATCHED ADAPTERS**

Do your research before you attempt to hook up anything to a mixer. Not only do you need to get connection hardware (an adapter) that is the correct size, but you need to make sure that the signal coming out of the mixer matches what your recording device wants (for example, matching line and microphone level outputs). Just because the plug fits doesn't mean it will not damage your expensive equipment.

Ultimately you need to sync this audio up with the video. This task might be difficult when using an analog tape machine, which might allow the tape to drift slightly because of variations in playback/recording speed. Synchronizing audio to video from two separate audio sources is simply a matter of finding a sharp and distinct noise (such as a drumbeat or handclap) and lining up the waveforms on the timeline. You would use the same process in your video editor when using multiple cameras for a single shoot; audio waveforms can be much easier to line up than trying to match video frames visually. Indeed, the clichéd Hollywood clapperboard is used not only to identify the scene and take before a shot, but is even more important for synchronizing the audio. Even a simple handclap before starting the action is very useful for synchronizing multiple cameras and audio later.

Fixing Poor Audio

Hollywood rarely ever uses any audio that was recorded in the field during shooting. Getting good audio is so difficult that almost all of the sound and dialogue you hear in a movie is meticulously redubbed in a studio. Audio that is recorded using an onboard camcorder microphone is usually of very poor quality. This is not a condemnation of the technology or the quality of onboard microphones, which do a remarkable job of recording in low-level noise situations. Most mics are directional, may respond to match the zoom level of the camera, and sometimes have sophisticated noise-reduction algorithms. The problem is that today's ultracompact camcorders are designed to make the camera easier to use and more portable; in the process, it has become impossible to get truly good audio from a camcorder without some kind of external microphone.

Camera motor noise is chief among the problems with a microphone that is physically in contact with (or even inside of) the camcorder body. Additionally, in the course of designing camcorders that are easier to use, camcorder microphones often get more and more sensitive in quiet situations because of automatic gain (volume) controls (AGC). This sensitivity can result in a breathing of the audio track, with the volume gradually getting louder when there is silence in the room, resulting in the background noise also growing louder. AGC is a type of compression and indeed acts very much like a compression or dynamics audio FX plug-in with the ACID software. To eliminate camera noise using the Track Noise Gate plug-in (as one example):

1. Click the FX button on the track with the camera noise.

2. In the Audio Plug-In window, click the Edit Chain button.

3. In the Plug-In Chooser dialog, double-click the Track Noise Gate plug-in and click OK to close the dialog.

4. Select an item on the Preset list and simultaneously play back the project to hear the changes in real time.

The Noise Gate plug-in reduces all low-level noises below the threshold level to zero, making these sections silent. The idea is to retain the content and eliminate the background (camera) noise, so you will need to play with the thresholds. A couple of other FX plug-in types are especially useful for camera noise:

* **Dynamics.** Several dynamics plug-ins can be used to apply Noise Gates and compression to tracks. You first eliminate background noise with the Noise Gate, then apply compression to reduce the peaks in the file, and finally increase the gain (volume) of the entire track. Without the compression, increasing the volume would cause clipping. Without the Noise Gate, the background noise would become too loud. See Chapter 8, "FX Dictionary," for more information, especially the explanation of the Noise Gate and the Graphic Dynamics plug-ins.

* **Equalization.** Camera noise is often isolated to a narrow range of frequencies or a couple of different, but narrow, frequency regions. Even the simplest of equalization plug-ins, such as Track EQ, can be used to isolate and eliminate camera noise. Again, see Chapter 8 for more information on using these plug-ins. The Multi-Band Dynamics plug-in is also an excellent tool that allows you to apply dynamics to specific frequencies.

FIX IT OR CONCEAL IT?
One excellent method of fixing a minor background noise problem in a video is to use a music bed to cover it up.

Ducking

Ducking is the term used for the process of temporarily lowering the volume of an audio track, usually music, under a voiceover narration. The basic process is very simple and can be quickly accomplished using Volume Envelopes in the ACID software.

As you might have guessed, ducking is not so easy if you need to perform it on the volume of a couple dozen tracks at the same time; such ducking in fact is not feasible. The easiest way to duck an entire project is by using a bus on the Mixer:

1. In the Mixer window, click the Insert Bus button. (For our example, let's say it is named "Bus A.")
2. Click the Device Selection button in the Track Header of a track that you want to assign to the new bus and, from the menu, select that bus (Bus A). You can use the Shift key to select a range of tracks or the Ctrl key to select multiple noncontiguous tracks, and then click one of the track's Device Selection buttons to assign them all to the same bus at once.
3. From the View menu, select Show Bus Tracks (or press B on your keyboard).

The bus track appears at the bottom of the timeline as another track. Initially, it might only appear as a single track labeled "Master" or "Surround Master," but you'll notice an independent vertical scroll bar on the far right of the track that you can use to scroll to the other bus tracks (one for each bus, assignable effect, or soft synth in your project). You can also expand the Bus Track section of the timeline to show all of your bus tracks by dragging the divider that separates the bus tracks from the main track area. The big benefit to this method, besides ease of use, is that you can now continue to refine the music mix as much as you want.

MIDI BUSSES
MIDI tracks cannot be assigned to audio busses and are instead assigned to soft synth busses in the Mixer window.

Another method you can use to duck a complex project is to downmix the project first to a single track. This method has the distinct disadvantage of not making future changes to the music portion of the project much harder. To duck a project in this way:

1. Mute any tracks that you don't want to duck under the voiceover (such as the voiceover narration itself, if it is already inserted).

2. From the Tools menu, select Render to New Track. Enter a name and press the Save button. This mixes down all of the tracks to a single file and inserts a new track into the timeline.

3. Delete (or mute) all of the tracks you mixed down so there is no duplication. You can select and mute (or delete) multiple tracks by holding down the Ctrl or Shift key while clicking on the Track Header.

4. Draw an event on the timeline that stretches for the duration of the media file and, in this case, the project.

5. Insert a Volume Envelope into the track: Right-click anywhere in the track and select from the context menu the Insert/Remove Envelope item, then click Volume.

6. Double-click the envelope to add nodes (keyframes). Each duck requires four nodes, as shown in Figure 11.9.

7. Drag the middle of the line (at the center of the four nodes) down to reduce the gain. The shorter segments between nodes one and two (and between three and four) serve as a brief fade-in and fade-out. These can be very short in length, often less than half of a second.

Figure 11.9

Two sections of the mixed-down background music track (bottom) have been ducked down to make the voiceover more clearly audible.

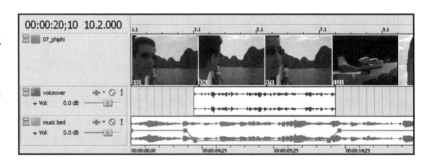

❋ **FREEHAND ENVELOPES**

Hold down the Shift key on your keyboard and use your mouse to draw envelope shapes by simply clicking and dragging on an envelope.

Clips on mixed-down tracks are inserted as Beatmapped clips by default. As such, the clip inherits the key and tempo of the project. If the project key or tempo is changed, the Beatmapped clip also changes.

Rendering Video

Although the fundamental procedure for creating video files is identical to that of creating audio files (from the File menu, click Render As, then select a video format), the actual rendering can be significantly more difficult. Video files tend to be much larger and can take much longer to render. For video that you are sending back to your Mini DV camcorder and television, the decision on format is easy: Render the video in exactly the same format. For video that is intended for the Internet, an intranet, or other distribution on a computer (such as via CD-ROM), the choices are much more complex because the files must be carefully compressed, balancing quality against file size. Of course, you might also want to make a DVD, too.

Render Once

For video that you want to send back out to your camcorder and television screen, file size and Internet bandwidth are not issues. You must maintain absolutely 100 percent of the quality of the original, so you do not want to re-render the video. The only way to maintain this level of quality is to use exactly the same settings as in your original video. To find the proper render settings, select the file in the Explorer window and look in the Summary view (see Figure 11.10). If the Summary view is not visible, click the arrow next to the Views button and make sure Summary View is checked.

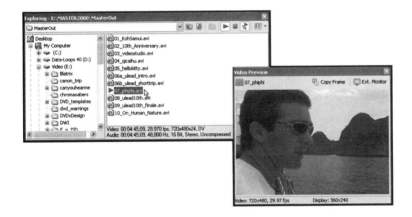

Figure 11.10

The Summary view at the bottom of the Explorer window displays the relevant video properties.

As shown in Figure 11.10, an NTSC standard consumer DV file in the United States would have dimensions of 720 × 480 at 29.970 fps. To render the file:

1. From the File menu, select Render As.

2. From the Save as Type list, select Video for Windows (.avi).

3. From the Template list, select NTSC DV.

4. Enter a name and click the Save button.

Rendering should be relatively fast, roughly equal to the duration of the file (that is, real time) or faster. This is because the video is not actually being rendered, but is being copied to a new file on your hard disk (which you can hear cranking away). If the render process takes a long time, it might indicate that something is wrong and that the file is indeed being re-rendered. To check the settings, from the Render As dialog, click the Custom button, which opens the Custom Settings Template dialog. For DV this is fairly easy, but the process might be more complex for other types of video. The list in Figure 11.11 shows two ASUS codecs that might be used to capture video from an analog camcorder (for example, Hi-8 or VHS-C). (See the following section to learn more about codecs.) When rendering video from these sources, you would want to use that particular codec. This list is found in the Custom Settings Template dialog, on the Video tab, in the Video Format list. The particular codecs vary from machine to machine and often depend on your hardware, in this case an ASUS capture card. Despite the apparent wide variety of choices, there is only one choice to maintain the highest quality: Whatever the codec of the source material is, that is the codec you should choose in the Video Format list.

Figure 11.11

Select a video codec from the Video Format list.

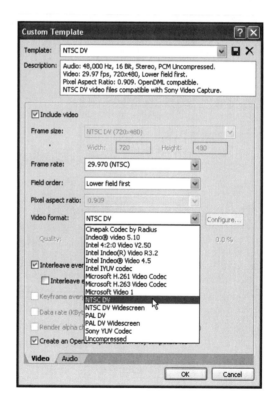

Compression

Video that is destined for playback on your computer or over the Internet is much more complex to render. This is because you must compress such video, reducing the file size and making video downloads more convenient. Compression occurs in a number of different ways and always results in some loss of quality:

❋ **Frame Size.** Full frame size video is typically 720 × 480 pixels for DV video in the United States. Reducing the frame size can dramatically decrease file size. Internet video should rarely be higher than 360 × 240.

❋ **Frame Rate.** Full frame rate video in the United States is almost 30 fps. Reducing this to 15 fps directly reduces the file size by half.

❋ **Compression Method.** Finally, you can use several different computer algorithms to compress video. A program that is used to compress video is known as a codec (compression decompression). Some are better than others, and some are better at specific applications. In addition, you need to understand who your viewers are, because they also need to have the same codec installed on their computer. Further, streaming technologies frequently require special Web servers to distribute the files over the Internet properly, so you need to verify that your Internet Service Provider (ISP) has the correct server installed. Specific compression methods are discussed in more detail in following sections.

What Compresses Well

Not all video compresses equally well. Talking heads, such as reporters on the evening news, and video with little action compress well. Fast-action sports with panning camera moves, ocean waves, and trees with quivering leaves all compress poorly. Unfortunately for the ACID application, music videos or anything with a lot of cuts and scene changes also tend to compress poorly. So, what is considered good compression? Anything can be compressed, but the obvious goal is to have something that still looks good after compression. On the Internet, what looks good is highly subjective, and almost all video, even of the very highest of quality using the latest twenty-first-century codecs, still do not compare well with even the lowest-quality television broadcasts.

Compression of video can be done a number of ways, but it is most commonly performed in two places: intraframe and interframe. Intraframe compression happens within single frames of video and is similar to how a JPG picture (a popular still-image format on the Internet) is compressed. Although an uncompressed picture (in the BMP or TIF format, for example) might identify every single pixel in an image with 100-percent fidelity and might take up 1 MB (1,000 KB) of hard disk space, the same picture saved as a JPG might be only 20 KB. Such compression is achieved by creating blocks of similar color. For example, an uncompressed image might represent four slightly different blue pixels with four pieces of information, but a JPG image might change all of those pixels to the same color blue and represent the entire block with one piece of information.

This does result in a loss of some quality and can sometimes be seen as blockiness in an image, especially along high-contrast lines.

The other way video is compressed is interframe, or between frames. In this case, a similar process compares blocks of color in a number of different frames and saves this information to a single piece of information, instead of many pieces for each frame. This is why video with little motion (little change between frames) compresses much better. Of course, this explanation greatly simplifies this decidedly high-tech process, but even a basic understanding will help you to make better choices about video for the Internet.

The ACID software can save video in any codec that you have installed on your computer, including AVI, MOV, Real, WMV, DivX, and MPEG. The AVI and MOV formats do not define individual codecs and should not be confused with the actual codecs that are used for compression. In other words, it is not possible to say that .mov files are better than .avi files, because each might use different underlying codecs or possibly even very similar codecs. There are situations when you might want to use one or the other, and the following sections will try to guide you a bit in making a decision.

Video for Windows (.avi)

The .avi file format is the Video for Windows general-purpose file format. AVI can use a large number of codecs, some suitable for professional-quality productions and some suitable for highly compressed Internet transmission. Figure 11.11 shows a list of the possible codecs that might be available on a typical Windows PC, although the exact codecs will vary depending on what you have installed.

1. From the File menu, select Render As and, from the Save as Type list, select Video for Windows (.avi).
2. Click the Custom button.
3. In the Custom Settings Template dialog, click the Video tab.
4. Select a codec from the Video Format list.

In most cases, the .avi format is best used for video that is not intended for high compression because Microsoft has a different format tailored for compression (.wmv). Still, the older Cinepak and Indeo codecs yield fairly good video, although the file sizes are larger. These codecs are also widely available, even on older PCs, so compatibility is usually not a problem. Typically, .avi files are used to capture and edit video that is being sent to television (see the previous "Render Once" section), although there is no reason that you could not use highly compressed codecs with the .avi format (such as VDOnet or the Microsoft H.263 video codec).

Most codecs on the Video Format list for .avi files have special configuration properties that you can access by clicking the Configure button next to the Video Format list.

Windows Media Video (.wmv)

The Windows Media Video (.wmv) format is up to version 10 in this installation of ACID. Just because you have the most recent incarnation of any format or codec does not mean your audience does, and many people resent having to download another application to view your video. However, the .wmv format for Internet distribution is often a very good choice for one simple reason: It is the most widely playable format by quite a large margin. We wish Real well and love our Mac, but, honestly, the quality of WMV is very high, and the vast majority of users will not have to install anything to play it back. The .wmv format is a streaming media format, although it doesn't have to be used that way. To use the .wmv format:

1. From the File menu, select Render As and, from the Save as Type list, select Windows Media Video V9 (.wmv).

2. Select a template based on your viewer connection to the source. (It is also possible to target a number of connection speeds for streaming.)

3. Click the Custom button.

4. Bit rate is the most critical factor in streaming video. The total bit rate is the audio bit rate plus the video bit rate together. No matter what you select on the other tabs, the final file will have a bit rate that is equal to the one selected on this tab. It is possible to select audio bit rates that are higher than the total bit rate on the Bit Rate tab, so be careful.

5. Set the balance of bit rates between the Audio tab and Video tab. The only way to find this balance is to experiment.

Finding proper bit rates and balancing the audio and video is not easy because you will always ruin your crystal-clear video and your elegantly mixed audio in the process. The trick is to determine the best possible acceptable quality for your target data rate. Audio takes up much less bandwidth (data rate) than video and, because this is the ACID software after all, you should be able to get pretty good sound. One other unfortunate aspect of this experimentation is that it takes a lot of time in rendering. Rendering compressed video is a slow process, and there is no way to speed it up.

The Video tab has a number of additional options on it to fine-tune the encoding of the visual portion of your file. Although all of these controls are very important, their effects can be subtle:

❋ **Mode** determines how the code operates. We like (and recommend) Quality VBR (*variable bit rate*) in almost all situations. Streaming video requires a CBR (*constant bit rate*) mode, so use CBR Two-Pass in that situation, although this option takes twice as long to render.

❋ **Format** asks you to select a codec or variation of Windows Media Video. Choose V7 or V8 if you are worried about backward compatibility with older machines, although V9 is becoming more universally used every day.

* **Image Size** is another straightforward variable that sets the dimensions of the movie. Why Microsoft suggests types of movies with the sizes (such as Animation or Presentation Small) is a mystery, but you should try to maintain the aspect ratio of the original or risk distortion. Select the Custom item from the list and manually enter the size you need. You can keep the Pixel Aspect Ratio at 1.000 (Square) unless you are using widescreen video.

* **Frame Rate** is the frame rate and is not subtle at all. U.S. television is almost 30 fps, movies are typically 24 fps, and low-quality television cartoons (such as *G.I. Joe*) are usually 15 fps. Frame rate is critical to the smoothness of the video, but lower frame rates dramatically and directly reduce file size. A frame rate of 15 fps is usually just about right.

* **Seconds per Keyframe** is a subtle and complex variable that has no easy answer. IFrames are the information frames (like keyframes) used by the codec. Keyframes are high-quality frames and thus take up more space in a file. The intermediate frames derive from the keyframes that surround them. In the simplest case, you could make every odd frame an IFrame and every even frame an interpolated frame. Every intermediate frame would then take up virtually no memory and would not be saved in the file, but would instead be rendered on the fly based on the surrounding keyframes (IFrames) and would be an amalgamation of the two. In practice, there are a number of intermediate frames between every pair of IFrames, and the rendering calculations can be quite complex. More pragmatically still, entering lower values (with fewer seconds between IFrames) in this box results in higher quality because keyframes are measured in the number of seconds between IFrames. Most other programs (codecs) measure keyframes in terms of IFrames per second instead of the other way around.

* **Quality** is the basic keyframe quality of the compressed file. Again, this subtle variable is constrained by the bit rate, and this might not be that important. There are few advantages to increasing the quality above 80 percent, yet 0 percent does not seem to negatively impact the video.

On the Bit Rate tab, you can select a number of different target bit rates for the final file. The size of the file must be large enough to accommodate the higher bit rate, but all of the selected bit rates are available on a Windows Media Video server.

WHAT'S NEXT?

This book details the latest and greatest formats. By the time you read it, however, there may very well be updates to these formats. Some might have new version numbers and others might even have completely different names (although the companies will probably still be around).

QuickTime (.mov)

The QuickTime video file format is an excellent choice for both Apple Macs and Windows computers. On many systems, there are more varied codec options that come with QuickTime Pro than you'd have with the AVI format. So, for example, you could select a DV/DVCPRO - NTSC codec to match footage shot with a MiniDV camcorder or you could select a Sorenson Video 3 codec (which is, incidentally, a very lovely codec) for efficient distribution on the Web.

Most codecs on the Video Format list for QuickTime files have special configuration properties that you can access by clicking the Custom button next to the Template item in the Render As dialog (Figure 11.12).

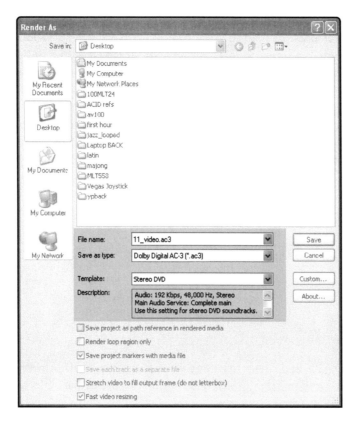

Figure 11.12
QuickTime Pro codec choices.

Streaming

Streaming is the process that enables you to watch a video as it is downloading. There is nothing magic about streaming video. Despite what you might have heard, streaming video does not download any faster than anything else. To watch an entire video from beginning to end requires the same amount of time, streamed or not. Some streaming methods do allow you to view the middle or end of a video file without downloading the entire video, however. The concept behind choosing an appropriate stream is to create streaming video files that match the bandwidth of the viewers' connection to the video, either over an internal company intranet or over the Internet. For example, you might want to stream video at 256 Kbps for viewers with DSL connections. The idea is that the video stream data rate should not exceed the connection speed data rate, allowing the video to be transmitted and played back at the same time. Of course, the real world is a complicated place, consisting of ISPs, routers, and Internet congestion, among a million other variables, so selecting a proper data rate for streaming video is not easy.

Properly streamed video also requires a server, such as a Windows Media Video server, and these cost money. You must install this software server on the computer on which you will store the accessible video file that people can download. Usually such a server is at an ISP, although you could run it yourself on any computer connected to the Internet. While the compression codec and player are free from Microsoft, the server is not. Your ISP may or may not offer this service at all and will probably charge to let you use it. Most likely, you will need to shop around for a company that specializes in streaming media service to stream your video properly.

DATA RATE AND STREAMING

Data rate is measured in bits per second (bps). Bits (b) are different from bytes (B), which are used to measure file size, where:

1 byte (B) = 8 bits (b)

So, if you wanted to stream a one-minute, 1-MB video file in real time, the minimum data rate you would need is:

(1,000,000 bytes × 8 bits/byte) / 60 seconds = 133 Kbps

Remember, this is the minimum data rate. In the real world, you will certainly need a connection with a higher rate.

Audio for DVD

MPEG-2 is the format used for DVD-Video. There are three ways to use the ACID software to make a soundtrack for your DVD, and selecting which one is right for your project is largely a matter of workflow and convenience. You inevitably will need a DVD-authoring application (and a burner) to burn a DVD disc. Although we will not cover the details of DVD video encoding in this book, we can offer an overview of the three audio options you will find in your authoring application, as well as in the ACID program. Although you must encode the video in an MPEG-2 format, the audio can take three different forms:

❋ **PCM audio** is the uncompressed audio format that your Mini DV camcorder shoots and is the digital format found on audio CDs. DVD audio (and Mini DV audio) uses a 16-bit depth at a 48- kHz sample rate. PCM audio is a part of the DVD specification and therefore is supported by all DVD players. The only disadvantage is that PCM audio takes up a lot of room on the disc because it is relatively uncompressed.

❋ **MPEG-1, Layer 3 audio** (otherwise known as MP3) is a compressed digital format that is part of the VCD and SVCD disk format, but is not in the DVD specification. Because the VCD and SVCD formats were popular in Asia and because most DVD players are made in Asia, many DVD players also support the MP3 audio format for DVD-Video discs, although they are not required to do so. The advantage to MP3 audio for DVDs is that you can fit a lot of audio on a disc, with the disadvantage being that it is not a universally supported (or required) format and thus presents some compatibility problems.

❋ **AC3 audio** is a licensed format from Dolby Labs, which means that it costs money to use. It comes in two flavors, stereo and 5.1 surround sound. It has the advantage that it is both a compressed data format and a part of the DVD specification, meaning that it is a required playback format for DVD players. Clearly, AC3 stereo encoding is highly desirable, and you should look for it as a feature when you buy a DVD-authoring application. AC3 5.1 surround sound is very cool and desirable, but you will pay a pretty penny for it (more accurately 30,000 or so pretty pennies).

So, that's the theoretical answer to the question of audio for DVD discs. The more pragmatic question is how do you output audio for your DVD from the ACID software? There are a few answers, depending on which video editing or DVD-authoring applications are installed on your computer. For our purposes here, we will assume that you have an editor and a DVD app because this discussion is moot without them. When you finish your project, you'll go to the File menu and select Render As. Then, in the Save as Type drop-down list (see Figure 11.13), choose one of the following:

❋ **MPEG-2** (for example, MainConcept MPEG-2 [.mpg]) renders a complete movie that is ready to be burned to a DVD with no further encoding. You will have to handle the specifics here, and the choices might be complex depending on your encoder. Furthermore, you'll have to make sure the file you create is compatible with the DVD-authoring software you are using. If your DVD app insists on re-encoding your video, something is wrong with your chosen settings.

❋ **AVI** is perhaps the easiest choice. Assuming your video is from a Mini DV camcorder, you should render out in an NTSC DV template. This enables you to create a high-quality master of your video for archiving back to tape, which is always a good idea. To create a DVD, you'll let your DVD-authoring application take care of all of the complexities of encoding for you. Again, if you have a choice, select stereo AC3 encoding in your app.

❋ **Dolby Digital AC3 (.ac3)** is a great option, provided you have purchased the encoder. For stereo projects, all you need is a stereo encoder. Surround projects require a much more expensive solution. Almost all DVD-authoring applications support AC3 audio as a valid file format, even if they don't actually perform the encoding. One other issue you might have to confront is that because you are encoding only the audio stream, you must synchronize the audio stream with your video in your authoring application. This is automatic 99 percent of the time, but you will certainly need to verify the results when you finish.

Figure 11.13
Optional DVD audio options in the ACID Pro software only.

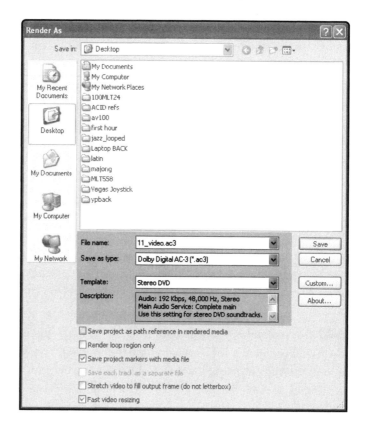

Ultimately, we recommend that you down-mix your project, render out your project at the highest-quality settings (NTSC DV), and let your DVD-authoring application take care of the compression, both for the video and the audio. If your authoring app doesn't include an AC3 encoder, you might want to use the ACID Pro application with the Sony Media Software encoder, or you might want to consider purchasing a new DVD-authoring app that includes such an encoder.

DVD-Video and DVD-Audio

DVD-Video and DVD-Audio are specific variations of the DVD disc format as defined in the DVD specification, just as the audio CD has a specific standard definition. The ACID software does not output or burn DVD disks, but several DVD-authoring applications do, including DVD Architect from Sony Media Software. Almost all consumer (that is, affordable) DVD-authoring apps burn DVD-Video discs, which is the format that Hollywood uses to distribute movies and that the DVD player in your living room doubtlessly plays. DVD-Audio is a different format that is not supported by most DVD-authoring applications or living-room DVD players at this time. If the app or the player does not specifically say that it supports this format, it likely doesn't. You could, however, create pseudo-DVD-Audio discs by encoding your music using an AC3 encoder and burning a DVD-Video disc with blank (black) video at an extremely low bit rate. This enables you to put a few hours of very high-quality 5.1 surround sound audio or even 10 (or more) hours of high-quality stereo music all on a single disc.

Video Editing?

Although the ACID software can handle finished video very well, it is not a video editing application. In addition to Sony Media Software's Vegas, a host of applications from many companies are available to edit video on your computer, but at the point that you are using the ACID application to score a project, the video editing should probably already be finished. One advantage to using Sony Media Software video editing software is that the audio is not an afterthought in these products. As discussed in the previous chapter, you can use the MTC and MIDI Clock features to synchronize and trigger these video editing applications, adding a new dimension in flexibility to video scoring. By linking the Vegas program and the ACID software together, you can edit video simultaneously with the musical soundtrack in the ACID application, using the Vegas application's Preview window to monitor the timing and synchronization. To use the Vegas software with the ACID application:

1. Run both the Vegas and ACID applications.

2. Configure the ACID software to output MIDI Timecode (MTC). (The ACID software and the Vegas application both chase MTC and not MIDI Clock.) To do so, open the Options menu, choose the Preferences item, and then click on the Sync tab. In the Generate MIDI Timecode Settings option, select one of the Sony Media Software MIDI Routers. See the previous chapter for details.

3. Configure the Vegas application to chase MIDI Timecode. Going through the same menus as in the previous step, select the same device you selected for the Trigger from MIDI Timecode Settings on the Sync tab. Place the Video Preview window in a location that the ACID software will not cover once it has the focus. Dual monitors would be handy at this point.

4. Enable (arm) the Vegas software to listen for MTC. From the Options menu, select the Time-code option, then select Chase to MIDI Timecode or (as in the ACID software) press Ctrl+F7. The Vegas time display shows the message "MTC Input Waiting."

5. Enable the ACID software to generate MTC. From the Options menu, select the Timecode option, and then select Generate MIDI Timecode or (as in the Vegas application) press F7. The time display shows the message "MIDI Timecode Out - Enabled."

6. Play back the ACID application. Vegas chases the ACID software, and the time display shows the message "MTC Input Locked."

Depending on the complexity of your project, the combination of using a professional-grade video editing application in synchronization with the ACID software can be taxing on your computer. Complex sections of your video project, especially areas with lots of overlay graphics and titles, might not preview at the full frame rate when working this way. This is a good way to fine-tune both the video and audio, although it is a bit clumsy and hard on your computer. Following the philosophy of rendering once for video, you might want to work with both applications, render the ACID project first, and then insert the audio from the ACID software into the video application. It is usually better to render audio twice (once in the ACID software and once in the video app) because you can render audio uncompressed (using PCM audio) and it still won't take up that much room. Video on a computer is almost always compressed in some way, and preventing recompression is critical.

Chapter 11 Quiz

1. The ACID software includes extensive video editing tools. (T/F)

2. The Video Preview window allows you to preview video:

   A. That has been selected in the Explorer window

   B. That is added to the timeline

   C. Either A or B

   D. Neither A nor B

3. The ACID software allows you to view your video on an external monitor. (T/F)

4. How many video tracks are allowed in an ACID project?

   A. 1

   B. 2

C. 3

D. Unlimited number of video tracks

5. Which of the following operations can you perform on video events?

A. Drag

B. Split

C. Trim

D. A and C

6. You will want to zoom in when marking video frames. (T/F)

7. Matching the tempo of your ACID project to the tempo of your video can be very important. (T/F)

8. The audio track of a video file is almost always beatmapped. (T/F)

9. The ACID software does not support which of the following formats of audio?

A. PCM audio

B. MP3

C. AC3 audio

D. DTS audio

10. Sony Media Software's Vegas application is a better option than the ACID application for editing video. (T/F)

12 } Publishing

As satisfying and fun as it has been to work and play in Sony Media Software's ACID® application, cooped up in your studio by yourself with the lights low and the volume high, at some point it is time to share your compositions with the world at large. Publishing your music breaks down into two separate, but interrelated steps: rendering and distributing. *Rendering* is the process of saving your music to an audio file that your listeners can play back independently of the ACID software. *Distributing* is a matter of selecting a destination for your music, whether streaming it over the Internet or burning it to an audio CD. This chapter covers everything from file formats and codecs to streaming media and copyright laws.

Rendering

ACID projects (.acd) contain all of the information about the loops, timing, envelopes, and effects necessary to create a song, but they are not audio files in and of themselves. You need to save these project files to an audio file format before the general public can listen to them. This is called *rendering*, which describes the process of creating audio files, video files, and 3D computer animations, among other things. Rendering in the ACID software is a fairly simple process on the surface:

1. From the File menu, select Render As.

2. In the Render As dialog, enter a name for the file.

3. From the Save As Type list, select a file format.

4. Click the Save button.

At first glance, this process couldn't be much simpler. But watch the third step: It's a long one. Explaining how to select the proper file format occupies a large portion of this chapter. After you've selected an appropriate format that meets your particular distribution needs, there are many controls and settings for each format that you can tweak and adjust. In most situations, you can achieve excellent results by selecting a template that matches what you want to do with your music file. In some situations, you might want to fine-tune the settings of the format to get the best results.

Render Options

The following render options are listed at the bottom of the Render As dialog (see Figure 12.1):

* **Save Project as Path Reference in Rendered Media** saves a path in the data header of the audio or video file that you save that points back to the original project file. This will let you find the project associated with a rendered song at a later date. This information can only be retrieved using Sony Media Software applications. The real trick here is that when you use a rendered file in another ACID project, you can right-click it and open the original project for instant editing.

* **Render Loop Region Only** lets you render a portion of the entire project. You might do this to create a loop file or to test a smaller section of your project.

* **Save Project Markers with Media File** saves all project markers with the rendered file. Project markers are used only for reference purposes and do not change the audio characteristics of a file. These markers are proprietary to Sony Media Software, and you can see them only when using the ACID software (in the Track Properties window) or other Sony Media Software products (such as the Vegas application).

* **Save Sections as Regions with Media File** allows you to save section markers with your project (to identify verses, refrains and so on).

* **Save Each Track as a Separate File** does exactly that. There are a number of reasons you might want to render individual tracks to separate files. The main reason is to send your creation to a post-production facility for professional mixing and mastering. The ACID software then renders the tracks one at a time to a media file that spans the length of the project, even if it is 90 percent silence. Thus if you have a 10-track project, the total combined file size will be 10 times as large as a normal render, and it will also take 10 times as long to complete. The files will be saved as Track ## trackname.wav (or whatever file type you have chosen).

* **Stretch Video to Fill Output Frame (Do Not Letterbox)** resizes the video, ignoring aspect ratio constraints to match your output video render settings. This will distort your video.

* **Fast Video Resizing** lets the ACID software perform quicker renders, with some minor sacrifices in quality. You might want to use this option while you are testing the output and then uncheck it for final renders.

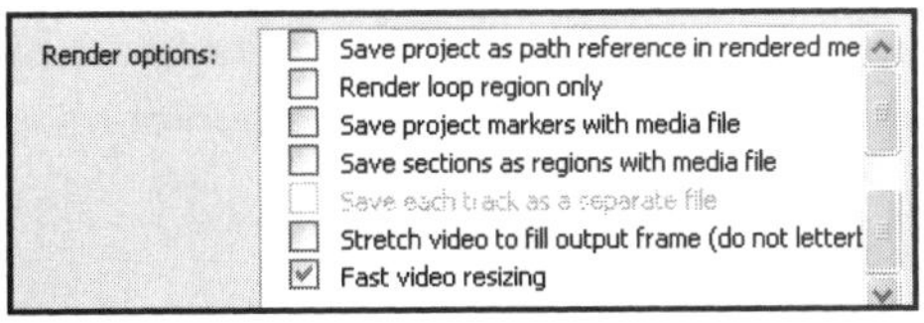

Figure 12.1
The render options at the bottom of the Render As dialog.

Digital Audio

All audio files on a computer are digital. Regardless of the format or encoding used to convert an analog audio source to digital, the digitization (quantization) process necessarily and discretely approximates the smooth analog world of sound. As a result, no matter the level of quality, some information is inevitably lost. This loss might be inaudible to most listeners and might even be considered theoretically imperceptible. Nonetheless, some information is always lost. Three major variables influence quality and file size of your output: sample rate, bit depth, and the number of channels.

Sample Rate

We call every digital piece of the analog world that we record a *sample*. The more samples we take per second, the greater the fidelity. This sample rate is measured in cycles per second or Hertz (Hz). So an 11,000-Hz (11-kHz) sample rate would collect 11,000 pieces of information in a second, which seems pretty high. Higher sample rates are better, but the quality, or fidelity, of the digital file compared to the original analog source depends on the frequency of the audio waves as well. Higher-frequency audio is, by definition, composed of more audio waves per second and thus requires higher sample rates for quality digital audio. In other words, lower-pitched audio can be digitized at lower sample rates and still retain a fair degree of fidelity. Figure 12.2 shows an example of how a continuous wave of analog audio might be digitized into discrete pieces of information. The top image shows how the waveform might appear over time. Notice that the waves on the right side of the graph are slightly closer together, representing higher-frequency sound waves. The middle graph is a simulated digitization of the waves at a certain sample rate; this type of graph does a poor job of simulating the higher-frequency waves. (Actually, this type of digitization does a poor job of simulating any kind of waves, but this is just an illustration, so accuracy is not important.) The bottom graph has a sample rate that is double the rate of the middle graph. It gets much closer to representing the original wave. Sound waves are much more complex and varied than any of these graphs can accurately represent, especially for music and other rich sources.

Bit Depth

Sample rate is only half of the quality equation. The other variable that determines quality is the bit depth. Bit depth determines how much information is used to describe each sample. Another way to say this is that bit depth determines the resolution or number of steps used to describe the amplitude of a sample. More information per sample yields higher-quality audio at the expense of larger file sizes. For one second of uncompressed CD-quality stereo audio:

(44,100Hz × 16 bits) × 2 stereo channels = 1,411,200 bits

Or, because eight bits are in a byte (for reasons we won't go into here):

(1,411,200 bits / 8) = 176,400 bytes

Figure 12.2
A continuous analog audio signal and how it might appear once digitized. The bottom graph represents a sample rate twice that of the middle graph.

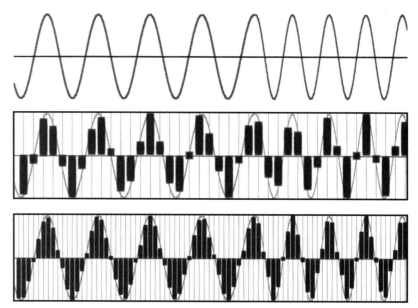

Since the dawn of CD audio, people have described 16-bit, 44.1-kHz digital audio as being close to perfection. From our discussion so far, it is easy to see that this is an exaggeration. When CD audio was new, it was argued that this level of digital quality could accurately represent the analog audio reality to a level that was indistinguishable from the original sound as far as human perception is concerned. This may be more or less true. Modern computers, camcorders, DAT machines, and studios can now exceed this quality level, as can the ACID software. In fact, depending on your hardware, 24-bit audio with a 192-kHz sample rate is not uncommon. Whether any human being could ever possibly detect the difference between one of these files and a standard CD audio file is debatable, although some audiophiles insist that the difference is not only detectable, but that the quality gap between these files is as wide as the Grand Canyon. Whether or not the difference is minor, it is undeniable that more information is saved with the higher bit depth and sample rate digital audio, and this is undoubtedly a good thing. Keep in mind that there is no point in converting 44.1-kHz, 16-bit audio files to a "higher-quality" format because this conversion will not increase quality. Recording source material at the highest possible sample and bit rates is a good idea, provided your recording equipment supports the target digital quality levels. You gain nothing by rendering projects at a higher bit depth, such as 24 bits, and then down-converting to 16 bits for CD audio or Internet distribution.

Channels

Every project will also have a number of channels. Monophonic projects have one, and stereo projects have two. Logically enough, stereo files are twice as large as monophonic files. Almost all recording is monophonic, but almost all projects are stereo. 5.1 surround mixes have six channels and are six times larger than monophonic files, but must be compressed using a special Dolby 5.1 surround sound encoder, which makes direct comparisons with other formats irrelevant. (See Chapter 11 for more information on AC3 encoding.)

Audio File Formats

You can save (render) the final song to a number of file formats. One file format isn't necessarily better than another, but you should base your choice on three factors:

- ❋ The destination of the file (for example, the Internet or CD audio)
- ❋ Whether the file needs to be compressed
- ❋ Your audience and their software

The rest of this discussion refers to some of the more common formats, many of which are already installed on your computer. These can be divided into archival formats (large files, high quality) and distribution formats (compressed files in formats that everyone else already has).

For archival files that will remain on your computer, you should select a potentially lossless file format. This means that the file will retain 100 percent of the quality and will not be significantly digitally compressed: .aif, .sfa, .pca, .w64, and .wav are all appropriate selections for high-quality storage. Take note of the qualification above: "potentially" lossless. File formats can use different kinds of encoding, which we'll discuss a little later.

When you distribute your files anywhere other than on CD-audio discs, you will probably select a format with a small data footprint. Compressed file formats are for use when you need to create smaller files, primarily for distribution on the Internet or for playback on portable digital audio players. All compressed file formats reduce quality somewhat, although this reduction can be very minor to practically inaudible. The balance between file size and quality is a delicate one that requires some experimentation and experience. Some compressed audio formats are .mp3, .ogg, and .wma. An additional consideration for compressed files distributed on the Internet is whether you want to stream the format.

> ※ **CODECS AND FILE FORMATS**
> Although you can recognize file formats by their file extensions (such as .wav, .txt, or .html), audio (and video) file formats might also be wrappers around the real format (codec) of a file. For example, a .wav file might use the PCM (uncompressed) format or the MPEG-1, Layer-3 format. See the section "Codecs and Compression" later in this chapter for more information.

Here is a partial list of available audio formats:

※ **Macintosh AIFF (.aif)** is the standard audio file format for Apple Macintosh computers, just as .wav is for Windows. It is a lossless file format that preserves the quality of your audio but creates rather large files.

※ **QuickTime (.mov)** is primarily a video format, but it can be used for audio-only files as well. This format allows you to select a number of different codecs for compression, so this format supports both uncompressed and compressed audio data.

※ **MP3 Audio (.mp3)** is a popular format that produces well-compressed files that retain a good level of quality. It offers many settings that you can tweak to adjust the balance of file size against quality. Because this format is so widely used, it is a good choice for songs distributed to a general audience over the Internet. Many portable media devices can play MP3 files.

※ **OggVorbis (.ogg)** is another compressed media file format that is appropriate for audio delivered over the Internet. It is an open standard audio format that anyone can and should use freely. Most other codecs (notably .mp3) require some type of payment for their use. (In most cases, you pay automatically when you buy software such as the ACID program.) OGG yields high compression ratios, maintains good quality, and supports streaming. This format is excellent, but, at the time of this writing, it is not as widely distributed as the .mp3 or .wma formats, although player software is free to download. Unfortunately, most portable music players do not support OGG. (Send your favorite manufacturer a polite letter requesting support today.)

※ **Sony Audio (.sfa)** is a proprietary format from Sony Media Software that is available only on computers that have software from Sony Media Software installed on them. As with some other formats, you can select a number of codecs for compression, so .sfa files can be compressed or uncompressed, using any codec available for .wav format files.

※ **Sony Perfect Clarity Audio (.pca)** is another proprietary format from Sony Media Software. This is a more advanced format that compresses files losslessly. This means that the file size of a .pca file is considerably smaller than standard uncompressed file formats, while still retaining 100 percent of the quality of the original file. For audio files that will remain on your computer, this format is an excellent choice because it enables you to save disk space without sacrificing quality. Use caution when distributing .pca files to others because they won't be able to use these files unless they have software from Sony Media Software on their computer. The amount of lossless compression depends on the complexity of the project and the source media used, but it can typically result in a file size savings of 30 percent or so.

❋ **RealMedia (.rm)** is a compressed file format that is suitable for distribution on the Internet. A direct competitor to the .wma format, RealMedia files are highly compressed, retain good quality, and can be streamed over the Internet. Listeners will need to download the latest version of RealPlayer (available as a free download) to listen to .rm files, but this major format is widely distributed. The format does not necessarily need a server to stream. (See the section "RealMedia (.rm)" later in this chapter.)

❋ **Sony Wave64 (.w64)** is similar to the .sfa format and allows compressed or uncompressed audio. The advantage to using this format is that it allows you to create much longer files than the standard Windows .wav format, which is limited to creating files of less than two gigabytes (2 GB) or over 3 hours and 20 minutes (3:20) of CD-quality audio. As with other Sony Media Software proprietary formats, most non–Sony Media Software programs cannot play back .w64 files.

❋ **Microsoft Wave (.wav)** is the standard audio format for Windows computers, just as the .aif format is the standard for audio on Macs. Like the .mov format, the .wav format is not defined by the codec used to achieve compression, but instead acts as a wrapper for a media file and allows you to select from a wide variety of codecs and compression methods.

❋ **Windows Media Audio (.wma)** is the default format for highly compressed audio from Microsoft. The latest version offers quality that is at least as good as that of the other highly compressed formats (such as .rm, .ogg, or .mp3) and can be streamed. It is also nearly universally available on Windows computers, thanks to Microsoft's controversial bundling practices. You still need to make sure your audience has the most up-to-date player if you use the latest version of the encoder.

Compression

As the previous discussion of file formats hinted, the real decision about how to render your final song boils down to digital compression. The first question is whether you need compression. For archiving masters on a modern computer (assuming that it includes a CD/DVD burner and large hard disk), you do not want to compress your audio because you must retain the absolute best quality. For distribution, you do want to compress the audio efficiently, so the second question is what kind of compression you should use. Audio compression is considerably easier to understand than video compression, and you have a number of choices that all produce quite good results. Although this topic might seem fairly complicated at first, always keep in mind that you can almost always get away with picking a compression method and selecting a template without giving the choices a second thought.

DYNAMIC OR DATA COMPRESSION?
Compression of file size and audio data is distinct from the dynamic compression of music, which is the process of reducing the dynamic range and is discussed in depth in Chapter 8.

Lossless Audio

The conversion from analog to digital automatically results in some information being lost (that is, the process is lossy), so no digital audio formats are lossless compared to an analog signal. Within the realm of digital audio, however, some formats are considered lossless—that is, you lose no audio information beyond the initial digital-to-analog conversion when saving to a lossless format. For example, if you are using a 44.1-kHz, 16-bit source file in the ACID software and you render using a lossless format, the rendered file is identical to the original. This does not mean that you won't lose information when mixing files together, however, but this loss is due to mixing and overlap of the audio, not to the process of rendering itself. As the previous calculations show, one second of lossless stereo audio at 44.1 kHz and 16 bits directly yields a file of about 176 KB.

Lossless means no loss of audio information. It is possible in many situations to eliminate unnecessary data from any computer file (including audio files) without losing any information. ZIP files are an example. This means that you can compress an audio file while still maintaining 100 percent of the original file's audio quality. The Sony Media Software Perfect Clarity Audio (.pca) format is an example of a lossless yet size-compressed file format.

Lossy Audio

Although all digital audio loses some quality when being converted to digital from analog, compressed audio uses sophisticated algorithms to create smaller files while retaining much, but perhaps not all, of the quality of the original. Most compression methods claim that the loss in quality is minimal, but the art of compression is balancing file size against quality. Every codec or compression method works in a different way. Some are targeted to compress spoken audio, and some are better at music. Finding the best compression method for your particular audio requires some research and experimentation.

Most often compression results in a loss of quality in the stereo image or spatial depth, in the dynamic range, and in the frequency range of the audio. Compression methods are developed using the principles of psychoacoustics, which is the study of how humans perceive sound. The goal is to remove information from the audio file that cannot be perceived by the human ear as interpreted by the brain. Of course, any science that involves perception and the human brain is bound to cover a lot of territory, which leaves plenty of room for discussion about which compression methods are the best. Again, the best compression method for your audio depends on what type of audio you are compressing (such as spoken words versus music), how much compression you need, and what sounds good to your ears. We'll deal with compression in more detail in the "Codecs and Compression" section later in this chapter.

Down-Converting

Source audio of a higher quality (bit depth and sample rate) can be rendered to a lower-quality format. For example, it is possible, and might even be necessary, to covert 24-bit, 192-kHz audio to CD-quality 16-bit, 44.1-kHz audio or even further down for Internet audio. This down-conversion results in smaller, and thus more portable, files. The process of down-converting or down-sampling is distinct from what a codec does in compressing a file. Combining careful down-converting with a good compression codec is the key to minimizing the size of an audio file.

Down-converting automatically results in some loss of quality and has the same problems inherent in converting analog audio to digital. Some type of down-conversion occurs for some files when you use source media files in the ACID software that are of a higher quality than the final rendered file. At times, this can introduce audible artifacts into the file that you can minimize or cover by using the Dither plug-in, which is discussed in detail in Chapter 8.

Codecs and Compression

When the ACID software renders audio (and video) files to minimize file size, they can be compressed. The files then need to be decompressed when played back. A codec performs this compression/decompression process. Any codec that you use to compress a file also needs to be installed on any computer that your audience wants to use for playback. Most file formats also define how the file is encoded (for example, .jpg files use JPEG encoding), but this is not necessarily the case with audio and video files, in which the file format can be distinct from the codec. The .wav file format does not define how the file is compressed, and, in this case, the file format and the encoding format do not need to be the same. Indeed, the .wav file format can use PCM (*Pulse Code Modulation*, or uncompressed) encoding or even MPEG-1, Layer-3 encoding, using any number of different codecs (see Figure 12.3). The .wav file format merely serves as a wrapper around the file, telling Windows about the file and how to play it back. Using a Windows computer does not guarantee that you will be able to play back all files in the .wav format because some might be encoded with codecs that are not installed on your computer.

Confusion can arise because of the language used in the dialogs when you are rendering audio files. As Figure 12.3 shows, the .wav file format Custom Template dialog allows you to select a format from a list. This is just a list of codecs, and you should not confuse them with the file format. You can check which audio codecs are installed on your computer by going to the Windows Control Panel, clicking the Multimedia option, and, in the Multimedia Properties dialog, clicking the Devices tab and expanding the Audio Compression Codecs tree, as shown in Figure 12.4. You'll notice that the list in Figure 12.3 is similar to, but not the same as, the list in Figure 12.4.

Figure 12.3

The .wav format can use any number of codecs to encode and possibly compress audio.

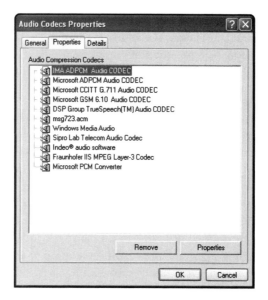

Custom Template

Template:	Default Template
Description:	Render 44,100 Hz, 16 Bit, Stereo PCM wave file.

Format:	PCM (uncompressed)
	CCITT A-Law
	CCITT u-Law
Attributes:	DSP Group TrueSpeech(TM)
	GSM 6.10
Sample rate (Hz):	IEEE Float (uncompressed)
	IMA ADPCM
Bit depth:	Microsoft ADPCM
	MPEG Layer-3
Channels:	PCM (uncompressed)

OK   Cancel

Figure 12.4

All of the audio codecs installed in Windows. Many more codecs may be available in the ACID software than are shown in this Windows registered list.

Audio Codecs Properties

General Properties Details

Audio Compression Codecs

- IMA ADPCM Audio CODEC
- Microsoft ADPCM Audio CODEC
- Microsoft CCITT G.711 Audio CODEC
- Microsoft GSM 6.10 Audio CODEC
- DSP Group TrueSpeech(TM) Audio CODEC
- msg723.acm
- Windows Media Audio
- Sipro Lab Telecom Audio Codec
- Indeo® audio software
- Fraunhofer IIS MPEG Layer-3 Codec
- Microsoft PCM Converter

Remove   Properties

OK   Cancel

As mentioned, sometimes a specific codec or encoding format defines a file format. The popular MP3 format defines a file format (.mp3) that is in turn defined by the MPEG-1, Layer-3 encoding used to compress the audio. This MPEG-1, Layer-3 standard for encoding comes from the Motion Picture Engineering Group, which precisely defines how the encoding works and the internal structure of what the file actually looks like. It does not define how to accomplish this encoding, however, and several different encoders are available to perform the actual compression, such as the Fraunhofer reference standard codec. Although the quality of the files produced by different codecs is a constant source of debate, the final file must still conform to the MPEG-1, Layer-3 standard.

There are far too many codecs to list and explain individually here. The section "Audio File Formats" previously explained some codecs because some file formats are defined by the codec they use. Following are a few of the more popular codecs:

* PCM (uncompressed) stands for *Pulse Code Modulation* and is a standard lossless format. It is widely used by many formats, notably the Windows .wav format, for the audio tracks on MiniDV camcorders and is an official part of the specification for DVD-video discs, although it is not often used because the file size is relatively large.

* ADPCM (*Adaptive Differential Pulse Code Modulation*) is a very popular audio compression system, widely used in telephony, HDTV, and many other applications. It is also a common codec used for compressed Windows .wav files. Not all applications can read ADPCM-encoded .wav files, but most can. Although ADPCM files are usually significantly smaller than PCM files, they are still not usually compressed as much as other Internet-targeted codecs, such as OGG or MP3.

* Some of the codecs listed in the Windows Control Panel are primarily used for compression of voice data. For example, μ-Law is used for digital telephony in North America and Japan, whereas A-Law is used in Europe. Other voice codecs include ACELP.net and DSP Group TrueSpeech. Voice codecs are not especially well suited to compression of music. Variations on these codecs can be found in both the .wav and .mov formats.

This is just a small sample to give you some idea of the available codecs. A more substantial discussion of a few of the more important codecs follows in the "Streaming" section later in this chapter.

Quality and Data Rate

Higher data rates yield higher-quality audio. As discussed earlier, quality can be directly measured in terms of sample rate (cycles per second or Hertz [Hz]) and bit depth. CD-quality audio has a data rate of:

(44,100Hz × 16-bit) × 2 stereo channels = 1,411,200 bps

or

1.4 Mbps (megabits per second)

Although this rate is fairly high for transmission across the Internet, remember that these rates pertain to uncompressed audio. You can decrease the data rate in a couple of ways. One way is to lower the sample rate.

> ❄ **DATA RATE CALCULATOR**
>
> Data rate is measured in bits per second (bps). Bits (b) are different from bytes (B), which are used to measure file size, where:
>
> 1 byte (B) = 8 bits (b)
>
> So if you wanted to stream a one-minute, 500-KB audio file in real time, the minimum data rate you would need is:
>
> (500,000 bytes × 8 bits/byte) / 60 seconds = 67 Kilobytes per second (Kbps)

FM radio is said to be equivalent in quality to a 22-kHz sample rate with 16-bit depth. Plugging this into our equation, we get:

$$(22,050 \text{Hz} \times 16\text{-bit}) \times 2 \text{ stereo channels} = 705,600 \text{ bps (or roughly 700 Kbps)}$$

This is too high for most Internet connections, but the audio is not yet compressed. This is where the compression codecs come into play. One of the most widely used music formats is undoubtedly the .mp3 format. If you select MP3 Audio (.mp3) in the Render As dialog and then select 64 Kbps, FM Radio Quality Audio from the Template list, you get what is claimed to be FM radio–quality audio at 22-kHz, 16-bit stereo audio. The preceding calculation shows that this stream would normally be 700 Kbps uncompressed. This gives a compression ratio of about 11:1 over an uncompressed PCM .wav file, which is quite good, but is not 22:1 as is suggested in the dialog. This is because the compression ratios listed are always measured against how compressed the audio is compared to the original CD-quality standard.

So we get 2:1 compression by lowering the sample rate (from 44 kHz to 22 kHz), and we get another 11:1 compression from the MP3 codec. How do we get this major 11:1 compression? This is the heart of any compression format and is where the differences between the various formats emerge. It is also where audible artifacts creep into the signal. Claiming that the audio is equivalent to FM radio is a bit disingenuous, because a broadcast FM radio signal is not digitally compressed and does not suffer from artifacts. This is not to pick on the MP3 format; all compressed formats claim compression that is equivalent to CD quality or FM quality (and so on), but these claims refer only to the sample rate, bit depth, and the arithmetic, not to the actual audible quality. Another example is DVD-video discs. DVDs certainly offer better visual quality than VHS tape, but you never see compression artifacts or color gradients on videotape. Likewise, how often did you ever see a baseball game break up into blocky digital artifacts in the old analog days before digital cable and satellite TV? Perhaps we're just old Luddite curmudgeons, but digital isn't always better.

Compression Artifacts

All compression codecs introduce some type of artifacts into the audio. Whether these artifacts are audible depends on how good your hearing is or whether you work for the marketing department at the company that sells the codec. Some types of artifacts are more noticeable than others, and some codecs are more prone to certain types of artifacts than others. Some codecs are better at some data rates and worse at others. Some codecs are better at music and some are better at voice. It is likely that some are better at encoding classical music with wide dynamic ranges, whereas others do a better job on loud (and always loud) rock music. In the end, deciding which codec produces the highest-quality output is a very subjective argument that depends on your personal preferences and particular audio application. In any case, compression artifacts can be heard as:

❋ Warbling or swishing, as if hearing music underwater

❋ Echoes, pre-echoes, flanging, and phasing, especially in the higher frequencies

❋ Tinny, metallic artifacts (again in the higher-frequency ranges), including chirping and ringing

❋ Excessive sibilance and plosives on vocal parts, noise bursts, and pops

❋ Loss of high frequencies

❋ Loss of stereo separation, space, and reverb

Although this sounds like a nightmare of artifacts that would completely ruin a song, these types of artifacts are infrequent and are, by design, difficult to hear. Unfortunately, they are more noticeable once you know what to listen for, as you now do. Sorry. These artifacts are truly a small price to pay when you consider the amazing 20:1 compression ratios (and higher) that you can get from most codecs, which still maintain a good level of quality. Just be happy that audio artifacts are much less apparent to the human ear than video artifacts are to the eye, which is why getting quality video over the Internet is extremely challenging. Of course, higher levels of quality in a codec will eliminate most, if not all, of these artifacts. For more information on lossless compression, see the discussion of Sony Media Software's Perfect Clarity Audio (.pca) format in the "Audio File Formats" section earlier in this chapter.

Media Destination

Regardless of whether you choose a lossless or a lossy and compressed file format, any file that you intend to make available to listeners using another computer needs to use a format that is compatible with their software. The following is a brief summary of some recommendations on which formats and codecs are appropriate for which destinations:

❋ Material that will remain on your computer or that you will back up to a data CD (DVD) as archival masters needs to maintain 100 percent of the quality and can use Sony Media Software's .pca format. Because archives are for your use only, compatibility is not important but quality is. Files using this format can be 70 percent as large as other lossless file formats, giving you some degree of space savings without compromising quality. If space is not an issue, use the more conventional .wav format.

❊ Music destined for the Internet needs to be compressed for portability, but must also use a format that is widely available. For example, if you use the popular .mp3 format, you can be reasonably sure that your audience can play back these files. You might also consider using a streaming format, although streaming involves a host of other considerations beyond simply making the file as small as possible. (See the "Streaming" section later in this chapter.) Streaming is also rapidly becoming less important as more and more people get broadband Internet connections.

❊ When burning audio CDs for playback on standalone audio CD players, you need to select a file format that your CD-writing software likes. The .wav format is the most widely accepted format, but many other standard formats may also work. Consult your audio CD-burning software for more information.

Sony Net MD

Mini Disc (MD) players never really caught on in the United States as they did in Asia, but they are still a fine portable player format that competes well with MP3 players in price and performance. They also make great portable recorders. If you are lucky enough to own a Sony Net MD player, you can output your ACID creations straight to disc by selecting Export to Net MD from the File menu and entering a name for the new track in the dialog that appears.

Publishing

Publishing your songs either on the Internet or on a record label is the absolute final step in song creation. Although signing a contract with EMI Classics might be the most formal way of publishing your music, the Internet and home audio CD creation have made independent publishing of music for the masses a reality.

ACIDplanet

ACIDplanet is an online community developed and run by Sony Media Software to promote the ACID software and offers a place where users can exchange ideas and inspiration and, of course, publish music. The ultimate motivation for the site may be marketing the ACID program, but don't let that dissuade you from taking advantage of this wonderful resource. There are always songs to listen to, arguments to engage in, free loops to download, and remix contests to enter. There is no better place to submit your ACID songs for critical review and get serious people to listen to and comment on your creations. Did we mention free loops?

Publishing to ACIDplanet

The first step to getting started with ACIDplanet is to register with the site. This involves standard username and password procedures, for security purposes, but you can also sign up for occasional newsletters and promotional messages from Sony Media Software. These messages are infrequent and always involve special discounts and introductions to loop series, usually with pointers to where you can get a few free samples from the new libraries.

To configure the ACID software for ACIDplanet, connect to the Internet and, from the File menu in the ACID application, select Publish. A small dialog opens (see Figure 12.5) as the program attempts to contact the ACIDplanet Web site. If this is your first time at the site, a registration Web page starts up. After creating an account, you can make all changes to your account, artist profile, and song uploading from the Publish Setup Web page.

Figure 12.5
The ACID software first attempts to make contact with the ACIDplanet Web site.

You can render songs and upload them to ACIDplanet in one easy operation by selecting Publish from the File menu. After you activate your account on ACIDplanet, a series of simple dialogs walks you through rendering to the .mp3, .rm, or .wma format and then automatically uploads the song when you are finished. You can also select files other than the current project if they are already encoded in a compatible format. Figure 12.6 shows the first dialog in this series.

AP Music

In the AP Music section of ACIDplanet, you'll find many projects created with the ACID program. Due to the large number of songs posted here every day, though, it is tough to find many true gems. The rating system doesn't always work that well because groups of people often collaborate to fix the ratings for each other. Stuffing the ballot box is part and parcel of this thing we call the Internet, and none of this is unique to ACIDplanet. The diamonds you'll eventually find in the rough make sticking around worthwhile, however. Of all the material in this book, the following suggestions are by far the most subjective, but here is how we get around the Lounge:

Figure 12.6

You can encode and upload the current song or select from songs you have previously created.

* Spend some time on the site. You won't need to browse around for more than an hour to start getting a feel for who's who. Go to the Community forum and see which posters are offering good, well-intentioned advice, then go and find their songs. Earnest folks don't always produce the finest music, but finding people who are serious about the ACID software is important. After a while, you'll have a few favorite names from whom you'll wait for new releases. Send them an e-mail and ask them for some names of other people they like.

* Although you can't always trust the reviews, look for specific, intelligent comments about a song, such as "Nice equalization on the slap bass line," or "The mix gets a little muddy at times, but I like it." Be skeptical of all-capital-letter reviews and excesses of exclamation marks, such as "AW3S0M3 d00d!!!!!"

* The other half of the interaction available in the Lounge is to get reviews of your own songs. It helps to have thick skin, and you will need to sort out who is serious and who is not, but most of the citizens of ACIDplanet are sincere and offer thoughtful critiques that are rarely without some encouraging compliments. Most of these folks want to like your music and will look for good qualities as well as traits that could be better. To get people to review your work, you should spend some time reviewing other people's work.

Contests

ACID remix contests are an extremely fun use for the ACID software beyond standard song creation from scratch. The site offers a few prizes every month or so, including loop libraries and software from Sony Media Software. There's also a chance that someone might recognize your work, and this could be the first step on the road to fame (and fortune). Loop packs and starter project files are provided for songs in a number of genres from today's top artists. These are good practice and great fun, but be careful you don't spend too much time with these contests at the cost of your own creative projects.

Community
As with all online virtual communities, the free nature of the Community forum means that you have to wade through a lot of crud to get to the good stuff. It won't take more than a week of casual browsing to begin to recognize the names of a few regulars who consistently post worthwhile advice. At the same time, you will also start to identify participants who rarely contribute anything but noise and whom you can safely ignore. It isn't hard to winnow the wheat from the chaff in the Community forum.

APRadio
If you find the free-for-all of the Lounge overwhelming, check out APRadio, which acts as an Internet radio station, streaming songs submitted by ACIDplanet citizens. This can be a good way to hear a variety of songs without having to make the selections yourself.

On the Web
Including links to media files created with the ACID software on a Web page is as simple as providing a link to the file. You can do this by hand if you know a little HTML, or you can use a Web-page editing program. On the other hand, embedding media files and players into sophisticated dynamic pages is also possible. Although advanced scripting techniques are beyond the scope of this book, the next few sections should give you a few ideas about what you can do with multimedia on the Web.

Simple Web Page
The easiest way to put media into a Web page is to provide a hyperlink to it in an HTML document. This can be as simple as:

```
<a href="my_song.rm">My Song</a>
```

Although a text hyperlink might be a bit boring, it is nonetheless simple and effective. When the user clicks on the link, the appropriate player loads and plays back the file in its own user interface outside of the Web page. Hyperlinks work for almost any registered file format.

Embedded Media
A more interesting and less obtrusive way of putting media files on your Web page is to embed the media player into the Web page. When you do so, the player and any controls you want to make available are actually visible as a part of your HTML layout. There are a number of ways to embed each of the various players (including OggVorbis, Windows Media, RealMedia, and QuickTime), but in its simplest form, you can embed the player using code such as the following:

<EMBED SRC="my_song.mov" VOLUME="50" HEIGHT="60" WIDTH="144">

The embedded player has a few attributes describing the initial volume as well as its height and width. You can even make the player invisible by not setting a HEIGHT or WIDTH attribute. Figure 12.7 shows a hyperlink to a media file, as well as a QuickTime player embedded with the preceding code.

Figure 12.7

A hyperlink and an embedded media player.

Different players accept (and might even require) different parameters and may allow you to create your own play buttons, sliders, and frames (that is, skins) or set the file to loop continuously. The simple example presented in Figure 12.7 automatically starts playing when the page loads, but you can use scripting to interact with the media, playing back or pausing in response to user input.

❄ **ANNOYING BACKGROUND MUSIC**
Embedded media with an invisible player allows you to create background music for a Web page. Most people find this very, very annoying. Younger people, however, have made an art of, well, being annoying to older folks and, to be perfectly honest, it's sometimes pretty funny. Do a Google search for "YTMND" to see some examples of Web pages with background music that are either incredibly funny or intensely annoying, depending mostly on how old you are.

Command Markers
Command markers in the ACID software are special temporal markers that allow you to execute a limited set of commands at a certain point in audio files (of a supported format—see the following table) embedded in a Web page. You could use these markers to include synchronized lyrics in a Web page or to open a Web page based on song playback. To add command markers to a project, move the timeline cursor to the position where you want to add a command marker and, from the Insert menu, select Command. Command markers appear as light-blue markers above the timeline and main Marker bar. The Command Properties dialog, as shown in Figure 12.8, lets you decide what command action is taken and when it occurs. For example, the URL Command

opens the Web page specified in the Parameter box at the time noted in the Position box (comments are optional).

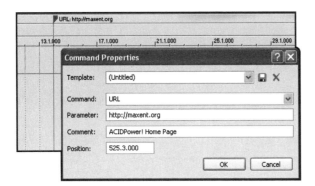

Figure 12.8
Add command markers by pressing C on your keyboard.

The ACID software supports command markers only for RealMedia (.rm) files and Windows Media (.wmv and .wma) files. Some commands are specific to the Windows Media format and begin with a *WM-* prefix. Some commands make sense only for video presentations. The following table lists the commands, what they do, and what parameters are acceptable. Some of these commands interact with the Web browser and the HTML document that contains the media file. Although the command marker itself is fairly simple, the interactions can be quite sophisticated and might require some pretty serious scripting (for example, in JavaScript).

Command	Description	Parameter Example
URL	Jumps to the specified URL.	http://acidplanet.com
TEXT	Displays text in the captioning area of the Windows Media Player located below the video display area. You enter the text that displays during playback.	Your text here!
WMClosedCaption	Displays the entered text in the captioning window defined with scripting.	Closed-captioned for the hearing impaired.
WMTextBodytext	Displays the entered text in the text window that is defined with scripting.	This is some narrative text in the body of the HTML document, such as the lyrics to a song, for example.
WMTextHeadline	Displays the entered text in the headline window that is defined with scripting.	My Great Song Title

Command	Description	Parameter Example
Title	Displays the entered text on the RealPlayer's title bar.	Rodrigue et Chimène
Author	Displays author information when the listener right-clicks RealPlayer and selects About This Presentation.	Claude Debussy
Copyright	Displays copyright information when the listener right-clicks RealPlayer and selects About This Presentation.	Copyright © 1890–1892
HotSpotPlay*	Video only. Plays the video specified when the listener clicks the HotSpot. Duration (Dimensions) "LABEL" FILENAME.rm MM:SS (LEFT, TOP, RIGHT, BOTTOM) "LABEL" FILENAME	00:10 (0, 0, 40, 25) "Play another file" next_video.rm
HotSpotBrowse*	Video only. Navigates to a new Web page in the browser when the listener clicks the HotSpot (RealMedia only). MM:SS (LEFT, TOP, RIGHT, BOTTOM) "LABEL" URL	00:10 (0, 0, 40, 25) "Go to ACIDplanet" http:\\acidplanet.com
HotSpotSeek*	Video only. Jumps to a new location in the video when the listener clicks the HotSpot (RealMedia only). MM:SS (LEFT, TOP, RIGHT, BOTTOM) "LABEL" MM:SS	00:10 (0, 0, 40, 25) "Go to exciting conclusion" 05:17

* In all of these commands, only the last command is required. If you do not specify a duration, the ACID software assumes that the command applies to the entire duration of the file. If you specify no dimensions, the program assumes that the command applies to the entire frame.

Streaming

Streaming refers to the technology that allows listeners to play back a file as the listener is down-loading it. Thus the user does not need to wait for the entire file to download before beginning to listen and can skip forward to a later point in the file without downloading earlier parts. Streaming is not some magical format that allows faster downloads or smaller file sizes, and the listener still needs to download the entire file to listen to the entire song. Streaming can occur only if the download time for the file over the entire connection, from server to client to everything in between, is less than the total playback time of the file. Many compressed audio formats can be primitively streamed over any Web connection. More and more people have broadband Internet connections, so streaming is really not all that important for individual songs, but it is an important consideration for longer-format programs, such as entire radio broadcasts. Streaming can also offer content creators more control over their digital copyrights by preventing users from downloading and redistributing the file.

> ❋ **STREAM WITHOUT A SERVER**
> A number of formats allow the listener to play back the audio file while it downloads without a special streaming server.

More advanced streaming properties will require a server to stream properly. The server controls how the stream is being sent and may be able to compensate for network traffic problems, allow variable bit-rate playback, and let the listener randomly access different parts of the file (instead of listening to the file linearly). Streaming media servers are sold by a number of streaming format companies and must be installed on the server. This means that you might need to find an Internet provider that specializes in streaming media to distribute your media, or you might need to work with your provider to get the proper server software installed.

A stream is a flow of data from a server to a client. Whereas standard audio files on your computer are measured by size in kilobytes (KB) or megabytes (MB), streaming media files are measured in terms of data rate or bits per second, such as Kbps (1,000 bps) or Mbps (1,000,000 bps). For example, a 56-KB modem can (theoretically) send and receive data at 56 Kbps, whereas a DSL or cable connection might support data rates that exceed your audio format's bit rate. Just because a device can theoretically handle such high data rates doesn't mean you will be able to stream data that fast in the real world. Internet traffic, server loading, routing, brownouts, DNS attacks, and just about anything else can cause your connection to the Internet to be much slower than what you should theoretically be able to receive.

Streaming Formats

Audio is not nearly as complex to stream as video is, primarily because the data rate for audio can be dramatically lower than the data rate for video, while still maintaining a relatively high level of quality. Because of this greater simplicity, streamed audio does not always necessarily need a server to stream. For example, although the MP3 format is not designed explicitly as a streaming format, in many situations you can play back .mp3 files as they are downloading, which is the essential definition of streaming. In other cases, a special server is required to stream audio. Streaming media servers also offer the possibility of more sophisticated streaming advantages, such as variable bit rates, multiple bit rates, and increased security.

> ❄ **STREAM FOR FREE**
> ACIDplanet uses both a RealServer and Windows Media Services server to stream media files. ACIDplanet is free, so it is a great way to stream your media over the Internet. However, your audience must also sign up with ACIDplanet to listen to your media files.

MP3 Audio (.mp3)

MPEG-1, Layer-3 audio encoding is very popular and widely used, and it provides good compression and audio fidelity. It can be streamed as is from any general-purpose Web server, in that the file can be played back as it is downloaded. The format does not allow random access. Following is a brief summary of some of the controls found in the Custom Settings dialog for the MP3 format:

- ❄ The **Quality slider** sets how carefully the encoder works. Dragging the slider to the right makes the encoding process slower, but it is recommended that you always take the time to encode at the highest quality level.

- ❄ The **VBR Quality slider** determines how the Variable Bit-Rate (VBR) encoding works. With VBR encoding, sections of the music that are easier to encode use lower bit rates, whereas more complex sections of music use higher bit rates. The slider controls the VBR within the file and does not affect the streaming attributes of the file.

- ❄ The **ID3 Settings tab** allows you to add artist and copyright information to the file.

QuickTime (.mov)

QuickTime is a do-all format that acts as a wrapper for everything from uncompressed lossless quality to streaming media. Because the codec you choose determines the particular properties of the .mov file, it is difficult to discuss the variables in creating streaming QuickTime files. Many of the codecs available in the Audio Format list can be streamed, although some are simply not appropriate for Internet streaming (for example, the 64-bit Floating codec). IMA 4:1, MACE 6:1, and Qdesign Music 2 codecs are all excellent choices for streaming. You can select these codecs from the Audio Format list on the Audio tab of the Custom Settings dialog for the .mov format. Unfortunately, not many audio templates are available for this format.

To create a .mov file that is properly wrapped for streaming, go to the Streaming tab in the Custom Settings dialog and select the Prepare for Streaming option (see Figure 12.9). In the Optimization list, the Fast Start and Fast Start with Compressed Header options create a file that can play back while downloading, but does not technically stream. The greatest disadvantage is that you cannot randomly access the file and thus skip ahead in the song.

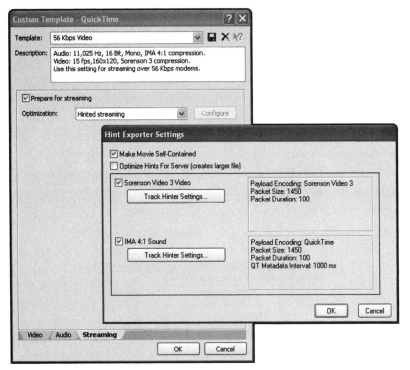

Figure 12.9

To create streaming QuickTime media files, you must select the Prepare for Streaming option.

To perform true streaming via a QuickTime streaming server, you must select the Hinted Streaming option from the Optimization list. With this option selected, QuickTime, while rendering your media, creates a hint track that tells the server exactly how to accomplish the streaming. Click the Configure button and make sure the Make Movie Self-Contained option is selected. Do not adjust the Track Hinter Settings unless you know about the particulars of packet sizes (and so on) on your server. For audio-only files, after you set the Optimization to Hinted Streaming, all the default settings are acceptable.

OggVorbis (.ogg)

The OggVorbis dialog contains relatively simple controls for setting up streaming. The quality and compression of this codec are very high and offer VBR encoding, which is similar to the MP3 VBR encoding. While OggVorbis does not require a server to stream, a free streaming server (Icecast) is available for Windows, Linux, and some UNIX platforms that improves streaming performance. Ask your ISP if they are willing to install and configure this server on their machines. Because OGG is an open-source format, you and your listeners can use it for free, which is a good reason to select it.

RealMedia (.rm)

The RealMedia dialog box is one of the simplest of any of the formats, but it is also very flexible.

❋ In the **Custom Template dialog**, select a template. You can add more later if you are using a streaming server.

❋ On the **Audiences tab**, select templates from the Available Audiences list and click the Add button to place them on the Selected Audiences list. Multiple audience selections can be made when streaming off of a RealServer. Click the Edit button to modify these templates (see Figure 12.10). For example, the actual bit rates for the 128k Dual ISDN option can be set on the tab that appears when you click the Edit button. The default bit rate is 96 kbps, but you can select any bit rate you like. This flexibility allows you to create preset bit rates that are completely unrealistic for the name of the target audience (for example, you can create a 176-Kbps preset to use for a 28K modem).

❋ The **Summary tab** allows you to add artist and copyright information to the file.

Figure 12.10

The Edit button allows you to configure the audio templates.

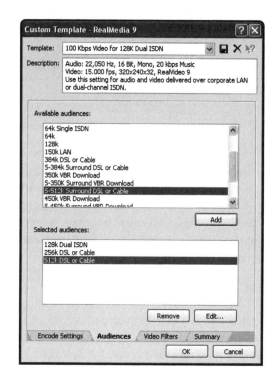

Windows Media Audio (.wma)

The .wma format from Microsoft is a direct competitor to the other highly compressed formats in terms of quality. You can achieve excellent results with any of these formats, but the .wma format has one (some say unfair) advantage over the others in that it is distributed by Microsoft. You can be certain that many of your listeners already have the software to play back .wma files on their computer.

This format has relatively simple controls and a solid list of templates to choose from in the Custom Template dialog:

❋ The **Mode drop-down** lets you select Quality VBR, which is the recommended mode unless you are streaming, in which case you'd choose CBR. CBR encoding is also good for voice.

❋ The **Format list** has three options in the ACID Pro software. For distribution, select the Windows Media Audio Professional format. The Windows Media Audio 9 lossless option is good for archiving. If you have selected CBR as your mode, you can also use a Windows Media Audio 9 Voice format, which is configured especially for spoken audio (and not for music) and produces very highly compressed, monophonic files.

❋ The **Attributes list** lets you select from a long list of coordinated internal templates that vary depending on the mode and format previously selected. There is no way to edit these attributes manually.

As with other formats, you do not need to place .wma files on a special server to allow downloading or even playback of media before the file is finished downloading. To stream properly, however, you must use the Windows Media Services server installed on your ISP's Web server.

Audio CDs

One of the best ways to distribute your songs is on an audio CD. No other format is more universally accessible that allows your music to be played back at 100-percent quality on a proper audio system. This solution is also cost-effective. CD burners are now available for less than $20 U.S. and are standard equipment on new computers. You can often find blank discs in 100-count spindles for less than 10 cents each.

❋ **RED BOOK STANDARD**
CD audio discs are formatted in a very specific way (the Red Book standard). CDs formatted as data CDs are distinct from audio CDs, although data CDs are still a great way to back up ACID songs and projects.

Burning Songs to a CD

Burning a single song to a CD is simple and does not require you to render the song first. There are two ways you can do this: one track at a time or an entire disc at a time.

Track-at-Once

To burn individual songs to a disc that you will eventually fill, from the Tools menu, select Burn Track-at-Once Audio CD. This opens a dialog with only a few buttons and a little information. Click the Start button to render the song and write it to the disc. Depending on the speed of your CD burner, this should take only a few tens of seconds or so for each song. The progress is displayed along the bottom of the dialog, as shown in Figure 12.11. The Write Buffer displays, as a percentage, the data that is in RAM and ready to be written to the disc. With older CD burners, this value could dip dangerously low and, if it reaches zero, ruin the disc. The buffer is likely to become low only if something goes wrong and the ACID software is not able to render data quickly enough or if your hard disk drive has problems. Typically, the buffer remains above 90 percent for the entire process. Although the dialog includes a Cancel button that you can use at any time, after the burn has started, you should click Cancel only as a last resort in case of a program lockup or crash; the Cancel button is only good for creating drink coasters after the writing process has begun.

Figure 12.11

The Burn Track-at-Once Audio CD dialog.

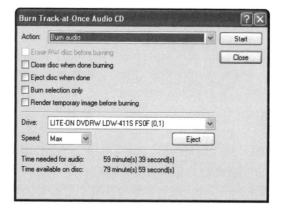

Some issues can arise when burning songs one at a time to a CD. Your CD burner needs to support writing to disc without closing it. Closing means the disc is finished, whether you have burned only one minute or 60, and it cannot be written to again. Some older computer CD-ROM units and nearly all standalone audio CD players require that you close a disc in order to play it. With most CD writers, however, there should be no conflicts with the ACID software, and you can write projects one at a time to the disc as you finish the song. Then, when the disc is full, from the Tools menu, select the Burn Track-at-Once Audio CD option again. This time, in the Burn Track-at-Once

Audio dialog, select Close and click the Start button. After a few seconds, the disc closes so you can play it in any audio CD or DVD player.

Disc-at-Once

The ACID software is a wonderful remixing tool and is very fun to use to create seamless hours of dance music, for example (see Figure 12.12). After you have an entire CD's worth of music to burn to disc, you can use CD markers in the software to identify the track breaks (without pauses between) and then burn a CD. To drop track markers, position the timeline cursor where you want to create a track split and, from the Insert menu, select CD Track Marker (or just press N on your keyboard). You probably want to create your first track marker right at the beginning of your project. Then, from the Tools menu, select Burn Disc-at-Once Audio CD and click OK. The dialog includes only a few options. It is usually a good idea to leave the Render Temporary Image Before Burning item selected because it makes burning more reliable and takes only a little more time.

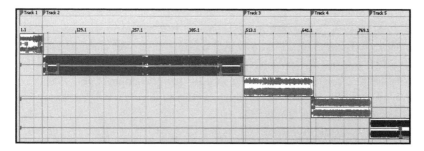

Figure 12.12
A simple remix project with CD track markers for a Disc-at-Once burn.

Dedicated CD-Burning Software

The ACID CD-burning capabilities are undoubtedly convenient, but they are also limited. Several CD-burning applications are available from other manufacturers that provide more features and options, including setting the delay time between songs. It is likely that a simple audio CD-burning software program was included with your CD-writing hardware. The ACID software does not interact directly with these programs. Your only concern is to make sure that you render media files that are of the right format and the right attributes. Most frequently, this means 44.1-kHz, 16-bit PCM (uncompressed) .wav files.

DVD-Audio discs

A few years ago, DVD-Audio seemed like the logical next step in high-fidelity audio distribution. At the risk of offending DVD-Audio aficionados everywhere, it looks like DVD-Audio is the laser disc of the twenty-first century. Like video laser discs, DVD-Audio seems to be just another fantastic format that failed to catch on and that eventually will be surpassed by other technologies. With the right encoding software, you can create DVD-Audio discs, but not many people can play them. DVD-Video, on the other hand, is the most successful and most rapidly adopted media format in history. That's a pretty darn good reason to use the DVD-Video format for distribution, even for audio-only recordings. For example, you can create DVD songs in fabulous 5.1 surround sound or you can distribute dozens or even hundreds of stereo songs on a single disc. Although there aren't many people doing this with DVD-Video discs, it is certainly a possibility that would be immediately and instantly compatible in almost every living room in the United States.

Copyright

Intellectual property in this age of effortless digital reproduction is a difficult issue at best. Technically, anything you create is your property and has an implied (and legal) copyright from the moment you save it in any medium. Music CDs are obviously copyrighted whether or not they have an explicit copyright statement, but so are all songs that are posted to ACIDplanet and even songs simply saved to your hard disk. In the Project Properties dialog for many formats is a field for entering and saving copyright information using the copyright symbol, ©, which you can add using the Windows Character Mapper or by pressing Alt+0169. This gives you some degree of additional protection, but it is pretty farfetched to believe that a court case over a stolen song would hinge on whether copyright information was saved with the song. Instead, a copyright notice is most useful in helping other people who want to use your song to contact you.

 AUTOMATIC COPYRIGHT PROTECTION
According to the U.S. Copyright Office, "Under the present copyright law, which became effective Jan. 1, 1978, a work is automatically protected by copyright when it is created."

This automatic copyright is not the same as registering (and paying for) an official copyright registration from your favorite government agency. The name of this agency will vary from country to country, and international copyright law is a hot issue that will be very lucrative for attorneys for many years to come. In the United States, however, you go to the U.S. Copyright Office:

Copyright Office
Library of Congress
101 Independence Avenue, S.E
Washington, D.C. 20559-6000
(202) 707-3000

Or, better still:

http://www.loc.gov/copyright

This excellent and well-organized Web site offers extensive information. Start with the Copyright Basics and FAQ, and then go to the Forms item to find the .pdf format files you need. Just download the proper form, print it, fill it out, and send it back. Two forms may be applicable to ACID projects:

❄ **Form SR** (*Sound Recording*) is used for sound recordings and is the most obvious form to use for ACID productions. This is used to copyright a particular performance of a song ("Phonorecords"). Registering the sound recording allows others to cover their own version of the song and possibly make remixes. It is also possible to copyright the musical composition of a song ("Copies") with this form, although it is difficult to tell what could be copyrighted in the case of ACID projects because the original intent was to copyright sheet music. Perhaps someday users will be able to copyright ACID projects along with the rendered song. Pragmatically, even writing out just the melody on staff paper is enough. Of particular interest to ACID users on this form is Space 6: Derivative Works. You can use this space to include information about the particular loops and samples used in your project. Commercial loop libraries almost always give you blanket permission in the license to use their loops in your own creations, so using loops is not really a legal issue, but it would certainly be appropriate to list those loops in this space even though it might not be required. You should not register a melody or bass line from a loop file as your own musical composition, however. So, one example of the complete process might be to register the actual sound recording as rendered from the ACID software, list the drum and bass parts created from Sony Media Software's loop files in Space 6, and also register your original electric piano and vocal performance as a musical composition, including the melody and lyrics.

❄ **Form PA** (*Performing Arts*) can be used for music, songs, and lyrics, either as sheet music or as sound recordings. You can use this form to copyright the song as an idea and as a performance. In other words, you would copyright a written play using this form, but not necessarily a particular performance of the play. In musical terms, you could use a sound recording to register the intellectual property of a song without registering the particular performance on the sound recording. This form seems appropriate for ACID songs, but Form SR is probably better. You definitely would need to use Form PA to copyright video productions.

> ❄ **USE A BOX**
> Unfortunately, security in our modern world has required the Copyright Office to put new procedures in place that can result in unintentional damage to CD and DVD media sent in envelopes. The office now recommends that you use a box when sending in discs to be registered.

The cost for filing one form is $30 U.S. This does not mean that you need to spend $30 for each song you register. In fact, one widely known trick is to register a bunch of songs on a single form as a single work. It could be that this was intended for multi-movement symphonies or possibly for albums, but the Copyright Office actively encourages the process of registering a compilation of sound recordings and collections of songs (see Circulars 50 and 56). By including all of your songs in a published collection, you can legally protect yourself for a minimal amount of money. Plus, in a few weeks, you'll get an official copyright certificate in the mail, suitable for framing.

Chapter 12 Quiz

1. To save your entire ACID project into an audio file:

    A. From the File menu, select Render As

    B. From the Toolbar, press the Get Media button

    C. From the Options menu, select Loop Playback

    D. From the Tools menu, select Render to New Track

2. Higher bit depths and sample rates offer better audio fidelity at the price of larger files on your hard drive. (T/F)

3. Which of the following is not an audio file format?

    A. AIFF

    B. MP3

    C. WAV

    D. All of the above are audio formats

4. Audio files can be compressed to reduce file size. (T/F)

5. Lossless compression means that some of the bits in your audio file will be discarded. (T/F)

6. Which of the following is not an example of a compression artifact?

   A. Warbling or swishing

   B. Echoes or pre-echoes

   C. Drastically reduced file size

   D. Loss of stereo separation

7. Publishing is the second-to-last step in your ACID project. (T/F)

8. ACIDplanet is:

   A. A drug rehab center

   B. Sony Media Software's online community for the ACID software

   C. A science research laboratory

   D. None of the above

9. An embedded media player gives the Web designer full control over what the listener will hear at all times. (T/F)

10. Streaming allows the listener to hear a file as it downloads. (T/F)

Appendix A

Preferences

These appendixes will wrap up many of the loose ends and background details that are important to getting the most out of Sony Media Software's ACID® application. Ultimately, the ACID software's own Help file is the definitive reference: If you don't find your answer here, check out the Help menu. The Preferences dialog (click the Options menu and select Preferences) contains a host of options to customize and optimize the software. Most of these options are covered in relevant sections of this book, but they are also listed in this appendix for your reference.

General Tab

Each of the following check boxes can be selected, or checked, in the dialog.

Check Box Name	Selected by Default	Description
Automatically open last project on startup	Y	The last project you were working on when you closed the ACID software is reopened on startup. Deselect this option if you want

(continued)

Check Box Name	Selected by Default	Description
		The ACID program to start a new, untitled, unsaved, and blank project every time it runs.
Show logo splash screen on startup	Y	This controls whether the ACID title screen is displayed during loading. Deselecting this option keeps this screen from being displayed, but does not decrease loading time.
Use Net Notify to stay informed about Sony products	Y	This option allows Sony Media Software to inform you automatically of product updates and patches. It works only when you are connected to the Internet while using the ACID software.
Draw contents of events	Y	This controls whether the waveforms are drawn inside events on the timeline. Deselecting this option can speed up the performance of the ACID software when you are scrolling or zooming on the timeline, but does not improve playback or rendering.
Create undos for FX parameter changes	Y	FX plug-ins can be considered as separate applications from the ACID software and operate somewhat independently. Undos (Ctrl+Z) for both the ACID program and FX plug-ins use up memory (RAM). If you are running short of RAM, you can deselect this option to recover a small amount.
Confirm media file deletion when still in use	Y	This option only warns you if you attempt to delete media files in the ACID Explorer window when they are currently being used in a project. Deleting files that are in use results in tracks and events that have (continued)

Check Box Name	Selected by Default	Description
		no corresponding media file. You can switch the media file used by a track and events in the Track Properties window.
Close media files when the ACID software is not the active application	Y	This option frees up RAM when switching to other applications.
Close audio and MIDI ports when the ACID software is not the active application	Y	When the ACID application is actively polling audio and MIDI ports, this polling occupies processor cycles and soundcard resources. Closing these ports allows other applications to work unimpeded.
Enable multimedia keyboard support	Y	Multimedia keyboards are simply keyboards that have special additional hot keys that are used to control the playback of media files. When this option is selected, you can also use these hot keys to control playback in the ACID software.
Automatically render large Wave files as Wave64	N	The Wave64 file format (.w64) is a proprietary format from Sony Media Software that allows much larger files than the standard Windows .wav format, which is limited to creating files of less than two gigabytes (2 GB), which is more than 3 hours and 20 minutes (3:20:00) of CD-quality audio. This is a useful option to select if you are doing very long mixes at higher bit rates and sample rates. As with other Sony Media Software proprietary formats, .w64 files cannot be played back with most applications other than Sony Media Software applications.
Prompt for region and marker names if not playing	N	This option automatically creates a text box with a flashing cursor to name markers and (continued)

Check Box Name	Selected by Default	Description
		regions as they are added. This does not happen when you are dropping markers on the fly during playback.
Create project file backups on save (.acd-bak)	Y	This option automatically creates a file with the same name but with a different file extension in the same folder every time you save. This file can serve as a backup in case the original is damaged or accidentally deleted. You can open these backup files by choosing the Open command from the File menu.
Preserve pitch for new Beatmapped tracks when tempo changes	N	Tempo changes speed up and slow down Beatmapped and Loop files. By default, the pitch of Beatmapped tracks changes slightly in response to tempo changes. Selecting this option changes this behavior, but requires more processing power and, in some cases, can result in distortions in these tracks.
Automatically start the Beatmapper Wizard for long files	Y	This option automatically starts the Beatmapper Wizard for long files, as defined by the Open Files As Loops If Between (Seconds) option on the Audio tab in the Preferences dialog. For example, long files are considered to be files more than 30 seconds long by default.
Use slower updates to prevent playback clicks during editing	N	Select this check box if you want to update the audio engine more slowly. Selecting this option can prevent unwanted artifacts during timeline editing.
Enable autosave	Y	No application is perfect, and the ACID software might crash on you someday.

(continued)

Check Box Name	Selected by Default	Description
		Wouldn't it be nice if your project had been saved automatically already? When you rerun the application after a crash, it prompts you and loads the autosaved version of your project. Make sure you save again right away.
Use SPTI for CD burning	N	SPTI (*SCSI pass-through interface*) might be needed for some SCSI interfaces when an ASPI driver is also installed.
Automatically detect plug-and-play CD/ DVD drives	Y	Almost all modern computers that can run the ACID software will be using devices that are compatible with Windows plug-and-play disc drives.
Autoname extracted CD tracks	N	If you don't want to bother naming tracks yourself, the ACID software can take care of this for you. Although the naming scheme that the ACID software uses is logical enough, it is quite cryptic to most humans.
Autoname new MIDI tracks	Y	The ACID software can automatically create names for the MIDI tracks you record. The naming convention is a very simple numerical one.
Keep bypassed FX running (to avoid pause on bypass/enable)	N	This option's name includes its own explanation. You might notice that the ACID software sometimes pauses briefly when you click the Bypass button when the project is playing back. In most cases, this option doesn't make a difference.
Confirm groove deletion when still in use	Y	Deselect this option if you are tired of the ACID software second-guessing your decisions to delete a groove.

(continued)

Check Box Name	Selected by Default	Description
Enable Windows XP Theme support	Y	If you are using a customized WinXP interface, the ACID software can fit right in with the look of the rest of your apps.
Save media-usage relationships in active media library	Y	This option automatically adds data to your Media Manager database on the usage of your loops. When you find loops that work together (however you personally define that), this option helps you identify these in the future.
Enable Media Manager	Y	This is actually a separate application from the ACID software that takes up memory. If you don't use the Media Manager (you probably should), deselect this option to free up some resources.
Allow snapping for Post-Groove Markers	N	This is off by default because you might want to drop markers based on the syncopation of the groove instead of the exact beat of a project.
Check .acd file type association at startup	Y	The ACID program will automatically run when you double-click an ACID project file (*.acd extension). It is possible to accidentally change this behavior when installing some other piece of software, and this option lets the ACID software check to see whether this has happened and then asks you if you want to correct the problem.
Do not query Gracenote for CD information	N	Gracenote is the online database that the ACID software queries for album name and track information when you rip a CD. Gracenote requires an Internet connection, and some people find the

(continued)

Check Box Name	Selected by Default	Description
		query process to be annoying or simply unnecessary.
Recently used project list	Y	This simply sets the number of projects that are listed at the bottom of the File menu list.

Audio Tab

The Audio tab sets up many of the ways the ACID software handles audio files by default.

Option	Description
Open files as loops if between (seconds)	This option simply defines what audio files the ACID software considers to be Loops and what files it considers to be potential Beatmapped files or One-Shots. By default, any media file with a duration of between 0.5 seconds and 30 seconds is opened as a Loop clip on a track, with shorter files being opened as One-Shot clips and longer files being opened as Beatmapped clips. On the General tab, select the Automatically Start the Beatmapper Wizard for Long Files option to run the Wizard for files longer than the upper end of the range.
Quick fade edit edges of audio events	This option prevents clicks and pops that may occur when audio events are cut or split. By default, this option is set to 10 ms. Quick fade edges can be seen as blue curved Fade Envelopes on event edges if you zoom in on the timeline far enough, as shown in Figure A.1.
Waveform display while recording	This option sets whether the ACID software draws the waveform as you are recording. While Show All Waveforms (the default) is the prettiest option, if you are experiencing any performance issues, hesitations, or stutters while recording, it isn't strictly necessary to watch the waveforms. Watch your meters first!

(continued)

Option	Description
ACID type for recorded audio	This option sets the default clip type for audio files you record. Beatmapped is the default and will save tempo information with your recorded files based on the project's tempo. This will allow your recorded files to be stretched or compressed in response to changes in tempo you make to your project. The One-Shot option will save your recordings without tempo information.
Record action when nothing is armed	This sets the behavior of the ACID software when you click the Record button on the Transport bar when you do not have a track (or tracks) already armed for recording. Your choices are to create a New Audio Track or a New MIDI Track, depending on what you most commonly record.
Include project name when naming recorded media	This option can help you remember later what files belong to which project. Of course, you can always change file names as you are recording, so this is strictly a convenience feature you can disregard if you don't find it convenient.

Figure A.1
Quick fade edges are visible on the split on the top event. The bottom event starts at the beginning of the media file and does not need a quick fade edge.

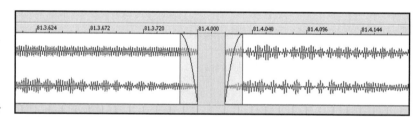

Audio Device Tab

The Audio tab is used to configure your soundcards and drivers. You can solve many performance problems in this tab, although the default values should work in almost all situations:

Option	Description
Audio device type	This option allows you to select the software drivers that the ACID software uses to interact with Windows and, ultimately, your soundcard. The Microsoft Sound Mapper option leaves all driver decisions to Windows, whereas the Windows Classic Wave Driver option might allow you to select from a number of different drivers listed on the Default Audio Playback Device option. Any ASIO drivers may be required for certain projects (such as a 48-kHz project for DVDs) and, indeed, ASIO drivers are often your best choice for minimizing latency anyway.
Default [channel] playback devices	This list is active (not grayed out) only for certain drivers and soundcards that support 5.1 surround sound. You can use this list to route playback to a particular purpose. For example, you can set up a 5.1 surround mix to go to the targeted speaker outputs.
Playback buffering	This option is set to 0.10 seconds by default, and you should adjust this setting only if playback is skipping or stuttering. Increasing the buffer can solve problems associated with the soundcard only.
Enable track buffering	This option is set to 0.25 seconds by default, and you should adjust this setting only if playback is skipping or stuttering in a particular track, often one with multiple FX on it. This option is mostly helpful if you have a dual CPU or dual-core CPU in your computer. For single processors, you can usually keep this option off.
Default audio recording device	This sets which audio device you will use to record, which is mostly useful when you have multiple audio devices connected to your computer. Many audio cards have stereo recording inputs, so you can set which channel to record from. For example, because (continued)

Option	Description
	almost all decent microphones are monophonic and many adapters will send a mono signal to the left channel, you can set this option to the left channel by default.
Automatically detect and offset for hardware recording latency	It might be better to let the ACID software handle recording latency problems. Select this item to do so, or deselect this item and use the User Recording Latency Offset (ms) slider to troubleshoot issues yourself.

MIDI Tab

The MIDI tab controls which MIDI devices are available on the Track Header for MIDI tracks for playback. More information on using this tab with MIDI tracks is detailed in Chapter 10.

Option	Description
Make these devices available for MIDI track playback	This item allows you to set up your external MIDI devices and controllers to be used for MIDI playback and timecode generation. Selected items show up on the device list in the Track Header for MIDI tracks.
Make these devices available for MIDI input	This option specifies the device (such as a MIDI keyboard connected to the MIDI In port) that can be used to record MIDI performances into a MIDI track and event in the ACID software. If you have multiple devices, you can select the one to use at the time of recording in the Track Header for the selected MIDI track.
Auto MIDI input routing	This option detects and configures attached MIDI devices in many situations.

Display Tab

The Display tab controls the default color assignments as applied by the ACID software to new tracks, envelopes, and icons. You can even adjust the icon color saturation and tint. Everything here is purely optional.

Option	Description
Track colors and Track	Click the Track drop-down first to select a track order (A through H) and then click the color box to select a color. The ACID software will cycle through these colors as new tracks are added to your project.
Envelope colors and Envelope type	Click the Envelope Type drop-down first to select a particular envelope (for example, Volume or Modulation), and then click the color box to select a color.
Section colors and Section	Click the Section option first to select a particular section (A through P) and then click the color box to select a color. The ACID software will cycle through these colors as new sections are added to your project.
Icon color saturation	This option lets you set the intensity of the colors of all of the icons in the ACID software—for example, all of the buttons on the toolbar.
Icon color tint	This option sets how much the ACID software's icons (the buttons on the toolbar) are tinted blue.

Other Tab

The Other tab determines how media files are previewed in the Explorer window.

Option	Description
Enable multiple-selection preview in Explorer window	This option allows you to select multiple items at a time (either using the Shift or Ctrl key) and preview them one after the other without any interruption.
Number of times to repeat each Loop	This option is pretty self-explanatory; 1 is the default setting.
Seconds of each One-Shot to play	One-Shot media can be longer in duration than the typical loops, so set the seconds of each One-Shot to play here. (Five seconds is the default.)
Number of Beatmapped measures to play	Likewise, set the number of Beatmapped measures to play. (Four measures is the default.)

Folders Tab

The Folders tab looks complex at first (see Figure A.2), but is simply used to set the default locations where the ACID software saves the many kinds and categories of files that it might generate. In each case, use the Browse buttons to set the location. Although this feature is simple, it is also powerful. Never again will you need to wonder where that take you just recorded went.

Figure A.2

The Folders tab sets where your recorded, saved, and rendered files will go by default.

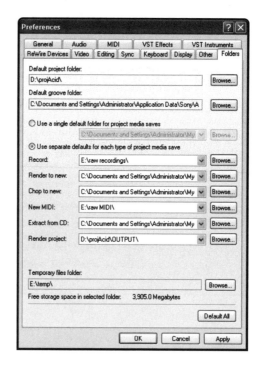

External Control & Automation Tab

The name of this tab is sort of backward because the Automation options are at the top. The top two options set up how effects automation (including recording Volume and Pan Envelopes) is saved. When recording effects automation, the ACID software sets dozens to hundreds of envelope nodes to accurately reflect your changes to a slider in real time. When the recording is complete, this can leave you with a mess, so use the Smooth and Thin Automation Data after Recording or Drawing option to optimize the final envelopes. This will make the resulting envelopes much easier to work with.

The Available Devices and Active Control Devices options are for special external controllers you can hook up to your computer to control the ACID application in a more intuitive and analog way. The sliders and knobs on a Mackie Control or TranzPort driver let you record effects automation in a very smooth way. These devices are also great in a live mixing situation.

VST Effects and VSTi Instruments Tabs

This tab sets up where the ACID software looks for VST (*Virtual Studio Technologies*) effects and instruments on your computer (see Chapter 10).

Option	Description
Default VST search folders	You can set up to three default locations here. VST effects and instruments are often found in a subdirectory under an audio application's installed location.
Select VST effects to be available as audio plug-ins or Select VST instruments to be available as Soft Synths	By default, the ACID software automatically makes any VST effects and instruments it finds on your computer available in the Audio Plug-In Chooser dialog. Deselect effects and instruments that are inappropriate for the ACID program or ones that you never use to reduce clutter.

ReWire Tab

The ReWire tab lists any active ReWire devices that are currently running on your computer so the ACID software can access them. (See Chapter 10.)

Video Tab

The Video tab is primarily used to configure DV FireWire cards to output a video signal to a television monitor for preview purposes. Chapter 11 discusses the reason for doing this and how to configure this feature. You can use the Video tab as follows.

Option	Description
Show source frame numbers on event thumbnails as Device	Thumbnail images of video can be labeled numerically in events on the timeline. Select how the frames are numbered from the list (or select none). The next option allows you to select an OHCI-compliant IEEE-1394/DV device to route a DV video signal through your camcorder and out to a television set. When an OHCI device is selected, additional information is displayed in the Details box.

(continued)

Option	Description
Details	A couple of additional options become available when an OHCI-compliant device is selected, as pictured at the bottom of Figure A.3.
If project format is invalid for DV output, conform to the following	This option selects the television standard you want to use to go out your FireWire card in situations where your project does not match the standard. For example, you might be working on a project for the Internet at 360×240, but you want to use an external device as your preview monitor, confroming to the NTSC DV standard for North America. Because only the video stream is sent over the IEEE-1394 cable to your tele-vision, synchronization can sometimes be problematic.
Sync offset (frames)	If you are experiencing synchronization problems between the audio from your soundcard and the video as it appears on your television, you can adjust the Sync Offset (Frames) option to fix it.
Record engage delay (frames)	This can help you when sending video to your camera if you are finding that playback of the timeline begins before the camera is rolling. This is not an uncommon problem because different camera mechanisms take different lengths of time to start up.
Recompress edited frames	Because you cannot edit video in the ACID software, this option is not available and is a relic of shared code with Sony Media Software's Vegas Video editing application.

Editing Tab

The Editing tab sets some of the more general features of how the ACID software works. There are only three simple options.

Option	Description
Project tempo range (40 to 300 BPM)	The default project tempo range is set from 70 bpm to 200 bpm, which is a very broad range of possible tempos, from slow ballads to trip-hop. These limits control what tempos are available on the Project Tempo slider at the bottom of the Track Header. Because

(continued)

Option	Description
	radical tempo differences between a project and the media files that it uses can cause distortions, this limited range is a pragmatic consideration only. You should not need to limit yourself to this tempo range if you use loops appropriate to your selected tempo.
Editing applications	This section allows you to set a number of outside editing applications for modifying media files—for example, Sony Media Software's Sound Forge. These applications show up on the Tools menu as, for example, Edit in Audition. To add applications to the list, click the Browse button and locate the .exe file that runs the chosen program. The Name item is for you to change as you see fit; the default is the .exe filename.
Check for latest version of Sony editors	The Check for Latest Sony Editors option is selected by default and allows the ACID software to detect and list other Sony Media Software applications (such as Vegas) on the Tools menu automatically.

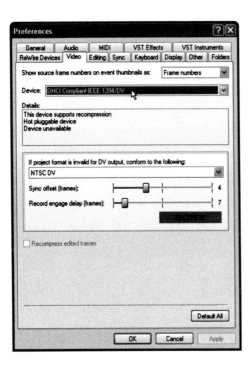

Figure A.3
Additional options become visible when an OHCI-compatible IEEE-1394 device is selected.

Sync Tab

The Sync tab is used to configure MIDI Timecode and MIDI Clock synchronization between the ACID software and other MIDI Timecode-capable applications. Chapter 10 deals with this topic in more detail. The tab's options include the following.

Option	Description
Generate MIDI Timecode settings	This option sets up the ACID software to send MTC to another application to allow the ACID program to trigger that application. The Output Device setting enables you to select the hardware used to generate MTC. The Frame Rate setting determines the format of the MTC and needs to be matched in the receiving application.
Generate MIDI Clock settings	This option configures a MIDI Clock signal to be created by the ACID software (instead of MTC, as previously detailed). The Output Device setting enables you to select the hardware used to generate the MIDI Clock and can be different from the MTC device.
Trigger from MIDI Timecode	The Trigger from MIDI Timecode setting allows the ACID software to listen for and respond to MTC as sent from another application. The Input Device control sets the hardware and software driver that the ACID software will listen to, and the Frame Rate control sets the format of the MTC and must be matched to the sending application.

Appendix B }

Shortcuts

The following is a partial list of shortcuts and keyboard accelerations available in the ACID®
software. Although it is not necessary (nor even possible for normal humans) to memorize this
entire list, you should always remember that the ACID software utilizes keyboard shortcuts extensively. If you find yourself using the mouse to push buttons or navigating the same set of menus
and submenus again and again, it is probably a good guess that there is some type of shortcut
associated with these actions.

> **YOUR OWN SHORTCUTS**
> If you don't like these default shortcuts, you can change anything and everything by going to the Options
> menu in the ACID software and selecting Customize Keyboard. This opens a very useful and flexible
> dialog that basically lets you customize everything.

Mouse Wheel

Press these keys while using the wheel:	In order to:
None (default behavior)	Zoom in and out on the project
Shift	Horizontal scroll
Ctrl	Vertical scroll
Ctrl+Shift	Move timeline cursor one grid line
Ctrl+Shift+Alt	Move timeline cursor one video frame at a time (only with video in a project)
Press (and release) mouse wheel button	Auto scroll (click mouse button to stop)
Ctrl (while cursor is over a slider)	Move slider in smaller increments

Marker Bar

Press these keys:	In order to:
K	Insert key change
T	Insert tempo change
M	Insert marker
R	Insert region
H	Insert time marker
N	Insert CD track marker
1–9 (not on number pad)	Jump to the specified marker or region

Keyboard Navigation*

Press these keys:	In order to:
W or Ctrl+Home	Go to start of project
Ctrl+End	Go to end of project
Home	Go to start of selection area (loop region)
End	Go to end of selection area (loop region)
Page Down	Move right (forward) through project by grid space

(continued)

Press these keys:	In order to:
Page Up	Move left (back) through project by grid space
Ctrl+G	Go to (and enter measure number)
\	Center project on position of timeline cursor
1–9 (not number pad)	Jump to marker
Left or right arrow	Move timeline cursor back or forward
Alt+left or right arrow	Move timeline cursor one video frame at a time
Ctrl+left or right arrow	Jump to previous or next marker
Ctrl+Alt+left or right arrow	Jump to previous or next event edge (or fade edge) in selected track

* These shortcuts allow you to navigate the timeline without using the mouse. Many of these shortcuts also work in the Chopper and Track Properties windows.

Keyboard Selection*

Press these keys:	In order to:
Shift+W or Ctrl+Home	Select to start of project
Ctrl+End	Select to end of project
Shift+Home	Select to start of selection area (loop region)
Shift+End	Select to end of selection area (loop region)
Shift+Page Down	Select right (forward) through project by grid space
Shift+Page Up	Select left (back) through project by grid space
Shift+1–9 (not number pad)	Select to marker
Shift+left or right arrow	Expand selection back or forward
Shift+Alt + left or right arrow	Expand selection one video frame at a time
Shift+Ctrl+ left or right arrow	Select to previous or next marker
Shift+Ctrl+Alt+ left or right arrow	Select to previous or next event edge (or fade edge)
I and O	Create a selection area at any time (on the fly during playback): Press I or [(In) to start and O or] (Out) to end.
-or-	
[and]	
Ctrl+A	Select all
Ctrl+Shift+A	Deselect all

(continued)

Press these keys:	In order to:
Ctrl+Shift+ drag mouse	Create (draw or drag) a selection area (regardless of edit tool selected)
Backspace	Recover previous selection areas

* As with Keyboard Navigation, these shortcuts allow you to make selections on the timeline without using the mouse. Almost all of these shortcuts are the same as the Keyboard Navigation shortcuts with the addition of the Shift key. Many of these shortcuts also work in the Chopper and Track Properties windows.

Playback (Transport) Controls

Press these keys:	In order to:
Spacebar	Play (start or stop playback)
Shift+spacecbar (Shift+F12)	Play from start
Ctrl+spacebar (F12)	Play from cursor
Enter	Pause
Esc	Stop
W (Ctrl+Home)	Go to start
Ctrl+End	Go to end
L or Q	Toggle loop playback
Ctrl+R	Record

Editing Commands

Press these keys:	In order to:
F5	Refresh loop waveforms
F7	Generate MIDI Timecode
Shift+F7	Generate MIDI Clock
Ctrl+F7	Trigger from MIDI Timecode
F8	Toggle snapping on and off
Ctrl+F8	Snap to grid
L	Toggle Loop Playback mode

(continued)

Press these keys:	In order to:
Ctrl+L	Ripple Edit mode
D	Change edit tool
Ctrl+D	Change to Draw tool
V	Insert or Show/Hide Volume Envelopes
Shift+V	Remove Volume Envelope
P	Insert or Show/Hide Pan Envelopes
Shift+P	Remove Pan Envelope
` (on ~ tilde key)	Minimize all track height (toggle)
Ctrl+Shift+up or down arrows	Change track height
Up or down arrows	Zoom in or out
Ctrl+up or down arrows	Zoom in (jump to high zoom) or out (to full project)
4 or 6 on the number pad	Move selected event left (back) or right (forward) on the timeline in small intervals (regardless of snapping)
Ctrl+4 or 6 on the number pad	Move event left or right one grid space
Alt + drag inside of event	Move the media around inside of an event (the event itself remains stationary)
Alt + drag edge of event	Change the size of the event, but the media inside remains stationary relative to the dragged edge
Ctrl+Alt + drag inside of event	Move the event while leaving the media stationary relative to the project

Chopper Commands*

Press these keys:	In order to:
A or /	Add media from cursor
Shift+A or /	Add media to cursor
, or . (comma or period)	Shift selection area left or right
Ctrl+, or . (comma or period)	Move timeline cursor left (back) or right (forward)
N	Link arrow to selection
; (semicolon)	Halve selection
' (apostrophe)	Double selection

* Many Keyboard Navigation and Selection shortcuts also work in the Chopper window, in addition to some playback (Transport) controls and zoom shortcuts.

Standard Windows Commands

Press these keys:	In order to:
F1	Help
Shift+F1, then click on an object	Context Sensitive or What's This? Help
Shift+F10 or Windows Command key	Context Sensitive menu
Shift+click two events	Select both events and all events between them
Ctrl+click multiple events	Select all clicked events (but not events between them)
Ctrl+Z	Undo (or Alt+Backspace)
Ctrl+Y	Redo (or Ctrl+Shift+Z)
Ctrl+C	Copy (or Ctrl+Insert)
Ctrl+X	Cut (Shift+Delete)
Ctrl+V	Paste from Clipboard (Shift+Insert)
Ctrl+B	Repeat paste from Clipboard
Ctrl+N	New project
Ctrl+O	Open project
Ctrl+S	Save project

Index

INDEX ♭

✳ ✳ ✳